Essentials

Autodesk® Nastran® In-CAD 2019.1

August 2018

AUTODESK.
Authorized Publisher

Contents

Introduction

Welcome to the *Autodesk® Nastran® In-CAD 2019.1 Essentials* learning guide, for use in Authorized Training Center (ATC®) locations, corporate training settings, and other classroom settings.

Although this learning guide is designed for instructor-led courses, you can also use it for self-paced learning.

This introduction covers the following topics:

- Course Description
- Prerequisites
- Using This Learning Guide
- Downloading and Installing the Exercise Files
- Feedback
- Free Autodesk Software for Students and Educators

This learning guide is complementary to the software documentation. For detailed explanations of features and functionality, refer to the Help in the software.

Course Description

The *Autodesk® Nastran® In-CAD 2019.1 Essentials* learning guide instructs students in the use of the Autodesk® Nastran® In-CAD software. This learning guide was written using the 2019.1.0.200 build of the Autodesk® Nastran® In-CAD 2019.1 software. The software is a finite element analysis (FEA) tool that is embedded directly in the Autodesk® Inventor® software as an Add-In. It is powered by the Autodesk Nastran solver and offers simulation capabilities specifically tailored for designers and analysts as a tool for predicting the physical behavior of parts or assemblies under various boundary conditions. Through a hands-on, practice-intensive curriculum, students acquire the knowledge required to work in the Autodesk Nastran In-CAD environment to setup and conduct FEA analyzes on part and assembly models.

After completing this course, you will be able to:

- Activate and navigate the Autodesk Nastran In-CAD environment to conduct FEA analyzes on part and assembly models.
- Create, edit, and assign idealizations and materials (linear and nonlinear) for use in an analysis (including composites).

- Manage the creation, setup, and modification of analyses and subcases that are used to analyze both static and dynamic models. Specific analyses types that are covered in this learning guide include:
  - Linear Static
  - Nonlinear Static
  - Nonlinear Transient Response
  - Normal Modes
  - Direct Frequency Response
  - Modal Frequency Response
  - Direct Transient Response
  - Modal Transient Response
  - Random Response
  - Shock/Response Spectrum
- Create constraints with the required degrees of freedom and assign them to entities in the model.
- Create loads that accurately represent the magnitude and location of the loads the model will experience in the working environment.
- Create Connector elements to simulate how a physical connector such as a rod, cable, spring, rigid body, or bolt will affect the model.
- Create Surface Contact elements to define contact between interacting components in an assembly.
- Assign global and local mesh settings.
- Run an Autodesk Nastran In-CAD analysis.
- Review and create result plots for analyzing the results of an Autodesk Nastran In-CAD analysis.

Prerequisites

This learning guide assumes that a student has Finite Element Analysis (FEA) knowledge, can interpret results, and in general, knows how a model should be setup for an analysis. The main goal of this learning guide is to teach a user that is new to the Autodesk® Nastran® In-CAD software how to navigate the interface to successfully analyze a model.

This learning guide was written using the 2019.1.0.200 build of the Autodesk® Nastran® In-CAD 2019 software. The software user-interface and workflow may vary if older or newer versions of the software are being used.

Using This Learning Guide

The lessons are generally independent of each other. It is recommended that you complete the lessons in the learning guide in the order that they are presented, unless you are familiar with the concepts and functionality described in those lessons.

Each chapter contains:

- **Lessons -** Usually two or more lessons in each chapter.
- **Exercises -** Practical, real-world examples for you to practice using the functionality you have just learned. Each exercise contains step-by-step procedures and graphics to help you complete the exercise successfully.

  - If a chapter's secondary exercise is dependent on a prior exercise, a prepared class file is provided for you. It will have all of the previous exercises' steps completed for you.
  - Depending on the analysis type, the FE model, and computer resources, an analysis can take some time to run. In some of the exercises in this learning guide, result files are provided that can be opened instead of running a full analysis during class time.

Downloading and Installing the Exercise Files

The Exercise Files page in this learning guide contains a link and instructions on how to download and install all of the data required to complete the exercises.

Feedback

We always welcome feedback on Autodesk Official Training Courseware. After completing this course, if you have suggestions for improvements or want to report an error in the learning guide or with the class files, please send your comments to *feedback@ASCENTed.com*.

Students and Educators can Access Free Autodesk Software and Resources

Autodesk challenges you to get started with free educational licenses for professional software and creativity apps used by millions of architects, engineers, designers, and hobbyists today. Bring Autodesk software into your classroom, studio, or workshop to learn, teach, and explore real-world design challenges the way professionals do.

Get started today - register at the Autodesk Education Community and download one of the many Autodesk software applications available.

http://www.autodesk.com/education/free-software/nastran-in-cad

Note: Free products are subject to the terms and conditions of the end-user license and services agreement that accompanies the software. The software is for personal use for education purposes and is not intended for classroom or lab use.

Exercise Files

To download the Exercise files for this guide, use the following steps:

1. Type the URL shown below into the address bar of your Internet browser. The URL must be typed exactly as shown. If you are using an ASCENT ebook, you can click on the link to download the file.

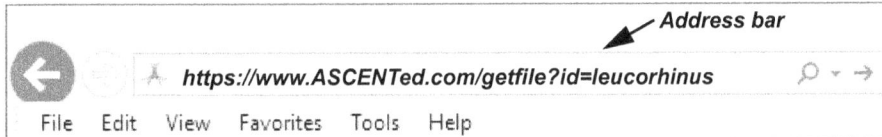

2. Press <Enter> to download the .ZIP file that contains the Exercise Files.

3. Once the download is complete, unzip the file to a local folder. The unzipped file contains an .EXE file.

4. Double-click on the .EXE file and follow the instructions to automatically install the Exercise Files on the C:\ drive of your computer.

   Do not change the location in which the Exercise Files folder is installed. Doing so can cause errors when completing the Exercises.

https://www.ASCENTed.com/getfile?id=leucorhinus

Getting Started

Finite element analysis (FEA) is a computerized method for predicting how a product reacts to real-world forces, vibration, heat, and other physical effects. Autodesk Digital Prototyping identifies the importance of FEA as a key stage in the design and development of a product and therefore, it provides a number of software tools that enable FEA. One such tool is Autodesk® Nastran® In-CAD, an add-in product to Autodesk® Inventor®. This tool enables you to integrate your analysis directly as a step in the modeling workflow. In this chapter, you will be introduced to Autodesk Digital Prototyping, the basics of finite element analysis, and how Autodesk Nastran In-CAD can be used to analyze your models.

Objectives

After completing this chapter, you will be able to:

- Identify the stages of Autodesk Digital Prototyping.
- Identify Autodesk's software products that can be used for Finite Element Analysis in the Autodesk Digital Prototyping workflow.
- Describe Finite Element Analysis and its importance in a design workflow.
- Describe how Autodesk Nastran In-CAD can be incorporated into a CAD workflow.
- Describe the analysis types available in the Autodesk Nastran In-CAD software.
- Activate the Autodesk Nastran In-CAD environment.
- Describe the Autodesk Nastran Model Tree nodes that are available when analyzing a model.
- Navigate between the Autodesk Nastran Model Tree and Autodesk Nastran Output views.
- List the files types that are generated when Autodesk Nastran In-CAD analysis is run.
- Describe the general steps in the Autodesk Nastran In-CAD FEA workflow.

Lesson: Autodesk Digital Prototyping

Overview

This lesson provides an overview of Autodesk Digital Prototyping and explains how incorporating a finite element analysis software tool in the testing and validation stage of a product's development helps get better products to market faster.

Objectives

After completing this lesson, you will be able to:

- Identify the stages of Autodesk Digital Prototyping.

- Identify Autodesk's software products that can be used for Finite Element Analysis in the Autodesk Digital Prototyping workflow.

Introduction to Autodesk Digital Prototyping

Autodesk Digital Prototyping enables you to explore your design ideas before they're even built. Traditional design environments provide individual tools that are used to develop each phase in a design independently. Using the intelligent, model-based approach of Autodesk Digital Prototyping integrated tools are used throughout the design process. You can explore design ideas, gather design data from all phases of the process into a single digital model, validate it against product requirements, and finally, reference all of the data as you build deliverables for release. The process enables team members to collaborate across disciplines with the aim of getting better products to market faster. From concept through design, manufacturing, marketing and beyond, the Autodesk Digital Prototyping software solutions streamline the product development process from start to finish.

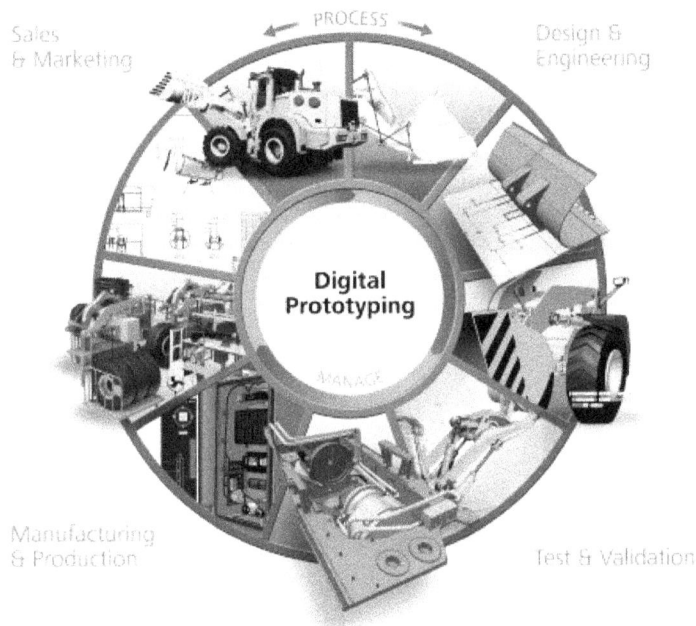

Finite Element Analysis

The Test and Validation phase is a key phase in the Digital Prototyping cycle and involves the use of Finite Element Analysis (FEA) tools. The overall goals for the use of FEA tools are to reduce reliance on costly physical prototypes and to improve product quality. Ultimately, this reduces support and warranty claims and it enables you to:

- Explore design options early in the design cycle.
- Optimize products for performance and material cost.
- Validate product designs to anticipate their performance in the field before expensive prototypes are created and tested.

Autodesk Digital Prototyping FEA Solutions

There are multiple Finite Element Analysis (FEA) tools that are available in the Autodesk Digital Prototyping solution. These solutions include:

- Autodesk® CFD
- Autodesk® Flow Design
- Autodesk® Fusion 360™
- Autodesk® Helius PFA
- Autodesk® Helius Composite
- Autodesk® Inventor® Professional Simulation
- Autodesk® Moldflow® Adviser
- Autodesk® Moldflow® Insight
- Autodesk® Nastran®
- Autodesk® Nastran® In-CAD (available for Inventor®)
- Autodesk® Robot™ Structural Analysis Professional

> This learning guide focuses on Autodesk Nastran In-CAD for Autodesk Inventor.

Lesson: Introduction to FEA

Overview

This lesson provides an overview of Finite Element Analysis (FEA) and how it can be used to predict and analyze a CAD model's reaction once it is manufactured and working in a real-world environment. The inclusion of FEA in the design workflow enables designers to anticipate how the model will react and make educated decisions on whether this anticipated reaction meets design requirements.

Objectives

After completing this lesson, you will be able to:

- Describe Finite Element Analysis and its importance in a design workflow.

The Basics of Finite Element Analysis

Finite element analysis (FEA) is a computerized method for predicting how a product reacts to real-world forces, vibration, heat, and other physical effects. FEA shows whether a product's material will yield, deform, wear out, or respond the way it was designed. It is called analysis, but in the product development process, it is used to predict what will happen when the product is used.

FEA works by breaking down a real object into a large number (thousands to hundreds of thousands) of finite elements, such as tetrahedrons, hexahedrons, and pyramids. Mathematical equations help predict the behavior of these elements. A computer then combines all of the individual behaviors to predict the behavior of the actual object.

Key Concepts in FEA Analysis

This section summarizes key concepts that must be understood when defining an FEA model. These include the analysis geometry, choosing the appropriate analysis type for the model and the element type that will be used, materials, meshing, loads, and constraints.

Geometry & Element Idealizations

The geometry that is being analyzed may be created directly inside of a CAD tool with an embedded analysis environment or it may be imported into a separate analysis tool. In either situation, FEA requires that the model be represented by finite elements that are used to test the model for the required reactions. The process of representing the model with the finite elements is called model idealization. The FEA software provides for multiple element idealization types. The selection of the type is dependent on the model geometry as well as the experience of the user. The element idealizations that are available in Autodesk Nastran In-CAD are listed in the following table. Different properties need to be defined when using each type. For more information on the element types, in Autodesk Nastran In-CAD, in the Help documentation, refer to User's Guide>Finite Elements.

Element Type	Example
Solid Elements (No element properties are required.)	

Element Type	Example
Shell Elements (Element thickness is required.)	
Line Elements (Cross section and orientation are required.)	

Materials

Materials are the physical substances that will be used in the fabrication of the model (aluminum, steel, etc.). In FEA, materials can generally be either imported from a predefined material library or you can manually input property data to define the required material. Autodesk Nastran In-CAD supports the following eight material types. Note that only the Isotropic material data can be loaded from the material library. However, you can create and save your own material properties.

- Isotropic
- Orthotropic 2D
- Orthotropic 3D
- Anisotropic 3D
- Hyperelastic
- Nitinol
- Viscoelastic

For linear analysis, note that only linear materials are available (Isotropic, Orthotropic, Anisotropic). For a nonlinear analysis, a linear or nonlinear material can be used.

You should consider if it is feasible to idealize a nonlinear material as linear. Determine whether you are in the linear elastic range or if you should be.

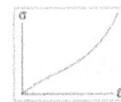

Linear   Nonlinear Elastic   Plastic   Hyperelastic (Elastomers)

Meshing Basics

Finite Element Analysis requires that the geometry that is being analyzed be broken down into smaller simplified volumes that approximate the shape of the model. These volumes are called elements. The collection of these elements is called an element mesh or mesh. Analysis is completed on the mesh to determine the overall results for the model. The selection of the element type (Solid, Shell, or Line) defines how the mesh is generated. Initially, a default mesh is applied based on the element type; however, the mesh can be further refined as required, by customizing additional mesh properties.

Boundary Conditions - Loads & Constraints

The loads and constraints used in the analysis software simulate the boundary conditions that the model will ultimately experience once manufactured and placed in a real-world working environment. Assigning the correct boundary conditions is a critical step in achieving an accurate and useful simulation. Ensure that the loads and constraints assigned to the model geometry realistically represent the operating conditions that the manufactured model will experience. The incorrect use of boundary conditions is the most common source of error in an analysis.

- Constraints are used to simulate a true support (rigid foundation), contacting geometry (adjoining structure), or other boundary conditions in your model. Constraints can be applied to the part's face, edges, or vertices.
- Loads are used to simulate the magnitude of the load that will be applied to the manufactured model in its working environment. Various load types are available in Autodesk Nastran In-CAD. Loads can be applied to the part's bodies, faces, edges, or vertices.

> The constraints and loads used to define the model's boundary conditions must not impose displacements, stresses, rigidity, or other behavior that would not be experienced in the model's working environment.

Analysis Types

Finite element analysis helps predict the behavior of products affected by many physical effects, including:

- Mechanical stress
- Mechanical vibration
- Fatigue
- Buckling
- Motion
- Heat transfer

With any analysis software product, including Autodesk Nastran In-CAD, the correct selection of the analysis type is essential for a successful and accurate analysis. Consider the following when deciding on an analysis type and what is to be studied in your model:

- Is the model and loading linear static?
- Do the parts experience large deflections or displacements? Should non-linear static be used?
- Are loads time-independent?
- Is it a dynamic analysis?
- Will buckling occur?
- Do temperatures influence loads, stiffnesses, or stresses?

Lesson: Introduction to Autodesk Nastran In-CAD

Overview

This lesson provides an overview of the Autodesk Nastran In-CAD software. You will learn how this add-in for Autodesk Inventor can be used in a modeling workflow to analyze a model.

Objectives

After completing this lesson, you will be able to:

- Describe how Autodesk Nastran In-CAD can be incorporated into a CAD workflow.

- Describe the various analysis types that are available in the Autodesk Nastran In-CAD software.

Overview of Autodesk Nastran In-CAD

The Autodesk Nastran In-CAD software is a finite element analysis (FEA) tool that is embedded directly in the Autodesk® Inventor® software as an Add-In. It is powered by the Autodesk Nastran solver and offers simulation capabilities specifically tailored for designers and analysts as a tool for predicting the physical behavior of parts or assemblies under various boundary conditions. Based on the predictions from an analysis, designers can easily return to the CAD modeling environment, make any required changes, and run the analysis again to verify the modifications are acceptable.

The Autodesk Nastran In-CAD software offers analysts a large range of solution capabilities, such as virtual simulation of linear and nonlinear stress, dynamics, and heat transfer. The following tables describe the basic and advanced analysis capabilities available in the software. In addition to these analysis types, you can also use Autodesk Nastran In-CAD to conduct Fatigue, Vibration Fatigue, and Response Spectrum analyses.

Basic Analysis Capabilities

Analysis Type	Description	Example
Linear Static	A Linear Static analysis that determines displacements, stresses, and strains resulting from applied loads.	
Buckling	The Buckling analysis determines the stability of a model under loads. Buckling examines structures for sudden failure modes caused by compressive forces. Use nonlinear buckling to simulate large deformations, contact, and nonlinear material behavior in calculation of buckling load.	
Prestress Static and Prestress Normal Modes	The Prestress Static and Prestress Normal Modes analysis types can be used to analyze models that are subjected to initial stress. The effect of the initial stress state is displayed on the model's displacements, stresses, and modes. Analyses can be conducted on part or assembly models.	

Analysis Type	Description	Example
Normal Modes	The Normal Modes analysis determines the undamped natural mode shapes and frequencies of structures. This enables design engineers to explore and resolve problems with noise and vibration. ■ Natural frequencies and mode shapes. ■ Flexible and rigid body motion. ■ Modal participation factors and effective mass/weight. ■ Linear and nonlinear prestress (stiffening). ■ Virtual fluid mass.	
Linear Steady State Heat Transfer	The Linear Steady State Heat Transfer analysis determines the temperature distribution using the principles of conduction and convection heat transfer. Compute steady state and time-dependent heat loading using: ■ Conduction ■ Convection ■ Radiation You can transfer temperature results to structural analyses as thermal loads.	
Thermal Stress (Static Analysis)	The Thermal Stress analysis type analyzes structures subjected to thermal loads. This is completed as a Static analysis.	

Advanced Analysis Capabilities

Analysis Type	Description	Example
Nonlinear Statics	The Nonlinear Statics analysis type provides the ability to add more realistic simulation with contacting parts, nonlinear elastic and plastic materials, and large deformations. Computes advanced nonlinear solutions such as large displacements/rotation, large strain, plasticity, hyperelasticity, creep etc.	

Analysis Type	Description	Example
Nonlinear Transient Heat Transfer	Simulate heat transfer with nonlinear thermal boundary conditions that vary through time. An example is transient heat generation caused by power fluctuations. ■ Conduction ■ Convection ■ Radiation	
Nonlinear Steady State Heat Transfer	Simulate heat transfer with nonlinear thermal boundary conditions or temperature dependent thermal properties.	
Random Response	Analyze structural behavior in response to random dynamic loads.	
Direct and Modal Frequency Response	Dynamic solutions add the ability to include time and mass in the solution. Capabilities include: ■ Enforced harmonic motion - frequency response. ■ Time dependent motion and loads - transient response. ■ Random excitation. ■ Shock loading. Use frequency response to determine the structural harmonic response based upon frequency-dependent loads.	
Shock/ Response Spectrum	A response spectrum is a plot of the peak or steady-state response (displacement, velocity, or acceleration) of a series of oscillators of varying natural frequency that are forced into motion by the same base vibration or shock. The resulting plot can then be used to pick off the response of any linear system, given its natural frequency of oscillation. One such use is in assessing the peak response of buildings to earthquakes.	

Analysis Type	Description	Example
Direct, Modal and Nonlinear Transient Response	Simulate the time-dependent response of a structure under the influence of constant or time-dependent loads. An example is impulse loading.	
Automated Impact Analysis (AIA) and Drop Test	Simulate drop tests and other impact type loadings easily and automatically. Define impacting parts, path, and velocity. Define initial conditions and loads, and run as a nonlinear transient analysis. Sophisticated treatment provides realistic and meaningful impact and drop test simulations. The only inputs required are projectile velocity and acceleration.	

This learning guide discusses the following analysis types:

- Linear Static
- Nonlinear Static
- Nonlinear Transient Response
- Normal Modes
- Direct Frequency Response
- Modal Frequency Response
- Direct Transient Response
- Modal Transient Response
- Random Response
- Shock/Response Spectrum

When a new model is setup in the Autodesk Nastran In-CAD environment for analysis, a Linear Static analysis is set as the default analysis type. This setting can be retained without having to make any changes or it can be modified to change the analysis type and/or its settings.

Lesson: Working in Autodesk Nastran In-CAD

This lesson explains how to navigate and use the Autodesk Nastran In-CAD interface.

Objectives

After completing this lesson, you will be able to:

- Activate the Autodesk Nastran In-CAD environment.

- Describe the Autodesk Nastran Model Tree nodes that are available when analyzing a model.

- Navigate between the Autodesk Nastran Model Tree and Autodesk Nastran Output views.

- List the folders and file formats that are generated when Autodesk Nastran In-CAD analysis is run.

- Describe the general steps in the Autodesk Nastran In-CAD FEA workflow.

Autodesk Nastran In-CAD User Interface

Autodesk Nastran In-CAD is an add-in environment that enables you to conduct FEA analysis directly in the CAD workflow while working in Autodesk Inventor. With a model active in Autodesk Inventor, select the Environments tab and click Autodesk Nastran In-CAD to activate the Autodesk Nastran In-CAD environment.

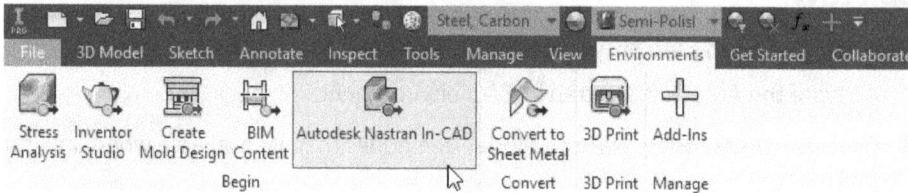

The model that was active in Inventor when the environment was launched is now available for use in Autodesk Nastran In-CAD for analysis. The interface consists of commands on the ribbon and the Autodesk Nastran Model Tree.

Ribbon

Similar to Autodesk Inventor, the Autodesk Nastran tab has multiple panels, which contain all the commands required to setup, run, and analyze a model. In general, the panels in the Autodesk Nastran ribbon are listed in the same order as the general workflow that is used to conduct an analysis (left to right). Throughout this learning guide, the panels and commands will be discussed in more depth.

Autodesk Nastran Model Tree

When the model is opened in the Autodesk Nastran In-CAD environment, the Autodesk Nastran Model Tree tab is displayed in the Model Browser, as shown in the following image. The top node in the Model Tree indicates whether the model being analyzed is a part or assembly model. The remaining nodes in the Model Tree provide a convenient outline view of the various finite element model entities that have been created in the model to define the analysis.

- When the Autodesk Nastran In-CAD environment is enabled, many of the nodes in the Autodesk Nastran Model Tree are automatically populated with default values.

- Other nodes are defined as the model is prepared for analysis and once the analysis is complete.

The Model Tree is broken into two sub-trees:

- Analysis sub-tree
- Model sub-tree

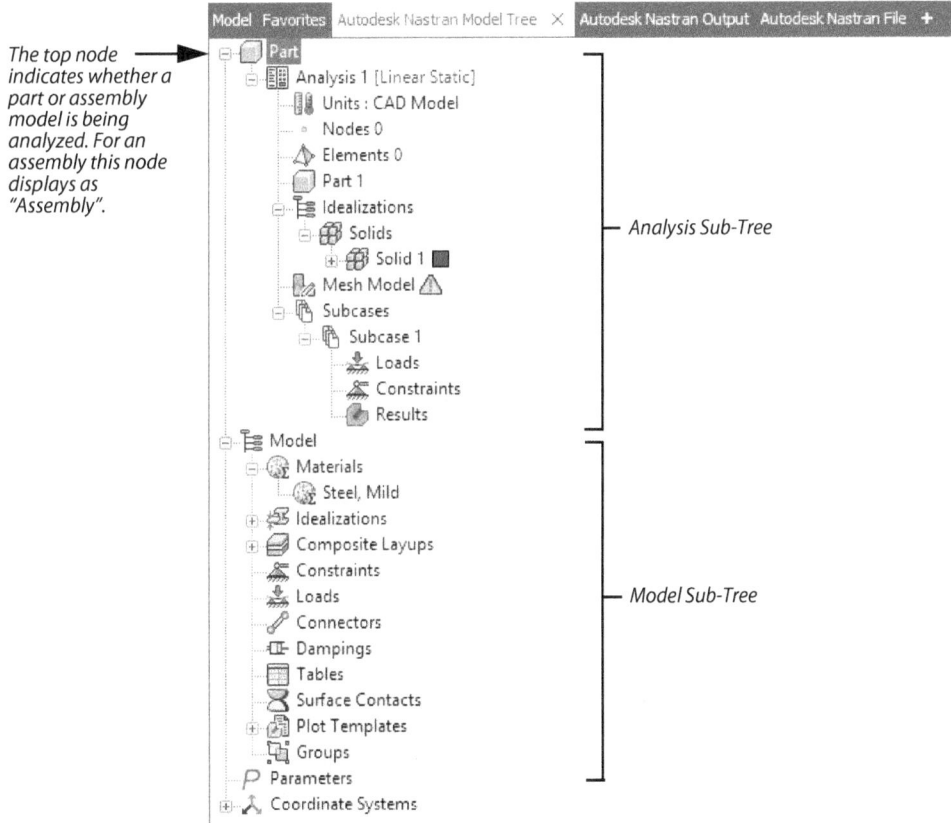

The Parameters and Coordinate Systems nodes are also available at the bottom of the Autodesk Nastran Model Tree. The Parameters node is intended for advanced control of the Autodesk Nastran solver Parameters. The Coordinate Systems node is where you must define any new model-specific coordinate systems that will be used for an analysis.

Analysis Sub-Tree

By default, when the model is opened in the Autodesk Nastran In-CAD environment, the Analysis sub-tree is listed at the top of the Autodesk Nastran Model Tree and contains a single Linear Static analysis called Analysis 1, which is automatically active. Multiple Analysis sub-trees can exist to represent the different analysis types, or different analysis setups that need to be run on the model. Each Analysis sub-tree is the primary location for defining the analysis. Which nodes are available to you depend on the active analysis type. The following nodes are standard in the default Analysis 1:

- **Idealizations**: Adds or edits idealizations for the analysis.
- **Mesh Model**: Defines the model's mesh settings. The number of nodes and elements that are generated are listed at the top of the Analysis sub-tree.
- **Subcases**: Manages the loads, constraints, and results for an analysis. Multiple subcases with varying loads and constraints can be set in an analysis. The subcases are run sequentially. You can add and edit settings from this node.
  - **Results**: Prior to an analysis being run, the Results node in any subcase is empty. Once run, the results are added to the node. The results that display depend on the results that were requested in the analysis. You can right-click on any of the results to display, animate, or create an AVI of the results. Additionally, you can edit, copy, delete, and rename a result.

> In a Nonlinear analysis, the results of one subcase are the initial conditions for the subsequent subcase.

To modify, create, or duplicate the analysis, right-click on the top-level Analysis node to access the context menu. Alternatively, each of the individual nodes in the Analysis sub-tree also provide a shortcut menu to work with the settings.

Model Sub-Tree

Once created, any FEA element definition is automatically stored in the nodes in the Model sub-tree. This applies to the settings defined in the Analysis sub-tree or the Model sub-tree; however, not all entities in the Model sub-tree have to be used in a current analysis. Therefore, entities can be defined here and saved for future use. The nodes available in the Model sub-tree define everything that can be included in an analysis and are described as follows:

- **Materials**: Contains the list of materials added to the model and enables the addition of new materials.
- **Idealizations**: Contains the list of idealizations added to the model and enables the addition of new ones that can be used in an analysis. A sub-node called Concentrated Masses contains the list of lumped mass elements that can be used to replace complex 3D model geometry in an analysis. This node also enables the creation of new concentrated masses.

- **Composite Layups**: Lists existing, and enables you to create new Laminates and Global Plies for association with the shell idealization for composite analyses.
- **Constraints**: Contains the list of all constraints added to the model and enables the addition of new constraints.
- **Loads**: Contains the list of loads added to the model and enables the addition of new loads.
- **Connectors**: Contains the list of specialized elements for connecting parts (Connectors) that have been added to the model and enables the creation of new connections.
- **Dampings**: Contains the list of damping instances that have been added to the model and enables the creation of new ones.
- **Tables**: Contains the list of tables that have been added to the model and enables the creation of new ones. Tables can be used for such things as defining transient loading (force vs. time) for an analysis. Tables can also be created as a Load but will be listed in the Tables node once created.
- **Surface Contacts**: Contains the list of automatic or manual surface contacts that can be used in an assembly analysis. This node also enables the creation of new surface contacts.
- **Plot Templates**: Contains specified results views that can be used to report on an analysis. This node also enables the creation of new views.
- **Groups**: Contains the list of Node and/or Element groups that are used in Contact definition and XY Plotting.

You can drag settings from the Model sub-tree into the analysis or any of the subcase nodes in the Analysis sub-tree, as required. If an entity is removed from a subcase, it is still available in the Model sub-tree, unless it is explicitly deleted from there.

Autodesk Nastran Output View

When the analysis is running, the Model Browser displays the Autodesk Nastran Output view to show the Autodesk Nastran Solver Log messages.

The log messages are tabulated as the solver is working. Once the analysis is complete you are prompted to click OK. Once you click OK, the Autodesk Nastran Output view is replaced by the Autodesk Nastran Model Tree.

When you are running an analysis and reviewing the Autodesk Nastran Output view, consider the following.

- Errors display in red in the log list.
- Click ⊗ to stop the analysis.
- Click 🖑 to pause the analysis.
- Click ➔ to resume a paused analysis.

To review the analysis log (once completed), select the Autodesk Nastran Output tab. This redisplays the solver output file (.OUT). Alternatively, you can use Windows Explorer to locate and open the .LOG file that was created. It is stored in the *<modelname>\InCAD\FEA* folder generated in the same directory as the source model.

Autodesk Nastran In-CAD File Formats

When a model has been analyzed using Autodesk Nastran In-CAD, a number of folders and files are created in the same directory as the source CAD model.

- The folder structure is generated when an analysis is run. The program creates a folder at the same level and with the same name as the CAD model being analyzed (e.g., Beam).
- The <model name> folder contains the \InCAD\FEA folders as shown below. This identifies Nastran In-CAD as the FEA tool that was used. If an analysis of the same model is run using the Inventor Simulation tool, an AIP folder is created for the results. This helps distinguish results that are generated between the two products.
- The generated file names that are stored in the \InCAD\FEA folder are unique for each analysis and subcase that is run. As design changes are made and the analysis is rerun, the system knows which analysis files to overwrite. If a second subcase or analysis is created, they will also have their own uniquely named files created in the same folder. Consider renaming these files if you need to keep any past results or if they need to be more easily recognizable.

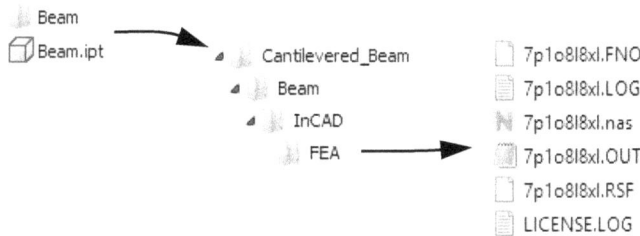

The generated file extensions are described as follows:

File Extension	Description
.nas	This file contains a complete description of the bulk data that was used to define the preprocessed model. It contains data on all model geometry, all elements, all nodes that make up elements, and the loads on the elements.
.LOG	This file contains the analysis data and information on what is happening in the solver as the process progresses through the analysis. The LICENSE.LOG file lists the license manager activity.
.FNO	This file is a binary file that contains the post-processed model information (results). This file can be used to load results that were previously run.
.OUT	This ASCII file is the information that is displayed as the solver runs. It summarizes the mass matrix, element results, warnings, and errors.
.RSF	This file provides a concise list of analysis results. The element results, warnings, and errors are not included.

FEA Workflow

A typical FEA workflow is also used in the Autodesk Nastran In-CAD software. As previously discussed, when working in Autodesk Nastran In-CAD, the panels in the ribbon generally progress you through the steps that are required to complete an analysis (left to right). The following general workflow can be followed; however, variations in the workflow order are possible:

1. Create the geometry that is to be analyzed, as required.

    ▪ Models can also be imported from other CAD software packages for analysis in Autodesk Nastran In-CAD.

2. Activate the Autodesk Nastran In-CAD environment.

3. Define the analysis type that is to be used to analyze the model and define its settings.

    ▪ The default analysis type that is automatically setup for any new model opened in the Autodesk Nastran In-CAD environment is Linear Static. This can be maintained, edited, or a new analysis defined.

4. Assign the properties (material and idealizations) to the model.

    ▪ The material can be defined independently of the idealizations or they can be assigned at the same time during the idealization definition.

    ▪ The material can be selected from a predefined material list or it can be created by entering appropriate property values.

    ▪ Inventor model properties are automatically imported into Autodesk Nastran In-CAD.

5. Apply constraints to the model to simulate supports (e.g., rigid foundation), contacting geometry (e.g., adjoining structure), or other boundary conditions in the model.

6. Apply loads to the model to simulate the magnitude of the load that will be applied to the manufactured model in its working environment.

7. Depending on the analysis type, additional analysis setup may be required. In general this setup is located in the subcase for the analysis.

8. Mesh the model.

9. Run the analysis.

10. Analyze and validate the results of the analysis.

11. Make changes to the model geometry, as required, and rerun the analysis.

> When analyzing a model with a consistent thickness that is small compared to its overall size, a thin body analysis workflow can be used. For this type of workflow, use the Prepare tab prior to assigning materials or idealizations, or ensure that you modify the element type to Shell Elements once the thin body has been properly represented. The thin body can be explicitly defined with an offset or mid-surface representation, or you can request Autodesk Nastran In-CAD to find bodies that match the shell feature criteria.

Exercise: Cantilever Beam Exercise

In this exercise, you will simulate a simple cantilevered beam with a fixed end and a load applied to the other end. The following assumptions will be used for this simulation:

- The displacement is small.
- The material exhibits a linear stress-strain response.
- The applied load does not change in magnitude, orientation, or distribution.
- The effects of gravity are negligible.

Open the Model & Start the Autodesk Nastran In-CAD Environment

1. Launch Autodesk Inventor, if not already running. If running, close any open files.

2. In the Get Started tab, in the Launch panel, click Projects. In the Projects dialog box, browse to and open the *Autodesk Nastran In-CAD.ipj* project file from the *C:\Autodesk Nastran InCAD 2019 Essentials Exercise Files* folder. Click Done to close the Projects dialog box.

3. Open the file *C:\Autodesk Nastran InCAD 2019 Essentials Exercise Files\Cantilevered_Beam\First Beam.ipt*.

4. Change the Material of the model.

   - Right-click on the model name in the Model Browser and select iProperties.
   - Select the Physical tab.
   - Note that Generic is the default material type assigned to the model.
   - In the Material drop-down list, select Steel, Carbon as the new material.
   - Click Apply to update the properties of the material.
   - Close the iProperties dialog box.

5. Save the model. If the model is not saved, the newly-assigned material will not be recognized in the Autodesk Nastran In-CAD environment.

6. Select the Environments tab and click Autodesk Nastran In-CAD to activate the Autodesk Nastran In-CAD environment.

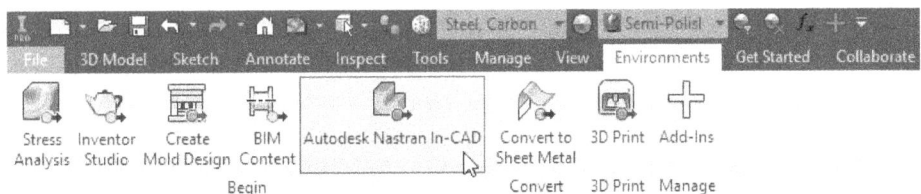

Review the Model Tree

In this task, you will review the Model Tree to identify the key areas of the interface as well as the default settings that will be used in your first analysis.

1. Three new tabs are added to the Model Browser. The main focus initially is on the Autodesk Nastran Model Tree tab. Ensure that it is the active tab, and if it is not, select it. Expand the Analysis 1 and Model nodes, if they are not already expanded.

2. In the Model node, note the following:

   - The Steel, Carbon material has been imported from the CAD model and is listed in the Materials node.
   - The Idealizations node contains a single solid idealization that was populated and assigned to the model by default.
   - No other nodes have any default settings preassigned.

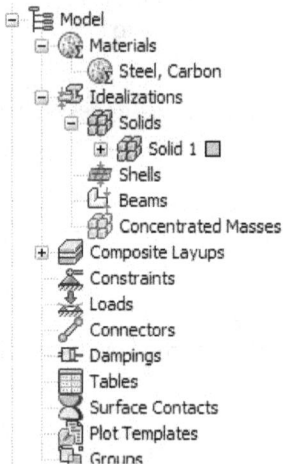

3. In the Analysis node, note the following:

   - The default analysis (Analysis 1) is a Linear Static analysis.
   - The Solid 1 Idealization has also been assigned to the analysis.
   - The Mesh node indicates that it needs to be updated (⚠).
   - In the Subcases node, no loads or constraints have been assigned.

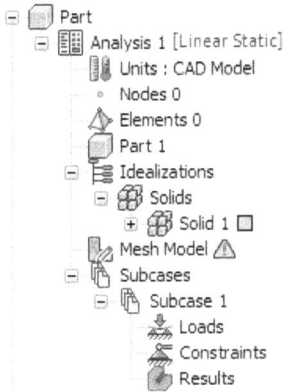

4. Right-click on Solid 1 and select Edit. This can be done from either the Analysis or Model sub-trees and any changes are reflected in both locations.

5. In the Idealizations dialog box, note the following:

   ▪ Solid Elements is the default type that was preassigned for this Linear Static Analysis. Maintain this option.

   ▪ The Steel, Carbon material is used.

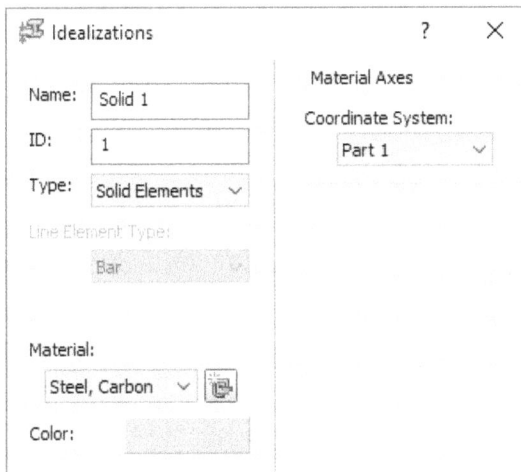

6. In the Color box, select the color swatch button. In the Color dialog box, select a dark green color and click OK.

   Note: The color that was initially assigned to Solid 1 was random.

7. Click OK in the Idealizations dialog box. Note how the color swatch that displays in the Model and Analysis sub-trees for Solid 1 updates to show its dark green color.

Constrain the Beam

In this task, you will assign a constraint that fixes the beam on one end, preventing movement in any direction. Constraints are assigned to entities in the model geometry and are not preassigned in any analysis. Later in this learning guide, you will learn more specifics about the Constraint dialog box; however, the purpose of this task is to quickly constrain the beam to run your first analysis.

1. In the Setup panel, click ⛏ (Constraints) to open the Constraint dialog box.

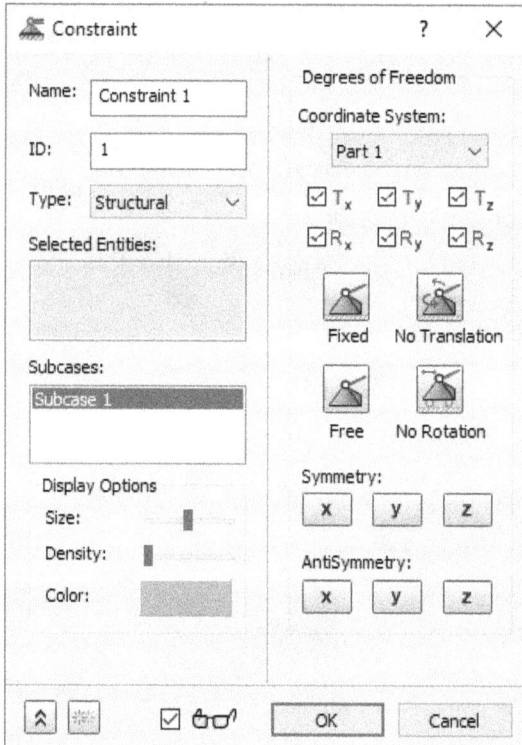

2. By default, all degrees of freedom are constrained (Fixed - no translation or rotation in any direction) and you can immediately select a face to constrain it. In the model, select the face at the end of the beam. Select □ 👓 at the bottom of the dialog box to preview the constraint. Drag the Density slider to the right to adjust the constraint symbol.

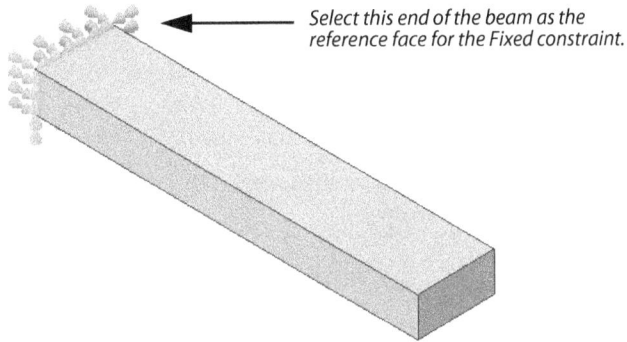

Select this end of the beam as the reference face for the Fixed constraint.

3. Click OK in the Constraint dialog box to close it without making any further changes. Later in this learning guide, you will learn about the other options in this dialog box.

4.   In the Setup panel, click ⬇ (Loads) to open the Load dialog box. Later in this learning guide, you will learn about the other options in this dialog box.

5.   Force is set as default type. Maintain this setting.

6.   Select the other end of the beam to assign the load to (the non-constrained end).

7.   Review the model coordinate system and note the Y direction. This is the direction that the force is required to be applied.

8.   In the Load dialog box, in the Fy field, enter **-1000lbf**. Select ☐ 👓 at the bottom of the dialog box to preview the constraint. Drag the Density slider to the right to adjust the constraint symbol.

9. Click OK in the Load dialog box.

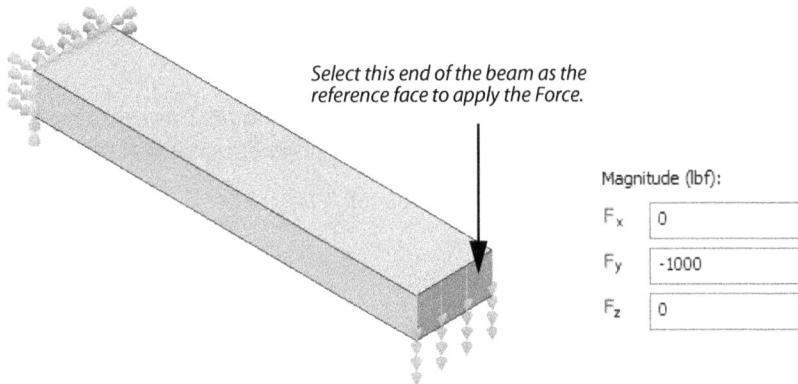

Select this end of the beam as the reference face to apply the Force.

Magnitude (lbf):

F$_x$	0
F$_y$	-1000
F$_z$	0

10. Review the Subcases node in the Analysis sub-tree and note the following:

- Subcase1 is the only subcase that currently exists in this analysis.
- A single load (Load1) and constraint (Constraint1) exist in Subcase1.

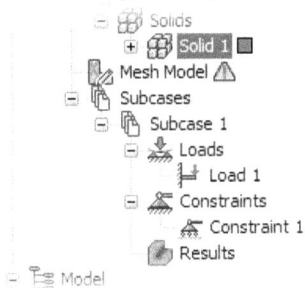

11. Review the Constraints and Loads nodes in the Model sub-tree and note the following:

- A single constraint (Constraint1) has been added to the model. This exists in Subcase 1. However, this constraint can be copied to any other Subcase that may be created at a later time.

- A single load (Load1) has been added to the model. This exists in Subcase 1. However, this load can be copied to any other Subcase that may be created at a later time.

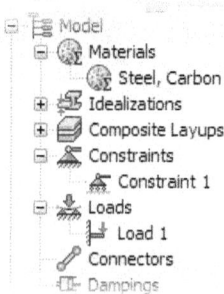

Mesh the Beam

In this task, you will generate the default mesh that will be used for the analysis based on the Solid Elements idealization assignment. No further changes will be made to the mesh at this time. Later in this learning guide, you will learn more specifics about the tools that can be used to modify the mesh.

1. In the Mesh panel, click (Generate Mesh). The mesh is displayed on the model in the color that was assigned to the Solid 1 Idealization (dark green). Note that once the mesh is generated, the Nodes and Elements nodes, at the top of the Analysis sub-tree, are updated with values.

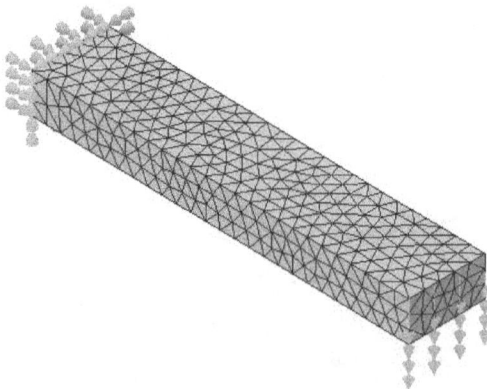

Run the Analysis

In this task, you will run the analysis that has been created and review the results in the Autodesk Nastran Output view.

1. In the Analysis sub-tree, note that in Subcase1 there are no Result nodes listed.

2. In the Solve panel, click [icon] (Run).

3. The Autodesk Nastran Output tab is activated in the Model Browser. This view displays a log of the results. Note that there were no errors at the bottom of the output list but that there was one warning.

4. Click OK to confirm the completion of the Nastran solution. The Model Tree is returned to the display.

5. At the top of the Model Browser, select the Autodesk Nastran Output tab to return to the output view.

Note: As an alternative to reviewing the log in the Output view, you can also open the .LOG or .OUT files in Notepad. These files are located in the *<model name>\InCAD\FEA* folder that was created at the same level as the source model file.

6. Scroll to the bottom of the report and note that there are no warnings or errors identified. Warnings are displayed in black, and errors are displayed in red. If there are errors or warnings, you can scroll up through the log and review them.

```
Model   Favorites   Autodesk Nastran Model Tree   Autodesk Nastran Output   ×   Autodesk Nastran File   +

PERCENT COMPLETE:   100

DELETING FILE:   7p1o818x1.ECD

MODEL ANALYSIS TIME SUMMARY

TOTAL CPU TIME = 3.3 SECONDS
WALLCLOCK TIME = 14.7 SECONDS

EXECUTION TERMINATED NORMALLY

TOTAL WARNINGS     = 0  ⟵
TOTAL FATAL ERRORS = 0
```

7. Return the display to the Autodesk Nastran Model Tree tab.

Display the Results

In this task, you will graphically display the Displacement and Stress (von Mises) results in the main window.

1. In the Analysis sub-tree, note that in Subcase1 there are now four Result nodes listed. These results were defined for the default Linear Static analysis. Later in this learning guide, you will learn how to set and customize the results that are to be displayed.

2. To visualize the displacement, right-click on Displacement in the Results node and select Display. The maximum displacement is 0.0687 inches.

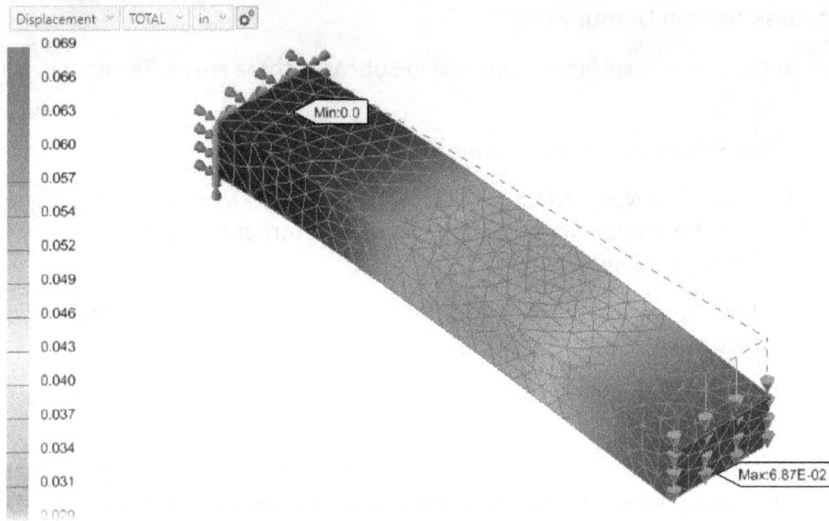

3. To visualize Stress, right-click on von Mises in the Results node and select Display. The maximum stress is approximately 30,021 psi.

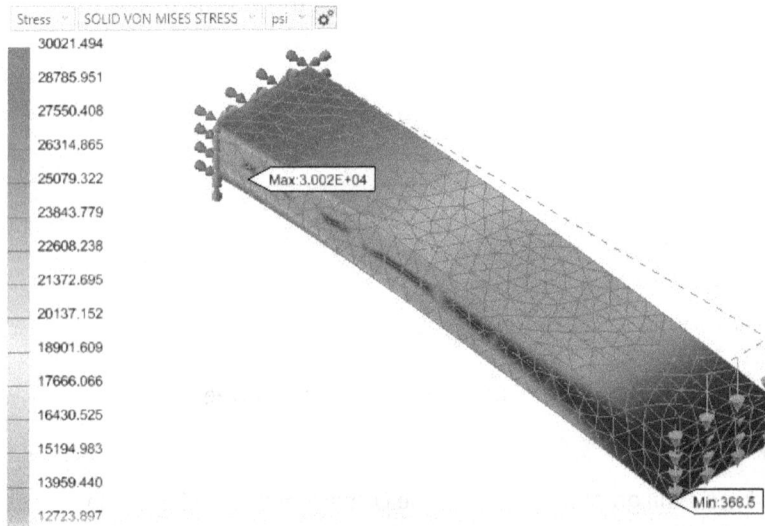

4. Continue to display the other two results.

5. In the Exit panel, click ✔ (Finish Autodesk Nastran In-CAD).

6. Save the model.

Review the Files that are Created from an Autodesk Nastran In-CAD Analysis

In this task, you will navigate to the working folder from which the First Beam.ipt part file was opened and review the folders and files that were created when the analysis was run using Autodesk Nastran In-CAD.

1. Open Windows Explorer and navigate to the *C:\Autodesk Nastran InCAD 2019 Essentials Exercise Files\Cantilevered_Beam\First Beam\InCAD\FEA* folder. Note that the *First Beam\InCAD\FEA* folders were created in the same folder as the source model that was analyzed. This occurred when the analysis was run. The files generated in the FEA folder store the following information:

   - *<unique name>.FNO* - Binary results file.
   - *<unique name>.LOG* - Analysis data.
   - *<unique name>.nas* - Nastran bulk data file.
   - *<unique name>.OUT* - ASCII Results file.
   - *<unique name>.RSF* - Results summary.
   - LICENSE.LOG - Summary of the license manager activity.

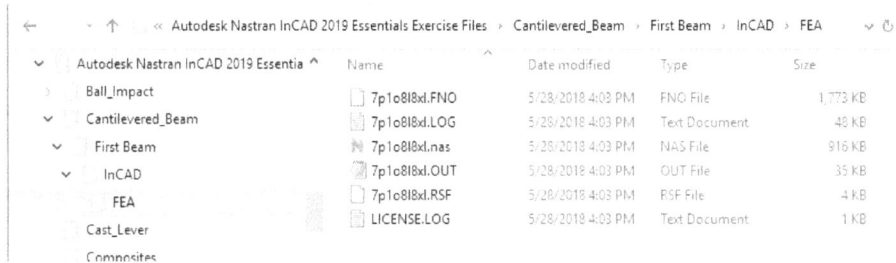

All but the .FNO file can be opened in a Notepad window for reviewing their content.

Working with the Default Analysis

The goal in this chapter is to become more familiar with navigating the Autodesk Nastran Model Tree and working with the nodes that are used to define an analysis. The default Linear Static analysis will be used throughout the chapter. You will learn to edit and create materials and idealizations that define how the model will be analyzed. Additionally, you will learn to assign the boundary conditions (constraints and loads) that will simulate the working conditions of the model.

Objectives

After completing this chapter, you will be able to:

- Duplicate an existing analysis in the Autodesk Nastran Model Tree.
- Create new or duplicate existing subcases in an analysis.
- Describe where currently used and additional idealizations and materials can be listed in the Model Tree.
- Create, edit, and assign idealizations for use in an analysis.
- Add a material from the Material Library or create a new material for use in an analysis.
- Edit and assign a material for use in an analysis.
- Create constraints with the required degrees of freedom and assign them to entities.
- Create loads that accurately represent the magnitude and location of the loads the model will experience in the working environment.
- Edit constraints and loads that exist in the model.
- Assign constraints and loads to subcases in an analysis.
- Create connectors with the required degrees of freedom and assign them to entities.
- Edit connectors that exist in the model.
- Assign connectors to the analysis.

Lesson: Analysis & Subcases

Overview

This lesson describes the Analysis sub-tree layout. You will learn how subcases can be used to test alternate loading and constraint scenarios in an analysis, as compared to simply creating multiple analyzes.

Objectives

After completing this lesson, you will be able to:

- Duplicate an existing analysis in the Autodesk Nastran Model Tree.
- Create new or duplicate existing subcases in an analysis.

Understanding an Analysis Sub-Tree

An analysis is stored as a sub-tree in the Autodesk Nastran Model Tree and defines the specific settings for how the analysis will be conducted on the model. Multiple analyzes can be included in the model. If multiple variations of a single analysis are required, subcases can also be used to define different scenarios (i.e., alternate loads and constraints). The benefit of using a subcase is that the analysis definition remains the same and only the subcase definition is changed.

By default, when the model is opened in the Autodesk Nastran In-CAD environment, a single Linear Static analysis called Analysis 1 is created. It contains a single subcase. The subcase definition is initially undefined.

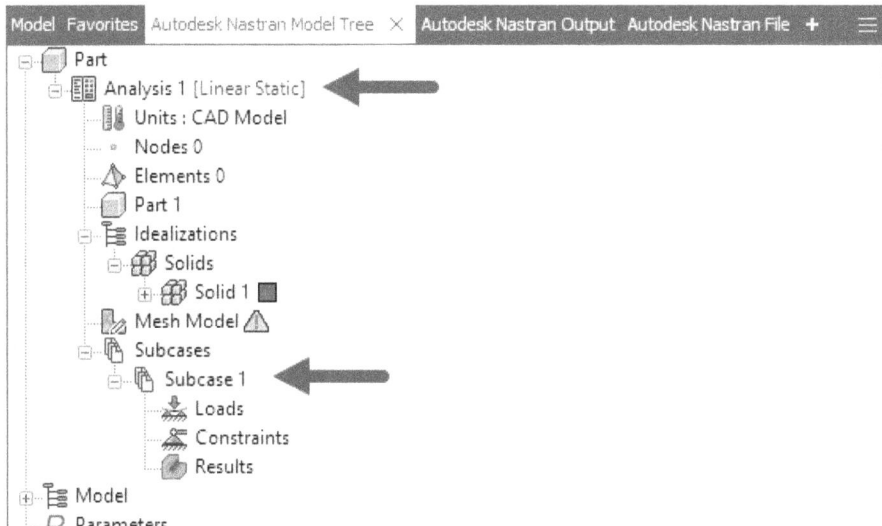

The Subcases node manages the loads, constraints, and results for a single instance of the analysis. Multiple subcases with varying loads and constraints can be set to run sequentially in an analysis. You can add and edit settings from this node. In the following lessons you will learn how to add loads and constraints to a subcase.

Working with Analyzes & Subcases

This section discusses some of the procedures that can be used to work with an analysis and its subcases to efficiently create, duplicate, and remove them from the Model tree. Later in this learning guide, you will learn how to create a new analysis.

- To duplicate an existing analysis, right-click on the Analysis node at the top of the Model Tree and click Duplicate.

- The new copy becomes the active analysis. Only one analysis can be active at one time. To activate an alternate analysis, select it, right-click, and select Activate.

- Consider renaming the analysis to a unique descriptive name. To rename, right-click on the analysis and select Rename.

- To delete an analysis, right-click on the analysis name and select Delete.

Procedure: To Create a New Subcase

1.   In the Analysis sub-tree, right-click on the Subcases node and select New. The Subcase dialog box opens.

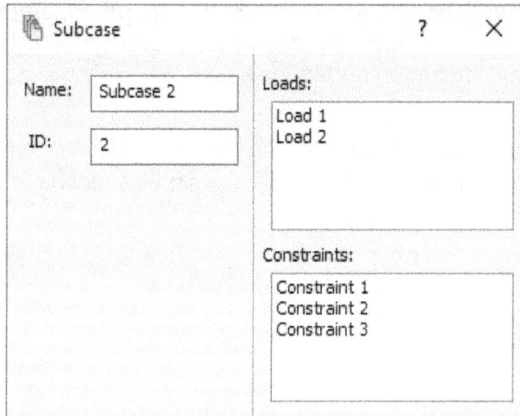

2.   Enter a new name for the subcase.

3.   In the Loads section select any of the existing model loads to assign them to the new subcase. If no loads exist, this list will be empty.

4.   In the Constraints section select any of the existing model constraints to assign them to the new subcase. If no constraints exist, the list will be empty.

5.   Click OK to create the subcase and close the Subcase dialog box.

Procedure: To Duplicate an Existing Subcase

1.   In the Analysis sub-tree, right-click on the Subcases name to be duplicated and select Duplicate. A copy of the subcase is created.

2.   (Optional) Right-click on the new subcase name and select Rename to edit its default name.

3.   Make changes to the loads, constraints, and result templates, as required.

Changes can be made to a subcase directly in the Subcase dialog box or you can manipulate its items directly in the Autodesk Nastran Model Tree.

- To edit a subcase, right-click its name and select Edit. Using the Subcase dialog box you can reassign, add, or remove loads and constraints or rename the subcase.
- To delete a subcase, right-click its name and select Delete.
- To deactivate a subcase, right-click its name and clear the Activate option.
- To rename a subcase, right-click its name and select Rename.
- Adding loads and constraints to a subcase are discussed in the Constraints & Loads lesson later in this chapter.

Lesson: Idealizations & Materials

Overview

This lesson describes the importance and how to define the materials and idealizations when setting up for an Autodesk Nastran In-CAD analysis. You will learn about the default material and idealization that are assigned when a model is opened in the Nastran In-CAD environment, and how to add new materials and idealizations for use in the model.

Objectives

After completing this lesson, you will be able to:

- Describe where currently used and additional idealizations and materials can be listed in the Autodesk Nastran Model Tree.
- Create, edit, and assign idealizations for use in an analysis.
- Add a material from the Material Library or create a new material for use in an analysis.
- Edit and assign a material for use in an analysis.

Idealizations

The Idealizations node in the Model sub-tree can contain a single or multiple idealization definitions. They are used to define and group all property elements and can include the following:

- Element type (Solid, Shell, or Line) and their associated options.
- Material assignment.
- Color that will be used to display the mesh.

When an Inventor model is opened for the first time in the Autodesk Nastran In-CAD environment, a default idealization is created called Solid 1. It is created such that it defines a Solid Elements analysis using the model's default material. It is automatically assigned for use. Only one idealization can be assigned to a part analysis at one time; however, multiple idealizations can exist in the Model sub-tree at one time.

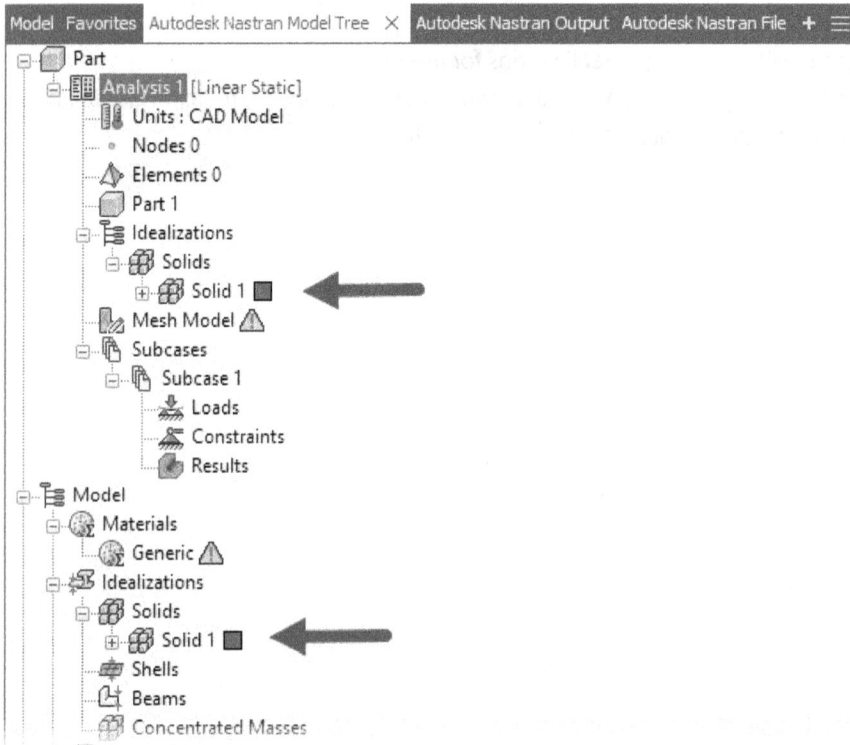

When analyzing an assembly file, multiple idealizations can be created and assigned to individual components in the assembly. By default, an idealization is created for each component that has a unique material assignment. When working in an assembly model analysis, it is recommended to rename the default idealization to help identify which is used and for which components. To rename an idealization, right-click its name and select Rename or double-click its name and enter a new name.

Overview of the Idealizations Dialog box

The Idealizations dialog box enables you to define the properties that will be used in an

analysis. In the Prepare panel, click 🔣 (Idealizations) to open the Idealizations dialog box. Alternatively, you can also right-click on the Idealizations node in the Model sub-tree and select New to open the same dialog box. You can create new Idealizations in the Analysis sub-tree by right-clicking on the element type in the Idealizations node and selecting New.

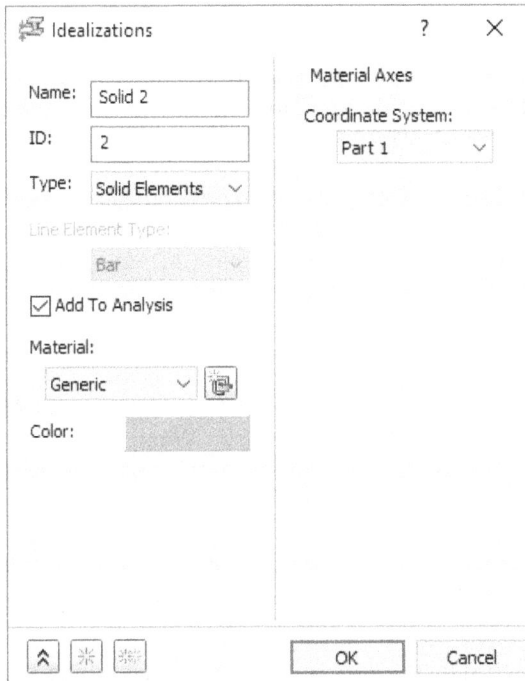

The following are available in the Idealizations dialog box for a Solid Elements analysis:

- **Name**: Defines the name for the new idealization.
- **ID**: Defines the ID of the idealization. This value is automatically updated sequentially as new idealizations are created so that it is unique.
- **Type** (default is Solid Elements): Assigns the element property for the model. Options include:
  - Solid Elements: 3D linear and parabolic tetrahedral elements.
  - Shell Elements: 2D quadrilateral and triangular elements.
  - Line Elements: 1D elements with 6 degrees of freedom.
- **Add to Analysis**: Assigns the idealization directly to the analysis once created. This option is not available when an idealization is being edited, it is only available during creation.
- **Material**: Defines the material for the idealization, which can be selected from the drop-

  down list or you can create a new material using the 🖼 (New Material). For more information on creating a new material, refer to the *Working with Materials* topic.

- **Color:** Assigns the color that will be used to display the mesh on the model. The color assignment of the idealization is random and can be changed as required, by selecting the color swatch and selecting a new color.
- **Associated Geometry:** Defines the geometry to which the idealization is assigned in multi-bodies or assembly model analysis. When using the Beam or Line Elements, this option varies to beam and line references.
- **Material Axes:** Assigns a material coordinate system for elements with orthogonal material. Global and User-defined Coordinate can be assigned.

> New coordinate systems must be created by right-clicking the Coordinate Systems node and selecting New. Once created, the coordinate system can be selected for use in an idealization. Alternate coordinate systems can also be used for loads and constraints.

Additional sections display in the Idealizations dialog box when either the Beam Element or Line Element types are selected. These are discussed later in this learning guide. For more information on the idealization types, refer to Autodesk Nastran In-CAD Help and search for "element properties" or "idealizations".

Idealizations in the Analysis

The Idealizations node exists in each analysis that is setup in Autodesk Nastran In-CAD. This node lists the idealization that is to be used when the analysis is run. When an Inventor model is opened in the Autodesk Nastran In-CAD environment, the default Idealization (such as Solid 1) is assigned to the analysis. For solid geometry, the default material in the model is represented using the Solid Elements type. For Frame Generator geometry, Beam Elements are used by default. If an analysis requires an alternate idealization, you must create it and assign it to the analysis. To replace and add idealizations in the analysis, use any of the following methods:

- Create a new idealization, assign it to at least one part, and ensure that Add to Analysis is activated.
- To replace an idealization in an analysis, select the idealization that is to be assigned in the Model sub-tree and drag and drop it to the Idealizations node. Click OK in the warning message that explains that the original one will be deleted. If working with an assembly, multiple idealizations can exist but only one can be assigned per component.
- To add an idealization to a new analysis, select the idealization name that is to be assigned in the Model sub-tree and drag and drop it to the Idealizations node.

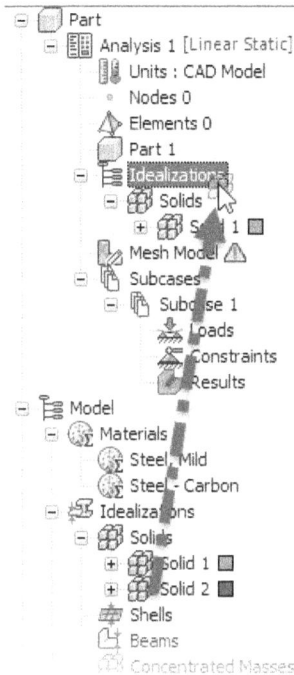

> 💡 To remove all idealizations of a particular type from an analysis, right-click on the element type in the Idealizations node and select Remove All. To remove an individual idealization, right-click on the idealization name and select Remove.

To edit and create new idealizations in the model, consider the following procedures. Additionally, consider copying existing idealizations and editing them.

Procedure: To Edit an Existing Idealization

1. Open the idealizations dialog box using any of the following methods:

   - Right-click on the idealization name in the Idealizations node, in the Model sub-tree, and select Edit. Alternatively, you can double-click on the idealization name.
   - If the idealization is assigned to the analysis, right-click on the idealization name in the analysis and select Edit. Alternatively, double-click on the idealization name.

2. To edit the idealization, you can make any of the following changes in the Idealizations dialog box:

   - Enter a new name.
   - Change the type of element that is being used.
   - Select a new material.
   - Define a new color by selecting the color swatch and assigning a new color.
   - Enter new values for the properties, as required.

3. Click OK to update and close the Idealizations dialog box.

Procedure: To Create a New Idealization

1. In the Prepare panel, click ☒ (Idealizations) to open the Idealizations dialog box.

2. Enter the name of the new idealization.

3. Select the Type of element (e.g., Solid Elements, Beam Elements, or Line Elements).

4. Select a material. Alternatively, you can create a new material. For more information on creating a new material, refer to the *Working with Materials* topic.

5. (Optional) Select the color swatch and select a new color to define the mesh color. No selection is required to maintain the default color.

6. Enter specific property data for the select element type, as required. The fields vary depending on the type selected.

7. Ensure Add to Analysis is selected if you want to include the idealization in the current analysis.

8. If working in an assembly, enable Associated Geometry and select the components to assign the property to. If you want the idealization to apply to all of the parts, no component selection is required.

9. (Optional) Assign a material coordinate system for elements with orthogonal material. Global and User-defined Coordinates can be assigned, but they must first exist in the analysis.

10. Click OK to create the new idealization and close the Idealizations dialog box.

As you progress through this learning guide, you will learn about the idealization settings for the various analysis and element types.

Working with Materials

By default, when an Inventor model is opened in the Autodesk Nastran In-CAD environment, the assigned model material is automatically created as a material for use in the Nastran In-CAD analysis. The following occurs:

- The material(s) are automatically added to the Materials node in the Model sub-tree.
- The material(s) are assigned for use in an idealization. An idealization is created per unique material in an assembly. If the model is a single solid part, the material is assigned to Solid 1.

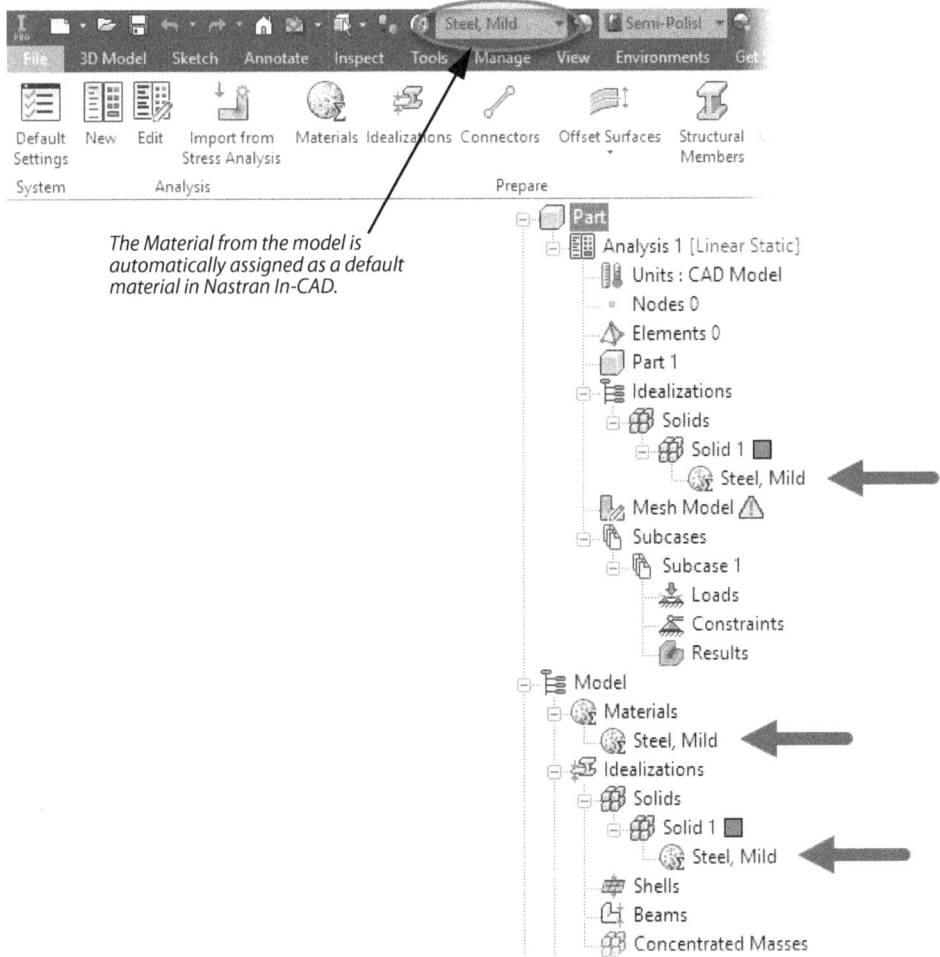

The Material from the model is automatically assigned as a default material in Nastran In-CAD.

> When an assembly is opened in the Autodesk Nastran In-CAD environment, the materials associated with every model in the assembly are automatically imported for use in an analysis.
>
> The model must have been saved prior to accessing the Autodesk Nastran In-CAD environment in order for the model's material to be recognized in the Materials node.

Overview of the Material Dialog box

The Material dialog box enables you to define a material. In the Prepare panel, click

(Materials) to open the Material dialog box. Alternatively, you can right-click on the Materials node in the Model sub-tree and select New to open the same dialog box.

The following are available in the Material dialog box:

- **Select Material**: Enables you to load a material from a material library.
- **Name**: Defines the name for the new material.
- **ID**: Defines the ID of the material. This value is automatically updated sequentially as new materials are created so that it is unique.

- **Type**: Defines the material type. The following are supported in Autodesk Nastran In-CAD. Depending on the type of material selected, the remaining fields in the Material dialog box change to provide for the required material properties. For more information on the material types, refer to Autodesk Nastran In-CAD Help and search for "material types".
  - Isotropic
  - Orthotropic 2D
  - Orthotropic 3D
  - Anisotropic 3D
  - Hyperelastic
  - Nitinol
  - Viscoelastic

> Only Isotropic material data can be loaded from the material library. To define non-isotropic materials, you can explicitly enter the material properties and save the material.

- **Sub Type**: Enables you to define a sub-type for the Hyperelastic material type. The options include Neo-Hookean, Mooney-Rivlin, Yeoh, Ogden, and Polynomial.
- **Idealizations**: Enables you to preassign which idealization the new material will be assigned to. By default, no idealization is selected, therefore, the material would only be added to the Materials node in the Model sub-tree.
- **Save New Material**: Saves a defined material property to a library file. The default library file is called ADSK_materials.nasmat and is stored in *C:\Program Files\Autodesk\Nastran 2019\In-CAD\Materials*. The ADSK_materials.nasmat library also contains a categorized list of all predefined materials. You can save custom materials to your own .nasmat file.
- **Analysis Specific Data**: Enables you to define additional data that is related to a specific analysis. The analysis types include Nonlinear, Fatigue, and PPFA (Progressive Ply Failure Analysis). However, their availability for customization is dependent on the material type that is active. For more information on the material types, refer to Autodesk Nastran In-CAD Help and search for "analysis specific data".

The remaining fields in the right-hand pane of the Material dialog box are dependent on the material type that is being created. The fields enables you to define such things as the following:

- General material properties.
- Structural material properties.
- Permittable strengths for failure analysis (e.g., tensile, compressive, shear) as well as the failure theory that should be used.
- Thermal material properties.
  Note: This can be toggled ON and OFF for a structural analysis.
- Hyperelastic material properties.

Assigning Materials from a Material Library

The Select Material option in the Material dialog box enables you to access a database of predefined Autodesk and Inventor materials. The Material DB dialog box enables you to navigate to and select a material for use in an analysis. Once a material is selected, click OK. The Material dialog box is immediately populated with the defined properties of the selected material.

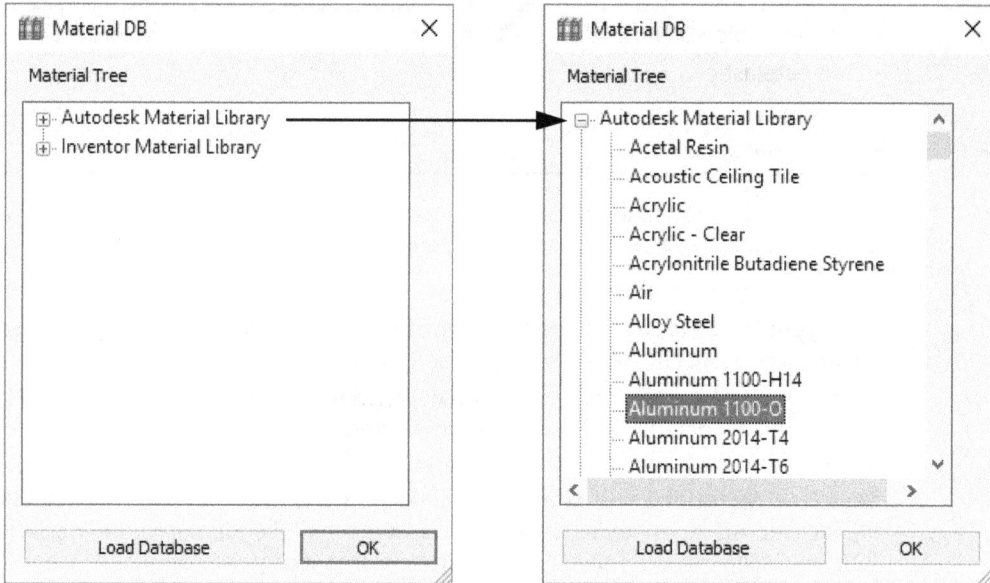

- Changes can be made in any of the property fields, as required. Changes made are not saved to the library. However, you can save a copy of the customized material to the custom Nastran material library using the Save New Material option.

- To load the custom database to access custom materials, select Load Database in the Material DB, navigate to, and select *C:\Program Files\Autodesk\Nastran 2019\Materials\In-CAD\ADSK_materials.nasmat* (substitute the actual filename if you have created your own material library). Materials you define are listed under the User Defined branch of the database. Once loaded it is listed in the Material DB and you can navigate to select a required material.

To analyze the model, the default material can be used, it can be edited to change any of its values, or new materials can be added to test alternate material behavior during analysis.

Procedure: To Create a New Material

1. In the Prepare panel, click (Materials). Materials are created by defining the material properties in the Material dialog box. Alternatively, use Select Material to select a predefined material from a library. This automatically populates all the fields.

2. Enter the name of the new material. If a material is being created from a library, you can maintain the default name or enter a new one.

3. Select the Type of material.

   Note: Only isotropic materials are available in the libraries.

4. (Optional) In the Idealizations section, select the name of a idealization to assign the new material to.

5. Enter specific property and analysis specific data for the material, as required. Not all the fields are required and the fields available are dependent on the type of material that is being created.

6. Click OK to create the new material and close the Material dialog box.

Procedure: To Create a New Material when Defining an Idealization

1. In the Prepare panel, click ⬚ (Idealizations).

2. In the Idealizations dialog box, click ⬚ (New Material). The Material dialog box opens to define the new material. For more information on completing the material creation, refer to *Procedure: To Create a New Material*.

3. Click OK to create the new material and close the Material dialog box.

4. Complete the definition of the idealization and click OK to close the Idealizations dialog box.

Procedure: To Edit an Existing Material

1. Open the Material dialog box using any of the following methods:

   - Right-click on the material name in the Materials node in the Model sub-tree and select Edit. Alternatively, you can also double-click on the material name.
   - If the material is used in an idealization, right-click on the material name in the idealization to which it is assigned and select Edit. This can be done in either the Analysis or Model sub-trees. Alternatively, you can also double-click on the material name.

2. In the Material dialog box, you can make any of the following changes to edit the material:

   - Enter a new name for the material.
   - Enter new values for the material's properties, as required.
   - Enter analysis specific data for the material.
   - Select or clear the selection of the idealization that the material is assigned to.
   - Save the material to the custom Nastran material library.

3. Click OK to update the material and close the Material dialog box.

To replace an existing material with a new material in an idealization you can use the drag and drop technique as follows. Alternatively, when editing the idealization, you can select a new material directly in the Idealizations dialog box.

- To replace the material in an idealization, select the material that is to be assigned in the Model sub-tree and drag and drop it to a an idealization. This can be done with idealizations in the analysis or in the Model sub-tree. Once dropped the material is immediately replaced.

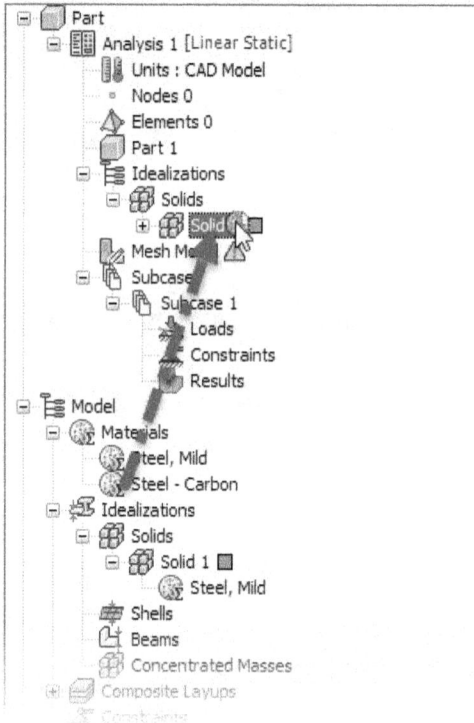

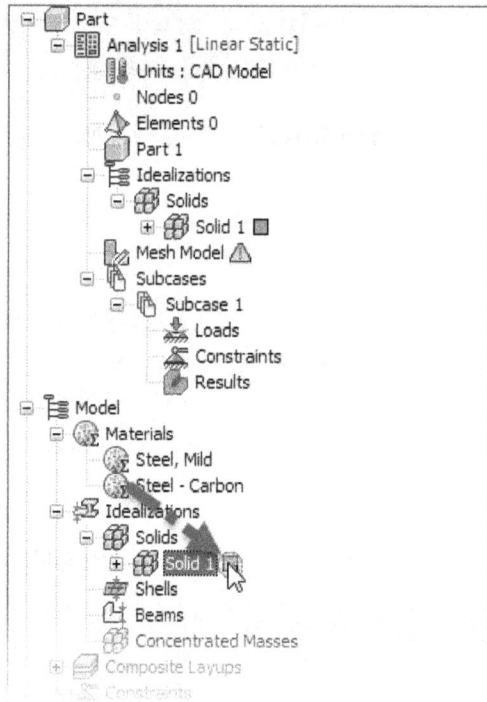

Lesson: Constraints & Loads

Overview

Loads and constraints simulate the boundary conditions that the model will experience in the working environment. Assigning the correct boundary conditions for FEA analysis is a critical step in achieving accurate and useful simulation results. Boundary conditions are defined by adding constraints and loads to the model. In this lesson, you will learn how to set the degrees of freedom for selected entities to define constraints in the model. Additionally, you will learn how to use loads to represent the forces that the model is required to withstand once manufactured.

Objectives

After completing this lesson, you will be able to:

- Create constraints with the required degrees of freedom and assign them to entities in the model.
- Create loads that accurately represent the magnitude and location of the loads the model will experience in the working environment.
- Edit constraints and loads that exist in the model.
- Assign constraints and loads to subcases in the analysis.

Working with Constraints

Constraints are used in the Autodesk Nastran In-CAD environment to simulate the boundary conditions of the model in its working environment. Assigning the correct constraint to accurately describe its physical boundary conditions is critical. Incorrectly representing a boundary condition can affect the accuracy of the results. In general, constraints are used to simulate the true supports (rigid foundation), contacting geometry (adjoining structure), or other boundary conditions in a model. Constraints can be applied to the part's face, edges, or vertices. Multiple constraints can be added to a model, as required.

> The constraints that are used to define the model's boundary conditions must not impose displacements, stresses, rigidity, or other behavior that would not be experienced in the model's working environment.

In the following model, a constraint was added to represent a pin that would be located through the lever component. This constraint fixes the model so that translational and rotational movement is prevented in all directions.

A fixed constraint was added to the inside surface of the model.

Overview of the Constraint Dialog box

The Constraint dialog box enables you to define a constraint in the model. In the Setup panel, click ![icon] (Constraints) to open the Constraint dialog box. Alternatively, right-click on the Constraints node in the Model or Analysis sub-tree and select New.

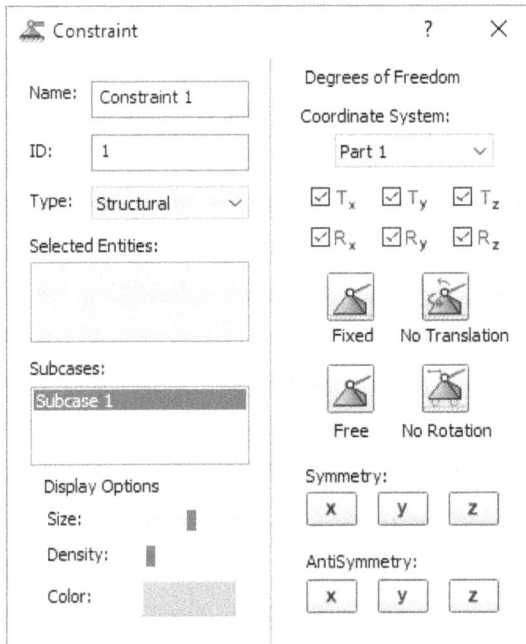

The following options are available in the Constraint dialog box:

- **Name**: Defines the name for the new constraint.
- **ID**: Defines the ID of the constraint. This value is automatically updated sequentially as new constraints are created so that it is unique.
- **Type**: Defines the constraint type. Structural, Pin, Thermal, and Response Spectrum are supported in Autodesk Nastran In-CAD. Depending on the type, the remaining fields in the dialog box change.
  - **Note:** The Pin constraint type only applies to cylindrical faces
- **Selected Entities**: Lists the various entities that were selected to be constrained. A face, edge or vertex can be selected.
- **Subcases**: Enables you to preassign which subcase the new constraint is assigned to. If no subcase is selected, the constraint is added to the Constraints node in the Model sub-tree.
- **Display Options**: Controls the display options of the constraint.
- **Degrees of Freedom**: Enables you to select the degrees of freedom of the nodes associated with the selected entities being constrained. Using the Coordinate System drop-down list, you can select an alternative coordinate system when the constraint is to be applied in a non-global direction (such as the radial direction of a cylindrical face).

Constraint Display Options

The Display Options section of the Constraint dialog box enables you to control how the markers that identify the constraint are displayed in the model. The options enable you to control the following:

- **Size**: Enables you to change the size of the constraint arrows.
- **Density**: Enables you to control the number constraint arrows.
- **Color**: Enables you to change the color of the constraint arrows.

Note: The constraint arrows are only visible when the constraint is assigned to an analysis and after ☐ 👓 (Preview) is enabled.

The following images show a constraint added to the end of the beam and how its constraint arrows can be modified using the Display Options.

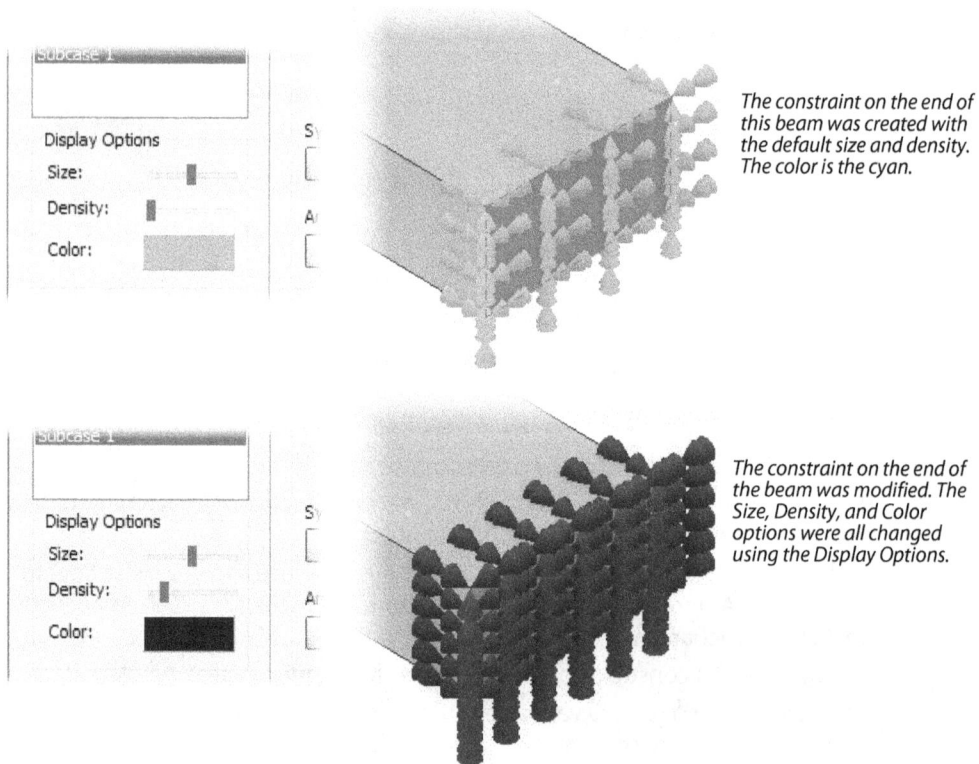

The constraint on the end of this beam was created with the default size and density. The color is the cyan.

The constraint on the end of the beam was modified. The Size, Density, and Color options were all changed using the Display Options.

Structural Degrees of Freedom Options

The Degrees of Freedom section of the Constraint dialog box enables you to fully define how the structural constraint is constrained by enabling or disabling the degrees of freedom options. By default, the constraint is assigned using the Part 1 coordinate system. This is the model coordinate system that was set when the model was opened in the Autodesk Nastran In-CAD environment. If a custom coordinate system was created in the Model Tree, it can be assigned for use in a new constraint.

Degrees of Freedom

Coordinate System:

Part 1

$\boxdot\,T_x$ $\boxdot\,T_y$ $\boxdot\,T_z$

$\boxdot\,R_x$ $\boxdot\,R_y$ $\boxdot\,R_z$

Fixed   No Translation

Free   No Rotation

Symmetry:

| x | y | z |

AntiSymmetry:

| x | y | z |

The four buttons located in the Degrees of Freedom section can be used to preset the degrees of freedom settings. Alternatively, you can explicitly enable or clear the degrees of freedom options to define the constraint, if one of these four buttons does not provide the correct degrees of freedom.

- Fixed ( ): Constrains translation and rotation in all directions.

- No Translation ( ): Prevents translation in any direction but enables rotation at each node on the selected entities.

- Free ( ): Enables translational movement in any direction and rotation about any axis.

- No Rotation ( ): Constrains nodal rotations for all axis directions but enables translational motion in any direction.

> Solid elements do not have rotational degrees of freedom. Therefore, rotational constraints have no effect on solid elements. A single node of a solid element acts like a frictionless ball joint when fully constrained (fixed).

Symmetry options are available at the bottom of the Degrees of Freedom section. These enable you to define symmetry or antisymmetry in the X, Y, or Z directions. Select any of these buttons and the symmetry options are preset for you. It is recommended that you verify the coordinate system to ensure that you are selecting the correct option.

> Symmetry is an important modeling technique that enables you to analyze a fraction of the structure without sacrificing quality. In some instances, it is used as a technique to improve solution quality. To accomplish this, the model geometry should be sectioned so that only half, quarter, or 1/8, or a radial section of the model geometry is displayed. This can be done in Inventor using an Extrude feature to remove half of the geometry. A constraint should then be added to the model geometry on the surfaces that define the symmetry plane. Symmetry constrains the "plane normal" translations and "in-plane" rotations. An example is shown in the following image.

> In the Constraint dialog box, you can use the X, Y, and Z symmetry options to preset the degrees of freedom that are to be constrained. Refer to the model coordinate system (or custom coordinate system) when defining the degrees of freedom. The normal vector to the symmetry plane should be parallel to the symmetry axis that is selected. For example, for symmetry in the XY plane, the Z symmetry axis should be selected to define the degrees of freedom.

Once the constraint is completed, it is added to the Constraints node in the Model sub-tree. If a subcase was selected, it would also be added directly to the selected subcase. If added to a subcase, the constraint markers display in the model.

> A Thermal constraint enables you to add a fixed temperature value to a selected entity.
>
> A Response Spectrum constraint enables you to set the degrees of freedom that are analyzed for a Shock/Response Spectrum Analysis. This constraint type is discussed further in Chapter 13.

Consider the following procedures when working with constraints.

Procedure: To Create a New Structural Constraint

1. In the Setup panel, click ⛫ (Constraints). Alternatively, you can right-click on either of the Constraints nodes in the Model sub-tree or an Analysis Subcase and select New.

2. Enter the name of the new constraint.

3. Select the Type of constraint (Structural, Pin, Thermal, or Response Spectrum).
    Note: The Pin constraint type applies only to cylindrical faces.
    Note: Only Structural and Response Spectrum constraints are discussed in this learning guide.

4. Select the entity or entities to which to apply the constraint. A face, an edge, or a vertex can be selected.

5. (Optional) In the Subcases section, select the name of a subcase to assign the new constraint to.

6. Select or clear the individual translational and rotational constraint directions in the Degrees of Freedom section, as required, to define how the constraint limits motion during the analysis. Alternatively, you can use the Fixed, Pinned, Free, No Rotation, Symmetry, and AntiSymmetry buttons to preset the degrees of freedom settings.

7. Select ☐ 👓 (Preview) at the bottom of the Constraint dialog box to preview the constraint prior to creating it.

8. (Optional) Use the display options to modify the display of the constraint arrows.

9. Click OK to create the new constraint and close the Constraint dialog box.

Procedure: To Edit an Existing Constraint

1. Open the Constraint dialog box using any of the following methods:
    - Right-click on the constraint name in the Constraints node, in the Model sub-tree and select Edit. Alternatively, you can double-click on the constraint name.
    - If the constraint is used in a subcase, right-click on the constraint name in the subcase and select Edit. You can also double-click on the constraint name.

2. In the Constraint dialog box you can make any of the following changes to edit the constraint:
    - Enter a new name for the constraint.
    - Select new or remove entities that have been selected as references for the constraint.
    - Clear the assignment of the constraint to a subcase or assign it to another subcase.
    - Modify the display options (size, density, or color) for the constraint.
    - Change the degrees of freedom or symmetry settings.

3. Click OK to update the constraint and close the Constraint dialog box.

Consider the following additional procedures when working with constraints:

- Similar to materials and idealizations, you can drag and drop constraints to include them in an analysis subcase. Multiple constraints can exist in a subcase.

- To remove a constraint from a subcase, right-click its name and select Remove. This removes the constraint from the subcase; however, it remains in the Model sub-tree. To remove it from the file, right-click its name in the Model sub-tree and select Delete.

- To clear the display of the constraint arrows, right-click its name in the subcase and clear the Display option. The constraint remains in the analysis but is just not visible.

Working with Loads

Loads are used in the Autodesk Nastran In-CAD environment to simulate the forces, motion, temperatures, or heat loads that the model is anticipated to withstand when in a working environment. Similar to assigning the correct constraints to represent the models boundary conditions, accurately describing how it will be loaded is critical. Loads can be applied to the part's face, edges, or vertices. Multiple loads can be added to a model, as required.

In the following model, a load was added to represent a force that will be applied to the top hole of the model when in a working environment. The load arrows are displayed in the model to identify that the load was added.

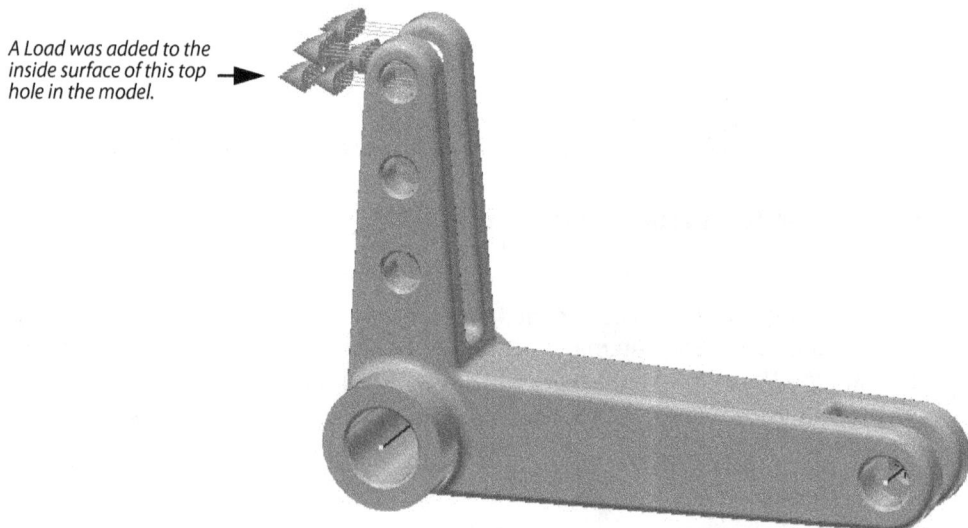

A Load was added to the inside surface of this top hole in the model.

Overview of the Load Dialog box

The Load dialog box enables you to define a load that is expected to be applied to the model in a working environment. In the Setup panel, click ⬇ (Load) to open the Load dialog box. Alternatively, you can also right-click on the Loads node in the Model or Analysis sub-tree and select New to open the same dialog box.

The following options are available in the Load dialog box:

- **Name**: Defines the name for the new load.
- **ID**: Defines the ID of the load. This value is automatically updated sequentially as new loads are created so that it is unique.

- **Type**: Defines the type of load. Depending on the type of load selected, the remaining fields in the dialog box change. For more information on the load types, refer to Autodesk Nastran In-CAD Help and search for "load type". Not all loads will be discussed in this learning guide. The following load types are supported in Autodesk Nastran In-CAD:

  - Force
  - Moment
  - Distributed Load
  - Pressure
  - Gravity
  - Remote Force

  - Bearing Load
  - Rotational Force
  - Enforced Motion
  - Initial Condition
  - Body Temperature
  - Temperature

  - Convection
  - Radiation
  - Heat Generation
  - Heat Flux
  - From Output

- **Selected Entities**: Defines the entities to which the load will be applied. The entity types that can be selected are bodies, faces, edges, and points.
  - **Tip:** Entities that are not supported for a selected load type are not selectable in the model.
- **Subcases**: Enables you to preassign which subcase the new load will be assigned to. If no subcase is selected, the load is only added to the Loads node in the Model sub-tree.
- **Display Options**: Controls the display options of the constraint. The display options are the same as those discussed for Constraints. For more information, refer to the *Constraints & Loads* lesson.
- **Load Definition**: Defines the specific settings that will define the selected load type.
- **Advanced Options**: Defines loads with varying load magnitudes across the geometry. Variable loads are not discussed in this learning guide.

Defining the Load

The Load Definition section varies depending on the Type of load selected. In general, the section has three sub-sections:

- Direction
- Coordinate system
- Magnitude

Direction

The Direction drop-down list provides options to define the direction the load will be defined. The options vary depending on the load type and coordinate system. The direction can be defined using the following options:

- **Components**: The load is applied based on the selected coordinate system from the model. Load values are applied based on the selected coordinate system (e.g., x, y, z or r, theta, phi).
- **Normal to Surface**: The load is applied normal to the selected surface.
- **Geometric Entity**: An edge or sketch is used to define the direction of load. It is the tangent vector at the start of the selected edge/sketch curve.

Coordinate System

The Coordinate System drop-down list enables you to select a global, CAD model, or a user-defined coordinate system when defining the load.

Magnitude

The Magnitude section enables you to enter load values in the x, y, and z directions. Forces on geometric entities (curves, vertices, surfaces) are on a per entity basis. For example, when you select two surfaces, the magnitude of that load will be applied to both surfaces resulting in a total load of two times the input magnitude. When Total Force is checked for the load on two selected surfaces, it will be applied to both surfaces by distributing the input magnitude.

Once the load is completed, it is added to the Loads node in the Model sub-tree. If a Subcase was selected, it would also be added directly to the selected Subcase. If added to a subcase, the load markers displays in the model.

Consider the following procedures when working with loads.

Procedure: To Create a New Load

1. In the Setup panel, click (Loads). Alternatively, you can right-click on either of the Loads nodes in the Model sub-tree or an Analysis Subcase and select New.

2. Enter the name of the new load.

3. Select the Type of load.

4. Select the entity or entities to which to apply the load. A body, face, edge, and point can be selected.

5. (Optional) In the Subcases section, select the name of a subcase to assign the new load to.

6. Define the Load Definition options to fully define the load.

7. (Optional) Select (Preview) at the bottom of the Constraint dialog box to preview the constraint prior to creating it. Use the display options to modify the display of the load arrows.

8. Click OK to create the new load and close the Load dialog box.

Procedure: To Edit an Existing Load

1. Open the Load dialog box using any of the following methods:

    - Right-click on the load name in the Loads node in the Model sub-tree and select Edit. Alternatively, you can double-click on the load name.

    - If the load is used in a subcase, right-click on the load name in the subcase and select Edit. Alternatively, you can double-click on the load name.

2. In the Load dialog box, you can make any of the following changes to edit the material:

    - Enter a new name for the load.

    - Select new or remove entities that have been selected as references for the load.

    - Clear the assignment of the load to a subcase or assign to another subcase.

    - Modify the display options (size, density, or color) for the load.

    - Change the load definition values and/or variable load settings.

3. Click OK to update the load and close the Load dialog box.

Consider the following additional procedures when working with loads:

- Similar to constraints, you can drag and drop loads to include them in an analysis subcase. Multiple loads can exist in a subcase.

- To remove a load from a subcase, right-click its name and select Remove. This removes the load from the subcase; however, it remains in the Model sub-tree. To remove it from the file, right-click its name in the Model sub-tree and select Delete.

- To clear the display of the load arrows, right-click its name in the subcase and clear the Display option. The load remains in the analysis but is just not visible.

Lesson: Connectors

Overview

The use of Connectors in an Autodesk Nastran In-CAD analysis enables you to simulate how a physical connector such as a rod, cable, spring, rigid body, or bolt will affect the model. The benefit of using connectors is that they enable you to accurately describe the degrees of freedom between components without physically modeling the connector geometry and analyzing the assembly model. In this lesson, you will learn how to create and assign connectors for use in an Autodesk Nastran In-CAD analysis.

Objectives

After completing this lesson, you will be able to:

- Create connectors with the required degrees of freedom and assign them to entities in the model.
- Edit connectors that exist in the model.
- Assign connectors to an analysis.

Working with Connectors

Connectors are used in the Autodesk Nastran In-CAD environment to simulate how a physical connector will affect the model. The benefit of using a Connector is that when assigned, the Connector eliminates the need to model the connector's geometry and include it in the model geometry that is being analyzed. The connector types that are available for use include the following:

- Rod
- Cable
- Spring
- Rigid Body
- Bolt

In the following model, a Rigid Body connector was added. The connector arrows are displayed in the model to identify that the connector was added.

A Rigid Body connector was added to a point at the midpoint of an axis. The dependent entities are the faces on the ends of the hole. ⟶

Overview of the Connector Dialog box

The Connector dialog box enables you to assign a Connector to geometry in the model. In the Setup panel, click ✐ (Connectors) to open the Connector dialog box. Alternatively, you can also right-click on the Connectors node in either the Model or Analysis sub-trees and select New to open the Connector dialog box.

Note: The Connectors node only displays in the Analysis sub-tree once the first connector has been added to the analysis.

The following are available for all types of connectors created using the Connector dialog box:

- **Name**: Defines the name for the new connector.
- **Type**: Defines the type of connector. Depending on the type of connector selected, the remaining fields in the dialog box change. For more information on the connector types, refer to Autodesk Nastran In-CAD Help and search for "connector type". Not all connector types will be discussed in this learning guide. The following Connector types are supported in Autodesk Nastran In-CAD.
  - Rod
  - Cable
  - Spring
  - Rigid Body
  - Bolt
- **Add to Analysis**: Defines whether the connector will be added to the analysis when it is created. If this option is disabled, the connector is added to the Model sub-tree and can be dragged and dropped to the analysis, as required.
- **Display Options**: Controls the display options of the connector. The display options are the same as those discussed for Constraints. For more information, refer to the *Constraints & Loads* lesson.

Defining the Connector Element Options

The Connector Element section of the Connector dialog box varies depending on the connector type that is being created. In all cases, it defines the entities to which the connector will be applied. Multiple elements can be assigned.

- **Rod/Cable/Spring**: The options available for these connector types enable you to define the end points for the connector's placement. Multiple rod, cable, or spring elements can be created in each connector. When these connectors are created, one line element at a time, you have the option of grouping additional elements under the same connector name, ID, and parameters (but with different endpoints). The first is "Element 1," the second "Element 2," and so on. Click "Next" to clear the endpoint fields, increment the element number, and prepare for defining the next segment's endpoints.
- **Rigid Body**: The Connector Element options available for the Rigid Body Connector type varies based on the type of rigid connector being added (Rigid or Interpolation). Both types require point and entity selection. For a Rigid type, the load is applied to all elements on the references or at the center of a reference, where in a Interpolation, the load is distributed based on loading direction across the references. Additionally, you can select the translational and rotational degrees of freedom that will be constrained with the placement of the connector.
  - In a Rigid type, all of the elements (independent point and dependent points) move in exactly the same way. It simulates a truly rigid body connection. Any type of point load, mass, or constraint can be applied to the independent point.

- An Interpolation type is not truly rigid. Instead of tying the displacements of the elements together, an interpolation connector distributes a force or mass placed at the reference point among the points belonging to the "Entities to be Averaged." There will also be relative displacement between the points on the selected entities (not like a rigid body connection). This type of connector does not support applying constraints or enforced motions at the reference point.

- **Bolt**: The options available for the Bolt Connector type enable you to define the surface or edge that represents the bearing surface or edge for the bolt head or nut that is being represented.

Defining the Connector Type Options

The options available on the right-hand side of the Connector dialog box enables you to define the specific settings for the connector that has been selected. These options all vary depending on the type. The sections that display for each type are described as follows:

- **Rod**: Enables you to define the rods cross-sectional area (A), its polar moment of inertia (J), its stress recovery location (C), and its non-structural mass. Additionally, you must assign a material that will be used for the rod.

- **Cable**: Enables you to define the initial cable slack (U_0), initial cable tension (T_0), its cross sectional area (A), its moment of inertia (I), and its permittable tensile stress (S_T). The Initial and Continuous PreLoad options define if T_0 is the initial preload of the cable (Initial) or whether T_0 is the actual tensile load and remains constant (Continuous). Additionally, you must assign a material that will be used for the cable.

- **Spring**: Enables you to define elemental Damping Coefficient (GE) to be used if elemental damping is used in a dynamic analysis and the coordinate system. Additionally, stress and strain recovery coefficients can be assigned. Typically these values are never changed.

- **Rigid Body**: Enables you to define whether the rigid body type is Rigid or Interpolation. Rigid defines RBE2 (fully rigid) element types and Interpolation defines RBE3 (interpolation) element types which is typically used to distribute loads or masses.

> When using RBE2 (Rigid) elements, the Dependent entities will move exactly how the Independent entity moves. When using RBE3 (Interpolation) elements, the displacement of the dependent entities is not tied to the displacement of the reference node. Instead, a force or mass applied at the reference point is distributed along the dependent entities on a proportional basis. The resulting nodal forces or masses depend on the size and location of the entities (relative to the reference point).

- **Bolt**: Enables you to define the specific settings for either a bolt and cap screw. The options that are available for each vary only slightly. It defines the bolt diameter, head washer height, the nut washer height (Bolt only), useful length (Cap Screw only), and the bolt's material. If the critical material properties (E, nu, alpha) are required, select User Defined and enter new values. The PreLoad options can be used to assign simple axial and torque preloads to the Bolt connection.

Once the connector is completed, it is added to the Connectors node in the Model sub-tree. If the Add to Analysis option was selected, it is also added directly to the analysis. If added to the analysis, the connector markers display in the model.

Consider the following procedures when working with connectors.

Procedure: To Create a New Connector

1. In the Setup panel, click ✐ (Connectors) to open the Connector dialog box. Alternatively, you can also right-click on the Connectors node in either the Model or Analysis sub-trees and select New.

2. Enter the name of the new connector.

3. Select the Type of connector.

4. Select Add to Analysis to add the connector directly to the active analysis.

5. Select the entity or entities to which to apply the connector. Depending on the type of connector that is being added the reference options will vary. A sketch point, nodes, sketched line, faces, and edges can be selected.

6. For Rigid Body connectors, select the translational and rotational degrees of freedom that will be constrained with the placement of the connector.

7. (Optional) Use the display options to modify the display of the constraint arrows.

8. Define each specific Connection option to fully define the new connection. The options vary depending on the type.

9. Click OK to create the new connector and close the Connector dialog box.

Procedure: To Edit an Existing Connector

1. Open the Connector dialog box using any of the following methods:
   - Right-click on the connector name in the Connectors node, in the Model sub-tree and select Edit. Alternatively, you can double-click on the load name.
   - If a connector is used in an analysis, right-click on the connector name in the analysis and select Edit. Alternatively, you can double-click on the connector name.

2. In the Connector dialog box, you can make any of the following changes to edit the material:
   - Enter a new name for the connector.
   - Select new or remove entities that have been selected as references for the connector.
   - Modify the display options (size, density, or color) for the connector.
   - Change the connector definition values.

3. Click OK to update the connector and close the Connector dialog box.

Consider the following additional procedures when working with connectors:

- Similar to constraints and loads, you can drag and drop connectors to include them in an analysis. Multiple connectors can exist for the analysis.

- All subcases in an analysis will incorporate the use of the connectors during analysis. If a scenario is required where connectors are to be included in one analysis and not another, multiple analyses must be created.

- To remove a connector from an analysis, right-click its name and select Remove. This removes the connector from the analysis; however, it remains in the Model sub-tree. To remove it from the file, right-click its name in the Model sub-tree and select Delete.

- To clear the display of the connector arrows, right-click its name in the analysis and clear the Display option. The connector remains in the analysis but is just not visible.

Using Rigid Connectors as a Constraint

A commonly used technique in FEA is the 'ball joint' constraint to control rotations. The ball joint constraint uses rigid elements to control a reference point. The rigid elements are often called 'spokes' or 'spider webs', given their appearance. The movement of an edge or surface is tied to a reference point to enable more natural movement. Rigid connectors can be used to represent a ball joint or pin joint constraint.

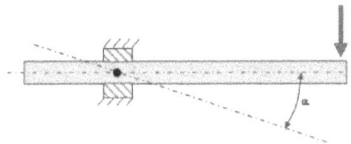

Exercise: Cast Lever Boundary Conditions I

In this exercise, you will conduct a linear static stress analysis of a simple lever arm part. You will use boundary conditions often found in entry-level CAD-based simulation systems. Note that in later exercises, you will build on the steps performed here to refine the analysis setup and improve the overall accuracy of the simulation.

The model is a lever arm as shown in the following image.

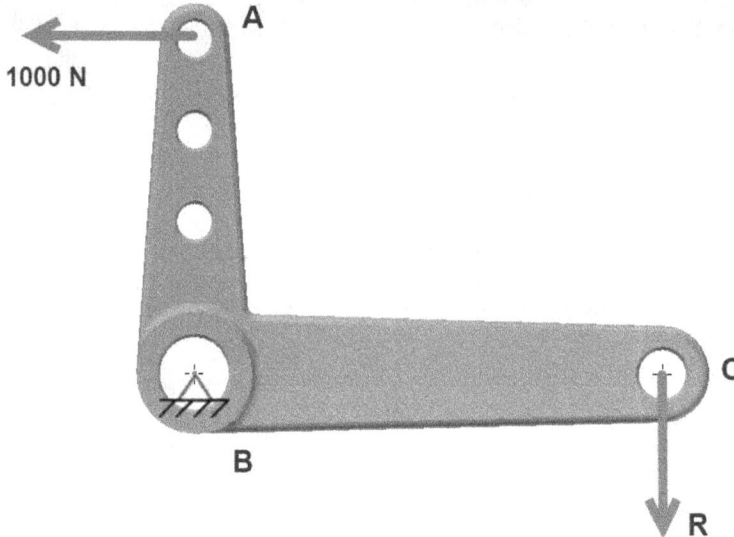

- A 1000 N load is applied to the top-most hole (A).
- The lever is pinned at the center (B).
- Assume a rod passes through hole (C) and is locked against movement.
- The reaction force, R, balances the loads, so the part is in static equilibrium. A force summation results in R = 687.5 N.

Open the Model & Start the Autodesk Nastran In-CAD Environment

1. Open the file *C:\Autodesk Nastran InCAD 2019 Essentials Exercise Files\Cast_Lever\Cast Lever.ipt*.

2. Select the Environments tab and click Autodesk Nastran In-CAD to activate the Autodesk Nastran In-CAD environment.

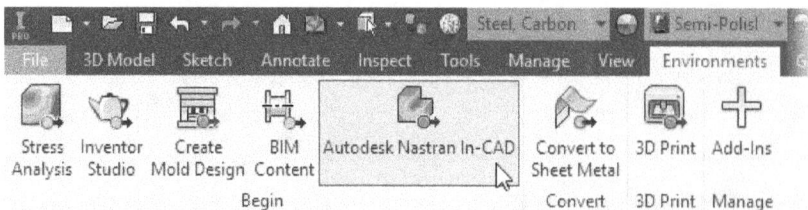

Assign New Materials

In this task, you will review the Autodesk Nastran Model Tree to identify the current material that was brought in from the Inventor model. You will also add additional material types that will be used in an analysis. You will learn how materials can be added using either the Materials or Idealizations options in the Prepare panel.

1. In the Autodesk Nastran Model Tree, expand the Idealizations and Materials nodes in the Model and Analysis sub-trees, as shown below. Note that by default, Solid 1 is created for you and the current material in the model is assigned (Steel, Mild).

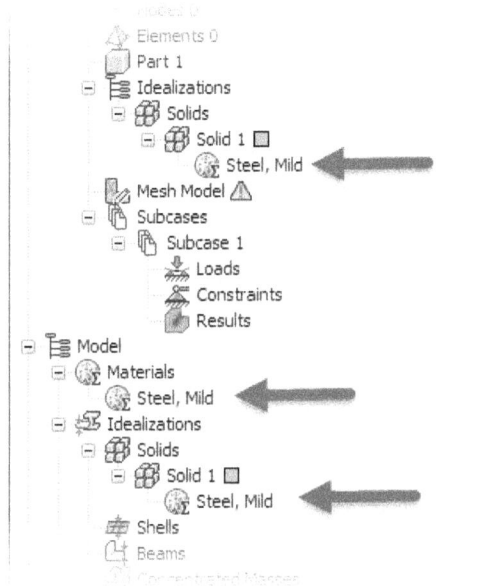

2. In the Prepare panel, click (Materials) to open the Material dialog box.

3. Click Select Material in the top-left corner of the dialog box.

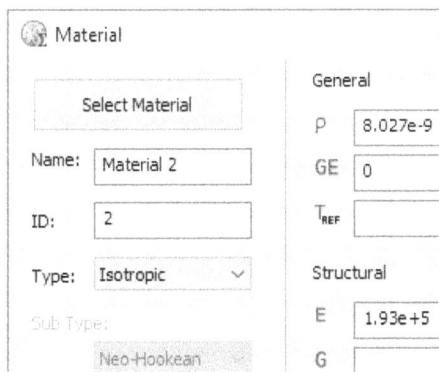

4. In the Material DB dialog box, expand Autodesk Material Library and select Steel - Carbon from the list. Click OK.

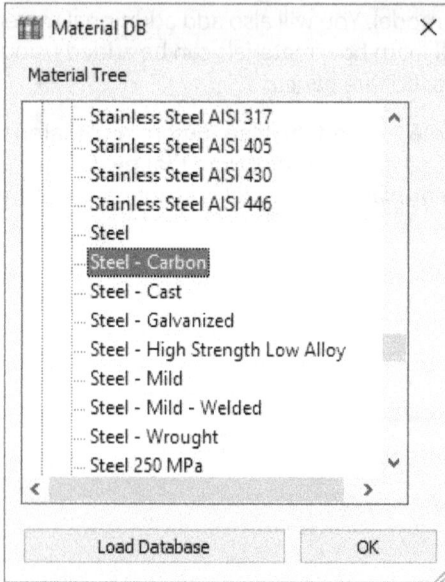

Material DB ✕

Material Tree

- Stainless Steel AISI 317
- Stainless Steel AISI 405
- Stainless Steel AISI 430
- Stainless Steel AISI 446
- Steel
- Steel - Carbon
- Steel - Cast
- Steel - Galvanized
- Steel - High Strength Low Alloy
- Steel - Mild
- Steel - Mild - Welded
- Steel - Wrought
- Steel 250 MPa

Load Database	OK

5. Note that the Material Name, Type, and many of the other properties are populated using the data that was stored for this material in the library.

6. Note the following in the Material dialog box:

- Solid 1 is not selected by default in the Idealizations section. This means that this new material will be added only to the Materials node in the Model sub-tree. From here, it can later be assigned to an idealization. Alternatively, if Solid 1 had been selected, the Steel - Carbon material would replace Steel, Mild and both materials would remain listed in the Materials node. Do not select Solid 1so that the material is added but not assigned to an idealization.

- New materials can be created by entering property values and selecting OK, as an alternative to using the library.

- New materials that are manually created can be saved for use in other models by selecting Save New Material to save to a materials file (.NASMAT) that is stored in the software installation location.

7. Click OK in the Materials dialog box. Note that the material is added to the Materials node in the Model sub-tree but it is not used in Solid 1.

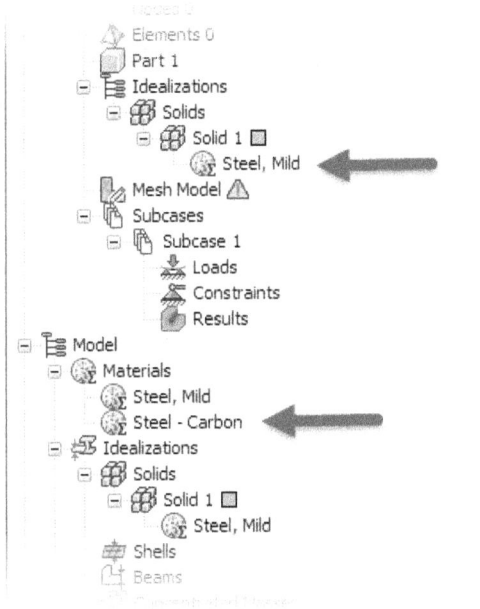

8. To assign Steel - Carbon to Solid 1, select it in the Materials node and drag and drop it onto Solid 1.

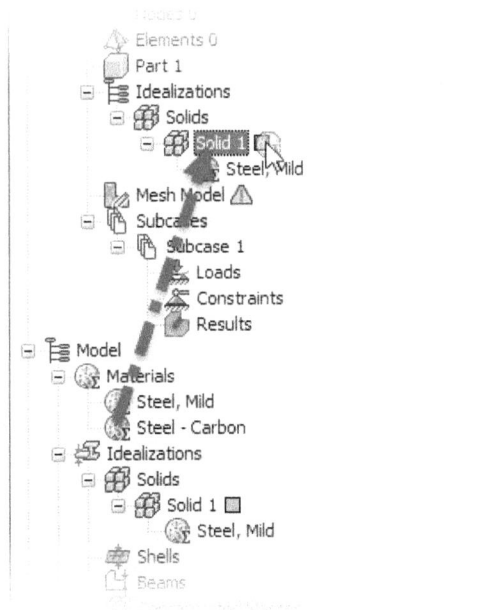

9. Alternatively, the next material will be created in the Solid 1 idealization. In the Idealizations node, in either the Model or Analysis sub-trees, right-click on Solid 1 and select Edit to open the Idealizations dialog box.

10. In the Material drop-down list, note that both Steel - Carbon (currently assigned) and Mild Steel are listed. You can select from this list as a method for changing the material that is assigned to Solid 1.

11. In the Idealizations dialog, click (New Material).

12. Click Select Material in the top-left corner of the dialog box.

13. In the Material DB dialog box, expand Autodesk Material Library and select Aluminum 1100-O from the list. Click OK.

14. In the Idealizations section, select Solid 1. This automatically assigns this new material for use in Solid 1without having to manually replace Steel - Carbon.

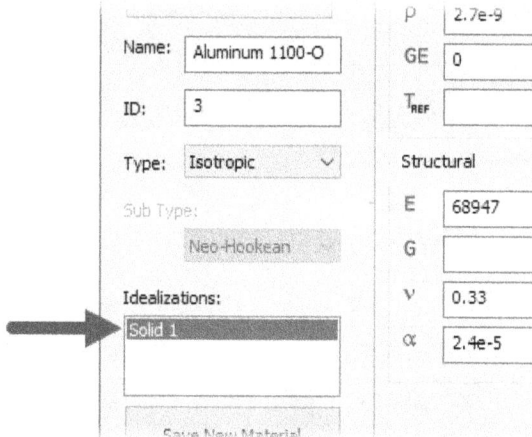

15. Click OK on the Material dialog.

16. In the Color box, select a dark orange color as the idealization color. Click OK.

17. Click OK on the Idealizations dialog box.

18. In the Model or Analysis sub-trees review the material associated with Solid 1. Aluminum 1100-O should be the material associated with this idealization.

Constrain & Load the Model

In this task, you will assign a constraint that fixes the lever at Point B, preventing movement in any direction. Additionally, loads will be added so that the model can be analyzed.

1. In the Setup panel, click (Constraints) to open the Constraints dialog box.

2. In the Degrees of Freedom section of the dialog box, select (Fixed). This presets the degrees of freedom options so that translation and rotation is constrained in all directions.

3. In the Subcases section of the dialog box, confirm that Subcase 1 is selected. This ensures that the constraint is automatically added to Subcase 1.

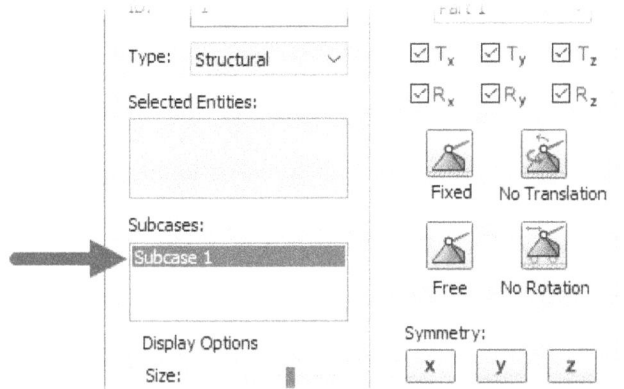

Tip: If a constraint is not yet required in a subcase, its selection can be cleared in the Subcases section. Once cleared, the constraint is only added to the Model sub-tree and it can be assigned to a subcase later, if required.

4. Select the inside surface of the center hole shown below.

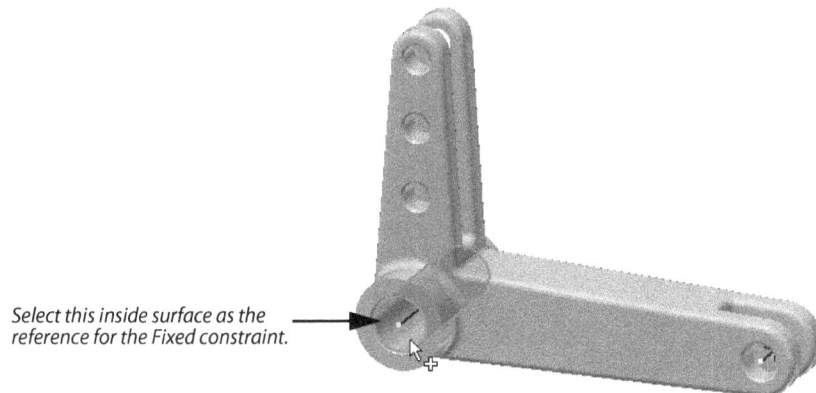

Select this inside surface as the reference for the Fixed constraint.

5. Select ☐ 👓 (Preview) at the bottom of the Constraint dialog box to preview the constraint prior to creating it.

6. In the Display Options section of the Constraint dialog box, complete the following:
   - Drag the Size slider to vary the size of the constraint vectors.
   - Drag the Density slider to vary the number of constraint vectors that are displayed.
   - Select the Color box to select a dark blue color as an alternate display color for the constraint vectors.

7. Click OK to complete the constraint.

8. In the Setup panel, click (Loads) to open the Loads dialog box.

9. By default Force is set as default type. Maintain this setting.

10. Select the two surfaces shown below to assign the load.

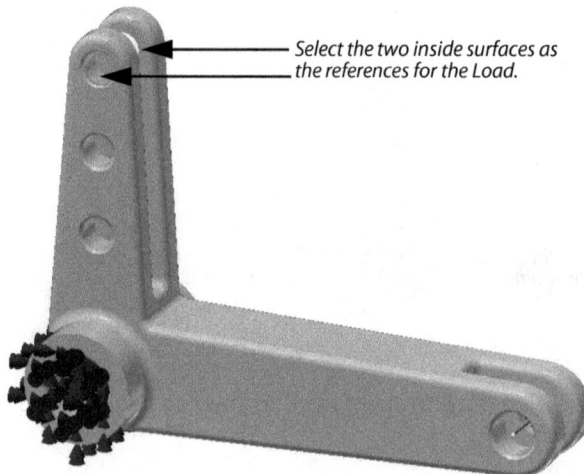

Select the two inside surfaces as the references for the Load.

11. In the Subcases section of the dialog box, confirm that Subcase 1 is selected. This ensures that the Load is automatically added to Subcase 1.

   Tip: If a load is not yet required in a subcase, its selection can be cleared in the Subcases section. Once cleared, the load is only added to the Model sub-tree and it can be assigned to a subcase later, if required.

12. Review the model coordinate system that displays on the model and note the Y direction. This is the direction that the force is required to be applied.

13. In the Load Definition section, select Total Force.

14. In the Total Force section, in the Fy field, enter **-1000**.

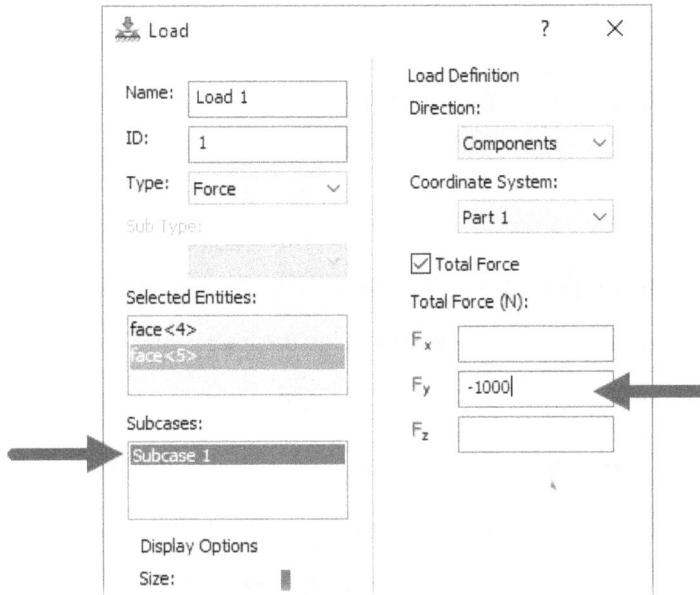

15. Select ☐ 👓 (Preview) at the bottom of the Load dialog box to preview the load prior to creating it.

16. Set the display options for this Load so that it displays as shown in the following image.

   Tip: The Size, Density, and Color or the load vectors can also be changed in the same way as the Constraint vectors.

17. Click OK in the Load dialog box.

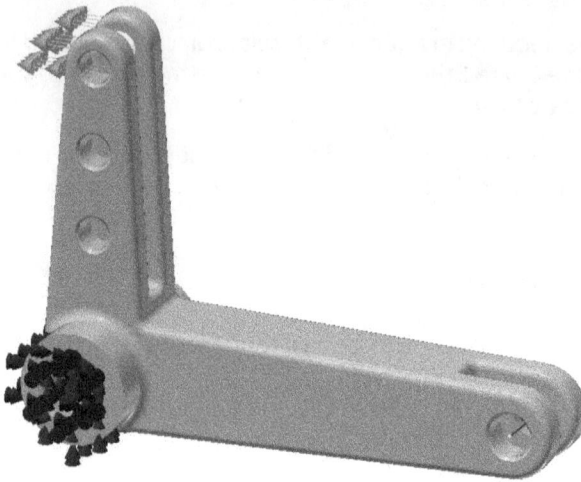

18. In the Setup panel, click ⬇ (Loads) to open the Loads dialog box.

19. By default Force is set as default type. Maintain this setting.

20. Select the two surfaces shown below to assign the load.

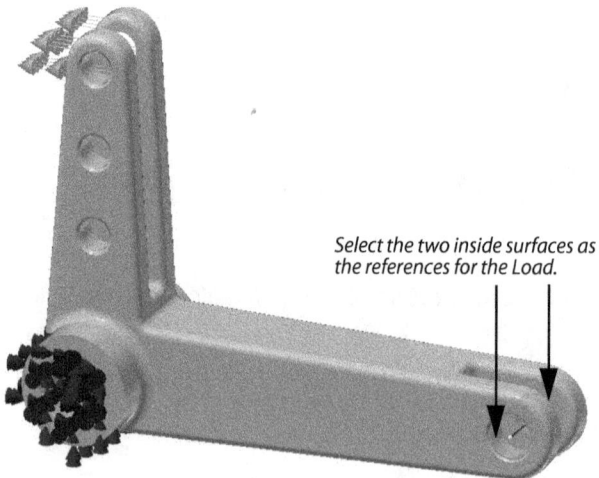

Select the two inside surfaces as the references for the Load.

21. In the Subcases section of the dialog box, confirm that Subcase 1 is selected to add the load to Subcase 1.

22. Review the model coordinate system that displays on the model and note the X direction. This is the direction that the force is required to be applied.

23. In the Load Definition section, select Total Force. This distributes the load evenly between the two selected faces, instead of assigning the same value to both faces.

24. In the Total Force section, in the Fx field, enter **-687.5**.

ID: 2	Direction: Components
Type: Force	Coordinate System: Part 1
Sub Type:	☑ Total Force
Selected Entities:	Total Force (N):
face<2>	F_x -687.5
face <3>	F_y
Subcases:	F_z
Subcase 1	
Display Options	

25. Select ☐ 👓 (Preview) at the bottom of the Load dialog box to preview the load.

26. Set the display options for this Load so that it displays as shown in the following image.

27. Click OK in the Load dialog box.

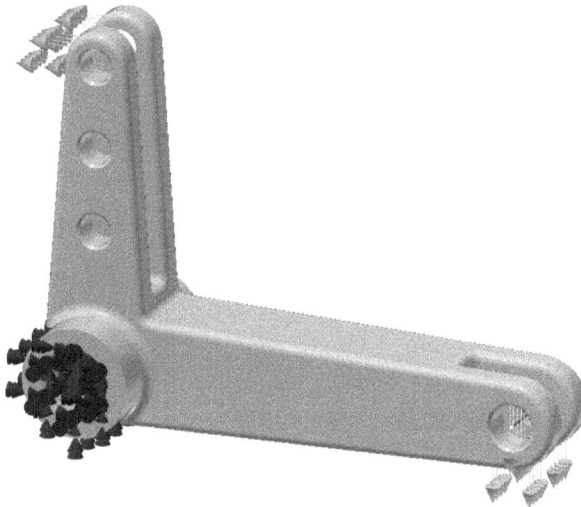

28. Review the Subcases node in the Analysis sub-tree and note the following:

- Subcase 1 is the only Subcase that currently exists in this analysis.
- Two loads (Load 1 and Load 2) and a single constraint (Constraint 1) exist in Subcase 1.

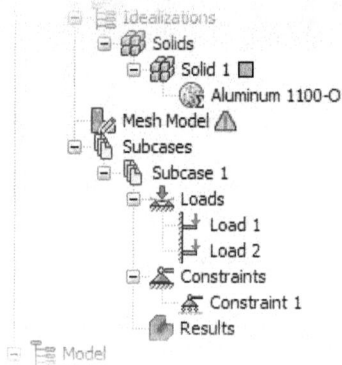

29. Review the Constraints and Loads nodes in the Model sub-tree and note the following:

- A single constraint (Constraint 1) has been added to the model. This exists in Subcase 1, however, it can be copied to any other Subcase created at a later time.
- Two loads (Load 1 and Load 2) have been added to the model. Both exist in Subcase 1 and can also be copied to any other Subcase created at a later time.

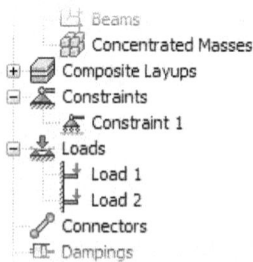

Mesh the Model

In this task, you will generate the default mesh that will be used for the analysis based on the Solid Element idealization assignment. No further changes will be made to the mesh at this time. Later in this learning guide you will learn more specifics about the tools that can be used to modify the mesh.

1. In the Mesh panel, click ![icon](Generate Mesh icon) (Generate Mesh). The mesh is displayed on the model in the color that was assigned to Solid 1 (dark orange).

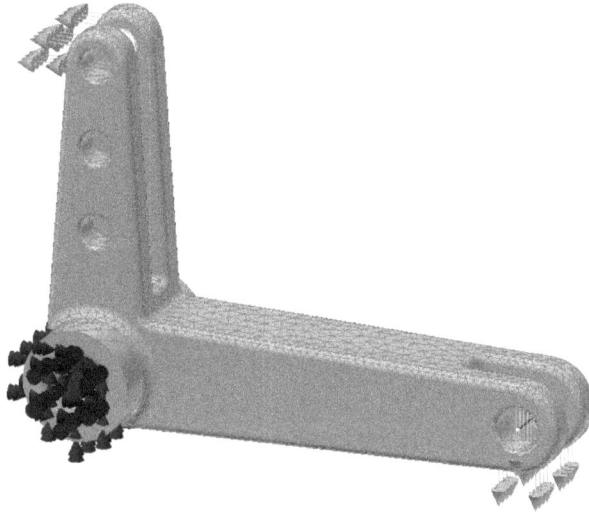

Note: Based on the model geometry, you may not see meshing across smaller entities. To verify that an entity has been meshed, consider clearing the display of the solid body geometry by right-clicking on the Part/Assembly node at the top of the Autodesk Nastran Model Tree and click Hide/Display Body. This enables you to verify that the meshing has been done.

Run the Analysis

In this task, you will run the analysis that has been created.

1.   In the Analysis sub-tree, note that in Subcase1 there are no Result nodes listed.

2.   In the Solve panel, click ![icon] (Run).

3.   The Autodesk Nastran Model Tree is replaced with the Autodesk Nastran Output view that displays a log of the results. Note that there were no errors at the bottom of the output view, but that there are a number of warnings.

4.   Click OK to confirm the completion of the Nastran solution. The Autodesk Nastran Model Tree is returned to the display.

5.   Select the Autodesk Nastran Output tab to return to the Output view.

6.   Scroll through the report and note that the warnings are all the same. They indicate that elements in the mesh have interior angles less than 10.0. This is just a warning and is not critical. It describes that there is a high aspect ratio in an element. For now, this will not be corrected. You will learn more about meshing in the next chapter of this learning guide.

7.   Return the display to the Autodesk Nastran Model Tree.

Display the Results

In this task, you will graphically display the Displacement and Stress (von Mises) results in the main window.

1. In the Analysis sub-tree, note that in Subcase1 there are now four Result nodes listed. These results templates were defined for the default Linear Static analysis. Later in this learning guide, you will learn how to set and customize the results that are to be displayed.

2. To visualize the displacement, right-click on Displacement in the Results node and select Display. The maximum displacement is 0.3146 mm.

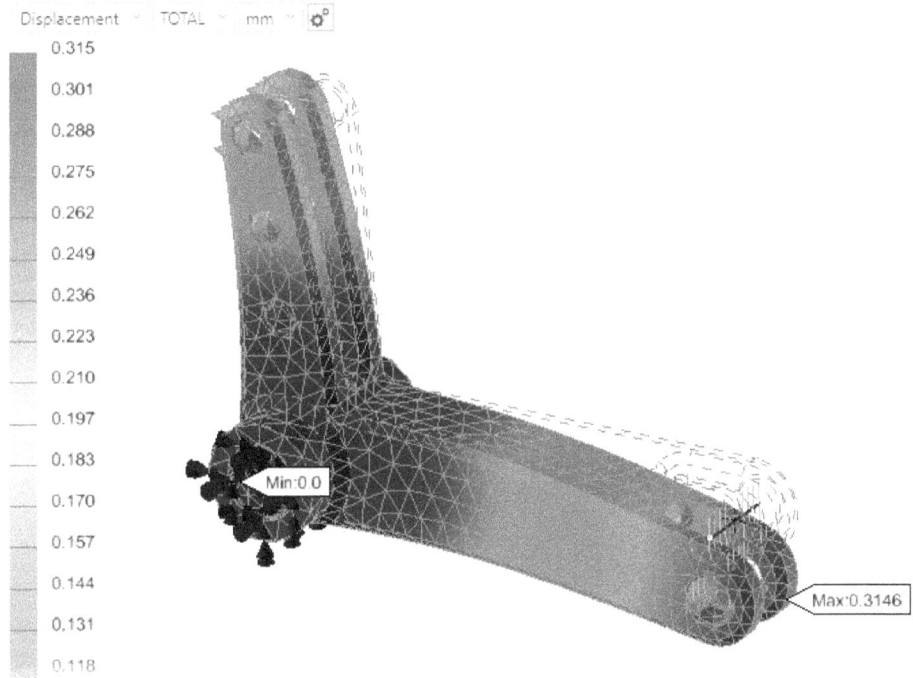

3. To visualize Stress, right-click on von Mises in the Results node and select Display. The maximum stress is approximately 102.2 MPa.

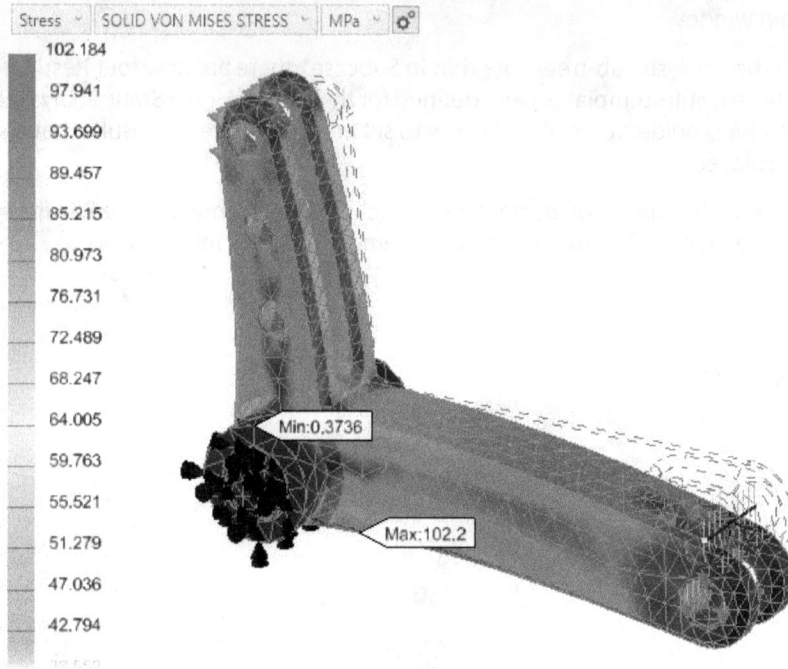

| Stress ˅ | SOLID VON MISES STRESS ˅ | MPa ˅ | ⚙ |

```
102.184
97.941
93.699
89.457
85.215
80.973
76.731
72.489
68.247
64.005
59.763
55.521
51.279
47.036
42.794
```

Min:0,3736

Max:102.2

4. Continue to display the other two results.

5. Save the model.

Exercise: Cast Lever Boundary Conditions II

Consider the modeling choices made in the previous exercise:

- Does the lever really move as it was defined?
- Although the part is in static equilibrium, the main bore can still rotate about the shaft. You can assume the axis is fixed, but must enable local rotation.
- The reaction force, R, is located at a pin. There is potential for local rotations there as well.
- The pin at Point C was locked in place so the end of the lever shouldn't bend as it did in the previous exercise.

In this exercise, you will modify the model from the previous exercise by applying advanced constraint techniques. This will provide a more realistic simulation of the pins that are not actually modeled.

Open the Model & Start the Autodesk Nastran In-CAD Environment

1. Open the file *C:\Autodesk Nastran InCAD 2019 Essentials Exercise Files\Cast_Lever\Cast Lever.ipt*, if not already open. If you did not complete the previous exercise, open the file *C:\Autodesk Nastran InCAD 2019 Essentials Exercise Files\Cast_Lever\Cast Lever2.ipt*.

2. Select the Environments tab and click Autodesk Nastran In-CAD to activate the Autodesk Nastran In-CAD environment, if not already active.

3. In the Autodesk Nastran Model Tree, expand the Idealizations and Subcase 1 nodes in the Analysis sub-trees, as shown below. Note the following:

   - Solid 1 is the active idealization being analyzed and it uses Aluminum 1100-O.
   - Subcase 1 defines the loads and constraints that were defined in the previous exercise.

   Note: If you opened and are working in the Cast Lever2.ipt model, the Results icons display in gray indicating they are unavailable because the results weren't loaded in the current session. To display them, rerun the analysis in the current session. Later in this learning guide, you will learn how to load previous results.

4.

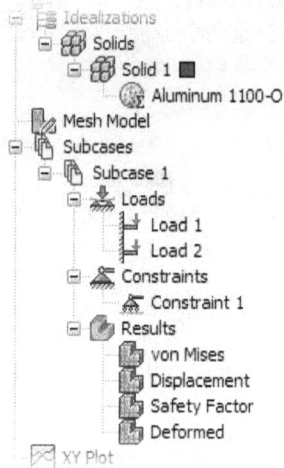

Create a New Subcase

In this task, you will create a new Subcase in the model to test alternate conditions.

1. In the Analysis sub-tree, right-click on the Subcases node and select New.

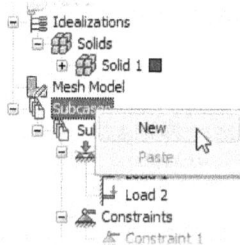

Tip: To create a duplicate of an existing Subcase, right-click on a Subcase and select Duplicate.

2. In the Subcase dialog box, select Load1 and Constraint1 to assign them to the new subcase.

3. In the Name field, enter **Exercise2**.

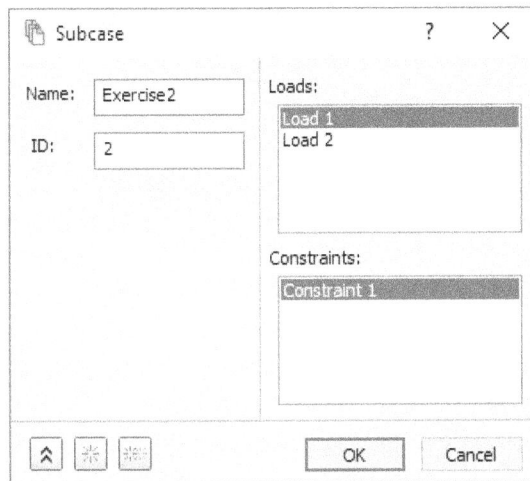

4. Click OK to create the new Subcase.

5. Right-click on Subcase 1 and select Rename. Enter **Exercise1** as its new name to help describe the differences between the two subcases as those loads and constraints assigned in each exercise in this chapter.

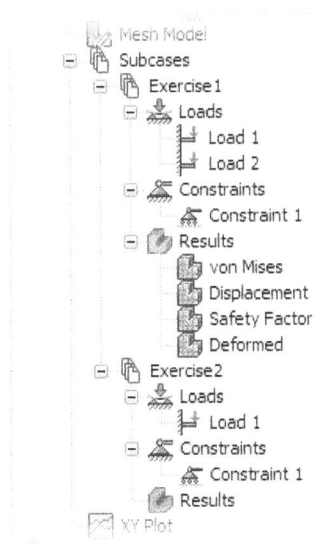

6. The Constraint 1 constraint was added to the Exercise2 Subcase in error. Right-click on Constraint 1 in the Exercise2 Subcase and select Remove to remove it.

7. On the model, note that all the load and constraint vectors are displayed. For this exercise, we are only interested in the Exercise 2 subcase. Right-click on the Exercise1 Subcase and clear the Activate option to deactivate the Exercise 1 subcase. Once Exercise1 is deactivated, only the Load1 vectors should be displayed as it is the only load/constraint in the Exercise2 subcase.

Add Rigid Connectors to the Model.

In this task, you will add two Rigid Body connectors to the model to more accurately represent how the model behaves using a pin constraint. You will apply a constraint to the center point (independent vertex) of the rigid joint, but only for the new subcase. Subcase 1 will continue to show the effects of a fixed constraint at the pivot hole.

1. In the Prepare panel, click ✎ (Connectors). The Connector dialog box opens. Alternatively, in the Model sub-tree, right-click on Connectors and select New.

   Tip: Connectors cannot be directly added through the analysis until the first connector is created and is added to the analysis.

2. In the Connector dialog box, select Rigid Body from the Type drop-down list.

3. Ensure that the RigidBody Type is set to Rigid.

4. Ensure that the Add to Analysis option is selected so that the connector is added directly to the Analysis sub-tree when it is created.

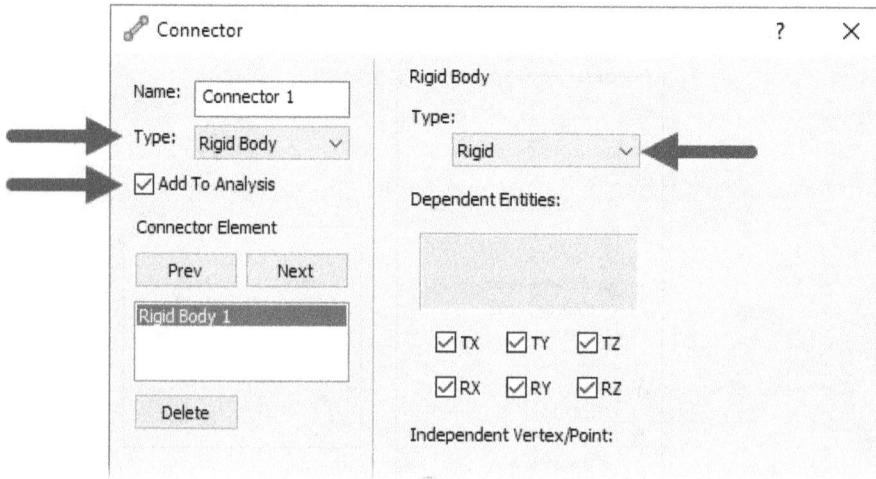

5. Select the two faces shown below as the references for the Dependent Entities.

   Note: If you previously toggled off the display of the body so that you could see the mesh, you will need to display it again to select the geometry.

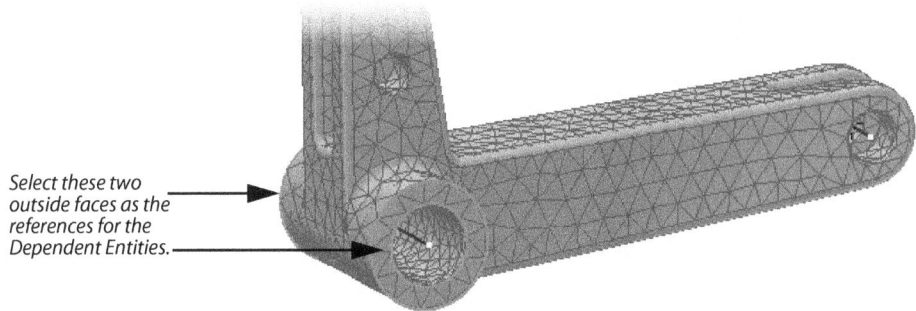

Select these two outside faces as the references for the Dependent Entities.

6. Activate the Independent Vertex/Point area, if not already active. Select the point on the axis as the Independent Vertex/Point reference.

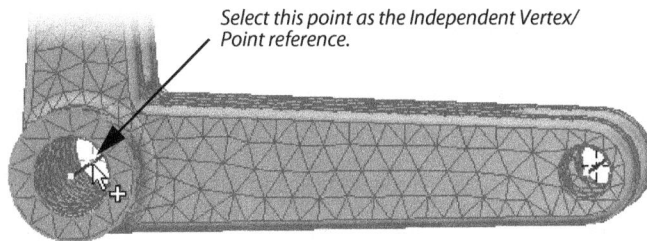

Select this point as the Independent Vertex/ Point reference.

7. Ensure that all the check boxes for the degrees of freedom are selected to remove translational and rotational movement.

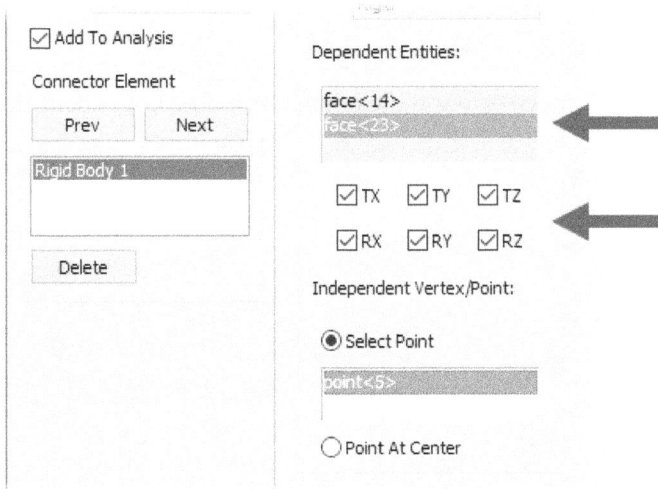

8. Maintain the display settings for the connector vectors; however, select the Color box and assign Red as the color for the new Connector, if not already set.

9. Click OK to create the connection.

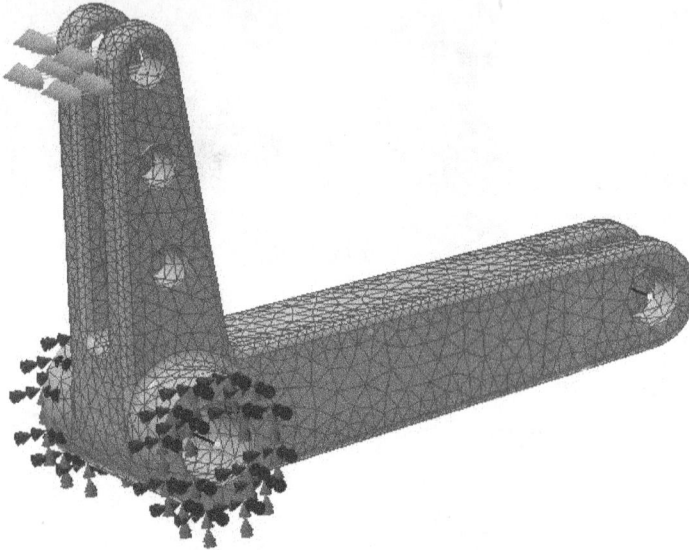

Note that Connector 1 is added to the Model and Analysis sub-trees.

10. Add a second connector to the hole that was previously loaded in the Exercise1 subcase. In the Analysis sub-tree, right-click on Connectors and select New. Now that one connection exists, you can add additional connectors using this approach.

11. In the Connector dialog box, select Rigid Body from the Type drop-down list and ensure that Add to Analysis is selected.

12. Ensure that the RigidBody Type is set to Rigid.

13. Select the two faces shown below as the references for the Dependent Entities.

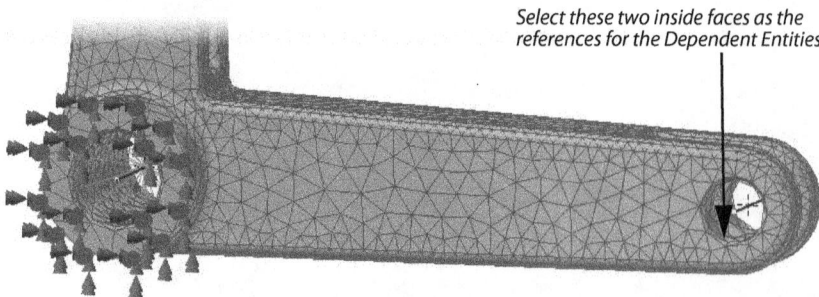

Select these two inside faces as the references for the Dependent Entities.

14. Activate the Independent Vertex/Point area, if not already active. Select the point on the axis as the Independent Vertex/Point reference.

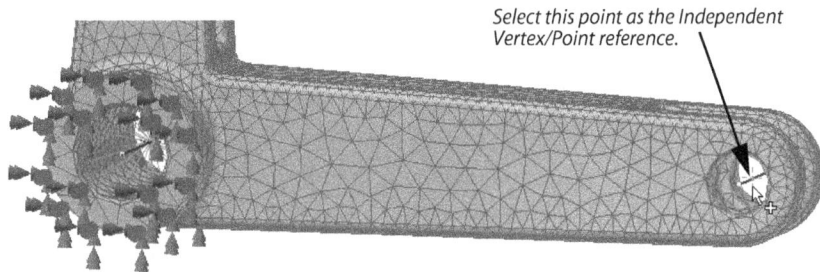

Select this point as the Independent Vertex/Point reference.

The hub of the lever is fairly long. In the actual assembly, bending deflection of the pin will cause most of the load to be transmitted through the outermost portions of the hole's surface (the pin will actually separate from the hole in the middle due to its bent shape). Attaching the constraint to the end faces is closer to reality than distributing it along the full length of the hole. This method also prevents artificial stiffening of the part because a rigid body attached to the full length of the hole would prevent the hub from deforming under load.

The holes on the end of the lever arms are relatively short. Assuming a rigid connection along the full length of the hole is reasonable. Since the hole is so short, there's not going to be much deformation along its length. Also, the end face in this case is the entire side face of the arm, which is much to great an area over which to impose a rigid connection.

Note: An alternative method of handling the hub hole would be to split the hole into three separate faces along its length (a wide one in the middle and a relatively narrow one at each end. Then, you would apply two rigid connectors, one to each narrow surface, with an independent vertex at the center of each narrow face. Then, both center points would be constrained in Tx, Tx, and Tz directions only (pinned). This method would give the most faithful representation of the actual application.

15. Ensure that all the check boxes for the degrees of freedom are selected.

16. Maintain the display settings for the connector vectors; however, select the Color box and assign Red as the color for the new Connector, if not already set.

17. Click OK to create the connection. The two connectors display on the model.

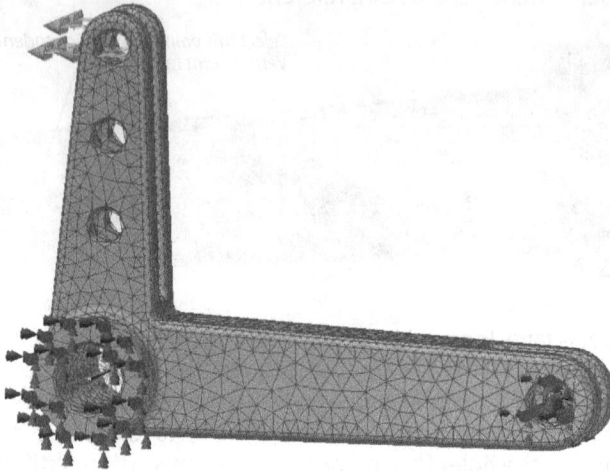

Add Constraints to the Subcase.

In this task, you will add a constraint to the model. The constraint will be added at the location of the Rigid Body Connector, to further capture how the model will react in a working environment.

1. In the Setup panel, click ⬛ (Constraints) to open the Constraint dialog box.

2. In the Subcases section of the dialog box, confirm that Exercise2 is selected and clear the selection of Exercise1. This ensures that the new constraint is automatically added only to the Exercise2 subcase.

3. Select the point at the center of the axis shown below.

Select point at the center of the axis as the reference for the Selected Entities field.

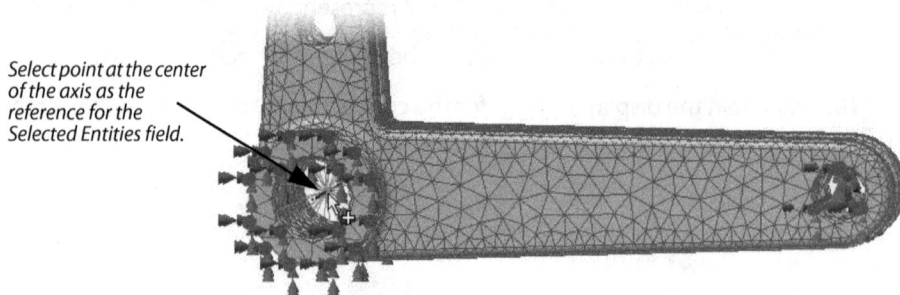

4. In the Degrees of Freedom section, ensure that all but the Rz degree of freedom is selected. By clearing the Rz checkbox, you enable rotation in the Z direction.

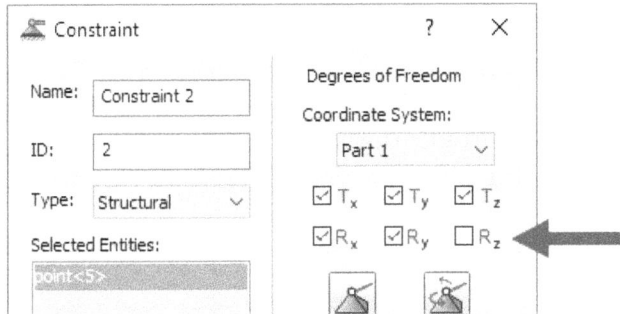

5. Select ☐ 👓 (Preview) at the bottom of the Constraint dialog box to preview the constraint prior to creating it.

6. In the Display Options section of the Constraint dialog box, complete the following:

   - Drag the Size slider to vary the size of the constraint vectors.
   - Drag the Density slider to vary the number of constraint vectors that are displayed.
   - Select the Color box to select a dark blue color as an alternate display color for the constraint vectors.

7. Click OK to complete the constraint.

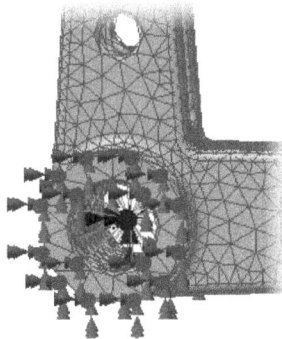

8. In the Setup panel, click to open the Constraints dialog box again. Create a Fixed constraint similar to the previous one.

- Assign the constraint to the Exercise2 subcase only.
- Select the reference point at the center of the axis in the small hole as the Selected Entities reference.
- Clear all of the degrees of freedom except for Tx.
- Select the Color box to select a dark blue color as an alternate display color for the constraint vectors.
- Preview the constraint prior to creating it and adjust the display settings, as required.
- Click OK to complete the constraint.

Select the point at the center of the axis as the reference for the Selected Entities field.

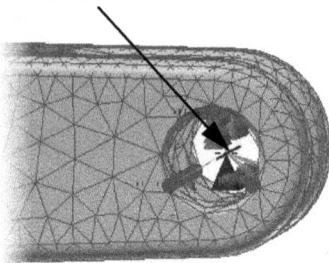

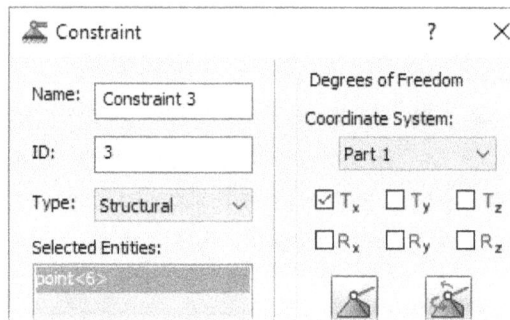

Note: The connector's vectors have been reduced in size in the above image for clarity to identify the constraint that has been added.

Run the Analysis & Review the Results

In this task, you will run the analysis that has been created. The model's mesh was previously updated so it is not required. You will review and compare the results to those found in the Exercise1 subcase.

1. In the Analysis sub-tree, note that in the Exercise2 there are no Result nodes listed.

2. In the Solve panel, click .

3. The Autodesk Nastran Model Tree is replaced with the Autodesk Nastran Output view that displays a log of the results. Note that there were no errors at the bottom of the output view, but that there are a number of warnings. Similar to the analysis completed in Exercise1, the warnings indicate that elements in the mesh have interior angles less than 10.0.

4. Click OK to confirm the completion of the Nastran solution. The Autodesk Nastran Model Tree is returned to the display.

5. To visualize the displacement, right-click on Displacement in the Results node for Exercise 2 and select Display. The maximum displacement is 0.412 mm and it is in a more realistic location. Previously, the maximum displacement was on the arm that was to be constrained in its working environment and simply applying a reaction force as a load did not yield realistic results. This displacement reflects more closely the behavior of the lever, in its actual application.

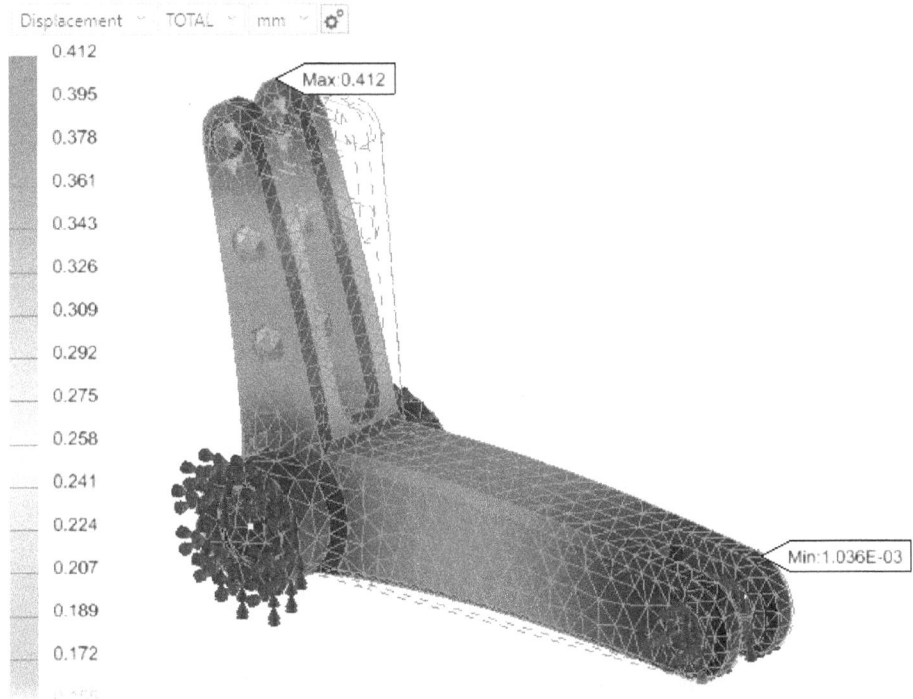

6. To visualize Stress, right-click on von Mises in the Results node for Exercise 2 and select Display. The maximum stress is approximately 129.1 MPa. The max stress is in a new location than the previous exercise with a higher stress value when using a more accurate representation of the constraints.

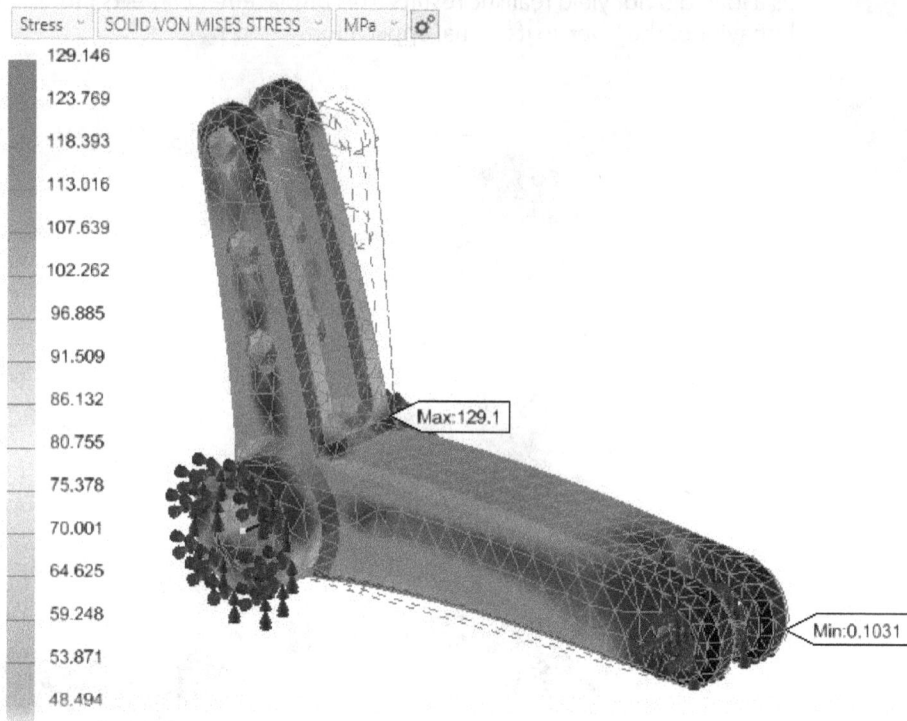

7. Continue to display the other two results and compare them.

   Note: Even with the improved boundary conditions, the controlling stress did not change appreciably. This should NOT be taken to mean that stress is insensitive to boundary conditions. It is, and this was simply a coincidence of this particular model.

Duplicate an Analysis

When Connectors are added to a subcase they are included at the Analysis level and are not subcase specific. In the current exercise, if the Exercise1 subcase had been rerun, the connectors would also have been applied to it. To avoid this situation, instead of creating multiple subcases in an analysis, you can create multiple Analysis nodes. In this task, you will duplicate Analysis 1 and manipulate all of the subcases so that both the Exercise1 and Exercise2 (with connectors) are represented in the model.

1. Right-click on the Analysis 1 [Linear Static] node at the top of the Model Tree and select Duplicate.

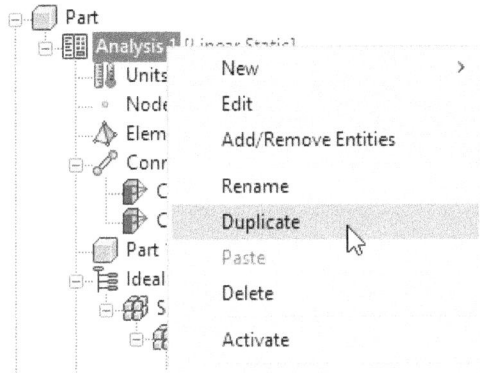

2. A copy of Analysis 1 is created. You are immediately prompted to enter a new name for the analysis. Enter **Analysis 2** as its new name.

3. Right-click on the Exercise1 subcase in the Analysis 2 [Linear Static] node, and select Delete. Click Yes to delete the subcase.

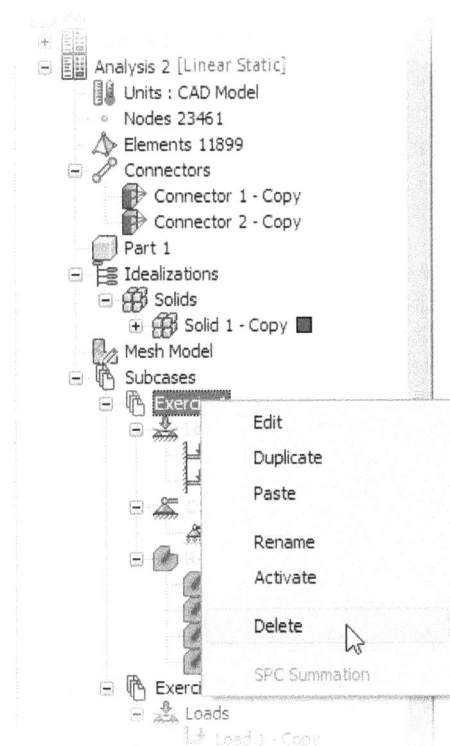

4. Right-click on the Analysis 1 [Linear Static] node, and select Activate.

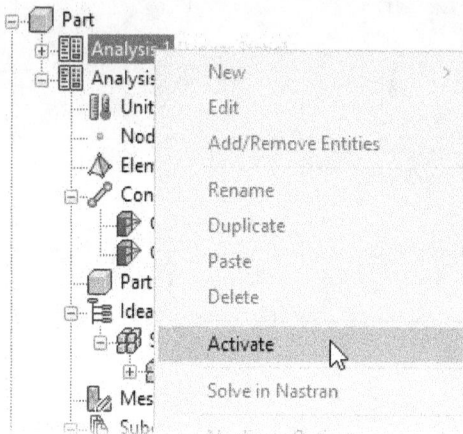

5. Right-click on the Exercise2 subcase in the Analysis 1 [Linear Static] node, and select Delete. Click Yes to delete the subcase.

6. In the Analysis 1 [Linear Static] node, right-click on Connector 1 and select Remove. Also remove Connector 2 from this analysis.

7. Review both the Analysis 1 and Analysis 2 nodes. Note that each can be run independently and connectors are only used in the second analysis.

8. Review the Model sub-tree. Note that when the analysis was copied, all of the properties (e.g., loads and constraints) are also copied. This enables you to go into each of these properties and make changes independently. To ensure that both analysis use the same properties, you must replace the copied property with the original. For example, in the case of the 1000N force, currently Load 1 and Load 1 - Copy are the same but if a change is required, the value would have to be changed in both locations. To avoid this you can replace the Load 1 - Copy used in Analysis 2 with Load 1 by dragging and dropping it into the Loads node and then delete the copied version. This can be done with all properties, if required.

9. Save the model.

Working with the Mesh and Result Plots

The goal in this chapter is to learn more about the mesh and result analysis. So far in this learning guide, you have run your analysis based on the system's default mesh settings. You will learn more about the mesh, how it is generated and customized, and the tools available to review it. Additionally, you will learn about the result plots that enable you to display and visually analyze the results.

Objectives

After completing this chapter, you will be able to:

- Identify the element types that are supported in the Autodesk® Nastran® In-CAD software and the properties that are required to define them.
- Represent structural members created using Inventor's Frame Generator as Beam or Solid element idealizations.
- Generate the mesh.
- Control the meshes display on a model.
- Query and highlight nodal and elemental information in a meshed model.
- Use the Check Mesh Quality option to identify areas of the mesh that might need further refinement.
- Customize the global mesh settings for a model.
- Customize the local mesh settings for selected entities, faces, and edges.
- Control the display of local mesh control elements.
- Use the Mesh Table to control visibility, global settings, and mesh generation for the components in an assembly.

- Load an existing .FNO results file into an analysis.
- Display and animate analysis plot in the graphics window.
- Edit the display setting associated with an existing analysis plot.
- Create a new analysis plot in an Analysis subcase.
- Create a new XY plot for an analysis.
- Display an XY plot that was created to display the results of an analysis.
- Edit the display settings associated with an existing XY plot.

Lesson: Meshing Basics

Overview

This lesson discusses some of the basics of element types that are used in the Autodesk Nastran
In-CAD environment to analyze a model. Additionally, you will learn of the importance of mesh convergence in obtaining results that have greater accuracy.

Objectives

After completing this lesson, you will be able to:

- Identify the element types that are supported in the Autodesk® Nastran® In-CAD software and the properties that are required to define them.

Understanding the Mesh

To mathematically solve the FEA solution, it is required to construct the mesh. The mesh consists of nodes and element. Nodes are points in 3D space and elements are areas or volumes defined by the nodes. A collection of settings in the Autodesk Nastran In-CAD software provides control over the element size, element order, and local refinement. Because the solution accuracy is very dependent on the fidelity of the mesh, it is important to take the time to define a high quality mesh when analyzing your models.

Element Types and their Properties

There are three types of elements supported in Autodesk Nastran In-CAD:

- Solid Elements
- Shell Elements
- Line Elements

The following sections introduce these three element types in more detail and describes the properties used to define them.

Solid Elements

When using solid elements, the geometry is entirely described by the CAD model geometry. Tetrahedrons are the element type for three dimensional, solid meshes. There are two types of tetrahedrons:

Type	Description	Example
Linear Tetrahedron	These elements have 4 nodes and are mathematically stiff. It is best to use these only for trend studies where absolute results are not as important as relative changes.	
Parabolic Tetrahedron	These elements have 10 nodes and are excellent general purpose elements suitable for most applications.	

Solid elements in Autodesk Nastran In-CAD only require the material properties to be defined.

Shell Elements

Autodesk Nastran In-CAD can mesh shells with triangles and quadrilaterals using these element types:

Type	Number of Nodes
Linear Triangle	3
Parabolic Triangle	6
Linear Quadrilateral	4
Parabolic Quadrilateral	8

The primary property of shell elements is the thickness (t). You can assign the property to geometric surfaces or to the faces of geometric solids.

Line (Beam) Elements

There are three types of line elements supported by Autodesk Nastran In-CAD:

- Bar
- Beam
- Pipe

Each of these line element types require you to define the geometry property data or cross-section and its orientation properties. Structural members created using Inventor's Frame Generator can also be selected. To input Property data, you can manually assign values in the Idealizations dialog box. To define Cross Section settings, it is recommended to use the Element Library. The cross-section for Bar and Beam line element types can be based on a number of different types (e.g., Rod, Tube, I, Channel, etc.), for the Pipe line element type the only cross-section that can be used is Tube.

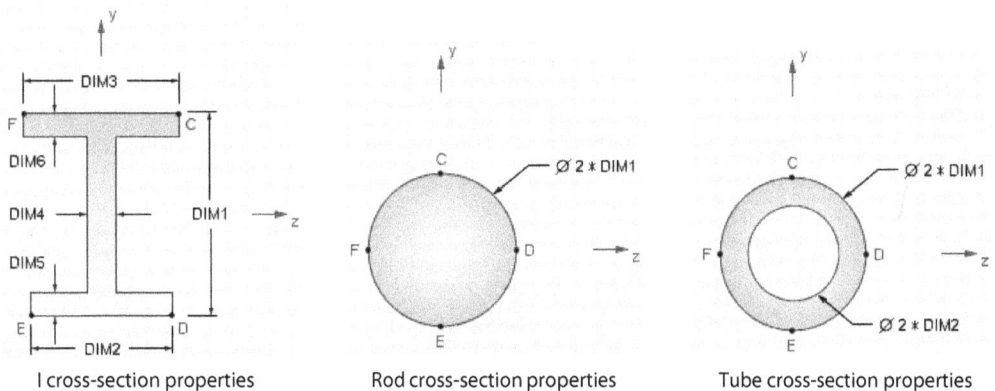

I cross-section properties   Rod cross-section properties   Tube cross-section properties

By using the libraries, you can create PBEAML and PBARL elements, which perform a maximum stress computation. Additionally, using libraries enables you to save individual cross-sections for reuse.

Inventor Frame Generator and Beam Elements

Components created using the Autodesk Inventor Frame Generator functionality are automatically recognized when brought into the Nastran In-CAD environment. Idealizations are automatically generated for each frame member. The cross-sectional properties are dictated by the section that was assigned during frame creation. Therefore, the Associated Geometry option does not display for Structural Member entities. The Idealization dialog box is shown below.

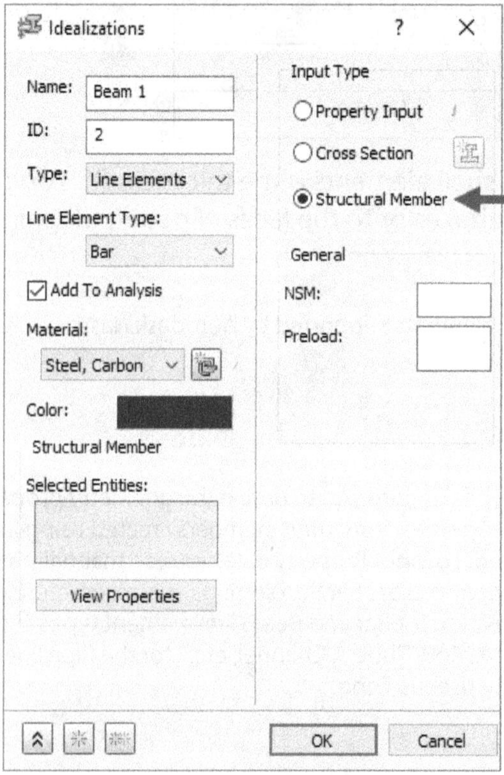

Although idealizations are created by default for all Frame Generator members, you can also use the Structural Members dialog box to choose whether to represent each member using beam elements or solid elements. When using beam elements, each structural member is divided into a series of shorter line elements when you generate the mesh. For solid elements, the volume of each structural member is discretized into smaller finite elements by the mesher, in the same manner that regular CAD solid parts are meshed.

To access the Structural Members dialog box, on the Prepare panel, click 🔧 (Structural Members). Using the double-arrow buttons you can move the members to the Solid column or back to the Beams column, as required.

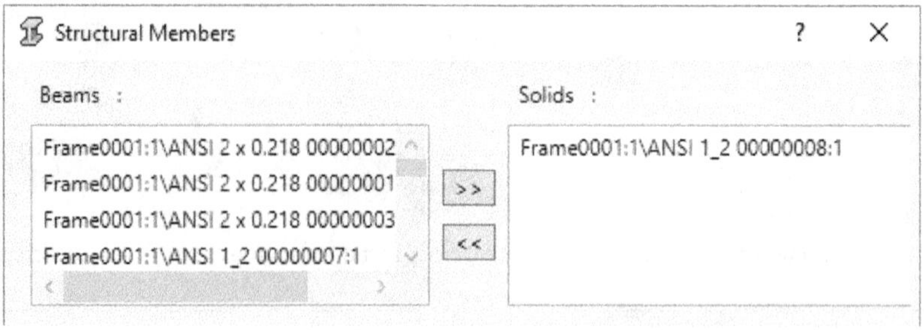

The remainder of the workflow for setting up a Beam Element analysis is similar to a Solid Element analysis.

Element Degrees of Freedom

Element degrees of freedom (DOF) link the mesh, element properties, and boundary conditions. It is important to note that nodes can only carry the loads they need to. For each element type, these are the degrees of freedom that nodes can carry:

- 3D Solids (Solid Elements): 3 DOF (TX, TY, TZ)
- 3D Plates (Shell Elements): 5 DOF (TX, TY, TZ, RX, RY)
- 3D Beams (Line Elements): 6 DOF (TX, TY, TZ, RX, RY, RZ)

Note that for adjoining elements of dissimilar types, the element with the lesser number of supported DOFs controls the behavior at the interface. For example, when a beam part is attached to a single node of a solid element part, no rotational loads can be transmitted between the parts because solid elements lack rotational DOFs. Similarly, a shell element part attached to a solid element part along a single edge forms a hinge connection in which the shells are free to rotate about the edge where the parts connect. For a rotationally stiff connection, beams or shells must be connected to three or more non-collinear points on the solid part.

> For more information on the supported element types and their properties that are available, refer to Autodesk Nastran In-CAD Help and search for "Finite Elements in Autodesk Nastran In-CAD".

Mesh Settings

The mesh should accurately represent the geometry and the physics you are simulating. A poorly defined mesh can produce results, but the accuracy of those results might be less than you require to make informed design decisions. In an upcoming lesson, you will learn how to customize the mesh.

The Importance of the Mesh on Convergence

In general, a higher element count leads to greater solution accuracy. This is because more nodes are available for calculating the response and because smaller elements minimize errors due to discretization. The practical limit to the effect of the mesh on the solution accuracy occurs when a mesh-independent solution is attained. This means that the solution does not change significantly, regardless of further reductions in element size.

You can control the mesh to lead to convergence by reducing the element size locally and globally and by monitoring the changes in results. Models will converge with fewer second order elements (Parabolic Tetrahedrons, for example) than with linear elements. This is because a single second order element can capture a more complex strain field than a linear element. However, the cost associated with second order elements is that they typically take longer to solve due to the higher node count.

The following image shows the effect of refining the mesh on the von Mises stress at a stress concentration point. As the mesh is refined from Mesh 1 to Mesh 3, you see a reduction in the amount of change in the stress at the point of interest. This means that the finer mesh is close to a mesh-independent solution, and smaller changes in the solution will occur as the mesh is further refined.

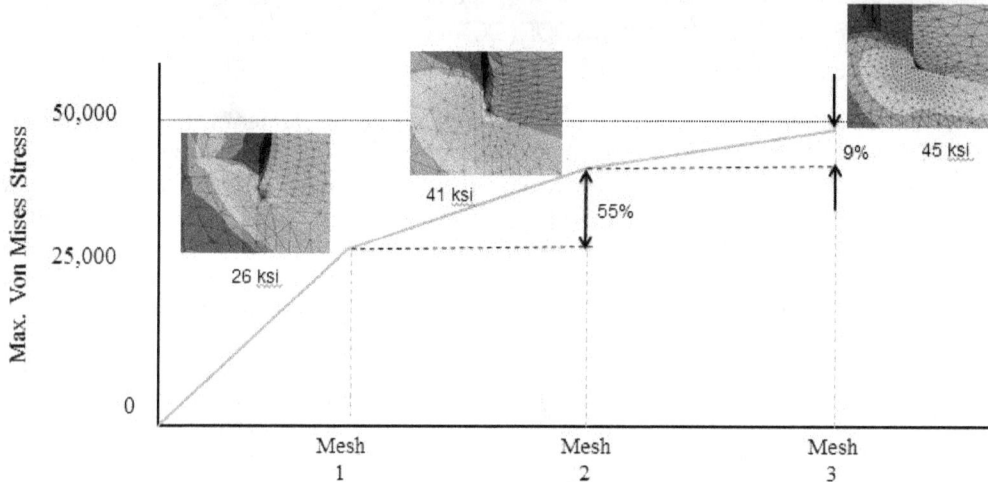

> When using shell and beam elements, it is best to use the linear quadrilateral element type to simplify the analysis.

Considerations for Meshing

Consider the following basic guidelines for meshing:

- Element recommendations:
  - Line elements are always good to help reduce the analysis time. Line elements converge easily and vastly reduce the number of elements required.
  - Linear quadrilateral elements are preferred in most shell models. The Autodesk Nastran In-CAD Shell mesher can produce a predominately quadrilateral mesh but might insert triangles to complete the mesh depending on the geometry.
  - Parabolic solid tetrahedrons are preferred. Linear tetrahedron elements behave too stiffly; however, they can be used for trend studies.
  - All FEA solvers expect quadrilaterals to be squares and all triangles to be equilateral. The closer the element are to these shapes the more accurate the results will be. Some variation is acceptable - Gross variation causes error.

- Not all meshes are good meshes:
  - If the mesh is too coarse (elements too large) the model will be too stiff, which can affect results.
  - Local stresses are most impacted. The regions where you already see high stress (whether due to contacts, constraints, or stress concentrations) will be affected the most by mesh refinement.
  - Convergence is the iterative process of using element size reduction where required, to ensure the correct results are calculated.

> When working with assemblies, multiple idealizations can exist and each may use a different element type.
> - Shell and beam elements can be combined.
> - Shell and solid elements can be combined directly (matching coincident mesh).
> - Solid and beam elements can be combined directly (matching coincident mesh).

Lesson: Generating & Reviewing the Mesh

Overview

This lesson describes how you can generate the mesh in a model and use the tools available in the Autodesk Nastran In-CAD environment to display and review the mesh to help ensure an optimal mesh for your analysis.

Objectives

After completing this lesson, you will be able to:

- Generate the mesh.
- Control the meshes display on a model.
- Query and highlight nodal and elemental information in a meshed model.
- Use the Check Mesh Quality option to identify areas of the mesh that might need further refinement.

Generating the Mesh

As soon as a model is opened in the Autodesk Nastran In-CAD environment, the default Analysis (Linear Static) is created. The Mesh node is added to the Autodesk Nastran Model Tree, as shown in the following image. The ⚠ icon displays adjacent to the Mesh Model node when it requires generating or updating.

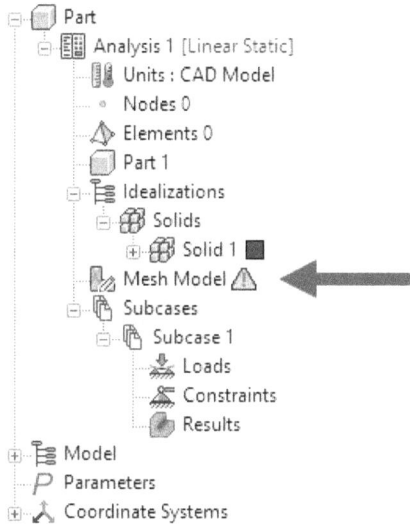

In addition to the Linear Static analysis being created, by default, one or more idealizations are also automatically assigned. Solid 1 is created using the current material in a single-part model. For assemblies, an idealization is assigned for each unique material in the assembly. Solid Elements are the default element type for the default idealization. With this information defined, you can immediately generate the default mesh for the model by selecting

 (Generate Mesh) in the Mesh panel on the ribbon. The default mesh is applied to the model using the color that was assigned in the Solid 1 idealization. The total number of nodes and elements are listed in the in the Analysis sub-tree.

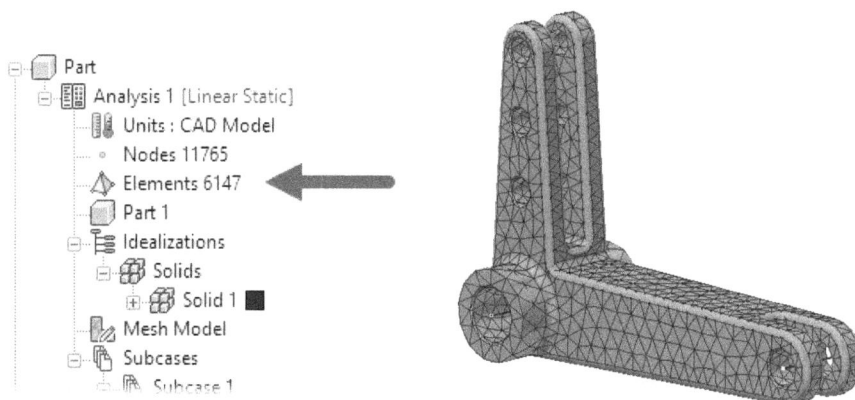

Consider the following when working with the mesh:

- The display of the CAD Body geometry in the model may cover the mesh display in areas with small geometry (i.e., fillets). Consider toggling off the CAD Bodies display in the Object Visibility drop down list to see the full mesh.

- To clear the display of the mesh from the model, right-click on the Mesh Model node in the Autodesk Nastran Model Tree and select Hide Mesh. To return the mesh to the display, right-click on the Mesh Model node and select Display Mesh.

- To delete the mesh from the model, right-click on the Mesh Model node and select Delete Mesh. This delete option will not delete any local mesh controls that might exist in the analysis. They must be deleted separately.

Nodes and Elements

Once the mesh is generated, the total number of nodes and elements are listed near the top of the Analysis sub-tree. Both of these nodes provide additional tools for reviewing the mesh. These tools are available in the shortcut menu when either of these nodes are selected, as shown in the following image.

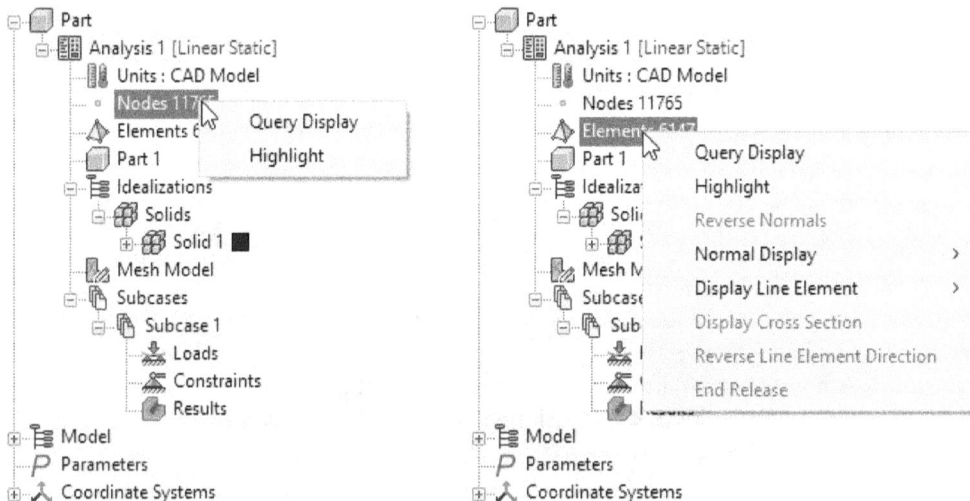

Query Display

The Query Display option is available for both nodes and elements. It enables you to place the cursor directly on a node or element to report information about it.

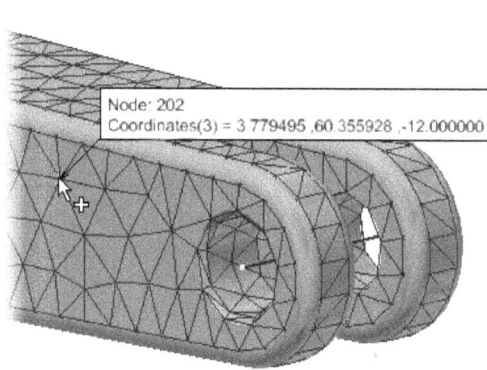

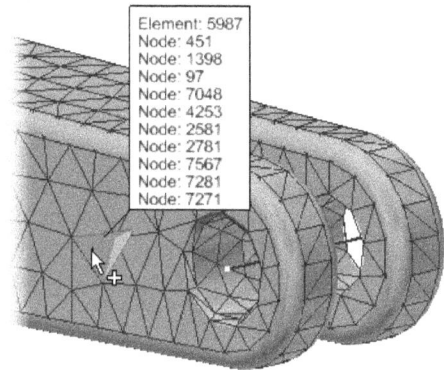

Node Query   Element Query

Highlight

The Highlight option is available for both nodes and elements. It enables you to identify a node or element in the model by highlighting it to show its location and properties. To use it, you are provided with the Highlight Nodes and Highlight Elements dialog boxes that enable you identify the Entity ID to be highlighted. If you know the ID, you can enter the value. Alternatively, you can select all entities (All) or define a range of entities that are to be highlighted (Define). Once defined, click Add to add to the Selected Entities list. The entities are immediately highlighted in the model. Nodes are highlighted in yellow and elements are highlighted in green. To clear the highlighting in the model, click OK to close the dialog box.

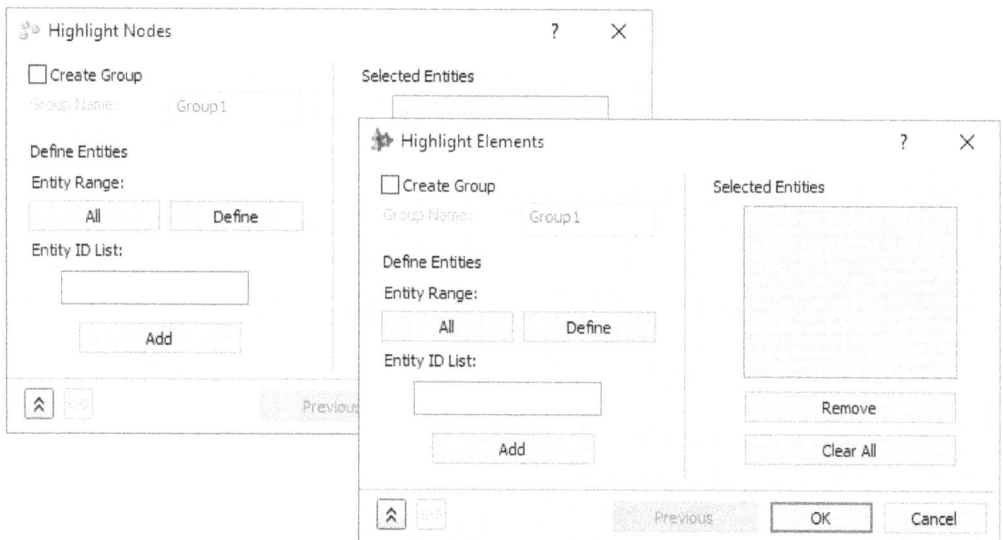

The remainder of the options that are available on the Elements shortcut menu enable you to control the normals display (when using the shell element type) and line display (for the line element type).

Reviewing Mesh Quality

> For the more experienced FEA users, this tool can be used in addition to your visual assessment to review the mesh quality against element shape criteria.

To determine if there are sub-optimal elements in the areas of interest (where stress is a significant concern), you can use the Check Mesh Quality tool. To open it, right-click on the Mesh Model node in the analysis and click Check Quality for Mesh.

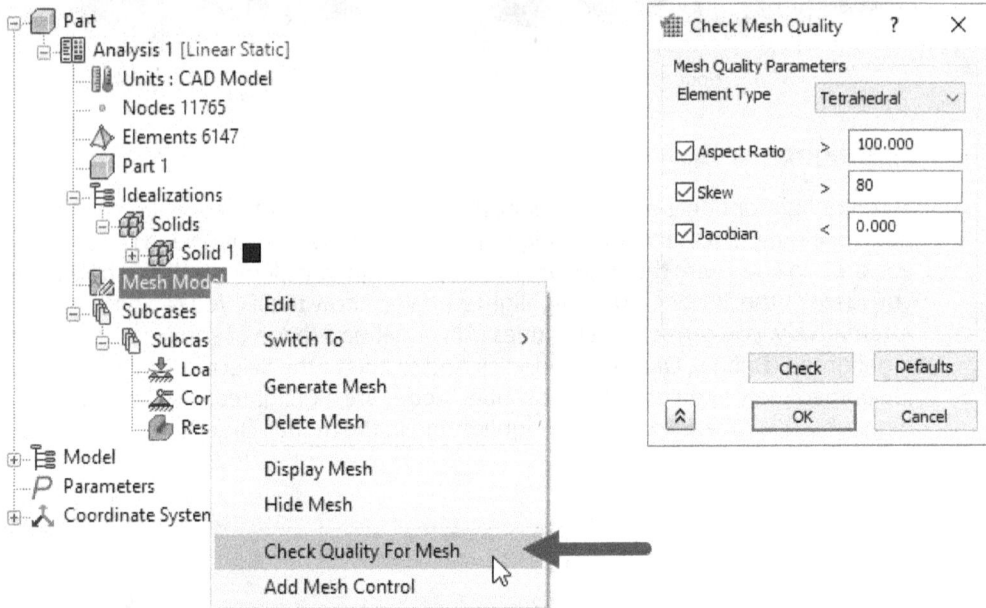

By setting the options in the Check Mesh Quality dialog box and running the check, areas that may need further refinement are identified. To help locate interior elements, consider creating the failed elements as a Group and review the group by changing the display to wireframe and possibly turning off the display of the idealizations.

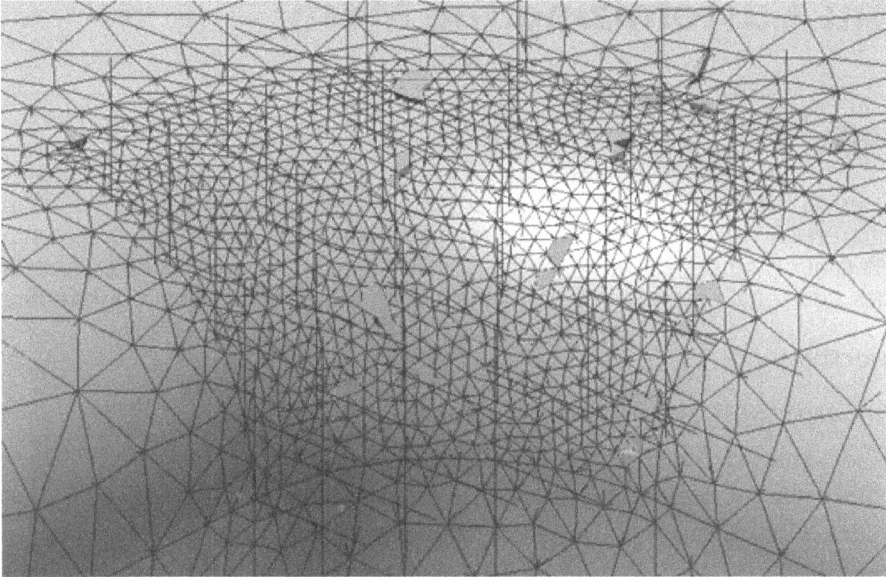

Depending on the type of Element, the following checks can be made:

- Aspect Ratio
- Skew
- Warping
- Taper
- Jacobian

> Jacobian provides a measure of the deviation of a given element from an ideally shaped element, defined as the ratio between the smallest and the largest value of the Jacobian Matrix determinant.

Lesson: Customizing the Mesh

Overview

This lesson describes how you can use both local and global mesh settings in the Autodesk Nastran In-CAD environment to refine the mesh in a model. You will learn that multiple local mesh control items can be added to the model to refine the mesh at vertices, faces, and edges. Additionally you will learn about the global mesh settings that affect the entire model.

Objectives

After completing this lesson, you will be able to:

- Customize the global mesh settings for a model.
- Customize the local mesh settings for selected entities, faces, and edges.
- Control the display of local mesh control elements.
- Use the Mesh Table to control visibility, global settings, and mesh generation for the components in an assembly.

Global vs. Local Mesh Settings

Once an analysis is run and interpreted it is often determined that the mesh isn't suitable for the specific analysis to provide the results that are required. For these situations you can modify the mesh settings to refine the mesh. Refinement can be done globally or locally.

Global Mesh Settings

The global mesh settings are the settings that are used to define the overall mesh of the model. To access the global mesh settings, use one of the following methods:

- Right-click on the Mesh Model node and select Edit.

- In the Mesh panel in the ribbon, click (Mesh Settings).

The global mesh settings for the model are controlled in the Mesh Settings dialog box.

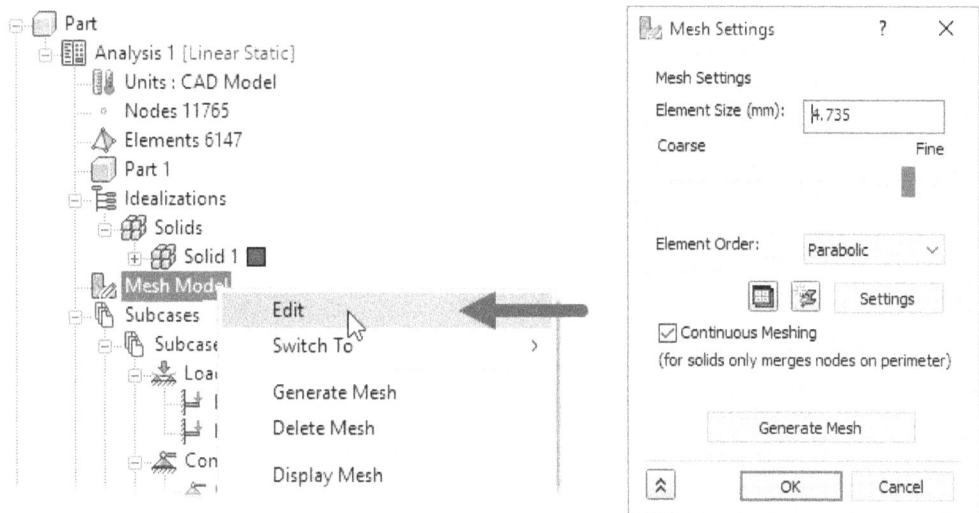

Basic Settings

The settings that are available in the Mesh Settings dialog box enable you to control the following on a global basis:

- **Element Size**: Meshes all faces with this nominal dimension unless a curvature setting overrides it.

- **Element Order**: Assigns the use of Linear or Parabolic for all elements in the model.

- **(Mesh Table)**: Opens the Mesh Table to control element attributes for the components of an assembly.

- **(New Idealization)**: Enables you to create a new idealization directly in the Mesh Settings dialog box. Once created, it is assigned as the idealization for the active analysis.

- **Continuous Meshing**: When checked, the mesher attempts to define compatible (matching) meshes on touching edges. This provides a higher level of load continuity than possible with the Welded Contact.
- **Generate Mesh**: Generates the mesh with the current settings.

Advanced Settings

Additional advanced settings are available by selecting Settings. These advanced settings enable you to further customize and refine the mesh by controlling the tolerance, sizing, geometry options, and midside nodes.

> Note that it is a good idea to use the default settings unless you have a good understanding of the impact of the different advanced settings on your model.

The following settings are the most commonly adjusted in the advanced settings. For more information on the options that are available in the Advanced Mesh Settings dialog box, refer to Autodesk Nastran In-CAD Help and search for "Mesh Model Edit".

- **Tolerance**: Adjusts the tolerance value of the mesh. This can be adjusted to help mesh parts that otherwise fail to mesh.
- **Max Element Growth Rate**: Reducing this value extends the region in which smaller elements transition to larger elements. This can help to smooth the mesh in high stress gradients areas.
- **Project Midside Nodes**: Maps midside nodes of parabolic elements to the geometry. This is particularly helpful in areas of high curvature. In the following example, the mesh on the left was created with this option disabled. The mesh on the right is with the option enabled.

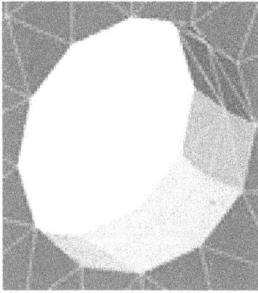

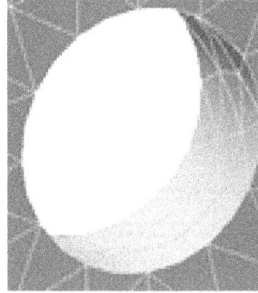

Local Mesh Settings

A Mesh can be customized locally such that selected faces have further refinements to their mesh as compared to the rest of the model geometry. To access the local mesh settings, use one of the following methods:

- Right-click on the Mesh Model node and select Add Mesh Control.

- In the Mesh panel in the ribbon, click (Mesh Control).

- If an existing Mesh Control element already exists in the model, right-click on the Mesh Control node in the analysis and select New.

All local mesh settings are controlled using the Mesh Control dialog box.

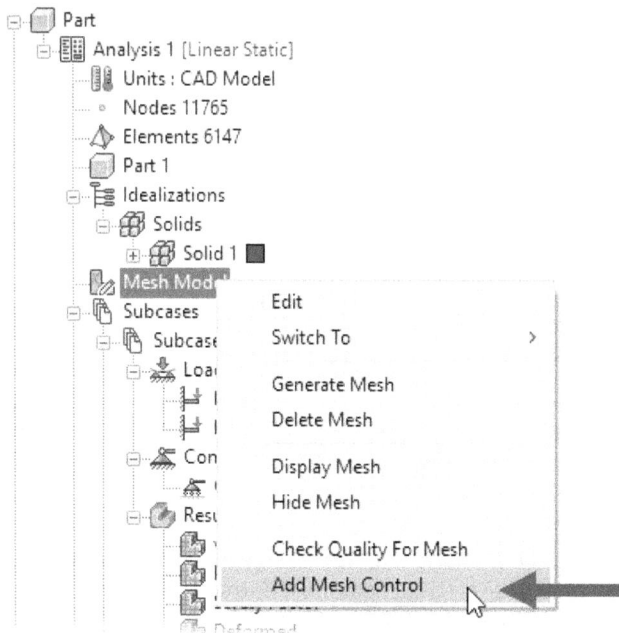

Mesh Control

Name: Mesh Control 1

Display Options
Size:
Density:
Color:

Vertex Data
Element Size (mm):
4.74487
Selected Points and Vertices:

Face Data
Element Size (mm):
4.74487
Selected Faces:

Edge Data
Specify By:
◉ Number of Elements
○ Element Size (mm)

Selected Edges:

OK   Cancel

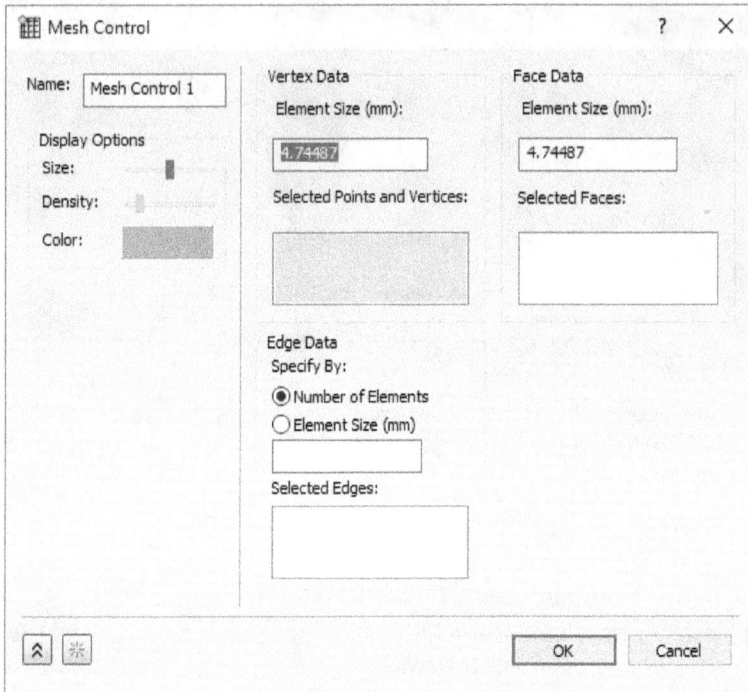

You can apply mesh control for local mesh sizing on points, edges, and faces. You can control the mesh definition on edges, either by specifying the number of elements or the element size. To assign the local meshing to a point, edge, or face simplify activate the entity selection field in the dialog box and select entities on the model. Multiple entities can be selected as required in each of the fields.

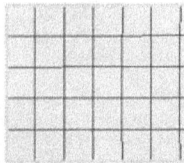

No Local Mesh Control   Edge Mesh Control   Vertex Mesh Control

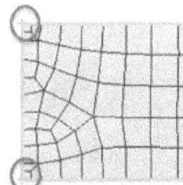

Face Mesh Control can also be assigned for 3D geometry (not shown).

To ensure that the color of the newly defined Mesh Control element is the same as the existing mesh, use the Color box in the Mesh Control dialog box when the local mesh control is added.

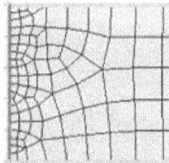

Once local mesh control is added to the analysis, a Mesh Control node is also added. Each Mesh Control element that is created is listed in the node. For example, in the following analysis, a single local mesh control element has been added.

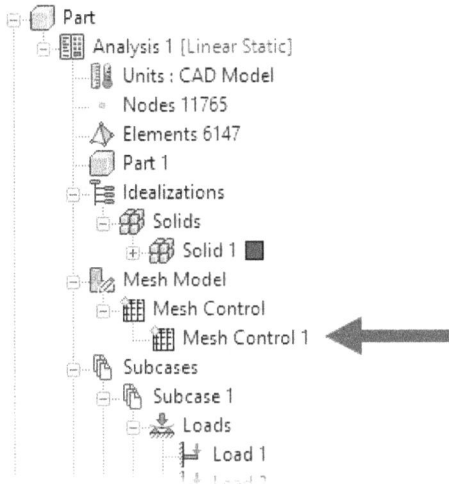

Consider the following when adding local mesh control:

- Multiple local mesh controls can be added to the model as required to refine the mesh.
- A local mesh control can be edited by right-clicking on the mesh control name and selecting Edit.
- Ensure that you update the mesh once local mesh control is defined.
- Local mesh controls can be displayed/hidden independently of the mesh lines (element edges) for the overall model. This is done by right-clicking on the Mesh Control node and selecting Display All or Hide All.

Mesh Tables

Mesh tables are used when analyzing an assembly model. It enables you to control the element size, order, and specify advanced settings for the each part in the assembly. To open the table, either click ⬛ (Mesh Table) in the Mesh Settings dialog or click ⬛ (Table) from the Mesh panel in the ribbon. All the components are listed in the table. Details on idealization color, element size, tolerance, element order, and the number of nodes and elements for each component is provided.

Part Name	Visibility	Color	Size (mm)	Tolerance (mm)	Element Order	Settings	Nodes	Elements
Mechanic...	✔		4.95974	9.91949e-05	Parabolic	Settings	0	0
Clip:1	✔	☐	1.50258	3.00515e-05	Parabolic	Settings	2964	1326
Cone:1	✔	☐	0.751141	1.50228e-05	Parabolic	Settings	9108	5117
Coupling:1	✔	⬛	0.326401	6.52802e-06	Parabolic	Settings	14503	8897
Dispenser ...	✔	☐	0.226937	4.53874e-06	Parabolic	Settings	11261	5916
Dispenser:1	✔	☐	0.397748	7.95495e-06	Parabolic	Settings	8442	4984
Eraser Ca...	✔	☐	0.622297	1.24459e-05	Parabolic	Settings	12412	6365
Eraser:1	✔	⬛	0.447257	8.94515e-06	Parabolic	Settings	19951	13155

Consider the following when working with a Mesh Table:

- To generate the mesh for any of the components, select its checkbox at the right-hand end of the row and click Generate Mesh. Multiple checkboxes can be selected at once to generate the mesh for multiple components. You can also use the checkboxes to delete a single or multiple meshes.
- Control the visibility of a component's mesh using the checkbox in the Visibility column. The visibility of the mesh in each component can be individually controlled.
- Access the advanced settings for individual components by selecting Settings in the Settings column for the appropriate component.
- Click (Mesh Settings) to switch from the Mesh Table to Global Mesh settings.
- New idealizations can be created using the button.
- Use the Continuous Meshing checkbox to enable continuous (matched) meshing between adjacent parts. Note that for two solid parts, the mesh is matched only along the edges (perimeter) of the parts. Nodes in the mated faces are not matched.

> Individual Mesh Controls can also be added to individual components in an assembly, in the same way as previously discussed for assigning mesh control to vertices, edges, and faces.

Lesson: Loading Analysis Results

Overview

This lesson describes how previously run analysis results can be loaded and reviewed in Autodesk Nastran In-CAD.

Objectives

After completing this lesson, you will be able to:

- Load an existing .FNO results file into an analysis.

Working with Existing Analysis Results

Autodesk Nastran In-CAD does not automatically load the results when a model is opened. This is true even if the results were previously run and the model was saved prior to closing the model. The results are released to save processing time and memory usage. You can identify whether the analysis results exist in the model based on the color of the analysis plot icons in the Results node. A gray icon indicates it isn't loaded, while a color icon indicates it is.

When an analysis is run, a new folder structure gets created in the same working folder as the model. The folder structure begins with a folder that has the same name as the working model and continues with the \InCAD\FEA folders. The *.FNO file is stored in the FEA folder and contains data for the active analysis that was run along with all of its subcases. The file name is randomly generated so that all results have unique naming conventions. Consider renaming the *.FNO file if specific data is to be maintained and easily identified.

Automatically Loading Results

To customize the software so that results are automatically loaded when the model is opened in the Autodesk Nastran In-CAD environment, click [icon] (Default Settings) in the System panel on the ribbon and in the Post-Processing settings, enable Automatically Load Results.

Loading Results

Previously saved results can be loaded into an analysis. This can be done to prevent having to rerun a in-depth analysis.

Procedure: To Load Analysis Results

1. Activate the analysis that is to be loaded.

2. Right-click on the Results nodes in a Subcase and select Load. If multiple subcases exist in the active analysis, the results for each will be loaded.

3. The results populate all subcases in the analysis that existed when the analysis was initially run.

Procedure: To Load Analysis Results from an .FNO file

1. Activate the analysis that is to be loaded.

2. Initiate the Load Results option using one of the following methods:

   - On Results panel on the ribbon, click 🗁 (Load Results).
   - Right-click on the Analysis name at the top of the Autodesk Nastran Model Tree and select Load Results.

3. In the Open dialog box, navigate to and select the *.FNO results file that is to be loaded.

4. The results populate all subcases in the analysis that existed when the analysis was initially run.

Tips for Working with Stored Results

- If the active Analysis is not the analysis that was active when the model was initially run/saved, the results will still load; however, the data on the loads and constraints is not listed. This can be misleading as to which loads and constraints the results were based on.

- Any result file can be loaded if you manually open the *.FNO file. If the result file from another analysis is loaded, an abnormal contour plot (or no plot) may be displayed because the loaded results do not correspond to the current model setup, mesh, or other parameters.

  Alternatively, the ⚠ icon may display adjacent to the Results node, indicating that the results may not be compatible. It is important to keep track of the results to ensure they match the model. If unsure, rerun the analysis. Loading the results directly from the Results node is recommended to ensure that the correct results are automatically located and loaded.

- Once a result file is created, you can rename the file in your working directory to include the name of the Analysis so that you can clearly identify which analysis the results are associated with.

Unloading Results

Unloading existing results that exist in the model can be used, as required, to release memory to improve system performance. It is not a requirement unless the postprocessing is lagging.

Procedure: To Unload Analysis Results

1. Activate the analysis name that is to be unloaded.

2. Initiate the Unload Results option using one of the following methods:

   - Expand the Results panel on the ribbon and click (Unload Results).
   - Right-click on the Analysis name at the top of the Autodesk Nastran Model Tree and select Unload Results.

3. The results are cleared from all subcases in the active analysis.

Lesson: Visualizing Result Plots

Overview

Result visualization is a key step in determining how the model reacts to its loads, constraints, and boundary conditions once an analysis is run. This lesson describes how you can display the default result plots that are generated in an analysis and how you can further edit their display to customize their output to show you exactly what is required in order to interpret the results.

Objectives

After completing this lesson, you will be able to:

- Display and animate an analysis plot in the graphics window.
- Edit the display settings associated with an existing analysis plot.
- Create a new analysis plot in an Analysis subcase.

Displaying Results

Visualizing your results is an important part of the analysis process as it enables you to assess the quality of your analysis model and to view the physical performance of the design. By default, some of the analysis types have predefined result plot templates that are assigned to them. These are automatically generated when the analysis is run. The settings that have been specified for these plot templates are based on generic settings; however, they can be further customized to modify how the plot is displayed. If default plot templates exist for an analysis, the results are listed in the Results node in the subcase when the analysis is run. In the following example, four default analysis plots were provided for this Linear Static analysis.

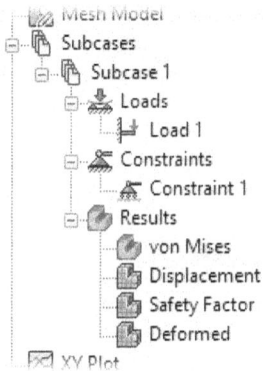

For example, in a Linear Static analysis the following default plot templates provided are:

- **von Mises:** This is the equivalent stress magnitude (which includes the effects of all stress tensors) and is best for predicting yield in ductile materials.
- **Displacement:** A scalar value showing how much the model changes in response to applied loading.
- **Safety Factor:** A scalar quantity that shows how much stronger a structure is beyond its applied loading.
- **Deformed:** Shows how the model changes shape in response to applied loading. Note that the deformed shape of the model is displayed, but no scalar results are shown.

Displaying a Results Plot

Autodesk Nastran In-CAD provides a range of tools and options for interacting with results and for controlling result appearance. To display a results plot you can view it as a static image or it can be displayed as an animation that enables you to see how the model changes under its assigned conditions. In both display styles, the model updates with the following information when a result is displayed:

- A gradient with values associated to the displayed plot display to the left of the graphics window.
- The model updates to show the contours and an outline showing the original position of the model prior to loading.
- A summary of the results are listed at the bottom of the graphics window.

Procedure: To Display a Results Plot

1. Right-click on the required result plot name in the Results node and select Display. Alternatively, you can double-click on the result plot's name to display it.

2. (Optional) To clear the display of the mesh from the results display, in the Display panel, expand ▭ (Object Visibility) and clear the Mesh and Mesh Control options.

3. Rotate and zoom the model as required to review the results.

Procedure: To Animate a Results Plot

1. Right-click on the required result plot name in the Results node and select Animate.

2. (Optional) To clear the display of the mesh from the results display, in the Display panel, expand ▭ (Object Visibility), and clear the Mesh and Mesh Control options.

3. Rotate and zoom the model as required to review the results.

4. To stop the animation, right-click on the plot name in the Results node and click Animate to clear its selection. Alternatively, in the ribbon, in the Animate panel, select Animate to clear is selection.

> To create an AVI of a result plot, right-click on the required Plot template's name in the Results node and select Create AVI. Once created, click OK and save the file, as required.

Results Panel

The Results panel in the ribbon provides additional options for displaying the results. Most of these options only display the default result plot for the analysis. If other result plots are required you must select ▱ (Options) on the ribbon or use the shortcut menu in the Results node to display and edit the plot. The assigned default is based on the element type used for the analysis. For example, for a Linear Static analysis, with solid elements the Solid von Mises result is the default. To verify the plot being displayed, note the active result in the Results node.

- Click ▱ (Contour) to display the contour plot for the default analysis plot.

- Click (Deformed) to display the deformed plot for the default analysis plot. The outline of the undeformed (original) geometry is displayed as dashed lines.

- Click (Stress Linearization) to display a graph of stress tensors along a selected stress classification line (SCL).

- Click (Animate) to animate the contour or deformed plot for the default analysis plot.

- The Contour and Deformed options can be displayed together to show the color contour on the deformed model.

- Click (Options) to access the Plot dialog box. This dialog box enables you to control the result type, deformed plot options, animation and visibility settings, and more.

Once an analysis is active, the Results panel updates as shown in the image below, with a few additional options.

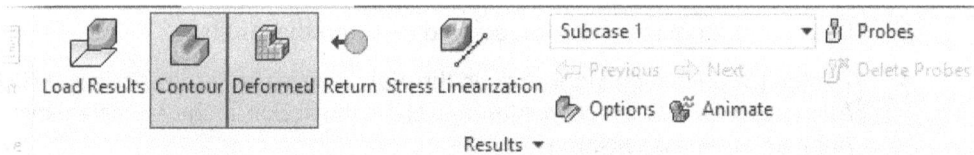

- The drop-down list (or the Previous and Next options) enable you to select the subcase that is being viewed. When reviewing other analysis types (e.g. nonlinear static) it can also be used to progress through the results of the default analysis plot.

> **Stress Linearization**
>
> Stress Linearization is primarily used to comply with design codes and requirements of the pressure vessel industry. However, the utility is applicable to other objects. You can use the Stress Linearization utility to graph local stress tensors along a linear path or to determine the relative contributions of bending and membrane stress for any type of structure. This option is located in the Results panel.
>
> For more information on Stress Linearization, refer to Autodesk Nastran In-CAD Help and search for "Stress Linearization".

Probing Values in a Result Plot

To view the exact value on the model the Probe tool can be used. This tool enables you to report the value at an exact position on the model. The value is reported in an information box that is attached to the cursor. The values that are reported depend on the result plot that is displayed. For example, if a von Mises plot is displayed, the probe will report the stress value, if the Deformed plot is displayed, the probe will report the X, Y, and Z translation values relative to the initial location.

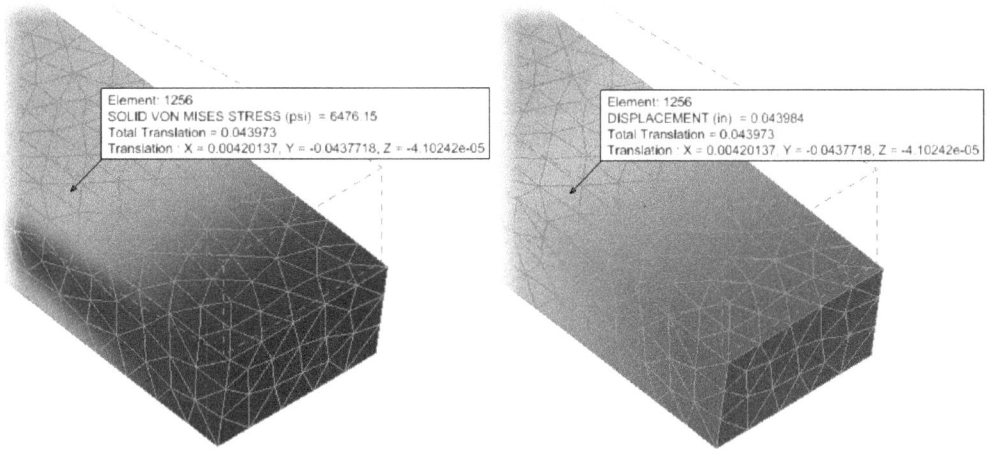

Element: 1256
SOLID VON MISES STRESS (psi) = 6476.15
Total Translation = 0.043973
Translation : X = 0.00420137, Y = -0.0437718, Z = -4.10242e-05

Element: 1256
DISPLACEMENT (in) = 0.043984
Total Translation = 0.043973
Translation : X = 0.00420137, Y = -0.0437718, Z = -4.10242e-05

Procedure: To Probe Values on a Displayed Result Plot

1. Right-click on the required result plot name in the Results node and select Display.

2. In the Results panel, select 📍 (Probe).

3. Position the cursor at locations on the model to report the element number and its value.

4. Continue to place additional probes on the model, as required. To prevent additional probes from being created, select 📍 (Probe) a second time to disable it. Once the Probe tool is disabled, you can select and drag the summary window to reposition it in the graphics window, if required.

5. To clear the display of all probes from the display, in the results panel, select 📍✕ (Delete Probes).

To clear the display of an analysis from the graphics window, right-click on the Plot template's name and clear the selection of either the Display or Animate options. Alternatively, you can double-click on the results plot in the Results node a second time to clear it.

Additional right-click options for the result plots enable you to do the following:

- Edit an existing plot. For more information on this topic, refer to the *Customizing the Plot Display* topic.
- Copy an existing plot to another subcase. Plots cannot be copied in the same subcase. As a work around, to duplicate a result plot in the same subcase, copy it to another subcase and then copy it back and change it as required.
- Delete an existing result plot from the Results node.
- Rename an existing plot.
- Create an AVI showing the results.

Customizing the Plot Display

By default, the plot settings are predefined with each default plot that is created for an analysis. These settings can be modified once the result has been generated to alter how the result is displayed to better meet your requirements. All customization of a result plot is done using the Plot dialog box. The predefined settings for the default von Mises plot is shown in the following image. The same dialog box is used to create a new result plot.

To access the Plot dialog box for editing, right-click on the result plot name in the Results node and select Edit. Alternatively, you can select [icon] (Options) in the Results panel. When using the [icon] option, the default result plot is initially accessed. You can choose a different results to plot using the Result Data and Type drop-down lists in the Contour Options tab of the Plot dialog box.

The Plot dialog box is made up of sections as well as tabs that are used for customization.

- The Name field is used to rename a result plot.

- The Plot section enables you to plot the result using the [icon] (Display), [icon] (Animate), or [icon] (Create AVI) options. These update the plot in the graphics window without having to close the Plot dialog box so you can continue to make changes, as required.

- The Display Options section controls the rendering display style and options for the result.
  - The Rendering drop-down list provides options to display the plot as Point, Line, Continuous, Fringe and Gouraud. The available options are dependent on the type of plot that is active in the dialog box.
  - The Levels field enables you to enter the number of contour levels required. Note that the Maximum number of levels permitted is 252. Additionally, you can flip the color range () for the color gradient.
  - The Min/Max option can be enabled to identify the nodes with the maximum and minimum values and display their corresponding values.
  - The Iso-Surfaces option can be enabled to display surfaces with the same contour plot level. The number of surfaces depends on the number of levels set in the plot.
- The tabs in the right-hand pane of the Plot dialog box enable you to access specific plot settings. Depending on the tab selected, the options will vary. For example, the Contour Options and Visibility Options tabs are active in the following image.

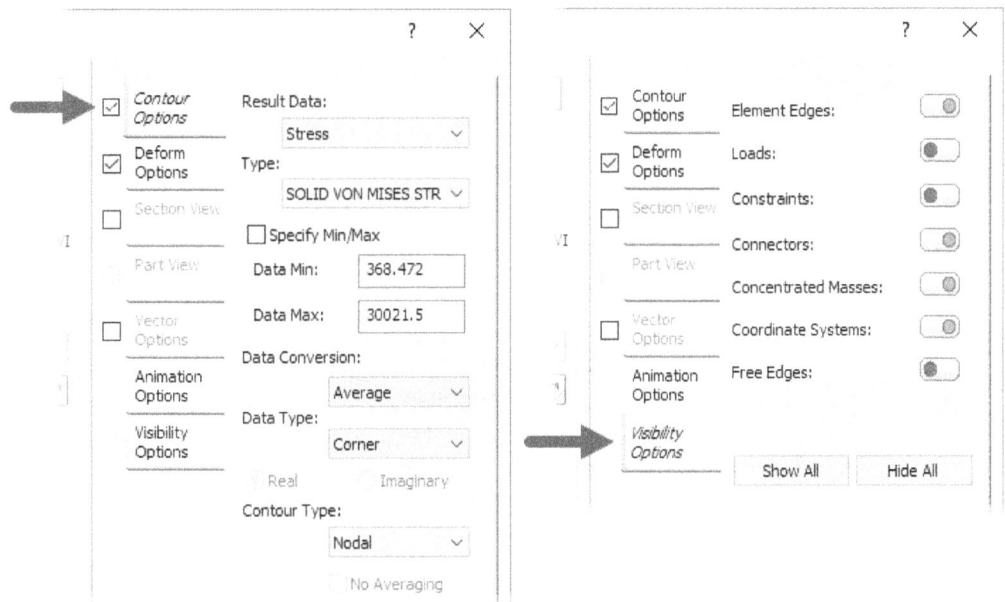

The options that are available on the 7 tabs enable you to customize the results plot display. These options are useful for isolating results in specific locations and determining the effect of the mesh on the results. With these tools, you can often determine if the mesh is too coarse. For more information on the options that are available on the tabs, refer to Autodesk Nastran In-CAD Help and search for "Plot Templates". Some of the commonly used customization fields in the available tabs include the options below. To enable the options in a tab, you must select the checkbox adjacent to the tab name.

- Contour Options tab
  - The Result Data drop-down list provides a list of result plot data that can be reported on. These include Stress, Displacement, Strain, etc. The Type list filters the available list of result plots based on the data that is required. This list is also filtered based on the idealizations (e.g., solid result types are only listed for solid element models, or shell stress results are listed for shell element models, etc.) For example, in the image below, only the Stress result plots are shown on the left and only the Displacement result plots are shown on the right.

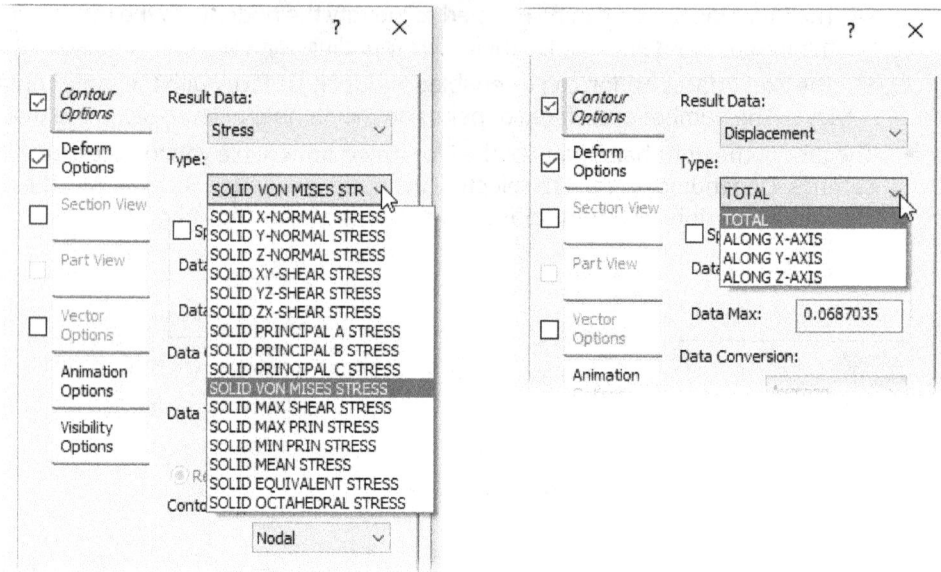

  - The Specify Min/Max field enables you to customize the minimum and maximum values that should be used in the gradient.
  - The Data Conversion options (Average, Maximum, Minimum) enable you to customize whether an average is taken for the surrounding values, or whether the max or min value from the surrounding elements is used.

> **Data Conversion Tips**
>
> The Min Data Conversion option should only be used when performing contours for vectors where the minimum values are actually the worst case (i.e. factor of safety or large compressive stresses). If there is a large difference between the three results (Average, Max and Min), especially at locations that do not have sharp corners or breaks in the model, your model may require a finer mesh.

  - The Data Type options (Corner or Centroidal) control how results are converted from pure data at element centroids and corners to the actual contour plot.
  - The Contour Type options enable you to select either nodal or elemental contouring. When Elemental is selected, several additional options are available. To create a plot in which each element face shows a single value, select Elemental and No Averaging.

- Animation Options tab
  - The animation options enables you to control the number of frames in the animation and the delay between frames (animation speed). You can also control how the animation cycles during playback. The Full option reverses the results (no load > full load > no load). The Half option produces a one-way animation (no load > full load). Additionally, the Oscillate option produces results both loading and unloading for positive and negative loads.
- Visibility Options tab
  - The options on this tab enable you to control the display of the additional items that are shown in the model. For example, the mesh (Element Edges), loads, constraints, etc. To control their display you can select the appropriate slider bar. Black indicates that the element is not displayed, and blue indicates that it is.

> **Element Visibility Settings**
> The visibility options that are set in the Plot dialog box only affect their display when viewing a results plot. If the results plot is toggled off, the element display settings for the analysis are used. These are set in the Object Visibility list ( ) on the Display panel.

Creating a Results Plot in a Linear Static Subcase

A new results plot can be added to the results of a subcase for a linear static analysis. The dialog box and options used for creating the new plot are the same as those used to modify an existing analysis plot.

Procedure: To Create a New Analysis Plot

1. Right-click on the Results node and select New. If multiple subcases exist, ensure that the new results plot is being created in the correct subcase. The Plot dialog box opens.

2. On the Contour Options tab, select the report data type in the Result Data drop-down list.

3. Select the type of report in the Type drop-down list.

4. Enter a name for the new analysis plot. Ensure that the name is descriptive to help identify the type of results that will be shown when the plot is displayed.

5. Define the options in the Display Options section of the dialog box.

   - For more information on these options, refer to the *Plot Templates* topic.

6. Define the options in the seven tabs, as required.

   - For more information on these options, refer to the *Plot Templates* topic.

7. Click OK to complete the results plot and save it to the Results node.

Lesson: Visualizing XY Plot Results

Overview

An XY Plot result provides an alternate way to visualize nodal or elemental data. This lesson describes how you can create and display XY plots and how you can further edit their display style to customize the output.

Objectives

After completing this lesson, you will be able to:

- Create a new XY plot for an analysis.
- Display an XY plot that was created to display the results of an analysis.
- Edit the display settings associated with an existing XY plot.

Creating an XY Plot in a Linear Static Subcase

Only a few of the analysis types in Autodesk Nastran In-CAD provide you with predefined XY plots. If so, they are automatically generated when the analysis is completed. For example, a linear static analysis does not create any XY plots; however, a nonlinear static analysis does. If a required XY plot is not automatically generated, it can be manually created. Once it is created and saved in the model, it will be retrieved when the results are reloaded. To create an XY plot you use the XY Plot dialog box.

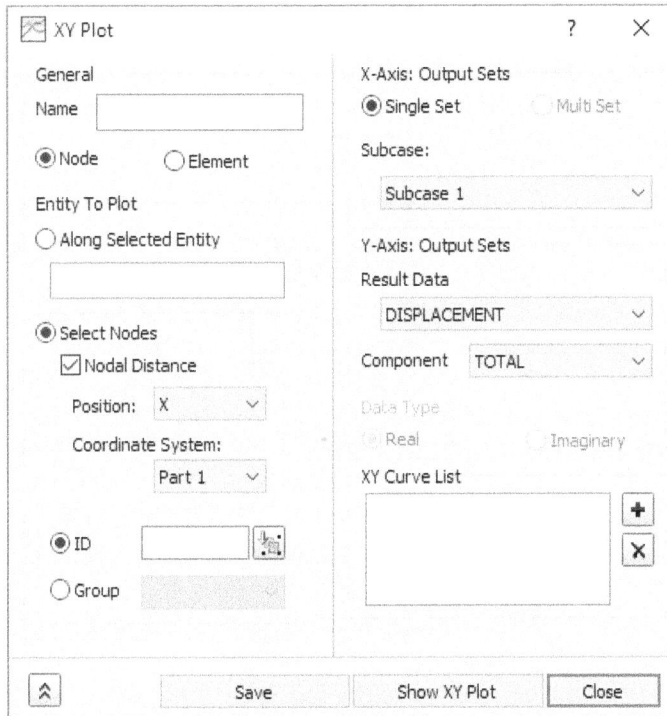

The following describes the key settings in the dialog box that can be used to define the XY plot. Once defined, you can select Show XY Plot to display the plot. To save the plot to the XY Plot node in the analysis, click Save.

- **General**: Defines the name of the XY plot and whether the plot will report nodal (Node) or elemental (Element) output quantities. The Node option enables plotting displacement, velocity, and acceleration and the Element option plots stress and strain.

- **Entity To Plot**: Defines the node or element to be plotted.
  - **Along Selected Entity**: Enables you to select sketch segments or edges to plot the results (i.e., results on the Y-axis and distance on the X-axis).
  - **Select Nodes/Elements**: Enables you to select the Node/Element IDs by setting the position and reference coordinate system.
    - **Nodal/Elemental Distance**: With this option enabled, it considers the Nodal or Elemental distance based on the position over X, Y or Z coordinates. You can also define the coordinate system to be used. With this option cleared, it plots the XY Plot based on Node/Element Index.
    - **ID**: Node or Element ID. You can click on the node or element of interest to populate the ID into the selection menu. You can use the Query Display (right-click on Nodes or Elements in the Autodesk Nastran In-CAD Model tree) to obtain your IDs to manually enter into the selection menu. It also enables you to enter the IDs successively by entering a comma between entries.
    - **Group**: Enables you to select from a predefined group of nodes or elements.
- **X-Axis Output Sets**: Enables you to define the output specifics for the X-Axis. If multiple subcases exist, ensure that the correct subcase is selected for the plot.
  - **Single Set**: This is applicable for all analyses. It enables you to plot the XY Plot for the results along sketch/edge selection using the Along Selected Entity option and also for some set of nodes/elements using Select Nodes/Elements.
  - **Multi Set**: This is applicable only for an analysis which consists of multi results for a subcase. It enables you to set the start and end sets of the range of output sets for the XY Plot.
- **Y-Axis Output Sets**: Enables you to define the output specifics for the Y-Axis.
  - **Result Data**: Defines which output vector will be plotted. (e.g, Displacement, Rotation, Force, moment, solid mesh convergence error)
  - **Component**: Defines which vector component (if applicable) will be plotted. (e.g, the total, or Tx, Ty, Tz)
  - **Data Type**: Defines the type of data that will be displayed. The availability of these options and the types of options available vary on the type of analysis. For more information on the options that are available, refer to Autodesk Nastran In-CAD Help and search for "Results XY Plotting".
- **XY Curve list**: Enables for plotting multiple curves on a single plot.
  - ⊞ (Add): Adds the curve to the XY Curve list. If multiple curves are added without selection, it will show all curves in the XY Plot graph. If any single curve is selected from the list and then plot the curve, it will show only the selected one.
  - ⊠ (Delete): Deletes the selected curve from the XY Curve list.

Procedure: To Create a New XY Plot

1. Right-click on the XY Plot node and select New. The XY Plot dialog box opens.

2. Enter a name for the new XY plot. Ensure that the name is descriptive to help identify the type of results that will be shown when the plot is displayed.

3. Select whether the plot will show node or element results by selecting their respective option.

4. Define the Entity to Plot options.

5. Define the X-Axis Output Sets.

    Note: If multiple subcases exist ensure that the new plot is being created in the correct subcase.

6. Define the Y-Axis Output Sets.

7. (Optional) If plotting multiple curves in one XY Plot result, define each curve and select [+] to add the curve to the XY Curve List.

8. Click Show XY Plot to display the newly created plot. If multiple XY curves have been added, ensure that the specific curve is selected if only its data is required, otherwise all curves will be plotted. If multiple plots are shown, each are assigned a unique color.

9. Click Save to save the newly created plot to the XY Plot node in the analysis. Any XY Plots that are saved in the model are retrieved when the results are reloaded.

    Note: When creating an XY Plot with multiple curves, the plot name of the last curve that was added will be used as the name of the XY plot in the Autodesk Nastran Model Tree.

10. Click Close to close the XY Plot dialog box.

    Note: Once saved an XY plot cannot be edited. It must be recreated if changes are required.

Displaying XY Plot Results

Any XY Plot that has been manually created or those automatically created during the analysis can be viewed in the same way. The XY plot displays the data and provides options to customize the plot's default line display.

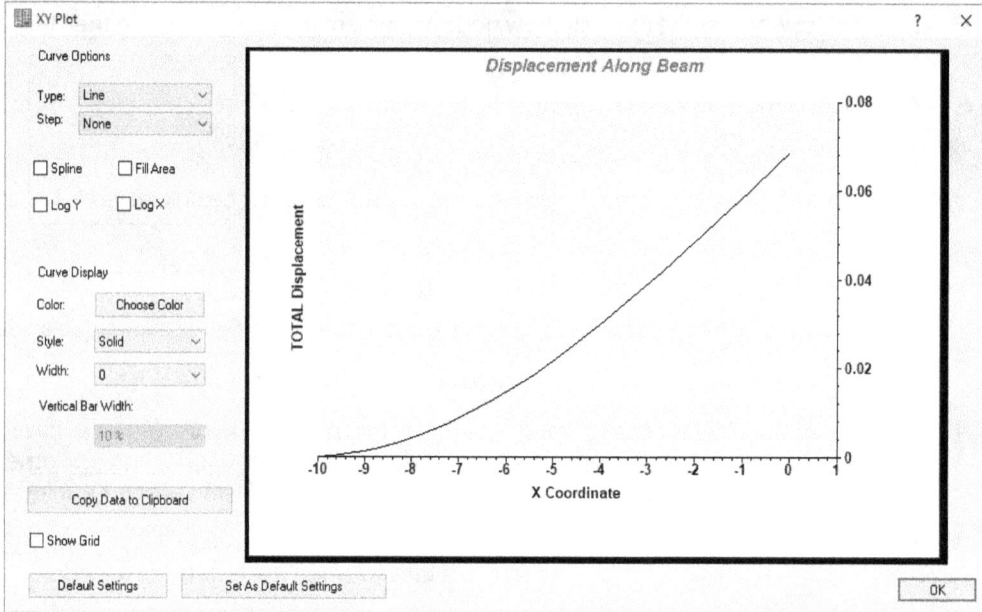

Procedure: To Display an XY Plot

1. Right-click on the required plot name in the XY Plot node and select Show XY Plot. Alternatively, you can double-click on the plot's name to display it.

2. (Optional) Customize the default line display, as required. For more information on these options, refer to the *Results XY Plotting* topic.

3. Click OK to close the XY Plot dialog box.

Customizing the XY Plot Display

Unlike working with the Result plots, you cannot edit an existing XY Plot to change the information that is being reported. However, you can modify the display of the plot once it is displayed for improved viewing. To customize the XY Plot, you can use the options on the left side of the XY Plot dialog box.

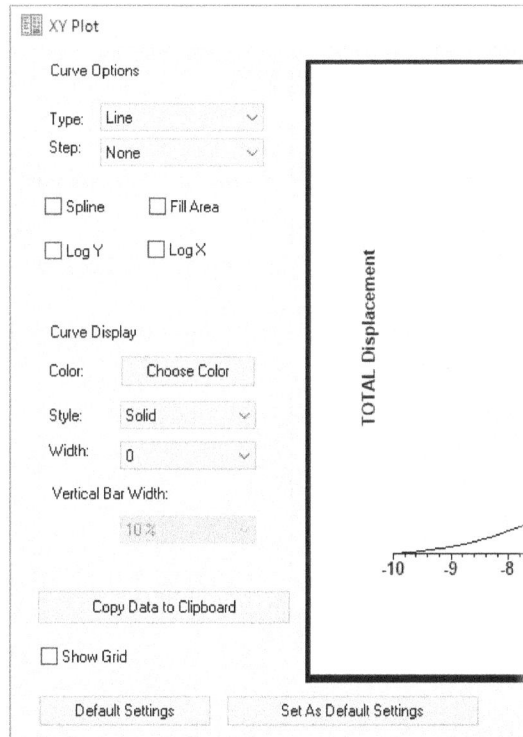

The options for customizing the display of the XY Plot include:

- Use the Type drop-down list in the Curve Options section to change the type of curve. The options enable you to display the results as a line, line and symbol, symbols only (Scatter), or vertical bars. For the line display you can further refine how the line is displayed between each point.
- Use the Curve Display section to change the visual style of the curve. You can customize its color, style (solid, dashed), and its width. For the vertical bar display you can also customize the bar size.
- Use the Copy Data to Clipboard option to copy the data for pasting into another document (e.g. Word Document).
- Click Show Grid to overlay a grid on the XY Plot.
- Once customized, click Default Settings to return to the original default settings. To set the customized settings as default, click Set As Default Settings.

Exercise: Refining the Mesh

In this exercise, you will examine the results from the last exercise, and determine if the mesh distribution played too strong an influence on the results. You will do the following in this exercise:

- Use an assortment of visualization customizations to determine the quality of the analysis results.
- Refine the mesh and compare the new mesh to the default mesh that was originally used in the model.
- Run the new mesh and examine the results.

Open the Model & Start the Autodesk Nastran In-CAD Environment

1. Open the file *C:\Autodesk Nastran InCAD 2019 Essentials Exercise Files\Cast_Lever\Cast Lever.ipt*, if not already open. This was the model that was used in the previous exercise.

    If you did not complete the previous exercise, open the file *C:\Autodesk Nastran InCAD 2019 Essentials Exercise Files\Mesh\Cast Lever3.ipt*.

2. Select the Environments tab and click Autodesk Nastran In-CAD to activate the Autodesk Nastran In-CAD environment.

Review the Results

In this task, you will review the result for the analyzed model. If you are working with the same model used in the previous exercise the results should be displayed or you can rerun them. If you are using the Cast Lever3.ipt, you will load results that were previously executed on the provided model. Additionally, you will use the Plot dialog box to control the results display.

1. If you are using the model from the previous chapter, ensure the results for the Exercise2 subcase in Analysis 2 are available. If not, run them again.

    If using the Cast Lever3.ipt, the results have been included and can be loaded. To load the results required for this exercise, complete the following:

    1. Ensure that the Analysis 2 analysis is active. The Exercise2 subcase is the subcase being reviewed.

    2. Right-click on the Results node in the Exercise2 subcase and select Load. If the Load option is not available, you likely need to update the Mesh (⚠). Right-click on the Mesh node in the Autodesk Nastran Model Tree and select Generate Mesh and rerun the analysis. Alternatively, in the Results panel, you can click 🖼 (Load Results). Using this method, you must navigate to *C:\Autodesk Nastran InCAD 2019 Essentials Exercise Files\Mesh\Cast Lever3\InCAD\FEA* and select the ry9z4i4sr.FNO results file. Click Open. The results are now available. Note: The other .FNO file in this folder contains the results for Analysis 1.

2. If you are using the Cast Lever2 file from the previous exercise, one of the analysis results may be displayed, If so, right-click on the displayed analysis and clear the Display option. The Meshed model should be displayed with no analysis.

   If you are using the Cast Lever3 file and loaded the results, no results should be displayed. If the results are displayed, right-click on the displayed analysis and clear the Display option.

3. For a Linear Static analysis, von Mises is the default analysis plot. Select (Contour) in the Results panel to toggle the display of the contour for the default von Mises analysis plot. In the Results node, note that the von Mises analysis is now active. The maximum stress is approximately 129 MPa.

4. In the Display panel, expand (Object Visibility) and clear the selection of the Mesh option, if displayed. This removes the element mesh from the display helping make the contours a little easier to see.

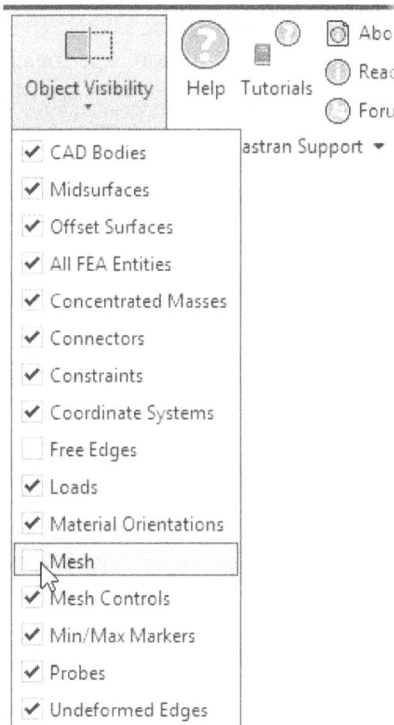

5. Select ![Deformed icon] (Deformed) in the Results panel to overlay the display of the original model geometry over the deformed geometry. Because the Contour option is still active, the stress contour and values are also displayed.

   Alternatively, you can control the analysis result display from the Results node in the

   Autodesk Nastran Model Tree. Clear the selection of both the ![Contour icon] (Contour) and

   ![Deformed icon] (Deformed) options in the Results panel. The model's loads, connectors, and constraints are only displayed.

6. To once again visualize the von Mises stress plot, right-click on von Mises in the Results node and select Display.

   Note: The displacement overlay and the mesh is still not included. The deformed overlay can be displayed using the option in the Results panel, if needed.

   Upon close inspection, the stress results show a few indicators of potential convergence issues. The local face tangency is intermittent because the element faces are flat, they can't form a perfectly curved face like that of the fillet. In the following image, you can see that the results on the surface look "rough" and the area of high stress is "spotty".

7. In the Results panel, click (Options) to open the Plot dialog box.

Note: Using the Plot dialog box, you can access all of the options for controlling the contour plot (result type, deform, animation, and visibility options, and more).

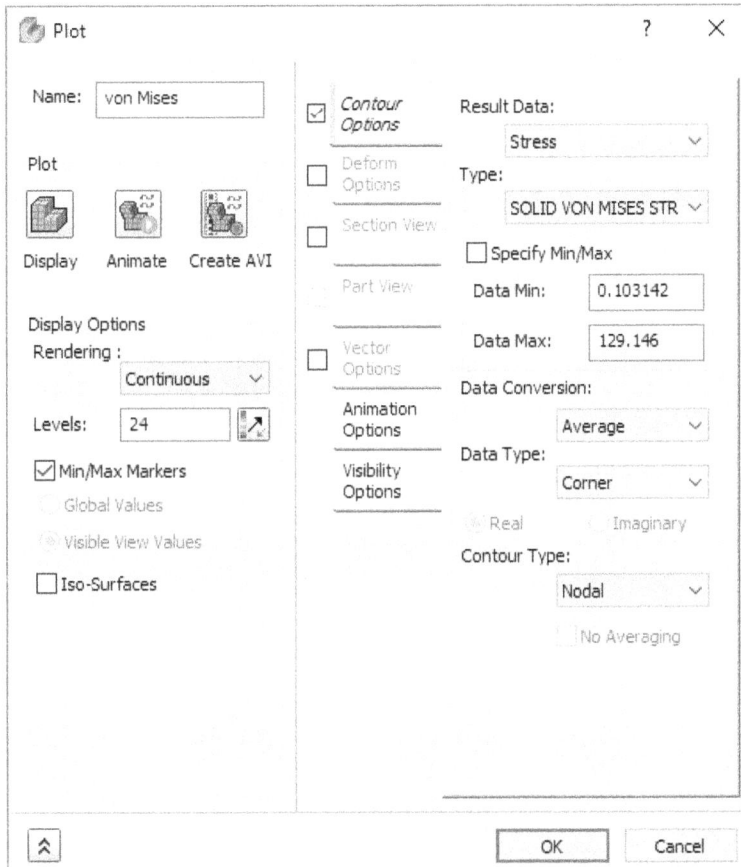

8. Ensure that Stress is selected in the Result Data list and that SOLID VON MISES STRESS is selected in the Type list. This verifies the plot that is being modified.

9. To further clean up the view, click the Visibility Options tab. Slider controls are presented to control the display of the elements that are added in the analysis. Note that the Element Edges are toggled off because this was previously done in the ribbon by clearing the Mesh option. By controlling the visibility options in this tab, you can control what is displayed in the result plot.

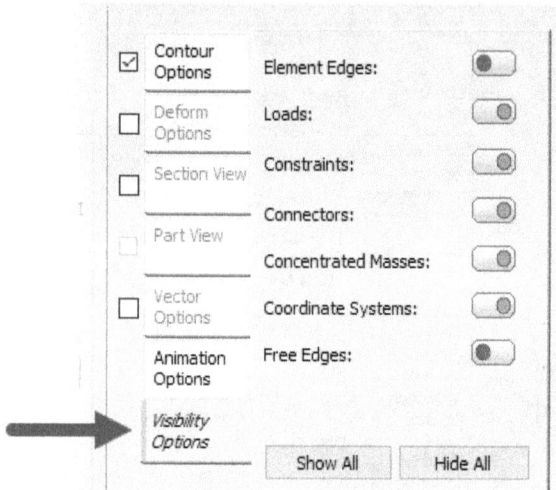

10. Using the slider controls drag the slider for Connectors to the left so that they are removed from the display.

11. Set the Rendering option to Fringe in the drop-down list.

12. In the Plot section of the dialog box, click ⬚ (Display) to preview the edits if they are not displayed. The connectors have been removed from the display and the fringe plot is displayed.

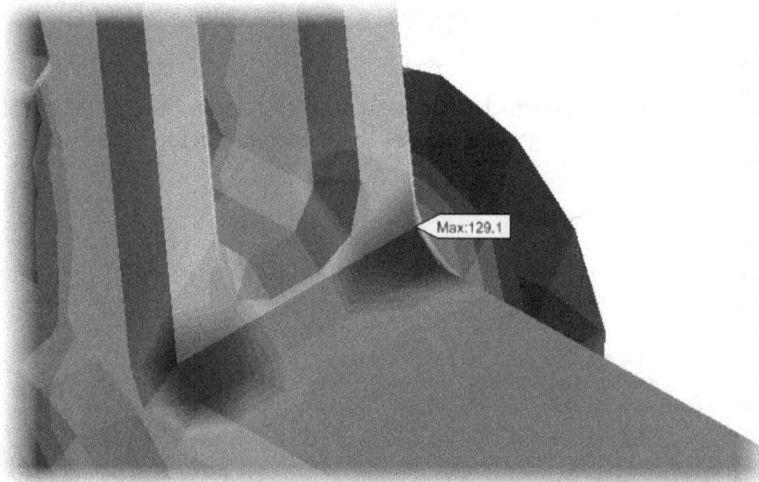

13. On the Visibility Options tab, drag the slider for Element Edges to the right so that they are included back in the display. If the display does not update, click .

Note that the boundaries of the contours are line segments instead of curved lines, and tend to be influenced by the element edges (follow the element edges and there shape). This indicates that you might need to refine the mesh to improve the results.

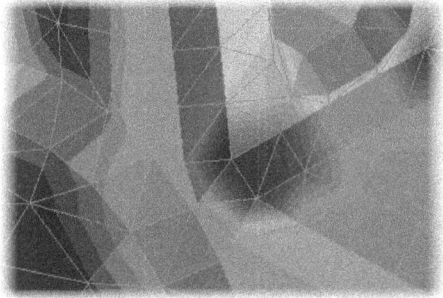

14. Set the Rendering option back to Continuous in the drop-down list. This is the default option for the default von Mises template.

15. Click the Contour Options tab and set the following options:

- From the Data Type list, select Centroidal.
- From the Contour Type list, select Elemental.
- From the Elemental Options section, select No Averaging.

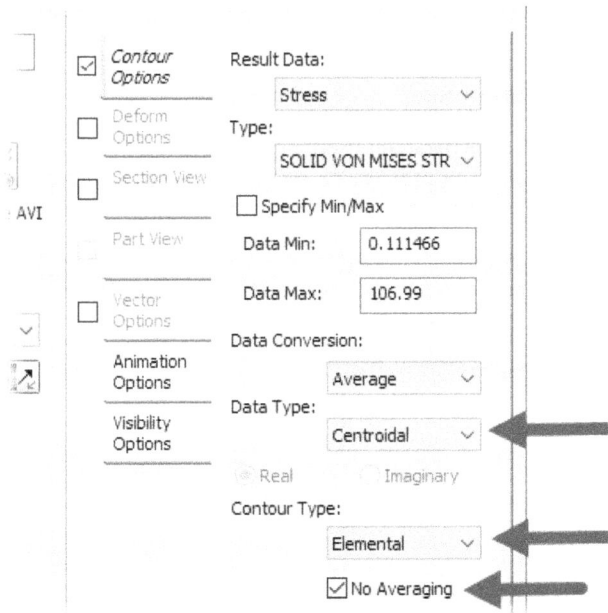

16. Note that the unaveraged centroidal plot shows large jumps in stress across adjacent elements. This is a clear indicator that mesh refinement is required.

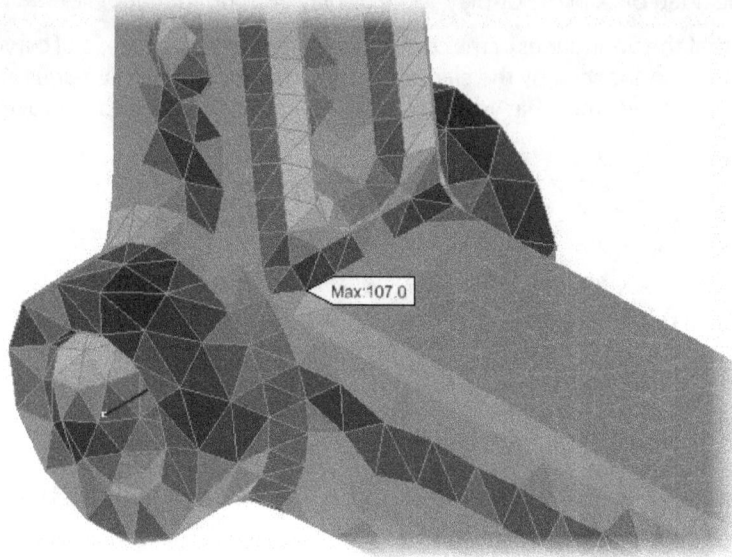

17. Click OK to close the Plot dialog box. If the von Mises result is displayed again later (e.g., by using the Autodesk Nastran Model Tree), the settings that have been defined will remain for the analysis. In this case the unaveraged centroidal plot will display.

18. In the Results node, right-click on von Mises and clear the Display option to remove its display from the model. Alternatively, you can double-click on the result plot name to clear it from the display.

Refine the Global Mesh Element Size

In this task, you will refine the global mesh element size for the model. Once the necessity for refinement is apparent, global refinement of the mesh is recommended prior to any local refinements.

1. In the Analysis 2 sub-tree, right-click on Mesh Model, and click Edit to open the Mesh Settings dialog box. The current settings are the default values that were assigned when the analysis was created.

2. Enter **4** as the new Element Size.

3. Click Generate Mesh to update the mesh in the model.

4. Click OK.

Refine the Mesh Locally

Local mesh control enables you to refine specific areas of the model without having to apply finer global mesh which can lead to unnecessarily longer analysis times. It can be useful in high stress/strain or highly shaped areas. In this task, you will refine the mesh for selected faces in the model. This will enable more precise strain calculation in this region, which will improve overall accuracy in the analysis.

1. In the Analysis 2 sub-tree, right-click on Mesh Model, and click Add Mesh Control.

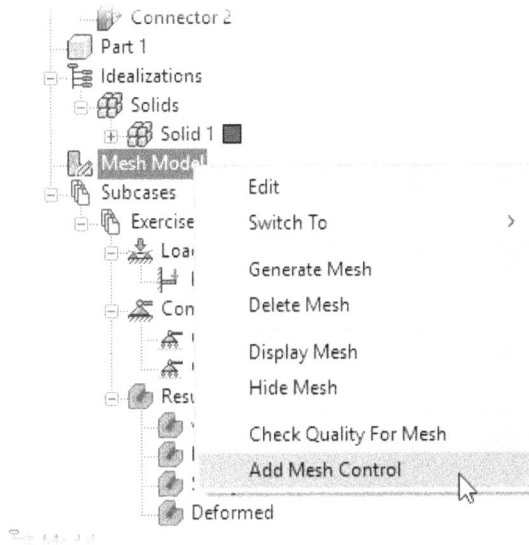

2. Set the color of the mesh to red in the Display Options, if not already set.

3. Enter **0.5** as the new Element Size value for the Face Data.

4. Click in the Selected Faces field to activate it so that faces can be selected on the model.

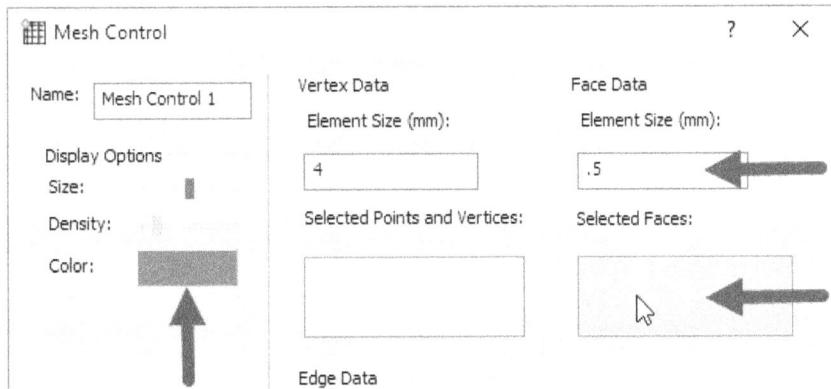

5. Select the 9 faces shown below to be customized with the new element size. Note that the Mesh elements, loads, and connectors have been cleared from the display to improve clarity in the image.

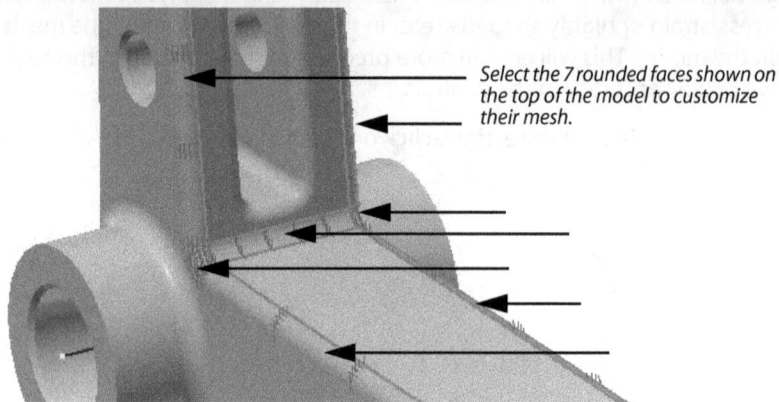

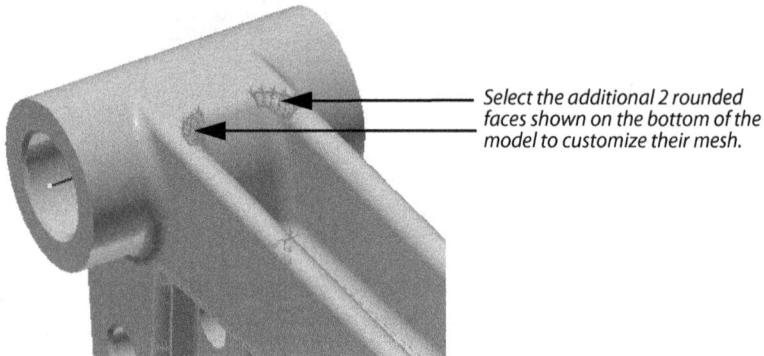

Select the 7 rounded faces shown on the top of the model to customize their mesh.

Select the additional 2 rounded faces shown on the bottom of the model to customize their mesh.

6. Click OK to complete the mesh modification on the selected surfaces. Note that a new Mesh Control element has been added to the analysis. To make further refinements to these surfaces you can edit this element.

7. Right-click on the Mesh Model node in the Autodesk Nastran Model Tree and select Generate Mesh to update the mesh after the refinement. Note that the number of total Nodes and Elements update.

Further Change the Global Mesh Settings

In this task, you will once again change the global mesh settings for the entire model. This will be done by changing the max element growth rate instead of entering a specific element size. This enables you to more tightly control the growth rate between elements. Additionally, you will enable the use of midside nodes to further refine the mesh, enabling it to contour to the curved shape of the model.

1. In the Analysis 2 sub-tree, right-click on Mesh Model, and click Edit to open the Mesh Settings dialog box.

2. In the Mesh dialog box, click Settings.

3. On the Advanced Mesh Settings dialog, change the Max Element Growth Rate to 1.1.

4. Select the Project Midside Nodes option.

5. Set the Quality Midside Adjustment to ON.

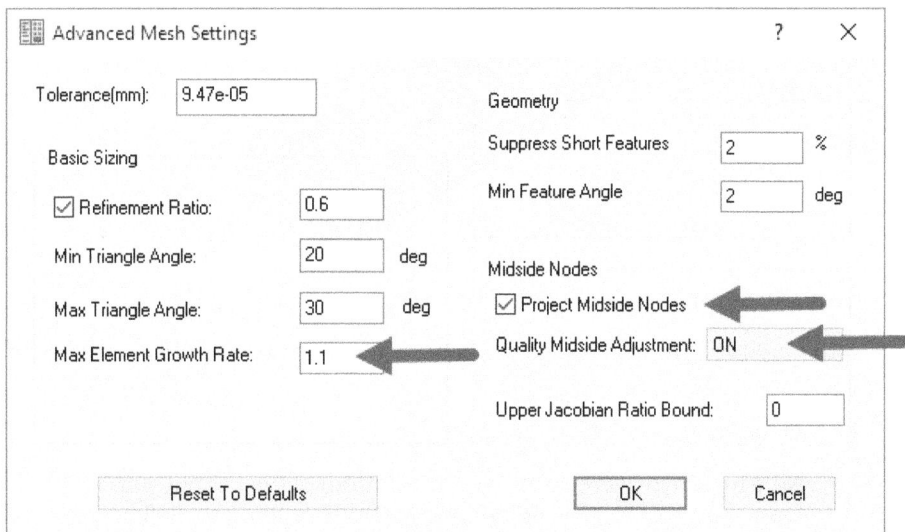

6. Click OK to close the Advanced Mesh Settings dialog box.

7. Click Generate Mesh to update the mesh.

8. Click OK to close the Mesh Settings dialog box. Note that the loads, connectors, and constraints have been cleared from the display to improve clarity in the image.

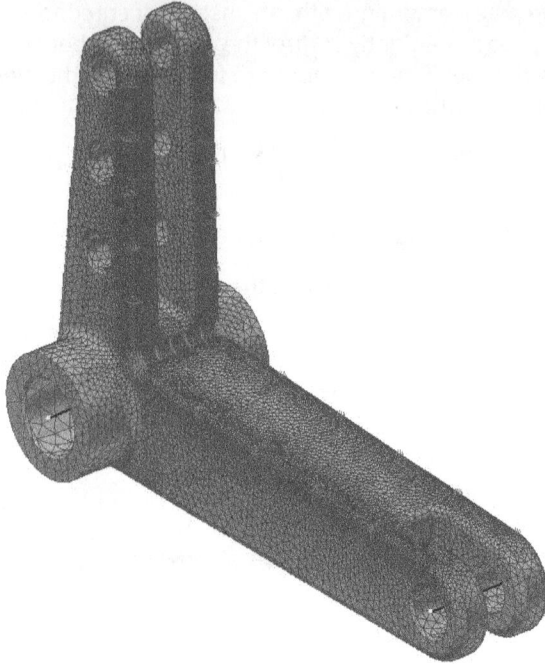

Run the Analysis

In this task, you will run the analysis again using the new mesh that has been modified.

1. In the Solve panel, click ▤ (Run).

2. Note that there were no errors at the bottom of the Output view, but that there are fewer warnings than were reported for the default mesh. Refining the mesh reduced the number of elements that had an interior angle less than 10.

    Note: To completely remove these warnings you could further modify the global mesh settings and change the Min and Max Triangle Angle values to a smaller size. For this exercise, these remaining warnings will be assumed acceptable and no further modifications are required.

3. Click OK to confirm the completion of the Nastran solution. The Autodesk Nastran Model Tree is returned to the display.

Display the Results

In this task, you will graphically display Stress (von Mises) results in the main window and compare the results to those that were obtained using the default mesh settings. Additionally, you will create an XY plot of the stress at points along an edge.

1. Right-click on von Mises in the Results node for the active analysis and select Display. Note that the stress increased in this fillet as compared to the previous max stress value. It is common to see an increase with correct meshing. By increasing the mesh density in the high stress region, you see that the local stresses are higher than previously thought because the course mesh wasn't permitting us to gather enough information for this important region.

   Note: Convergence should always be checked, even if you are focusing on trend analysis. If two designs are not similarly converged, you won't know if the stress change was due to design variations or is mesh related. This could lead to bad design decisions.

2. Right-click on the XY Plot node and select New.

3. Enter **Upper Edge Stress Plot** as the name for the new XY plot.

4. Select Element in the General section.

5. Press and hold <Ctrl> and select 10 elements along the edge shown below. Note that the loads, connectors, and constraints have been cleared from the display to improve clarity in the image. The selected elements display in green.

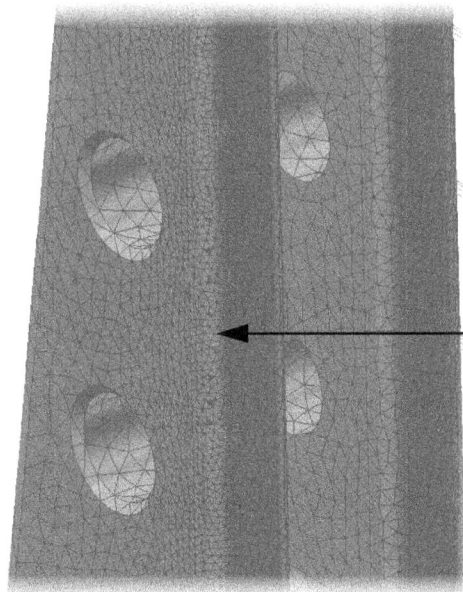

Select the 10 elements along this filleted face (from the bottom to the top).

6. Maintain the default options in the X-Axis Output Sets section. The Exercise 2 subcase should be automatically selected.

7. In the Y-Axis Output Sets section, select SOLID VON MISES STRESS in the Result Data list.

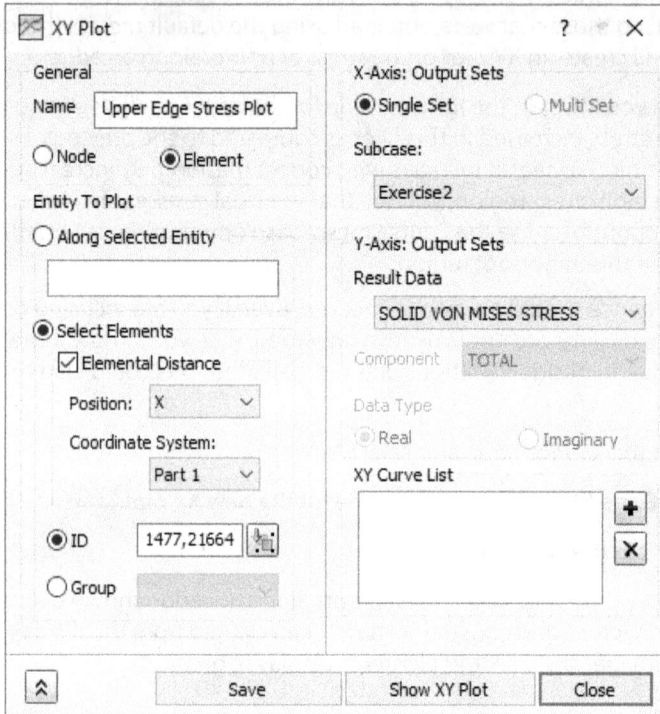

8. Click Show XY Plot to display the newly created plot. Your plot will vary as it depends on the elements selected.

9. Use the options on the left-hand side of the XY Plot to customize the curve options:

    - Change the curve Type to Line+Symbol.
    - Change the curve color to red.

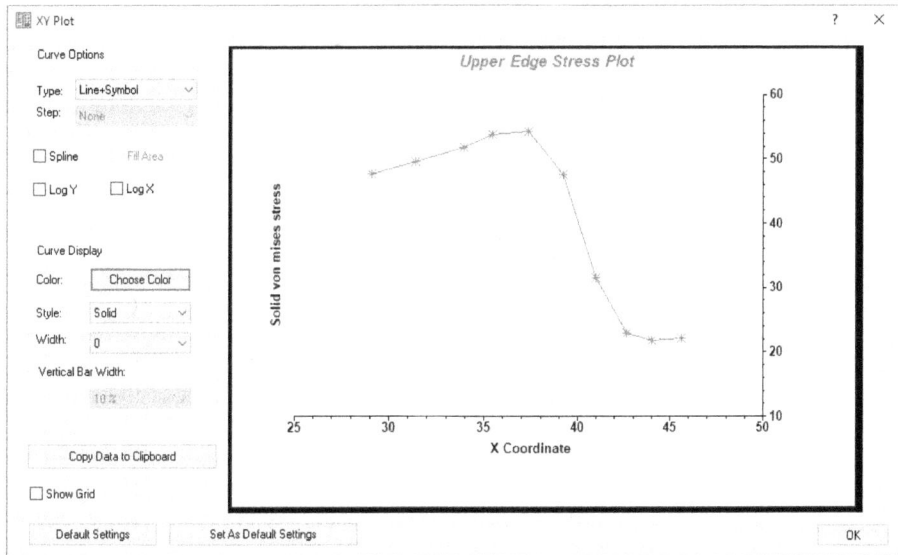

NOTE: Your plot will vary depending on the order and location of point selection.

10. Click OK to close the XY Plot.

11. Click Save to save the newly created plot to the XY Plot node in the analysis.

12. Click Close to close the XY Plot dialog box. Note that the new XY Plot is displayed in the XY Plot node. To display it again, double-click on its name or right-click and select Show XY Plot.

13. Save the model.

Exercise: Working with Line Elements

In this exercise, you will set up, solve, and review results of a beam element analysis based on Inventor Frame Generator structural members. A linear static analysis will be used to determine the displacement and stress that a railing will experience when loaded both horizontally and vertically. These loads will be assigned as two separate subcases, both of which will also include gravity. This analysis will use a model that was created using the Inventor Frame Generator tool. Because it was created in Frame Generator, Nastran In-CAD automatically generates Idealizations for a Line Element analysis that uses the cross-section from the defined structural member.

Prepare the Model for use in Nastran In-CAD

1. Open *C:\Autodesk Nastran InCAD 2019 Essentials Exercise Files\Railing\Railing.iam*.

    This railing model was created in Autodesk Inventor using Frame Generator and will be analyzed using Nastran In-CAD. The Frame Generator tool enables you to easily create frame assemblies. To begin, a skeleton of the overall frame is created using sketched line entities. From there, each frame member is generated from a library of frame components, corresponding to each line in the reference skeleton part. The type of frame member that is created is defined during placement and includes, among other placement type references, the selection of the standard (e.g., ANSI, DIN, ISO, etc.), the family (e.g., rectangular, circular, flat, square, etc.), its size, and its orientation. In addition, end treatments can be customized, ensuring that the beam members are correctly intersected and terminated. In this assembly, four different member types (cross-sections) have been used.

2. Activate the Autodesk Nastran In-CAD environment.

3. If the frame members are displayed in the Nastran environment, complete the remainder of this step, otherwise skip to step 4.

In the Analysis sub-tree, expand the Railing.iam node. Right-click on Frame0001:1 and clear the Visibility option. This toggles off the display of the frame members and shows only the line elements that represent the overall frame.

Note: If you do not see the line elements, click Save to save the model and refresh the graphic display.

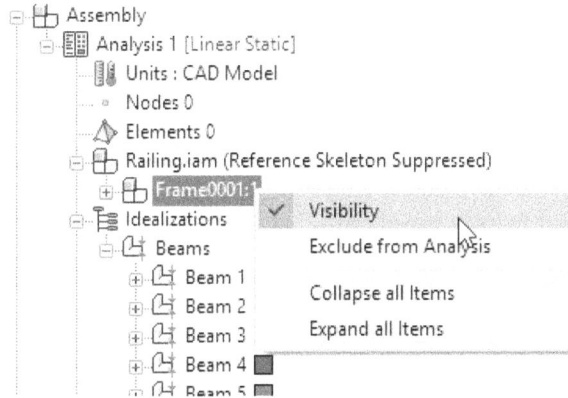

4. In the Idealizations node, expand the Beam 1 node. As this assembly was created using Frame Generator, the default idealizations that are generated use the Beam element type. A separate color is assigned to each idealization, and they are sequentially numbered. The Mild Steel material that was assigned in Autodesk Inventor when the frame was created is used for all idealizations in the analysis.

5. In the Analysis sub-tree, right-click on the Subcases node and select New. In the Name field, enter **Vertical Load and Gravity**. Click OK.

6. In the Analysis sub-tree, right-click on the Subcase1 node and select Rename. Enter **Horizontal Load and Gravity** as the new name.

Constrain the Model

In this task, you will constrain the model to be fixed where the three circular members would be attached to the floor. Additionally, you will add constraints that prevent translation where the four members would attach to a wall or another segment of railing.

1. In the Setup panel, click ⚓ (Constraints) to open the Constraints dialog box. Create a constraint using the following options.

- In the Degrees of Freedom section of the dialog box, click 🔧 (No Translation). Only rotation should be allowed, and Tx, Ty, and Tz remain selected to constrain against translation.
- In the Name field, enter **Constraint 1 (Beam)**.
- Select the four endpoints of the railing, as shown below, as the references for the constraint.
- Assign the constraint to both subcases.

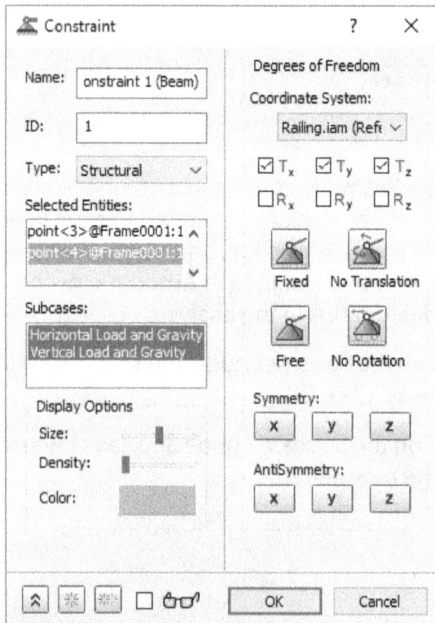

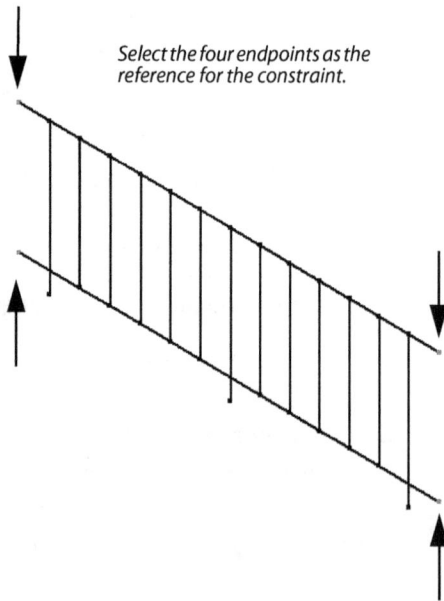

Select the four endpoints as the reference for the constraint.

- Select ☐ 👓 (Preview) to show the constraint on the model.
- Click OK.

NOTE: As of the printing of this learning guide, the display of constraints and loads were unpredictable as to whether they would display or not. The following is a suggested workaround that can be used to display them, if enabling the Preview option is not working as expected. Begin by exiting the Autodesk Nastran In-CAD environment to return to the Inventor modeling environment. Then return to the Nastran In-CAD environment, and edit the constraint to refresh the display. Subsequent loads and constraints added to the model should display as expected.

2. Add an additional constraint to the model using the following options. This constraint will constrain the bottom vertices that attach to the floor such that they are fixed, preventing any translation or rotation.

- In the Degrees of Freedom section, click (Fixed).
- In the Name field, enter **Constraint 2 (Beam)**.
- Select the three vertices shown below as the references to place the constraint.
- Assign the constraint to both subcases.

- Select ☐ 👓 (Preview) to show the constraint on the model.
- Click OK.

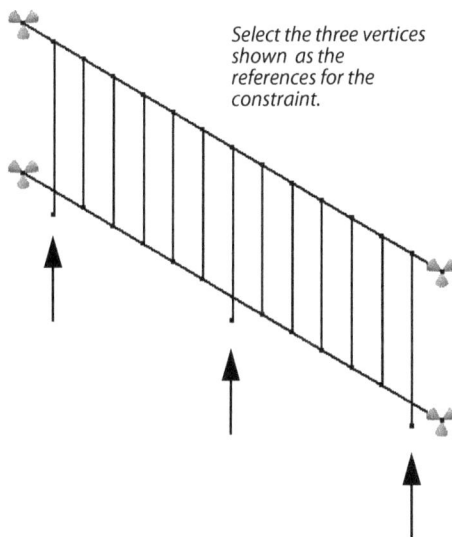

Select the three vertices shown as the references for the constraint.

Load the Model

In this task, you will add two different distributed force loads to the model and a gravity load. One of the distributed force loads will be assigned horizontally to the top member of the railing and the second will be assigned vertically to the bottom member of the railing. Each will be analyzed as separate subcases. The gravity load will be assigned to both subcases.

1. In the Setup panel, click ![Loads icon] (Loads) to open the Load dialog box. Create a load using the following options.

   - Select Distributed Load as the load type and Force as its Sub Type.
   - In the Name field, enter **Horizontal Load (Beam)**.
   - Select the top entity as shown below as the reference for the load.
   - Enter a Magnitude of **20** lbf/in in the Fz field.
   - Assign the load to the Horizontal Load and Gravity subcase. Ensure that it is only assigned to this one subcase.

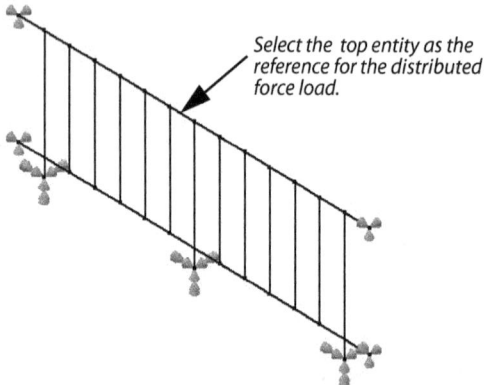

Select the top entity as the reference for the distributed force load.

   - Select ☐ ![Preview icon] (Preview) and modify the Density slider to better view the load similar to that shown below.

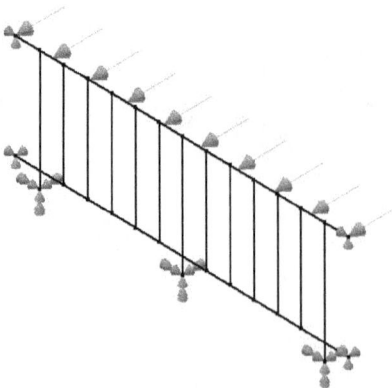

   - Click OK.

2. Add an additional load to the model using the following options. This load assigns a vertical distributed force load to the bottom horizontal member.

- Select Distributed Load as the load type and Force as its Sub Type.
- In the Name field, enter **Vertical Load (Beam)**.
- Select the bottom entity shown below as the reference to place the load.
- Enter a Magnitude of **-20** lbf/in in the Fy field.
- Assign the load to the Vertical Load and Gravity subcase. Ensure that it is only assigned to this one subcase.

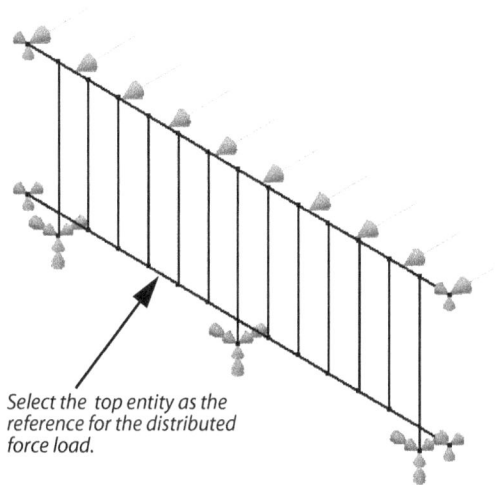

Select the top entity as the reference for the distributed force load.

- Select ☐ 👓 (Preview) and modify the Density slider to show the constraint on the model.
- Click OK.

3. Create a load to represent gravity using the following settings.

    - Set the Type of load as Gravity.
    - In the Name field, enter **Gravity**.
    - Enter **-386.4** as the Fy value.
    - Assign the load to both Subcases.
    - Select Preview to show the load on the model. Only a G is displayed in the graphics window indicating this load.
    - Click OK. The loaded model displays as shown below.

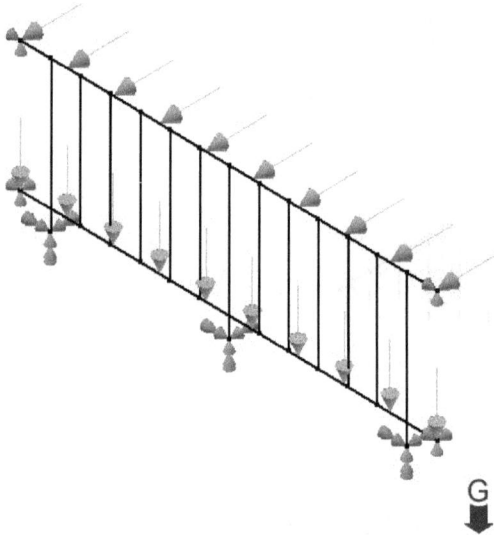

Mesh the Model

In this task, you will specify a custom mesh size and tolerance, and then mesh the model.

1. In the Analysis 1 sub-tree, right-click on Mesh Model, and click Edit.

2. Enter **1** as the new Element Size value.

3. Select the Settings option. Enter **0.01** as the new Tolerance value. Click OK.

4. Ensure the Element Order option to set to Parabolic in its drop-down list.

5. Select Continuous Meshing.

6. Click Generate Mesh to update the mesh.

7. Click OK to close the Mesh Settings dialog box. Ensure that all beam entities are meshed similar to that shown below. Note that the loads and constraints have been removed from this image for clarity in seeing the resulting mesh.

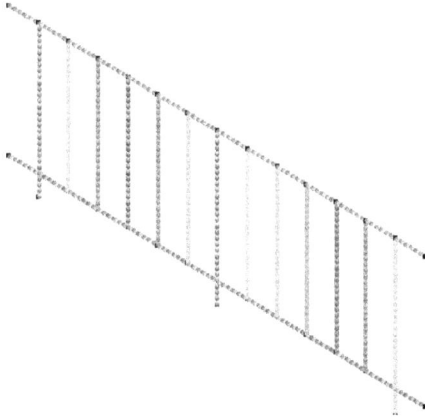

Run the Analysis and Review the Results

In this task, you will run the analysis and then analyze the displacement and stress result plots.

1. In the Solve panel, click (Run).

2. Click OK to confirm the completion of the Nastran solution. The Autodesk Nastran Model Tree is returned to the display.

3. The Frame Members are returned to the display to show the undeformed geometry.

To clear the members from the display, in the Display panel, expand (Object Visibility) and clear the CAD Bodies option.

4. Additionally, in the Object Visibility list clear the selection of Loads and Constraints. This clears them from the display so that you can more easily review the results.

5. To visualize the displacement, right-click on Displacement in the Results node for the Horizontal Load and Gravity Subcase, and select Display. The maximum displacement is 0.1002 in.

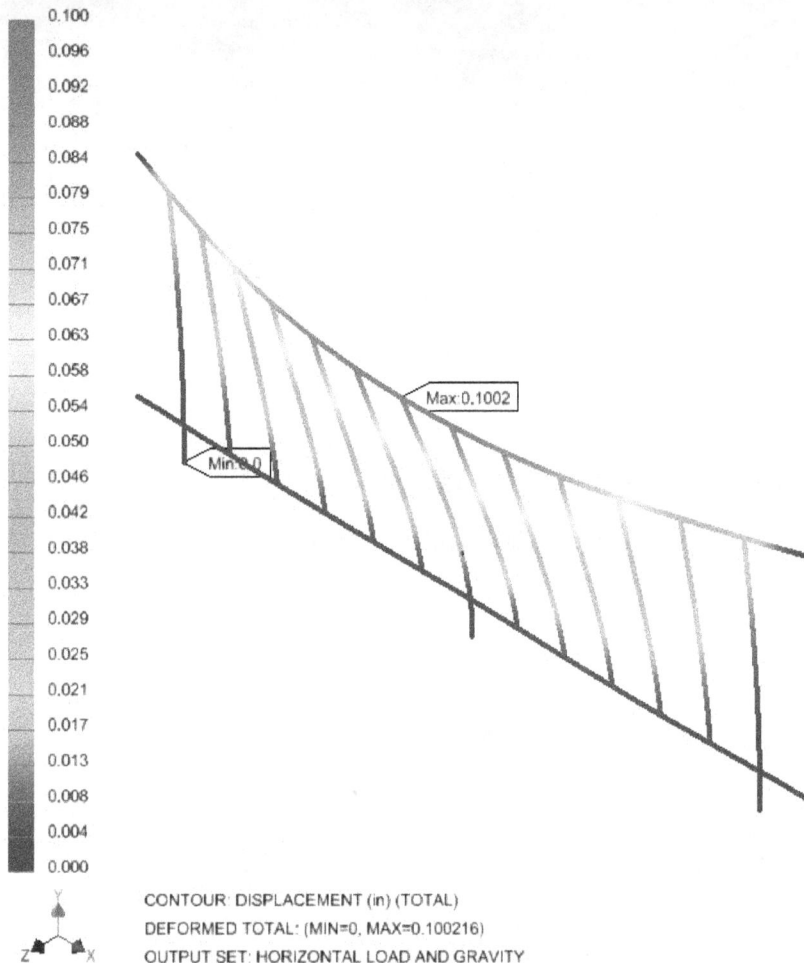

0.100
0.096
0.092
0.088
0.084
0.079
0.075
0.071
0.067
0.063
0.058
0.054
0.050
0.046
0.042
0.038
0.033
0.029
0.025
0.021
0.017
0.013
0.008
0.004
0.000

Max:0.1002

Min:0.0

CONTOUR: DISPLACEMENT (in) (TOTAL)
DEFORMED TOTAL: (MIN=0, MAX=0.100216)
OUTPUT SET: HORIZONTAL LOAD AND GRAVITY

6. Display the von Mises results plot for the Horizontal Load and Gravity Subcase. The maximum stress is approximately 1.506 E^+04 psi.

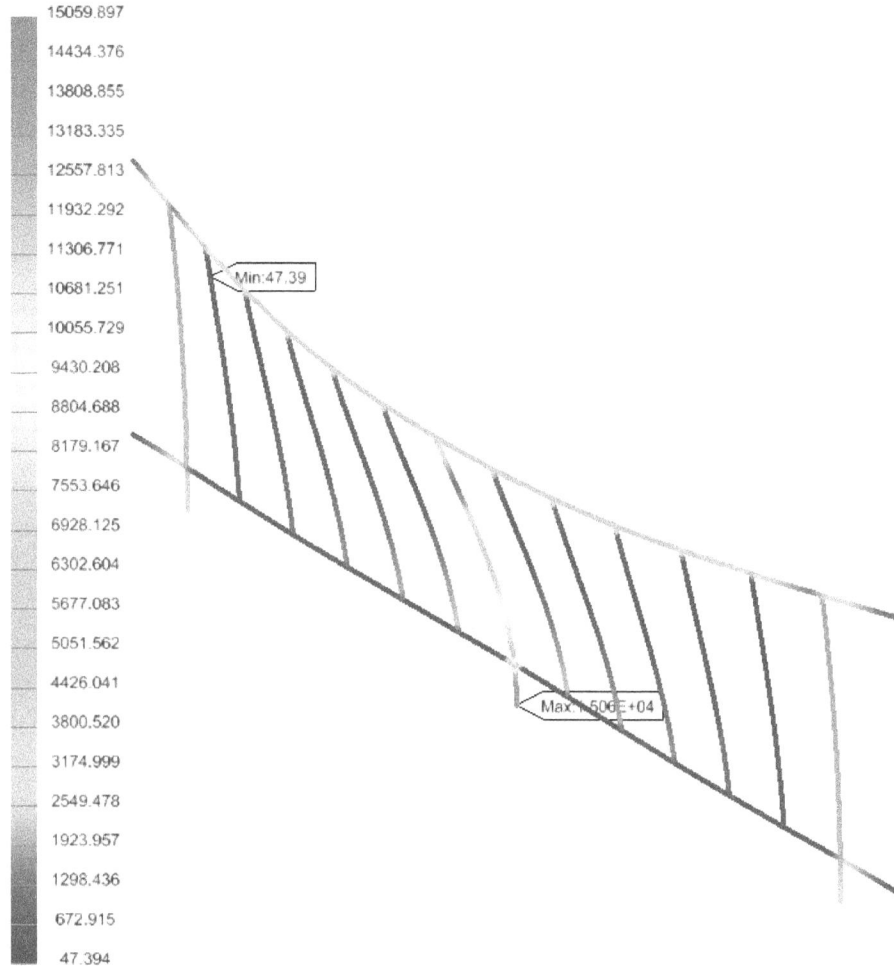

15059.897	
14434.376	
13808.855	
13183.335	
12557.813	
11932.292	
11306.771	
10681.251	
10055.729	
9430.208	
8804.688	
8179.167	
7553.646	
6928.125	
6302.604	
5677.083	
5051.562	
4426.041	
3800.520	
3174.999	
2549.478	
1923.957	
1298.436	
672.915	
47.394	

Min:47.39

Max 1.506E+04

CONTOUR: BAR VON MISES STRESS (psi)
DEFORMED TOTAL: (MIN=0, MAX=0.100216)
OUTPUT SET: HORIZONTAL LOAD AND GRAVITY

7. Display the results for the Vertical Load and Gravity Subcase.

- Maximum displacement is 0.00786 in.
- Maximum von Mises stress is 3446.5 psi.

8. Clear the display of the analysis results by right-clicking on the displayed analysis, and clearing the Display option.

9. Save the model.

(Optional) Compare with a Solid Element Linear Static Analysis & Review the Results

This task provides you with an alternate design for use in comparing the results of a Beam Element analysis to that of a Solid Element analysis. The Solid Element version of the railing study has been set up and solved for you in this design. Please note the following special considerations when modeling structural members using solid element idealizations:

- Distributed loads are only applicable to line elements. An equivalent total force has been applied to the faces of the solid model.

- Pinned constraints (no translations, rotations allowed) do not behave in the same way for solid representations as they do for beam elements. To allow rotation at the end of a span, the axial translation constraint must be omitted, otherwise the beam will behave as if it has a built-in end constraint. This behavior occurs because the constraint is not applied to a single point but rather to a number of nodes along a surface. Rotation of the member is not possible without translation of the end face.

- The meshes typically will not be matched where solid structural members meet. On the other hand, meshes between beam elements match automatically by virtue of the shared endpoints of the lines representing the members. To provide correct connectivity for solid structural members, create a manual contact pair that acts globally (that is, do not specify the contact regions). Specify a generous Maximum Activation Distance (approximately twice the element size) to ensure correct bonding of all of the nodes on the end faces of the intersecting members.

1. To continue with this exercise, open the file *C:\Autodesk Nastran InCAD 2019 Essentials Exercise Files\Railing\Completed_Analysis\Railing_Complete.iam*.

2. Activate the Autodesk Nastran In-CAD environment.

3. Ensure that the Analysis 2 - Solid Elements analysis is active.

4. Right-click on either of the Results nodes in the Analysis 2 - Solid Elements analysis and click Load. The 2fob7ur89.FNO results file is loaded.

   Note: The s7em6e27b.FNO results file can be used to load the results for the Beam analysis, if required.

5. Review the results and compare with the results obtained with the Beam Elements analysis.

    Horizontal Load and Gravity Subcase (Solid Elements)

    - Maximum displacement is 0.09832 in.
    - Maximum von Mises stress is 2.652E+4 psi.

    Vertical Load and Gravity Subcase (Solid Elements)

    - Maximum displacement is 0.007285 in.
    - Maximum von Mises stress is 3691 psi.

    The displacement results closely agree between the beam and solid element analyses. However, the stress results in the solid element model were approximately 75% higher than the beam model for the horizontal load and approximately 10% higher for the vertical load. This in not too surprising. Solid elements capture details about the connections between structural members that cannot be captured using beam element theory (where a perfectly rigid connection is assumed at the endpoints of the neutral axes). However, if the mesh and element connectivity between adjacent parts of a solid element model are not good, the stress results at the connections might be exaggerated. The reason for the exaggeration is that a limited number of nodes may carry a disproportionately large share of the load between members.

    Outside of the connection areas between adjacent members, the stress results are typically in good agreement between beam and solid structural member representations. Again, the significant differences are in the local stresses captured at connections when analyzing a solid representation.

6. Save the model.

Surface Contacts

The goal in this chapter is to learn how to add Surface Contacts to your model when analyzing an assembly model.

Objectives

After completing this chapter, you will be able to:

- Create Surface Contact elements that are automatically generated by enabling the Autodesk® Nastran® In-CAD software to locate and define the contacts.
- Create Surface Contact elements that are manually generated by selecting references in the model.

Lesson: Surface Contacts

Overview

This lesson discusses how Contacts can be used between interacting components in an assembly to model their real-world behavior. You will learn how to automatically and manually create contacts and how you can edit an existing contact.

Objectives

After completing this lesson, you will be able to:

- Create Surface Contacts that are automatically generated by enabling the Autodesk® Nastran® In-CAD software to locate and define the contacts.
- Create Surface Contacts that are manually generated by selecting references in the model.

Working with Contacts

The use of Contacts in the analysis simulates the real-world interactions of two separate parts or different surfaces on the same part. Examples include if the parts are bonded together and simply cannot move, if one part can slide relative to another, or if two parts can separate from one another but cannot slide.

> **Using Contacts vs. Boundary Conditions**
>
> Using Contacts between interacting components in an assembly is more accurate than the use of modeling constraints (Boundary Conditions). The "Rule of Differential Stiffness" can be very useful for determining the best way to model certain reactions:
>
> - If the stiffness of the part of interest is MUCH LESS than that of the supporting parts, use Constraints.
> - If the stiffness of the part of interest is MUCH MORE than that of the supporting parts, use Loads.
> - If the stiffness of the part of interest is SIMILAR to that of the supporting parts, add the supporting parts to the model, and use Contacts.

There are two primary methods that can be used to define contacts: automatic and manual.

Automatic Contacts

Using the automatic creation method for defining contacts enables the Autodesk Nastran In-CAD software to identify contact pairings throughout the model and assign a contact condition to each. To run an Automatic contact calculation, click (Auto) from the Contacts panel in the ribbon.

By default, all automatically-computed contact pairs are set to Bonded. This means that the two parts move together at the contacting surface as loads act on the model. To change the contact definition, you can specify the required default contact settings in the analysis setup before using the Automatic command. Alternatively, you can edit the Automatic contact definition settings from the Autodesk Nastran Model Tree after using the Automatic contact command.

- Contacts that are added using the Automatic option are only added to the analysis. They are not included in the Model node for use in other analyzes that might be set up in the model.
- To remove Contacts that have been created using the Automatic option, select them in the Surface Contact node in the Analysis sub-tree and drag it outside the Model Tree window. There is no right-click Delete option.

Manual Contacts

Assigning contacts manually enables greater control over the contacting surface pairs. To manually assign contacts, click ⬓ (Manual) from the Contacts panel in the ribbon.

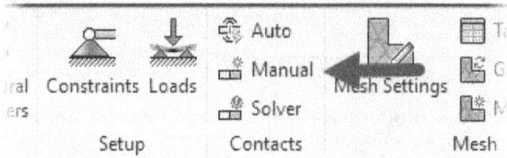

The Manual option enables you to specify the master and slave surfaces or edges involved in the contact. Two references are required.

Initially, when defining the references, you can select two methods to define the surface contact:

- Surface to Surface
- Edge to Surface

Both of these types require the selection of a master and slave entity. The Master surface usually has the more coarse mesh and must be a surface selection. The Master surface is highlighted in blue once selected. The Slave Entity selection field must be manually activated once the master surface has been defined. It enables both surface and edge selections in Surface to Surface and Edge to Surface types respectively. The Slave surface is highlighted in pink once selected. The slave cannot penetrate the master. The use of a Symmetric Penetration Type eliminates the distinction.

The remaining options are available in the Surface Contact dialog box to complete the definition of the contact.

- **Add To Analysis**: Enables you to determine whether the defined contact is immediately added to the analysis, or just included in the Model sub-tree for inclusion at a later time.
- **Contact Type**: Defines the type of contact.
  - **Separation**: This type of contact is true surface to surface contact. Both sliding and opening are enabled. This is available in a nonlinear analysis. In a linear static analysis, it uses the linear contact solution. Only the areas that are initially in contact are being used. The areas that are not in contact are ignored and will include friction effects. The following image shows 3 blocks, the bottom block is pushed up and free surface contact is used between the touching surfaces.

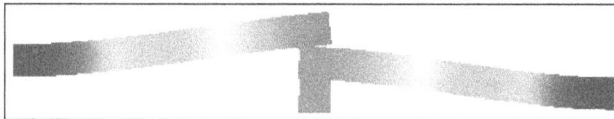

  - **Bonded**: This type of contact is used to bond the touching surfaces together. It moves together with loading. The advantage with this type of contact is that the mesh does not have to be the same. It can be useful in cases where touching surfaces on different parts have dissimilar meshes and do not undergo relative displacement. It is available in linear and nonlinear analysis. The bonded contact response between the beams is shown in the following image.

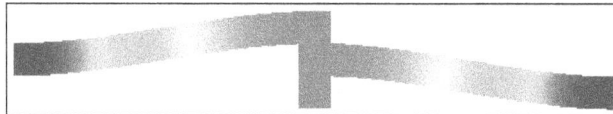

  - **Sliding / No Separation**: This type of contact enables the element to act similar to a bonded contact element in tension and compression, but will slide in-plane. Slide contact can be used in linear and nonlinear solutions. It works best for planar surfaces, since curved surfaces require a little bit of lifting to accomplish sliding relative to one another (due to faceting of the mesh).

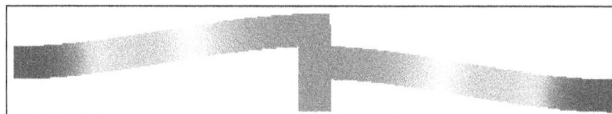

- **Separation / No Sliding**: This type of contact enables the element to act similar to a separation contact element in tension and compression, but will not permit sliding in-plane. It is essentially infinite friction. It is available only in nonlinear analysis.

- **Offset Bonded**: This type of contact is intended for welded connections with significant separation between contact surfaces. It is available in linear and nonlinear solutions, and it works for edge to surface contact, typical of what you would see with shell models or midsurface models.

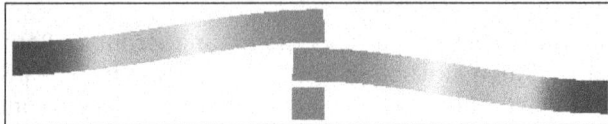

- **Disable:** This type of contact is intended for use disabling a contact without having to remove it from the analysis. Using this option enables you to maintain all of the settings and temporarily disable the contact type.

There are two penetration types that can be assign for a Manual contact.

- **Penetration Type**: Defines the type of penetration.
  - **Unsymmetric Contact**: For this method, only the penetration of the slave nodes into the master surface segment would be checked and adjusted.
    - This may lead to master nodes penetrating into slave surface segment that can be reduced with a finer mesh.
    - When some penetration of the master surface is expected, this method can be a good way to speed up the analysis. In reality there is always some degree of master slave penetration.
  - **Symmetric Contact**: For this method, the segments of the contact pair, master and slave are also made to be slave and master respectively and both penetrations are checked and adjusted.
    - More accurate results can be obtained with this method at a cost of increased computational time depending on the model size.
    - In the case of Edge to Surface contact, it is not applicable.
    - This is the default option for all contact types.

- **Stiffness Factor**: Controls the stiffness scaling of the contact.
  - The Stiffness Factor is the stiffness of the contact joint. This value is based on the stiffer of the two joined sections. Use the default value if the two entities have similar stiffness values.
  - The higher this value, the stiffer the contact and the less the penetration, but too high a value may cause convergence issues and chatter.
  - Setting this to a lower value may sometimes help convergence, but usually the default (1.0) works well for an analysis.
- **Coefficient of Friction**: Sets the coefficient of static friction.
- **Penetration Surface Offset**: Defines a numerical offset value for instances, such as plate to plate or solid to plate contact.
- **Max Activation Distance**: This is a tolerance value that specifies the distance that contact elements should be activated. This helps limit the number of contact elements and therefore decreases solution time. It also prevents unnecessary (and possibly conflicting) contact elements. When no value is specified, the default solver distance will be used. This is a large distance that is based on the model size. When a value is input, the solver will use that value.
- Additional, more advanced settings can be configured to further control the contact parameters using the Advanced Settings option.

Procedure: To Create a Contact

1. Click ⬚ (Manual) from the Contacts panel in the ribbon.

2. (Optional) Enter a name for the surface contact.

3. Select the required references to define the surface contact by selecting the master and slave surfaces or edges involved in the contact.

4. Select the required contact type in the Contact Type drop-down list.

5. Define the remaining Contact Data options, as required.

6. Click OK to close the Surface Contact dialog box and create the contact.

Solver Contacts

The Solver option (🖳) enables you to generate contacts between elements at runtime. Contact is created by the solver wherever two surfaces are within the distance from each other that is specified in the Tolerance or Max Activation Distance fields. This command acts globally on the model, but you can limit the contact scope by specifying the contact regions to consider.

Solver contacts do not create individual contact pair nodes in the Model or the FE Model Analysis sub-tree branches of the Model Tree. The solver creates the individual contact interactions during the solution phase. The following describes the additional options that are available in the Surface Contact dialog box, as compared to the options available when defining contacts manually.

- **Specify Contact Regions**: Enables you to select the entities for which to generate contact elements when they are in contact.
- **Max Allowable Penetration**: Sets the adjustment of penalty values normal to the contact plane. A positive value activates the penalty value adjustment.

- **Frictional Stiffness for Stick**: Sets a frictional stiffness for stick.
  - One method of choosing a value is to divide the expected frictional strength (MU * expected normal force) by a reasonable value of the relative displacement before slip occurs. A large stiffness value may cause poor convergence, while too small a value may result in reduced accuracy. An alternative method is to specify the value of relative displacement using SMAX.

Basic Guidelines

- In general, when selecting the Manual option to setup contact, choose the master as the contact segment that has the least amount of curvature, or if it is cylindrical contact choose the master as the outside segment (and use unsymmetrical penetration).

- Generally, when setting up a nonlinear analysis, use 5 increments for contact with no sliding, 10 increments for contact with sliding, and 20 increments for contact with nonlinear materials.

- For nonlinear analyses, run your model in a static/modal analysis first, and ensure that it runs fine, and that the results look good. Note that the contact elements will behave as bonded (weld) elements during a static/modal analysis. If the results are as expected, proceed to a nonlinear analysis.

> For more information on Contacts, refer to Autodesk Nastran In-CAD Help and search for "Surface Contacts".

Exercise: Contacts & Symmetry in an Assembly Model

In this exercise, you will continue to work with the cast lever model; however, in this exercise the lever and the pins have been combined in an assembly model. Because all of the models have similar stiffness values, contacts will be used to simulate their interaction. Symmetry will also be used to simplify the definition of the analysis.

Symmetry is an important modeling technique for analyzing a fraction of the structure without sacrificing quality. In some instances, it is considered a better technique for improving solution quality than other methods. In the previous exercise with the lever arm, the lever could still slide along the length of the pins. In a linear static analysis, however, rigid body motion is not permitted. In this exercise you will use symmetry in the model to constrain the rigid body motion. This method reduces the model size while naturally adding the required constraint. Symmetry constrains the "plane normal" translations and "in-plane" rotations

Prepare the Model for use in Nastran In-CAD

1. Open the file *C:\Autodesk Nastran InCAD 2019 Essentials Exercise Files\Contact_Symmetry\Lever-Pins.iam*. The Cast lever component in this assembly is the same model that you have been using in previous chapters; however, it is assembled here with other components.

2. This assembly model is symmetric and has been cut in half to only enable half of model to be analyzed. Review the Model Browser and note that Extrusion 1 has been added to cut the model in half to enable the symmetry analysis.

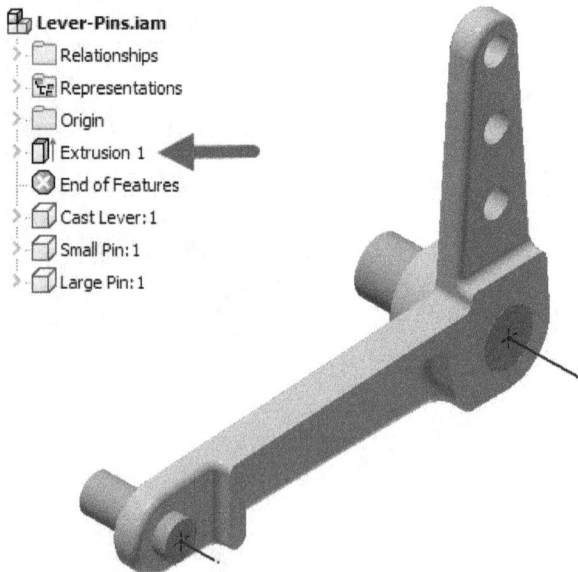

3. Activate the Autodesk Nastran In-CAD environment. Note the following:

   - By default, two idealizations are included in the assembly. Solid 1 uses Mild Steel and is assigned to the Cast Lever. Solid 2 uses the Generic material and is assigned to the two Lever Pins.

4. To identify which idealization is associated with each model in an assembly it is recommended that you rename it to include the component name. Right-click on Solid 1 and select Edit. In the Select Entities section, note that this is assigned to the Cast Lever component.

5. In the Name field, enter **Cast Lever - Mild Steel**. This is the default material that was assigned to the model. Click OK.

6. Solid 2 uses the Generic material. Edit this idealization and note that it is not explicitly assigned to the pins; however, as it is the only idealization that isn't assigned, it is used for the pins. Rename this idealization to **Pins - Generic**.

7. Remove the two idealizations from the Idealizations node by right-clicking each of their names and selecting Remove. They will remain listed in the Model sub-tree if they are ever required again, but they will not be used for the analysis.

Assign new Idealizations to the Assembly Components

In this task, you will create two new idealizations and assign them to their appropriate models.

1. In the Prepare panel, click ⌗ (Idealizations) to open the Idealizations dialog box.

2. Enter **Cast Lever - Aluminum** as the name of the new idealization.

3. Ensure that Solid Elements is selected as the Type of element for the property.

4. Click ⌗ (New Material)

5. Click Select Material in the top-left corner of the dialog box.

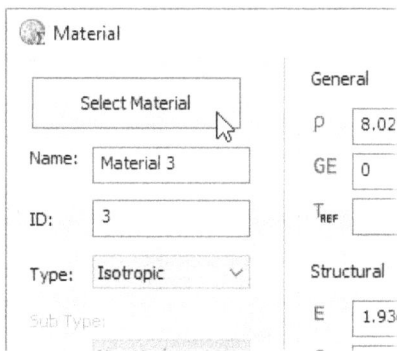

6. In the Material DB dialog box, expand Autodesk Material Library and select Aluminum 1100-O from the list. Click OK.

7. Note that the Material Name, Type, and many of the other properties are populated using the data that was stored for this material in the Material Library.

8. Click OK in the Material dialog box.

9. Change the idealization material to green.

10. In the Idealizations dialog box, select Associated Geometry and select the Cast Lever.ipt model directly in the graphics window.

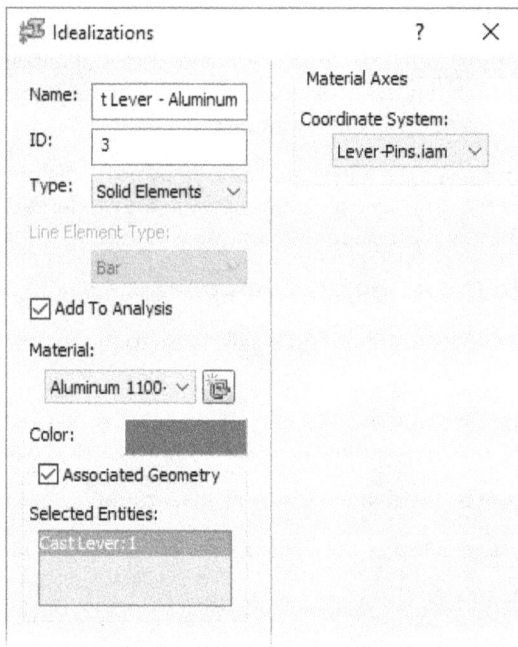

11. Ensure that Add to Analysis is selected. Click ⚹ (New) to create the new idealization and keep the Idealizations dialog box open to create another. The new idealization has been assigned for use in the analysis.

12. Create a second idealization as follows:
    - Enter **Pins - Steel** for the property name.
    - Assign the Alloy Steel material from the Autodesk Material Library.
    - Change the idealization material color to different shade of green.
    - Assign the new idealization to the two pin components in the assembly.

    Click OK to create the idealization and close the dialog box.

Assembly
  Analysis 1 [Linear Static]
    Units : CAD Model
    Nodes 0
    Elements 0
    Lever-Pins.iam
    Idealizations
      Solids
        Cast Lever - Aluminum ▤
        Pins - Steel ☐
    Mesh Model ⚠
    Subcases
      Subcase 1
        Loads
        Constraints
        Results
  Model

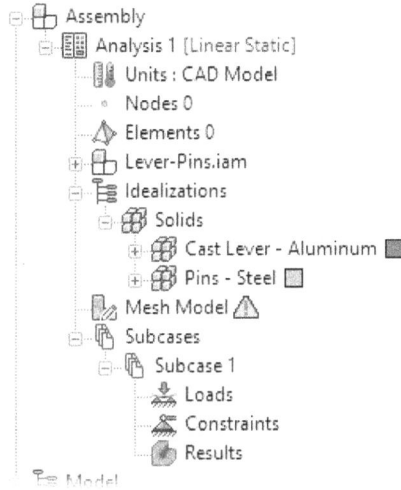

Constrain & Load the Model

In this task, you will assign a constraint that fixes the two pins, preventing movement in any direction and that assigns symmetry to the model. Loads will also be added to the model.

1. In the Setup panel, click ⛏ (Constraints) to open the Constraints dialog box.

2. In the Degrees of Freedom section of the dialog box, ensure that ⬔ (Fixed) is selected to remove all degrees of freedom.

3. In the Subcases section of the dialog box, confirm that Subcase 1 is selected to automatically add the constraint to Subcase 1.

4. If not already defined, set the display color for the constraint to cyan.

5. Select the two planar faces of the pins shown below. Select ☐ 👓 (Preview) at the bottom of the dialog box to display the constraint on the model. Modify the density and size of the constraint's display, as required.

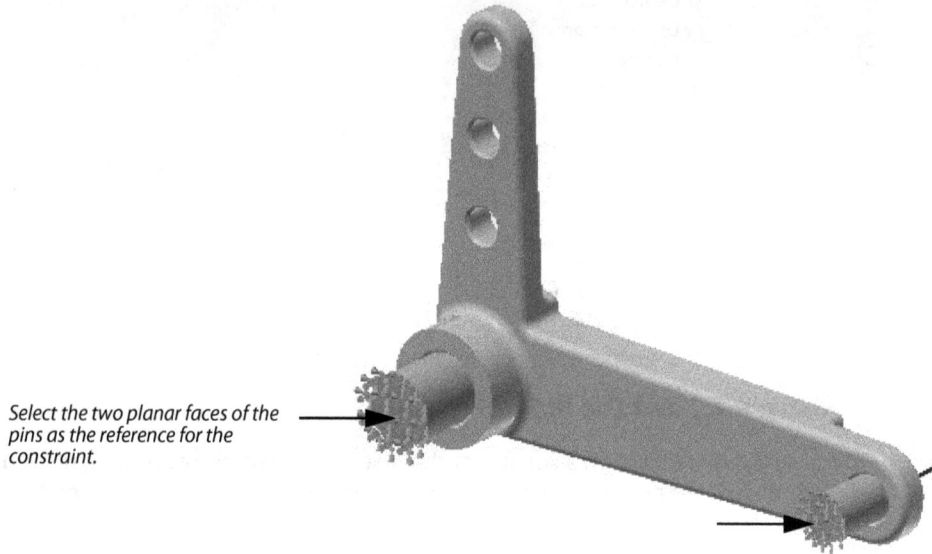

Select the two planar faces of the pins as the reference for the constraint.

6. Click ⚹ (New) to create the constraint and begin the creation of a new one.

7. Add an additional constraint to the model using the following options:

- In the Symmetry section, click ⊠ . Note that the normal for the plane of symmetry is in the x-direction. Choosing this option sets the constraint in the Tx, Ry, and Rz directions.
- Select the three faces that lie on the symmetry plane.
- Select Preview to show the constraint on the model.
- Modify the density and size of the constraint's display, as required.

Click OK.

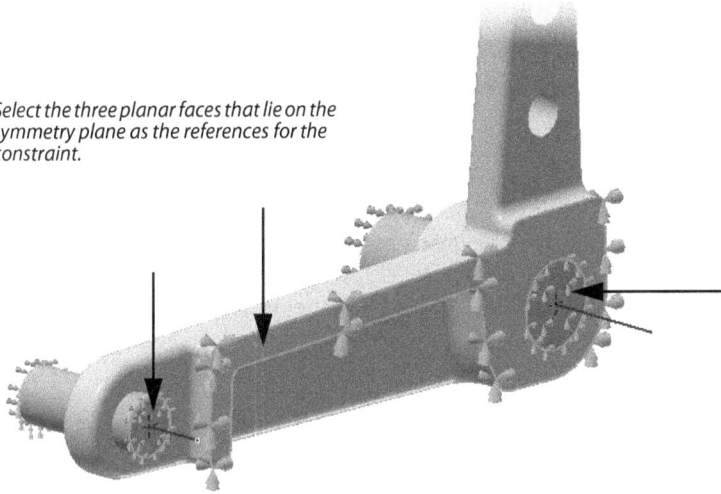

Select the three planar faces that lie on the
symmetry plane as the references for the
constraint.

8. In the Setup panel, click ⬇ (Loads) to open the Load dialog box. Define the load as
   follows:

   - Add a Force load of **-500** for Fz. (Because you are assuming symmetry, you only
     need half of the original -1000 load.)
   - Select the inside surface of the top-most hole.
   - Assign the load to Subcase 1.
   - Assign a display color of green, if not already defined.
   - Select Preview to show the load on the model.
   - Modify the density and size of the load's display, as required.
   - Click OK.

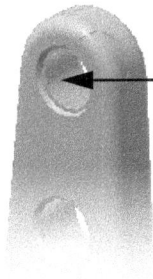

Select the inside surface as the
references for the load.

Assign Contacts to the Model

In this task, you will use the Automatic option to detect contacts and assign them to the analysis. Additionally, you will change the default Bonded contact type so that movement is permitted.

1. In the Contacts panel, click 🖼 (Automatic) to launch automatic contact creation.

2. In the analysis, expand the newly created Surface Contacts node. Two contacts have been identified and were automatically created. Note that one is between the Cast Lever and Small Pin components and the other is between the Cast Lever and the Large Pin components.

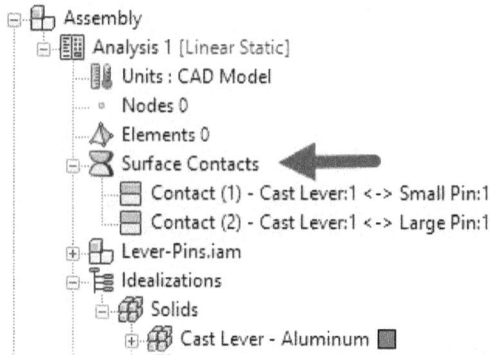

3. The default contact type for both contacts is Bonded. For this assembly, some movement is to be permitted. Right-click on Contact (1) and select Edit.

4. In the Surface Contact dialog, select Separation and set the Max Activation Distance to 2. Click OK.

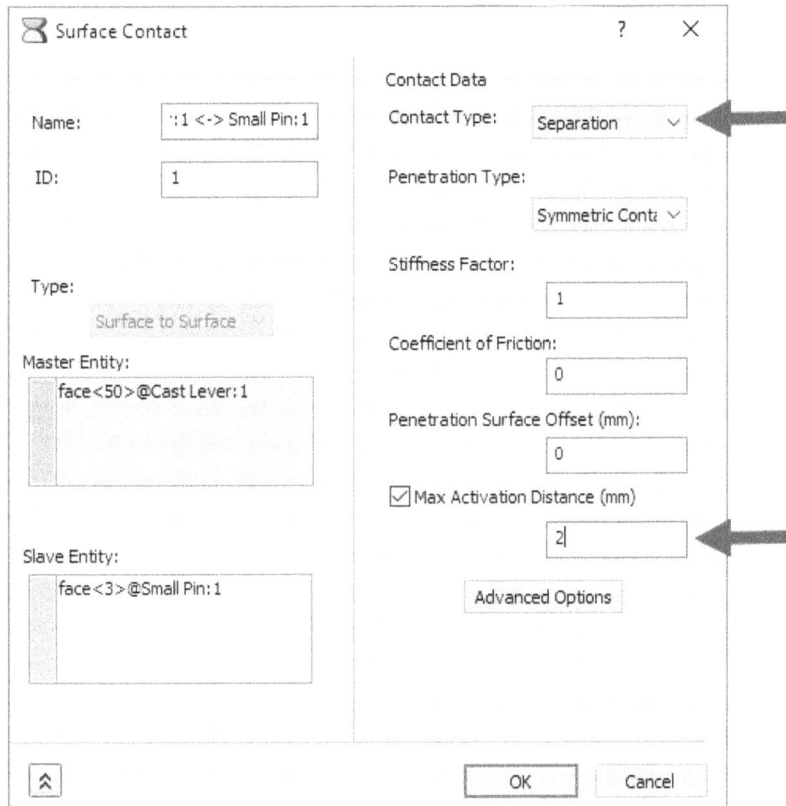

5. Edit Contact (2) and set the same two options.

   Note: The icons associated with the contacts now indicates that there is separation.

Change the Global Mesh Settings & Mesh the Model

In this task, you will change the mesh settings globally for the entire model prior to meshing.

1. In the Analysis 1 sub-tree, right-click on Mesh Model, and click Edit.

2. For the Element Size, enter **2.5**.

3. In the Mesh dialog box, click Settings.

4. On the Advanced Mesh Settings dialog, change the Max Element Growth Rate to 1.1.

5. Select Project Midside Nodes.

6. Set the Quality Midside Adjustment to ON.

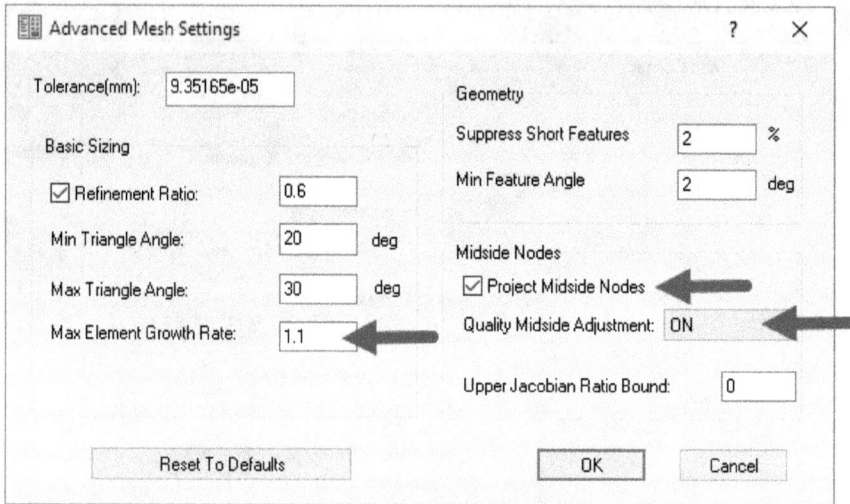

7. Click OK to close the Advanced Mesh Settings dialog.

8. Click Generate Mesh to update the mesh.

9. Click OK to close the Mesh Settings dialog box. The mesh updates on each of the components using the colors that were assigned with their associated idealizations.

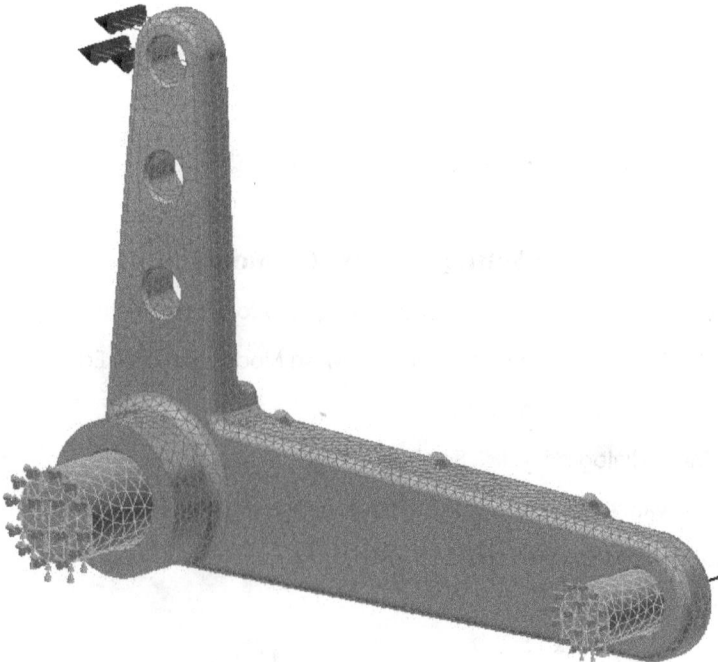

Run the Analysis

In this task, you will run the analysis using the customized mesh.

1. In the Solve panel, click ▦ (Run).

2. Note that there were no errors at the bottom of the Output view, but that there are warnings similar to those listed in the previous chapter. No further changes are required to the model.

3. Click OK to confirm the completion of the Nastran solution.

Review the Results

In this task, you will review the result for the analyzed model.

1. To visualize the displacement, right-click on Displacement in the Results node and select Display. Toggle off the display of the mesh in this results plot by clearing the Mesh option in the expanded Object Visibility list, in the Display panel. The maximum displacement is approximately 0.3662 mm.

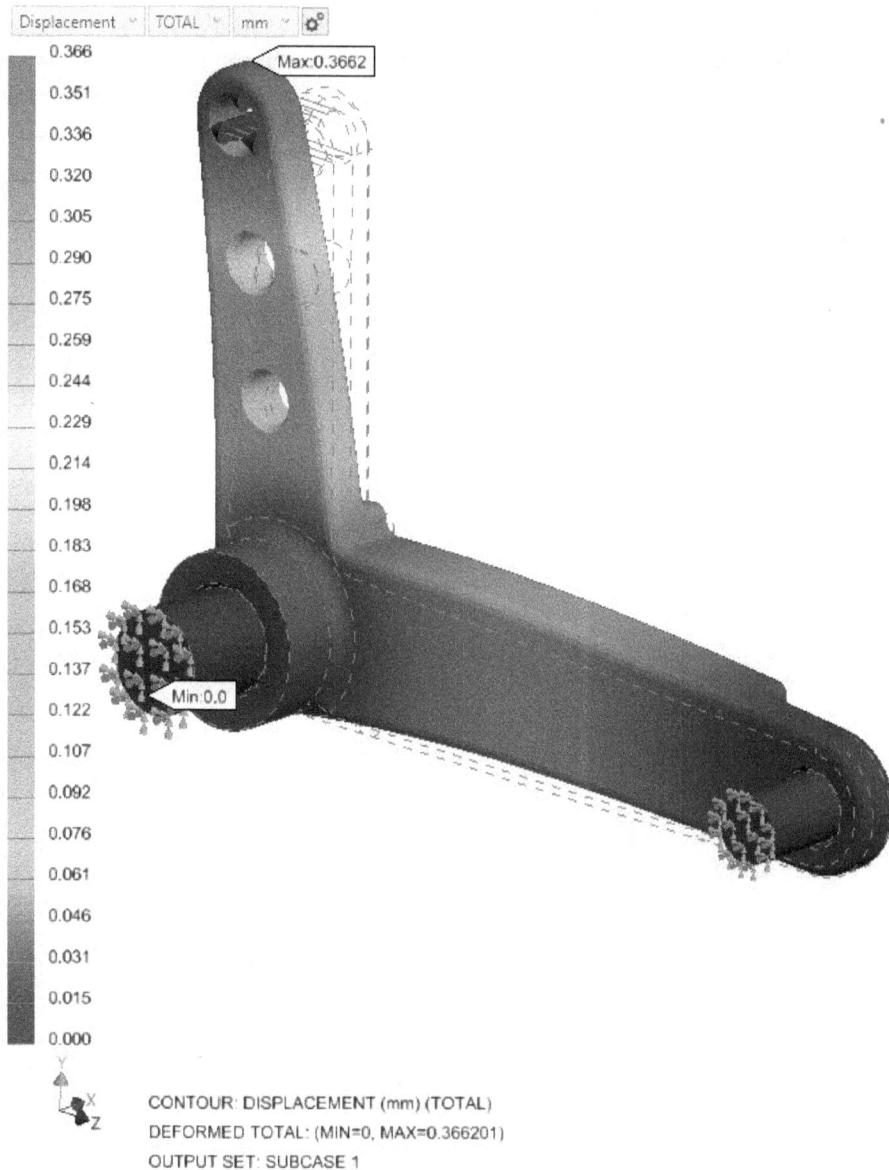

CONTOUR: DISPLACEMENT (mm) (TOTAL)
DEFORMED TOTAL: (MIN=0, MAX=0.366201)
OUTPUT SET: SUBCASE 1

2. Display the animation of the Displacement results plot.

3. Display the von Mises results plot and clear the display of the mesh, if shown. The maximum stress is approximately 150 MPa.

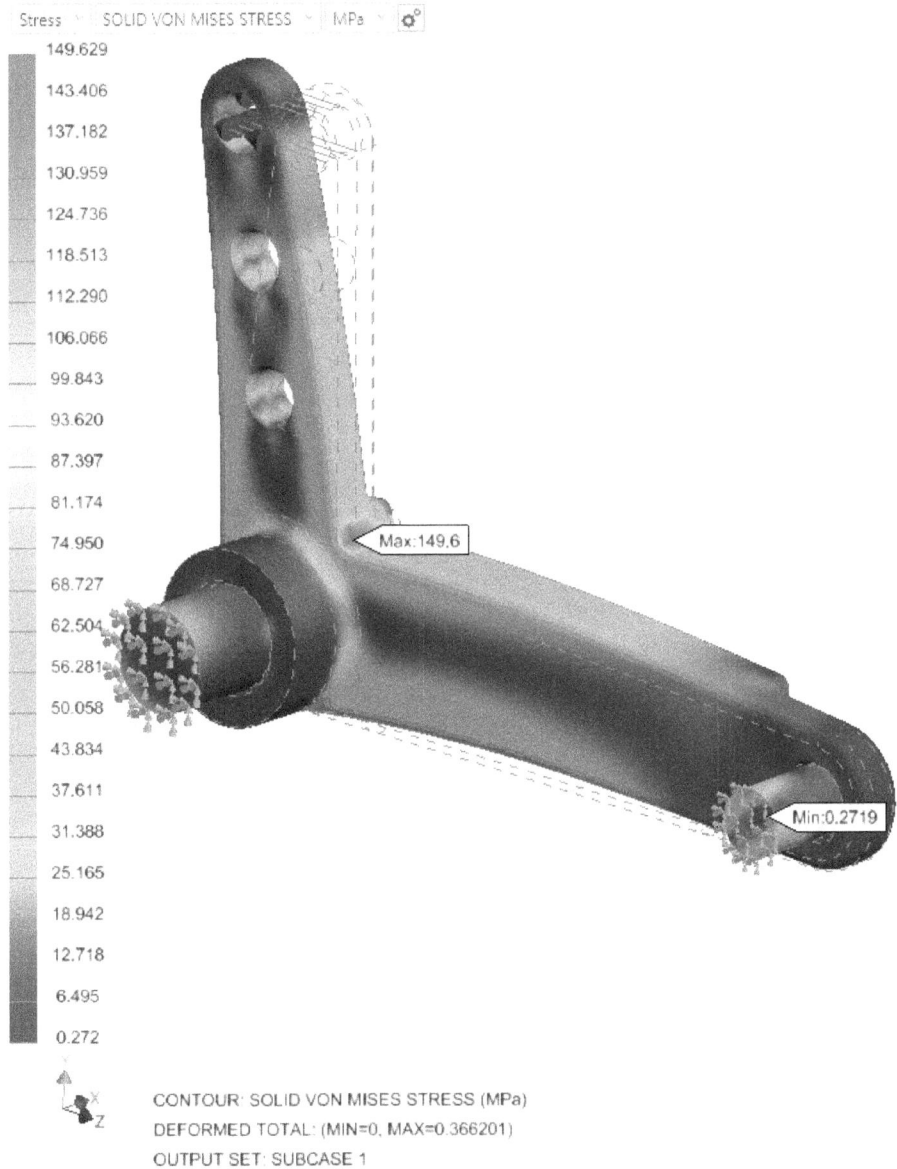

Stress ∨   SOLID VON MISES STRESS ∨   MPa ∨   ⚙

149.629
143.406
137.182
130.959
124.736
118.513
112.290
106.066
99.843
93.620
87.397
81.174
74.950
68.727
62.504
56.281
50.058
43.834
37.611
31.388
25.165
18.942
12.718
6.495
0.272

Max:149,6

Min:0.2719

CONTOUR: SOLID VON MISES STRESS (MPa)
DEFORMED TOTAL: (MIN=0, MAX=0.366201)
OUTPUT SET: SUBCASE 1

4. Right-click on the Safety Factor plot and select Edit. A Safety Factor plot enables you to visualize the multiple of the current stress level the structure is able to withstand before yielding.

5. Select Specify Min/Max in the Contour Options tab to activate it, if not already enabled. This will set the actual Data Min value as the minimum SF in the display range.

6. Set the following values for the Data Min and Data Max values:

    - Maintain the default Data Min value. The Data Min value is automatically set to the actual minimum result value for the model.

    - Enter **20** as the Data Max value.

    Note: Changing the Data Max produces a full spectrum of color in the contour plot. If the difference between the two limits is large it skews the colors all towards red or blue (depending upon whether the predominant safety factors are low or high). Reducing the Data Max value typically helps when reviewing the contour plot.

7. Click (Display) to display the plot. Clear the display of the loads and constraints using the options in the Visibility Options tab.

8. Click OK to close the Plot dialog box.

9. Clear the display of the mesh and review the results.

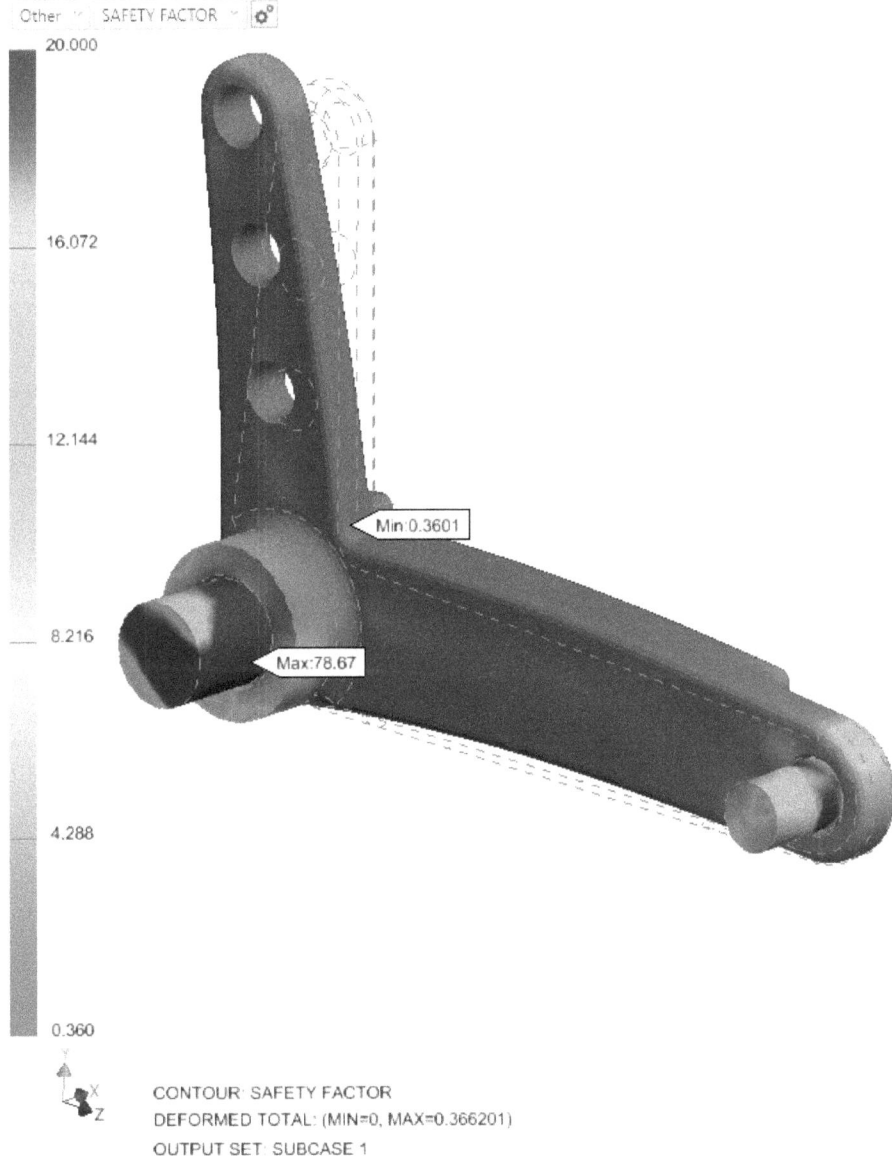

Other ⌄ SAFETY FACTOR ⌄ ⚙
20.000

16.072

12.144

Min:0.3601

8.216

Max:78.67

4.288

0.360

CONTOUR: SAFETY FACTOR
DEFORMED TOTAL: (MIN=0, MAX=0.366201)
OUTPUT SET: SUBCASE 1

The minimum SF (0.3601) is significantly less than 1, meaning that the structure can only withstand a fraction of the applied load. Therefore, the lever is not suitable for the assumed load. The load rating must be reduced, or a stronger material specified for the lever, in order to produce minimum safety factor results in excess of 1.0.

10. Save the model.

Consider the following alternate strategies for solving this assembly model instead of using symmetry.

- Enable friction with the contact definition to provide resistance to the sliding movement. This method is sensitive to the contact force, and can slow down the analysis.
- Connect the lever to the ground or connect it to a pin using a soft spring (connector). This adds an additional step, but does not affect the solution time.
- Place or create a point on the geometry at the symmetry plane, and constrain this in the direction of free motion.

Working with Composites

The goal in this chapter is to learn how to create a composite for use in an analysis. The creation of a composite in Autodesk® Nastran® In-CAD involves a number of steps, including defining the ply materials that will be used and the composite layup (material type, its thickness, stacking order, and ply orientation of each ply). The composite layup is also referred to as laminate or ply stacking. Once the layup is defined, an idealization can be setup for the laminate and it can be assigned to shell elements in the model.

Objectives

After completing this chapter, you will be able to:

- Create a ply material and assign it physical properties.
- Create a composite layup/laminate.
- Create an idealization that references the laminate and assigns it to geometry in the model.
- Define the material orientation for the composite.

Lesson: Working with Composites

Overview

This lesson discusses how to create a composite for use in an analysis.

Objectives

After completing this lesson, you will be able to:

- Create a ply material and assign it physical properties.
- Create the composite layup/laminate.
- Create an idealization that references the laminate and assigns it to geometry in the model.
- Define the material orientation for the composite.

Introduction to Composites

Laminated composites are materials created by bonding two or more layers (plies) of material. The use of composites in a design provides materials that are lighter or stronger than a traditional material. The materials used to create each ply in a composite laminate may or may not vary. However, the material orientations generally differ between adjacent plies. This technique is employed to provide good overall strength and stiffness in every direction. Composites are used in a variety of industries to meet a number of design goals. The following are examples of industries where composites are used:

- aerospace
- automotive
- recreation
- wind energy
- musical instruments
- construction

Autodesk Nastran In-CAD supports using composites when conducting an analysis. To create a composite, consider the following general workflow:

1. Define the ply material type and physical properties.

2. Define the composite layup.

3. Create an Idealization of the composite for use in an analysis.

4. Define the material orientation on the model geometry.

Defining Ply Material Properties

Similar to a standard material, ply material properties are defined using the Material dialog box. This can be accessed by clicking [icon] (Materials) in the Prepare panel or by right-clicking the Material node in the Model sub-tree and selecting New. The Material dialog box opens to create the new ply material and define its properties.

- Click Select Material to access the Autodesk or Inventor Materials libraries. These libraries contain some of the more commonly used ply materials and can be selected to predefine property values.
- Select the Type of material from the Type drop-down list. Orthotropic 2D is the most commonly used type for composite materials. This type enables property differences for the in-plane directions.
- If an Idealization already exists for the ply material, select it in the Idealizations list to assign the new material.
- Enter the ply material properties using the General, Structural, Allowables, and Thermal sections in the Material dialog box.
- Consider using the Save New Material option to save any custom ply material properties.

If required, refer to the *Working with Materials* topic in the *Idealizations & Materials* lesson in Chapter 2 for more information on accessing and creating a Material.

Define the Composite Layup (Laminate)

The material properties alone are not sufficient to fully define a composite. A composite layup or laminate is required to define the layers that will be used to complete the definition of the composite. The Laminate option enables you to define each layer by defining the ply material being used one at a time, along with its thickness, angle, and Stress/Strain values. The following steps detail the procedure for creating a new composite layup or laminate.

Procedure: To Create a Laminate

1.   Right-click on the Laminates node in the Model sub-tree and select New. The Laminate dialog box opens.

2. Click ⬙ (Add) in the Ply Options area to add the first ply to the laminate.

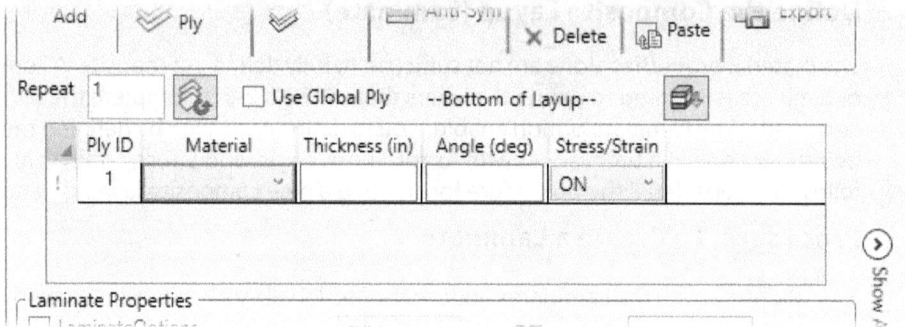

- By default, the plies are created from bottom up, as indicated by the "Bottom of Layup" title above the table. To switch to top down, click ⬚.

3. Click in the Material cell for Ply ID 1 and select a material from the drop-down list.

- Only the materials that were assigned to the model will display in this list.

- To create a new material, click ⬚ (Material) in the Ply Option area.

4. Click in the Thickness cell for Ply ID 1 and enter a thickness value for the ply.

5. Click in the Angle cell for Ply ID 1 and enter the ply orientation angle. This angle is measured with respect to the material orientation angle. A zero angle ply corresponds to alignment with the principle material orientation.

6. Select the drop-down list in the Stress/Strain cell for Ply ID 1. To control the stress output on each ply, set the value to ON, otherwise set the value as OFF.

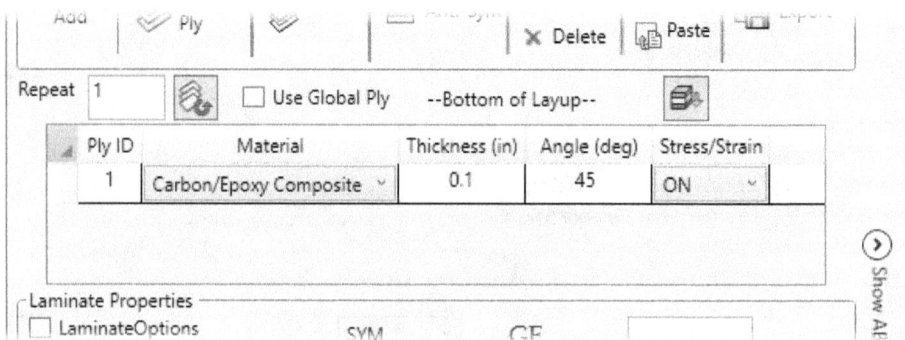

7. Continue to add additional plies to the laminate using any of the following techniques:

- Click (Add) in the Ply Options area a second time, select a new material, and define its Thickness, Angle, and Stress/Strain setting.

- Select an existing row, enter a repeat value in the Repeat field, and click . The selected row is repeated as entered.

- With multiple rows selected, use either the (Sym) and (Anti-Sym) options in the Ply Option area. The Symmetric option creates mirrored plies to those selected, while the Anti-Symmetric option creates mirrored plies with opposite signs for the ply angles.

- Use the (Import) option in the Ply Option area to import any previously exported ply tables. Plies are saved as .CVS text files.

Ply ID	Material	Thickness (in)	Angle (deg)	Stress/Strain
1	Carbon/Epoxy Composite	0.1	45	ON
2	Carbon/Epoxy Composite	0.1	-45	ON
3	Carbon/Epoxy Composite	0.1	45	ON
4	Carbon/Epoxy Composite	0.1	45	ON
5	Carbon/Epoxy Composite	0.1	-45	ON
6	Carbon/Epoxy Composite	0.1	45	ON

8. Define the properties in the Laminate Properties area of the dialog box.

- Enable the Laminate Options check box and select a form of laminate. The options include SYM, HCS, FCS, ACS, SME, or SMC. These options are defined in more depth in the product Help documentation.

- In the Failure Theory drop-down list, select the Ply failure theory that you want to use. If left blank, no failure calculation is performed. Hill is set as the default failure theory. The other options include HOFF, TSAI-Wu, Max Stress, Max Strain, NASA LaRC, PUCK, and MCT.

- Set the Strength Ratio setting to ON or OFF, as required. It controls the output of Tsai Strength Ratio, which is provided in place of Failure Index for composite element ply results output. When it is set to ON, it allows to define Parameter PARAM,STRENGTHRATIO,ON, and the Tsai Strength Ratio is calculated. Strength Ratio is considered more useful than Failure Index because it indicates exactly how to change applied loading to achieve optimal ply performance.

- Enter the Allowable Bond Shear Stress value. This value defines the interlaminar shear stress of a Bond Material and it is required to get Bond Failure Index output.

- Enable the Bottom Fiber Distance and enter a new value, if the default value is not appropriate. The default value is half of the total thickness.

- Enter a GE (Damping Coeff.) value. This defines the structural element damping coefficient, which is twice the critical damping ratio to be used in dynamic analyses.

- Enter a NSM value to define the nonstructural mass per unit area.

- Enter a Ref. Temperature value to define the reference temperature of the composite plies (all plies) to be used for temperature dependent material properties.

For more information on the laminate properties including the failure theory, refer to the Autodesk Nastran In-CAD Help and search for "Laminates".

9. Prior to completing the Laminate, you can preview it by clicking 🔍 (Preview) at the top of the Laminate.

- The Show Layup area provides a graphical representation of the plies.

- The Show ABD Matrix shows laminate equivalent properties in an ABD matrix with the number of plies and total thickness defined in the ply.

- Select the ⊙ icon associated with the Show Layup and Show ABD Matrix to show them individually.

10. Click OK to create the new laminate.

Manipulating Existing Plies in the Table

The Up (move up), Down (move down), Undo, Redo, Delete, Cut, Copy, and Paste commands in the Ply Options area of the dialog box are all standard commands that can be used to manipulate existing plies in the table.

Global Ply

The Global Ply option in the Laminate dialog box can be used to quickly create and save a ply for reuse. This acts as a template and avoids having to define the Material, Thickness, Angle, and Stress/Strain options individually for every lamina in the stack. Instead, it enables you to select a predefined laminate (global plies). This technique is useful if properties are repeated for several different layers. For example, you might have four or more layers of the same material and thickness alternating between +45 and -45° orientation angles. Define two global plies, one with Angle=45 and the other with Angle=-45. Then, just specify a repeating pattern of Global Ply 1, Global Ply 2...

- To create a global ply, select 📚 (Global Ply) in the Ply Option section of the Laminate dialog box. Define the ply using the options in the Global Ply Definition dialog box.

- To convert a normal ply to global ply definition, right-click on it in the table and select Convert to Global Ply. Once converted, it can be reused as required.
- To use a global ply when creating the laminate, select Use Global Ply at the top of the table to enable the Global Ply column. Once this row is included, you can select an existing global ply from the drop-down list. While adding global plies to the layup, the Use Global Ply option must be enabled. While adding manual plies, it must be disabled. Once a global ply is added and the option is disabled, it is subsequently treated like any manual ply and can be edited (i.e. change its angle). **Note:** If you later re-enable the Use Global Ply option, overrides to previous global plies are discarded. They revert to the global ply definition.

Any laminates or global plies that have been created in a model are listed in the Composite Layups node of the Model sub-tree.

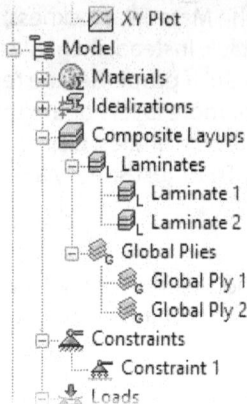

Defining an Idealization

The Idealizations dialog box enables you to select the element type to which the laminate properties will be assigned. In the Prepare panel, click ⤴ (Idealizations) to open the Idealizations dialog box. Alternatively, you can right-click on the Idealizations node in the Model sub-tree and select New to open the same dialog box. You can create new idealizations in the Analysis sub-tree by right-clicking on the element type in the Idealizations node and selecting New.

- To create an idealization for a composite, you must select the Shell Elements type in the Type menu. Selecting this element type provides you with the Laminate options as shown in the following image.
- Enable the Associated Geometry option so that you can select geometry on the model to assign the idealization to.

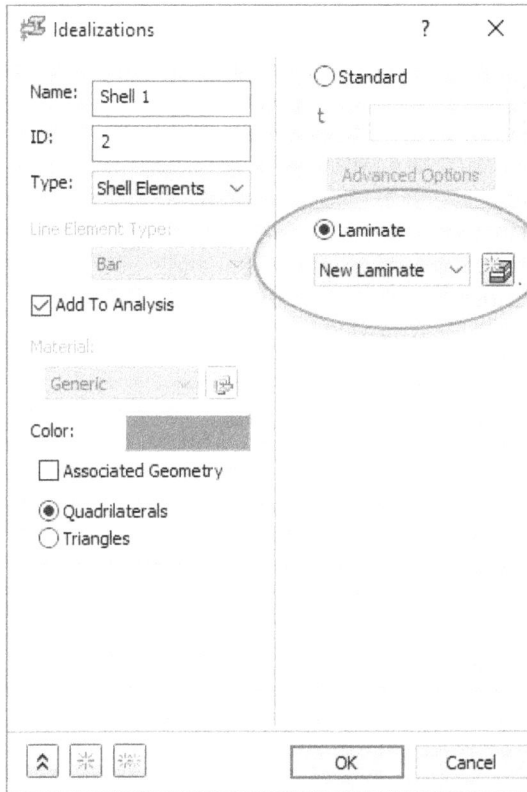

Procedure: To Assign a Laminate to an Idealization

1. Select the Laminate option to enable it.

    -   Once selected, you are no longer able to assign a material directly in this dialog box. Material plies are assigned through the laminate.

2. Assign the Laminate for use in the Idealization.

    -   If the laminate already exists in the model, select it from the drop-down list.

    -   To create a new laminate, select (New Laminate).

3. Assign the idealization to the model, as required, using the Associated Geometry area.

    Note: The remaining options in this dialog box are described in the Idealizations & Materials topic in Chapter 2.

4. Click OK.

For more information on assigning an Idealization, refer to the *Idealizations & Materials* lesson in Chapter 5 of this learning guide.

Material Orientation

Material orientation must be defined when using an idealization that incorporates the use of a composite for an analysis. This is an important step when working with composite materials to ensure that the material is oriented correctly on the model. Incorrect orientation will affect the results of an analysis. In composite analyses, a zero angle ply means that it is aligned in the direction of the material orientation.

To add a material orientation, right-click on the Analysis node and select New>Material Orientation. If another material orientation already exists in the analysis, you can right-click on the Model Orientation node in the Analysis sub-tree and select New. The Material Orientation dialog box opens as shown in the following image.

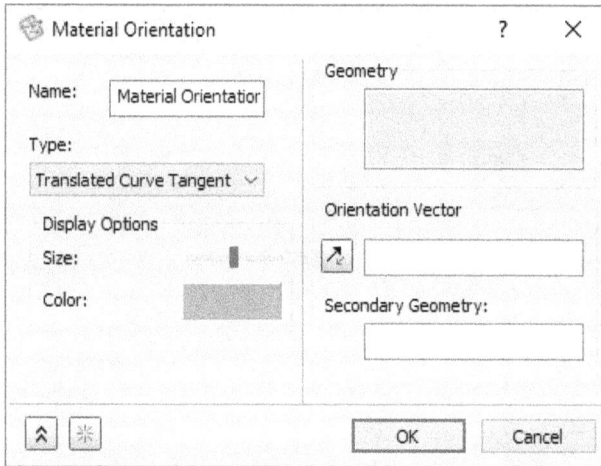

There are eight options to specify material orientation on a surface. Click on the Type menu to select from the following methods:

- Vector Projection
- Curve Tangent
- Rotated Curve Tangent
- Translated Curve Tangent
- Surface U Direction
- Surface V Direction
- Surface -U Direction
- Surface -V Direction

For a complete description of these options, refer to the Autodesk Nastran In-CAD Help and search for "material orientation".

Procedure: To Define a Material Orientation

1. Enter a name for the material orientation. Use a descriptive name to help identify it.

2. Select the type of material orientation that is required.

3. Set the display options and color for the resulting vector that will be added to the geometry. The vector identifies the "0 angle" direction.

4. Click in the Geometry field to activate it and select the geometry on the model to assign the idealization.

5. Depending on the type of orientation being used, additional options may display in the dialog box to fully define the orientation of the vector.

6. Click OK. The material orientation is listed in the Material Orientation node of the Analysis sub-tree.

Exercise: Using Composite Materials in a Bike Frame

In this exercise, you will use a Linear Static analysis to analyze a portion of a bike frame. The bike frame is made of carbon/epoxy composite.

Prepare the Model for use in Nastran In-CAD

1. Open the file *C:\Autodesk Nastran InCAD 2019 Essentials Exercise Files\Composites\ Bike Frame Section.ipt.* This component represents a portion of a bike frame that will be used in the analysis.

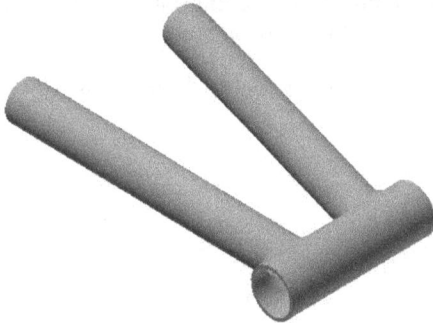

2. Select the Environments tab and click Autodesk Nastran In-CAD to activate the Autodesk Nastran In-CAD environment.

Create a Ply Material, Laminate, and Idealization

In this task, you will create a new 2D orthotropic ply material and composite layup that will be assigned for use during model analysis. The composite layup will be created during idealization creation.

1. Expand the Materials node in the Model sub-tree. Note that the only material listed is the Generic material that was assigned when the model was created in Autodesk Inventor. The material is used in the default Solid 1 idealization assigned to the analysis.

2. Right-click on the Materials node and select New. Alternatively, in the Prepare panel,

    click ![Materials icon] (Materials) to open the Material dialog box.

3. In the Name field, enter **Carbon/Epoxy Composite** as the new ply material name.

4. Select Orthotropic 2D in the Type drop-down list.

5. Set the values for material properties under the General, Structural, and Allowables sections as shown in the following image. Click OK in the Material dialog box.

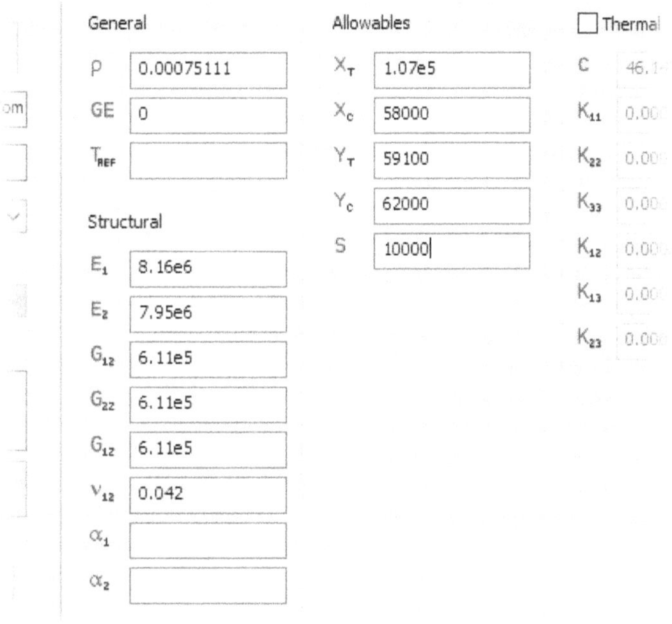

General

ρ	0.00075111
GE	0
T_{REF}	

Structural

E_1	8.16e6
E_2	7.95e6
G_{12}	6.11e5
G_{22}	6.11e5
G_{12}	6.11e5
V_{12}	0.042
α_1	
α_2	

Allowables

X_T	1.07e5
X_c	58000
Y_T	59100
Y_c	62000
S	10000

☐ Thermal

C	46.1
K_{11}	0.00
K_{22}	0.00
K_{33}	0.00
K_{12}	0.00
K_{13}	0.00
K_{23}	0.00

6. Right-click on Solid 1 in the Idealizations node and click Edit. The default idealization is not required so it will be modified instead of creating a new one.

7. In the Name field of the Idealizations dialog box, enter **Carbon/Epoxy Layup**.

8. Select Shell Elements from the Type drop-down list.

9. Select the Laminate option and click (New Laminate) to create a new laminate. The Laminate dialog box displays.

10. In the Laminate dialog box, ensure that the Failure Theory is set to Hill in the Laminate Properties section. This will enable you to review failure index information when the analysis is complete.

11. In the Ply Option section, click  (Add) to create a new ply.

12. Define the first ply for the laminate as follows:
    - Click in the Material cell for Ply ID 1 to activate it. Select Carbon/Epoxy Composite in the Material drop-down list.
    - Click in the Thickness cell for Ply ID 1 to activate it. Enter **0.01** as the Thickness value.
    - Click in the Angle cell for Ply ID 1 to activate it. Enter **45** as the Angle value.
    - Leave Stress/Strain output to ON.

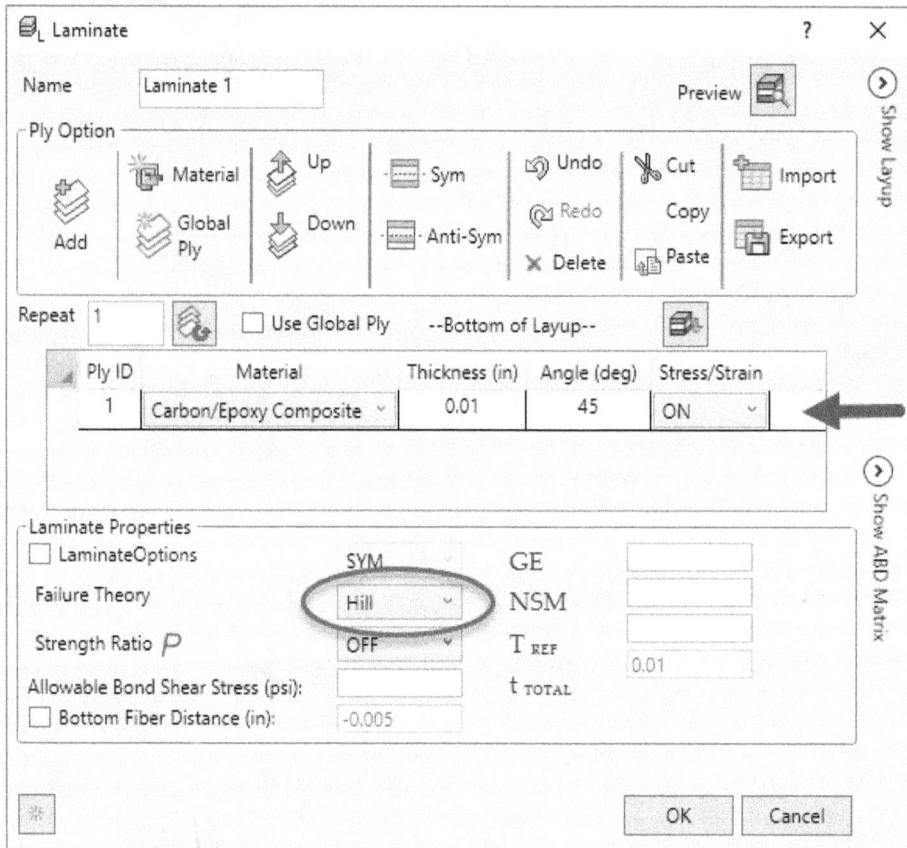

13. Select the Ply 1 row. Enter 5 as the repeat value and click ![Repeat icon] (Repeat) to create 5 additional copies of the first ply.

Ply ID	Material	Thickness (in)	Angle (deg)	Stress/Strain
1	Carbon/Epoxy Composite	0.01	45	ON
2	Carbon/Epoxy Composite	0.01	45	ON
3	Carbon/Epoxy Composite	0.01	45	ON
4	Carbon/Epoxy Composite	0.01	45	ON
5	Carbon/Epoxy Composite	0.01	45	ON
6	Carbon/Epoxy Composite	0.01	45	ON

Repeat 5   Use Global Ply   --Bottom of Layup--

Laminate Properties

Show ABD Matrix

14. Change the Angle values so that they are **45**, **-45**, **45**, **-45**, **90**, **0** for ply 1 through ply 6, respectively.

Ply ID	Material	Thickness (in)	Angle (deg)	Stress/Strain
1	Carbon/Epoxy Composite	0.01	45	ON
2	Carbon/Epoxy Composite	0.01	-45	ON
3	Carbon/Epoxy Composite	0.01	45	ON
4	Carbon/Epoxy Composite	0.01	-45	ON
5	Carbon/Epoxy Composite	0.01	90	ON
6	Carbon/Epoxy Composite	0.01	0	ON

Repeat 5   Use Global Ply   --Bottom of Layup--

Laminate Properties

Show ABD Matrix

15. In the Ply table, click ◢ in the top left corner to quickly select the entire list of plies in the table. In the Ply Option section, click ▦ (Symmetric). This automatically creates a symmetric set of the selected plies in the table. There are now 12 plies in the table, as shown in the following image.

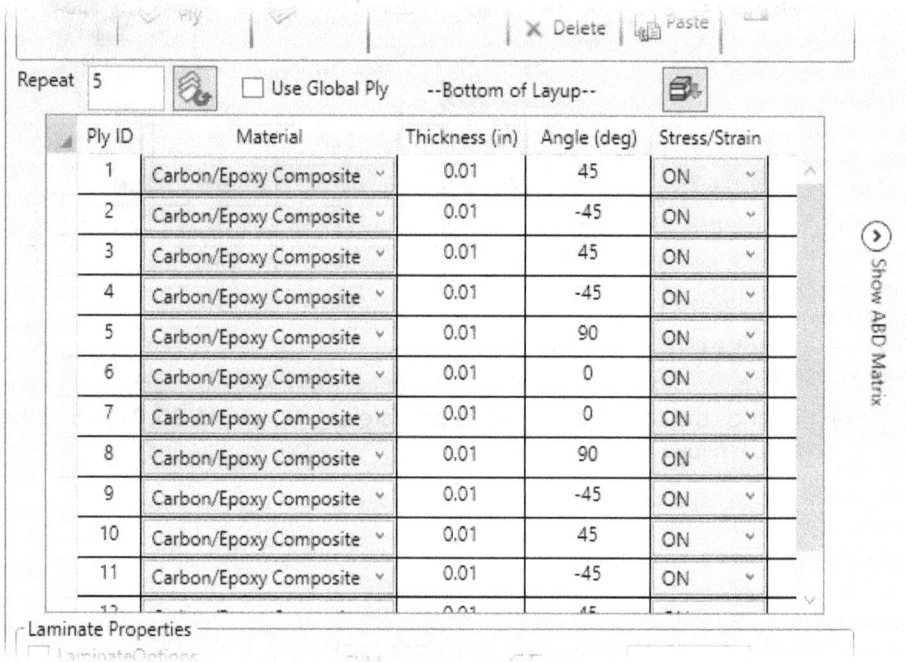

Ply ID	Material	Thickness (in)	Angle (deg)	Stress/Strain
1	Carbon/Epoxy Composite	0.01	45	ON
2	Carbon/Epoxy Composite	0.01	-45	ON
3	Carbon/Epoxy Composite	0.01	45	ON
4	Carbon/Epoxy Composite	0.01	-45	ON
5	Carbon/Epoxy Composite	0.01	90	ON
6	Carbon/Epoxy Composite	0.01	0	ON
7	Carbon/Epoxy Composite	0.01	0	ON
8	Carbon/Epoxy Composite	0.01	90	ON
9	Carbon/Epoxy Composite	0.01	-45	ON
10	Carbon/Epoxy Composite	0.01	45	ON
11	Carbon/Epoxy Composite	0.01	-45	ON
12		0.01	45	

Repeat 5 ☐ Use Global Ply --Bottom of Layup--

Laminate Properties

16. Click OK to complete the laminate definition.

17. In the Idealizations dialog box, select Associated Geometry. With the Selected Quadrilaterals section active, select the outer surfaces of the model (three cylindrical surfaces and two fillet surfaces). Ensure that you are only selecting the outer surfaces.

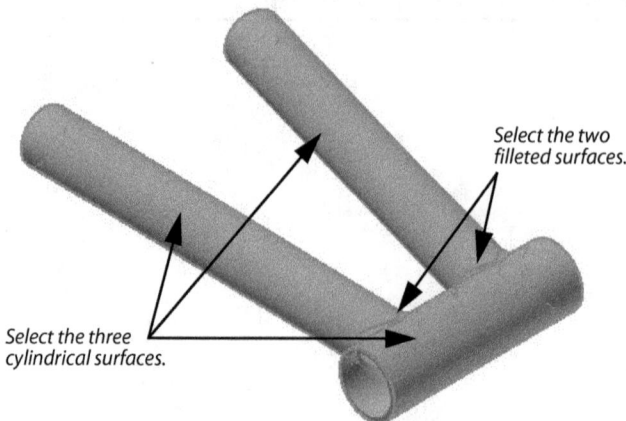

Select the two filleted surfaces.

Select the three cylindrical surfaces.

18. Change the idealization color to maroon. The Idealizations dialog box should display as shown in the following image.

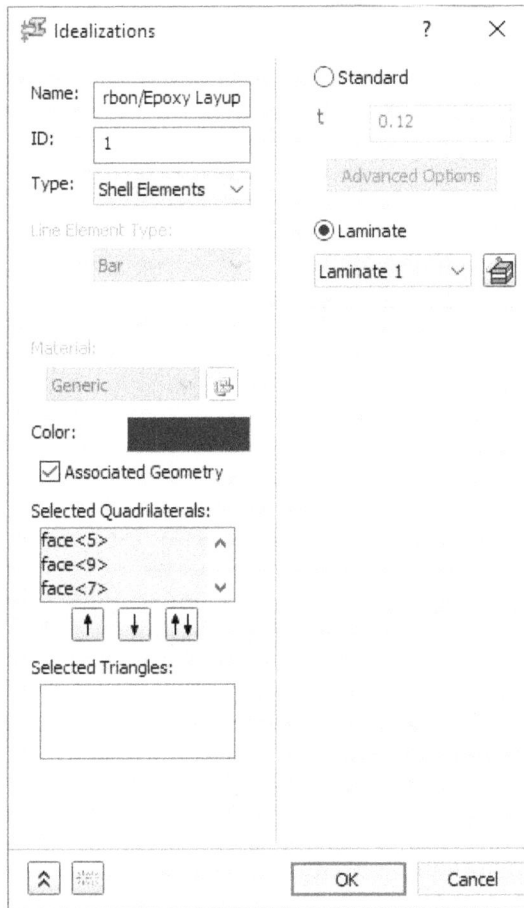

19. Click OK to complete the Idealization. Note that Solid 1 is no longer available in the model and that the Carbon/Epoxy Layup is the Shell Idealization assigned to the analysis.

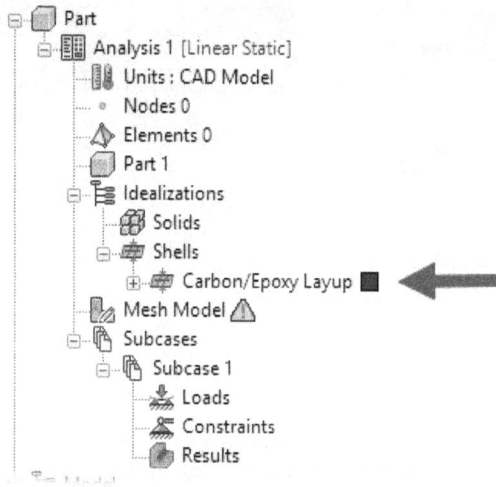

Constrain & Load the Model

In this task, you will assign a constraint that fixes the ends of the two tubes, preventing movement in any direction. Loads will also be added to the model.

1. In the Setup panel, click (Constraints) to open the Constraints dialog box. Define the constraint using the following options.

- In the Degrees of Freedom section of the dialog box, ensure that (Fixed) is selected to remove all degrees of freedom.
- Select the two edges on the end of the two long tubes as shown in the following image.
- Confirm that Subcase 1 is selected to add the constraint to this subcase.

- Select (Preview) to show the constraint on the model.
- Modify the density and size of the constraint's display, as required.
- Click OK to create the fixed constraint.

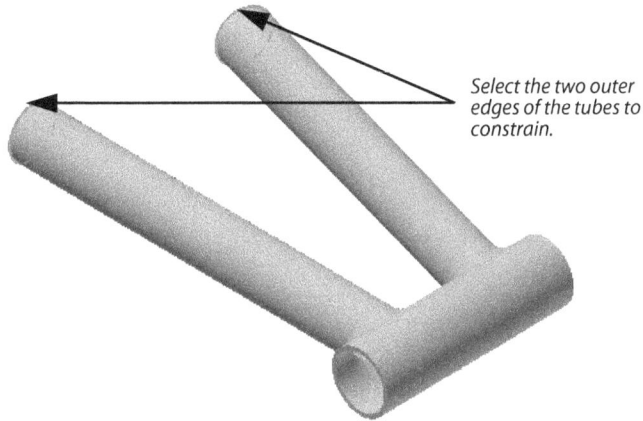

Select the two outer edges of the tubes to constrain.

2. In the Setup panel, click ⟱ (Loads) to open the Load dialog box. Define the load using the following options:

- Add a Force load of **100** for Fx.
- Select the outer edge shown in the following image to assign the load to.

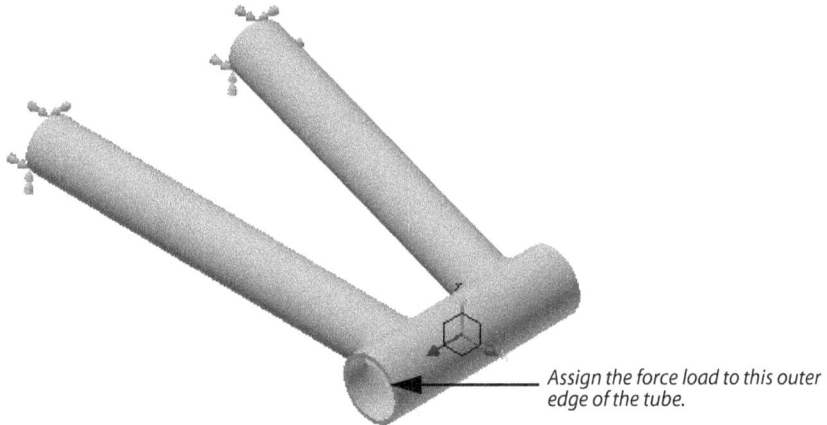

Assign the force load to this outer edge of the tube.

- Confirm that Subcase 1 is selected to add the load to this subcase.
- Assign a green display color, if not already defined.

- Select ☐ ᏠᏠᎧᎧᏠᎧ (Preview) to show the load on the model.
- Modify the density and size of the load's display, as required.

- Click ⬚ (New) to complete the load and leave the dialog box open to create another load.

3. Define a second load using the following options:
   - Add a Force load of **-100** for Fx.
   - Select the outer edge shown in the following image to assign the load to.

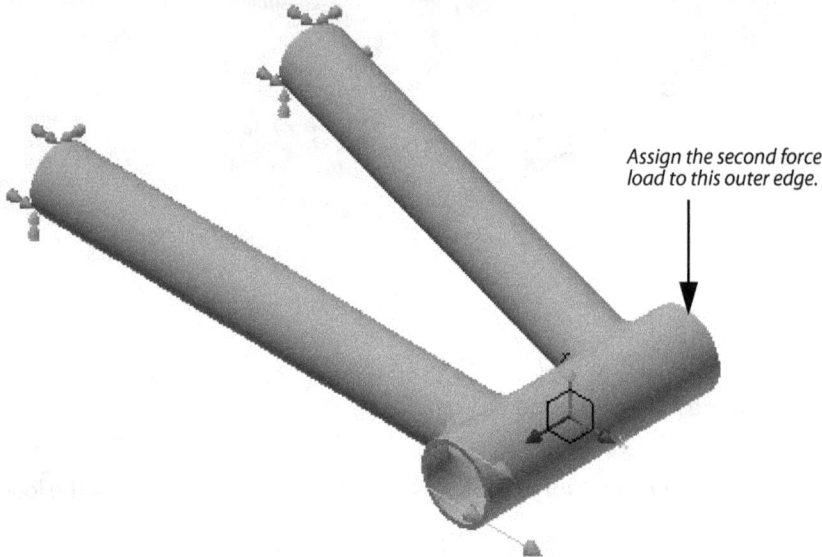

Assign the second force load to this outer edge.

   - Confirm that Subcase 1 is selected to add the load to this subcase.
   - Assign a green display color, if not already defined.
   - Select ☐ 👓 (Preview) to show the load on the model.
   - Modify the density and size of the load's display, as required.
   - Click OK.

Change the Global Mesh Settings & Mesh the Model

In this task, you will change the mesh settings globally for the entire model prior to meshing.

1. In the Analysis 1 sub-tree, right-click on Mesh Model, and click Edit.
2. Enter **0.2** as the Element Size.
3. Ensure that Continuous Meshing is selected.
4. Click Generate Mesh to update the mesh.

5. Click OK to close the Mesh Settings dialog box. The mesh updates as shown below.

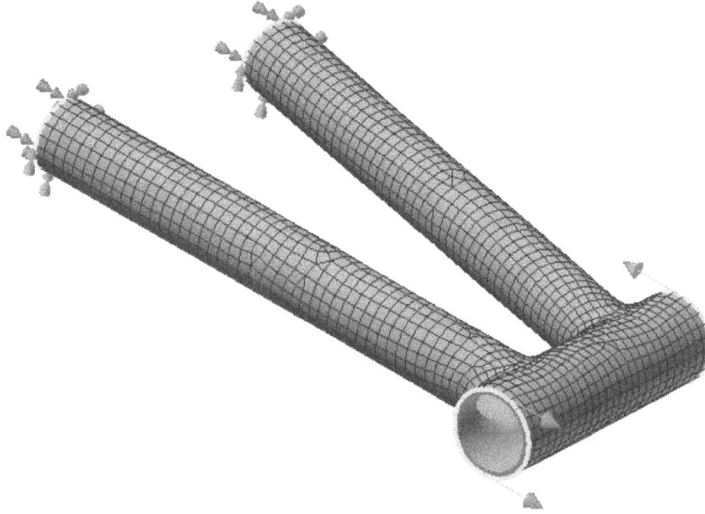

Define the Material Orientation

In this task, you will define the material orientation on the model. This is an important step when working with composite materials to ensure that the material is oriented correctly on the model. Incorrect orientation will affect the results of an analysis. In composite analyses, a zero angle ply means that it is aligned in the direction of the material orientation.

1. Right-click on the Analysis 1 node at the top of the Analysis sub-tree and select New>Material Orientation. The Material Orientation dialog box opens.

2. In the Type drop-down list, select Surface V Direction.

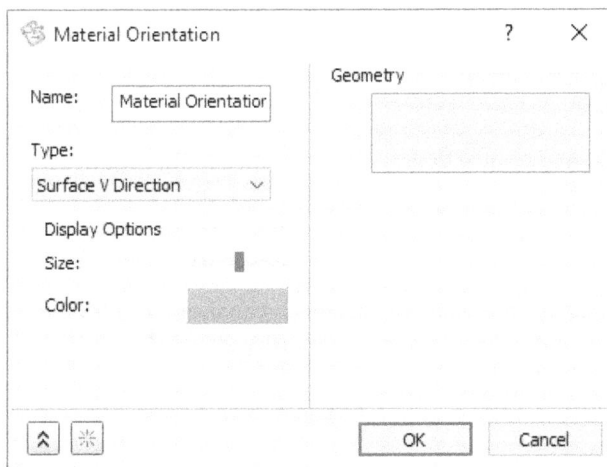

3. Select the same five outer surfaces of the model (three cylindrical surfaces and two fillet surfaces) that were selected when assigning the idealization.

Note: At the time of the printing of this learning guide, a message would occasionally incorrectly appear stating that the selected face does not have any shell elements associated with it. Ensure that the faces you have selected were previously assigned to the Shell idealization. This warning will not prevent the Material Orientation from being assigned.

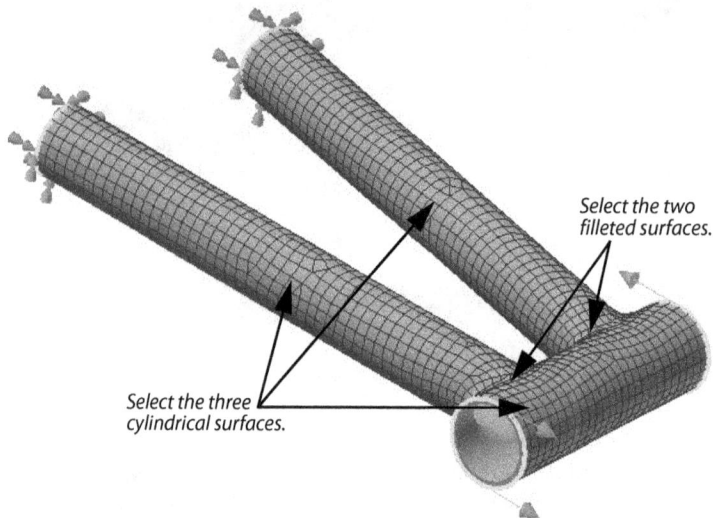

Select the two filleted surfaces.

Select the three cylindrical surfaces.

4. Click OK to close the Material Orientation dialog box.

5. Zoom in on an area of the mesh and note the green arrows that display in the mesh segments. These identify the 0 angle direction.

Run the Analysis

In this task, you will run the analysis.

1. In the Solve panel, click 📋 (Run).

2. Click OK to confirm the completion of the Nastran solution.

Review the Results

In this task, you will review the composite results for the analyzed model. First, we will look at the maximum ply failure index result for the composite elements.

1. To visualize the COMP MAX PLY FAILURE INDEX result, complete the following. When the failure index is over 1.0, the first ply failure is predicted, meaning that at least one ply has failed. When the failure index is less than 1.0, no failure is predicted to occur.

   - In the Results panel, select ![Contour icon] (Contour) and ![Deformed icon] (Deformed) to toggle on the default results display (von Mises), if not already enabled.

   - In the Results panel, click ![Options icon] (Options) to open the Plot dialog box.
   - In the Contour Options tab, select Composites in the Result Data drop-down list and select COMP MAX PLY FAILURE INDEX in the Type drop-down list.
   - In the Contour Options tab, select Centroidal in the Data Type drop-down list, select Elemental in the Contour Type drop-down list, and select No Averaging.

   - The result should be displayed. If not, select ![Display icon] (Display) in the Plot area.

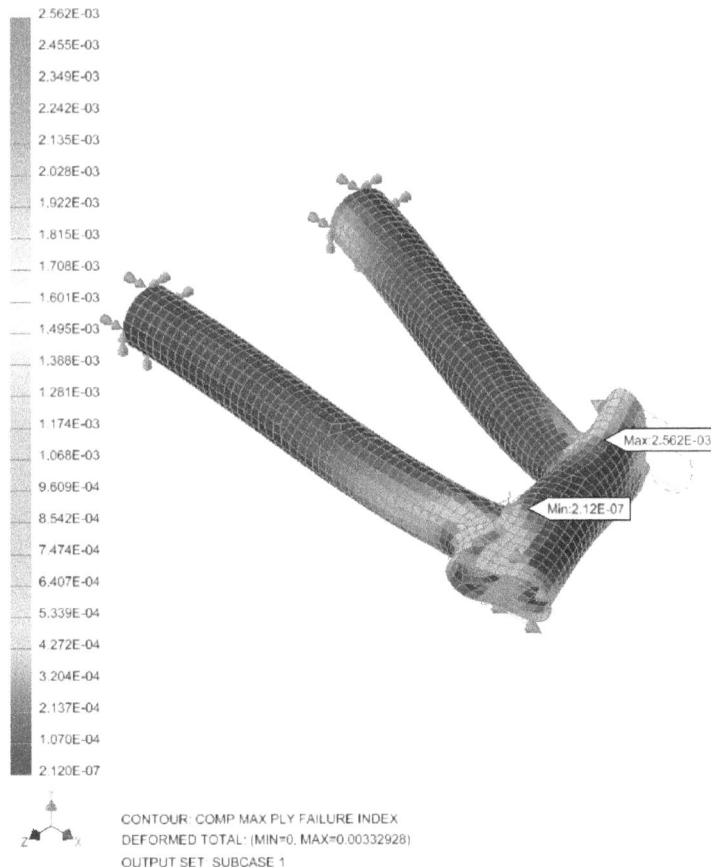

CONTOUR: COMP MAX PLY FAILURE INDEX
DEFORMED TOTAL: (MIN=0, MAX=0.00332928)
OUTPUT SET: SUBCASE 1

This result output vector shows the maximum occurring failure index on each element (using the Hill composite failure theory). The plot shows a maximum failure index value of much less than 1.0, indicating no ply failure is predicted to occur.

2. To visualize the COMP MAX FAILURE INDEX PLY result, complete the following. This
    result indicates what ply is most critical and has the highest failure index. In other
    words, this result indicates the critical ply number at each element, not the failure
    index value.

    ▪ The Plot dialog box should still be open. If not, in the Results panel, click

       [icon] (Options) to open the Plot dialog box.

    ▪ In the Contour Options tab, select Composites in the Result Data drop-down list
      and select COMP MAX FAILURE INDEX PLY in the Type drop-down list.

    ▪ In the Display Options area, ensure that the Rendering option is set to Fringe and
      the level is now set to **12**. Additionally, clear the Min/Max Markers option, if
      enabled.

    ▪ The result should be displayed. If not, select [icon] (Display) in the Plot area.

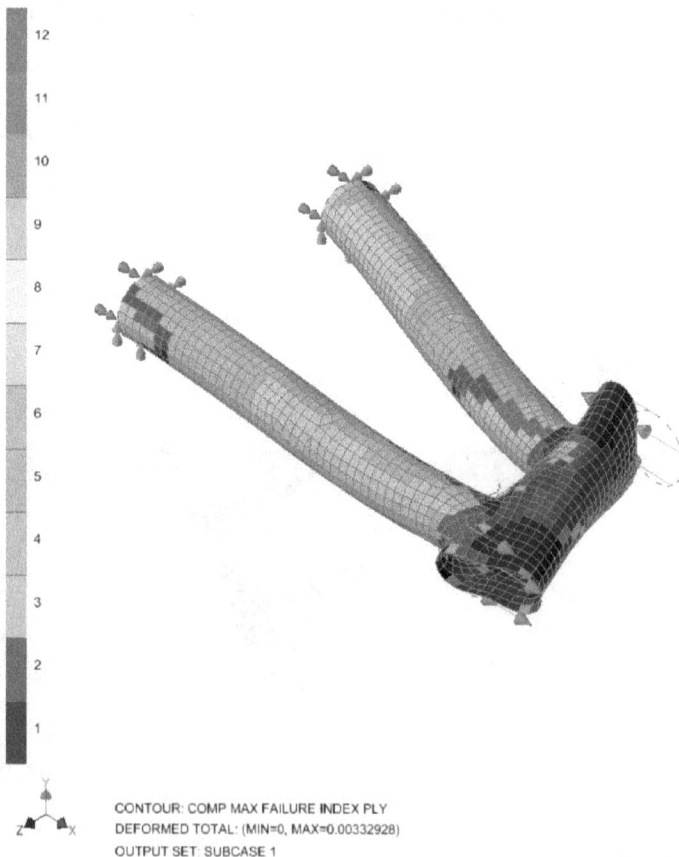

CONTOUR: COMP MAX FAILURE INDEX PLY
DEFORMED TOTAL: (MIN=0, MAX=0.00332928)
OUTPUT SET: SUBCASE 1

In the two long arms, plies 6 and 7 are the most critical. These two are 0-degree plies,
but due to the global material direction, the 0-degree plies are loaded perpendicular
to the fibers. In the short tube, plies 1 and 12 are the most critical plies.

3. Since Ply 1 was one of the critical plies in the short tube, we can visualize the normal stress along the fiber direction for Ply 1, which is COMP PLY 1 NORMAL-1 STRESS. To visualize this result, complete the following. Alternatively, COMP PLY 1 NORMAL-2 STRESS is the stress in the transverse fiber direction for ply 1.

- Open the Plot dialog box, if not already open.
- In the Contour Options tab, select Composites in the Result Data drop-down list and select COMP PLY 1 NORMAL-1 STRESS in the Type drop-down list.
- In the Display Options area, ensure that the Rendering option is set to Continuous and the level is now set at **24**.
- Display the results if they are not already visible.

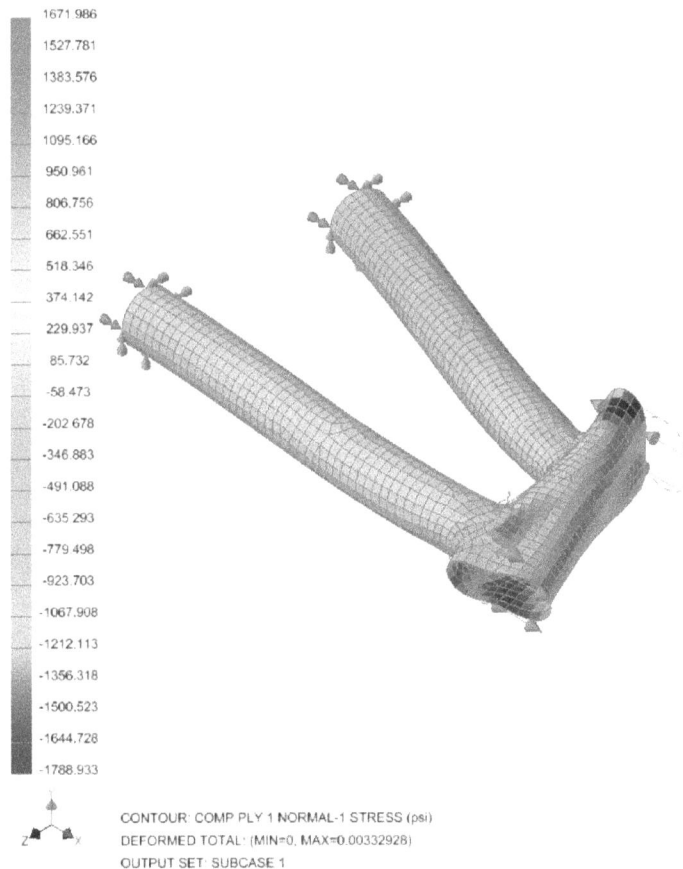

CONTOUR: COMP PLY 1 NORMAL-1 STRESS (psi)
DEFORMED TOTAL: (MIN=0, MAX=0.00332928)
OUTPUT SET: SUBCASE 1

We see a combination of tensile and compressive stresses, which means the ply is experiencing bending. The results show that the max normal stress for Ply 1 is approximately 1672psi.

4. Save the model.

Nonlinear Static Analysis

The goal in this chapter is to learn about nonlinear analysis, specifically how to create a nonlinear static analysis. To begin the chapter you, will learn about the various behaviors that should be considered for any nonlinear type of analysis. Additionally, you will learn how to create a nonlinear static analysis and how to analyze the results that are presented after an Autodesk® Nastran® In-CAD analysis.

Objectives

After completing this chapter, you will be able to:

- Describe the differences between linear and nonlinear analysis and which behaviors are considered nonlinear.
- Create a new nonlinear static analysis.
- Display a nonlinear static analysis' result plot, incremental plots, and XY plot results.

Lesson: Basics of a Nonlinear Analysis

Overview

There are many types of behaviors that may be referred to as nonlinear. Some examples of nonlinear behavior include displacements that cause loads to alter their distribution or magnitude, materials that change properties as they are loaded, gaps that may open or close. The degree of nonlinearity may be mild or severe. This lesson introduces and discusses these behaviors.

Objectives

After completing this lesson, you will be able to:

- Describe the differences between linear and nonlinear analysis and which behaviors are considered nonlinear.

Linear vs. Nonlinear Analysis

The defining line between linear and nonlinear is gray at best. Traditionally, in finite element analysis, there has been a set of criteria that determines if nonlinear effects are important to a particular model. If any of these criteria are present, a nonlinear analysis is required to accurately simulate real-world behavior. While this criteria still holds true, new capability, such as linear contact, and new materials, such as composites, further blur the line regarding when it is required to carry out a full nonlinear analysis.

In linear static analysis we assume the following:

- Displacements and rotations are small.
- Supports do not move or settle under load.
- Materials remains linear (stress remains directly proportional to strain).
- Loads (magnitude, orientation, distribution) remain constant as the structure deforms.

Most problems can usually be considered linear because they are loaded in their linear elastic, small deflection range. For these types of problems, the slight nonlinearity does not significantly affect the results, and the difference between a linear and nonlinear solution is negligible.

While many practical problems can be solved using linear analysis, some or all of its inherent assumptions may not be valid:

- Displacements and rotations may become large enough that equilibrium equations must be written for the deformed rather than the original configuration. Large rotations cause pressure loads to change in direction and also to change in magnitude (if there is a change in the area to which they are applied).
- Elastic materials may become plastic or the material may not have a linear stress-strain relationship at any stress level.
- Part of the structure may lose stiffness because of buckling or material failure.
- Adjacent parts may make or break contact with the contact area, changing as the loads change.

Note that many problems can exhibit all of these nonlinear effects combined. The corresponding FEA equations are described as follows:

Type	Equation	Graph
Linear	$[K]\{U\} = \{F\}$ where: K is the global tangent stiffness matrix U is the global displacement vector F is the global load vector	

Type	Equation	Graph
Nonlinear	$[K(U)]\{\Delta U\} = \{\Delta F\}$ where: K is the global tangent stiffness matrix U is the global displacement vector ΔU is the global incremental displacement vector F is the global load vector ΔF is the global incremental load vector	 The difference (F – Fi) is called residual force. The process is repeated until F = Fi.

- The global tangent stiffness matrix [K] is a function of the global displacements {U} because the problem is nonlinear.
- The current global displacement vector {U} is the sum of the preceding {ΔU}.

A Nonlinear effect can be broken down into three main categories:

- Geometric (large displacements)
- Material (plasticity, nonlinear stress-strain curves)
- Boundary condition (moving loads and constraints, contact interaction)

Geometric Nonlinearity

Geometric nonlinearity becomes a concern when a model deforms such that the small strain assumptions are no longer valid. The large displacements effects are a collection of different nonlinear phenomena, such as:

- Large deflections
- Stress stiffening/softening
- Snap-thru and Buckling
- Large strain

The following sections introduce and describe these properties in more details.

Large Deflections

When considering large deflections, we refer to movements or rotations of a part. For instance, if a part is expected to rotate or deflect 45 degrees, then a nonlinear analysis is required. In fact, in linear analysis, rotations greater than 10 degrees will generally cause significant errors in the results. This is because linear analysis assumes small displacement theory in which $\sin(\theta) \approx (\theta)$.

Stress Stiffening

Stress stiffening effects are caused by tensile stresses which result from larger displacements, not by the displacements themselves. The actual displacement in the model is not a clear indication of the degree of nonlinearity, nor is the tensile stress magnitude. A similar tension in one geometry or load orientation may result in significantly less stress stiffening than in another. The stress stiffening effect (sometimes referred to as geometric stiffening) is most pronounced in thin structures where the bending stiffness is very small compared to the axial stiffness.

- Consider a prestiffened drum membrane subjected to a uniform pressure load. The structure is fixed around the perimeter. This thin walled structure will undergo significant stress stiffening as the part transitions from reacting to the load in bending, to reacting to the load in-plane.

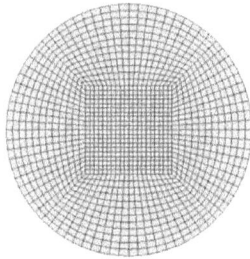

- The images below show two results of the prestiffened drum membrane. The image on the left is an actual deflection with large displacement effects toggled on (peak deflection is 0.8 inches). The second image is the deformed shape with large displacements toggled off. Note that in the second image the deformation is scaled down, as the peak deflection is over 5,000 inches.

- Flat plates under out of plane loading with 3-4 pinned sides are also common stress stiffening cases. In the paper tray below, as the distributed load on the face of the part is increased, a linear model predicts a proportional response, whereas the nonlinear model shows that the displacement tapers off as load increases due to the stress stiffening effect.

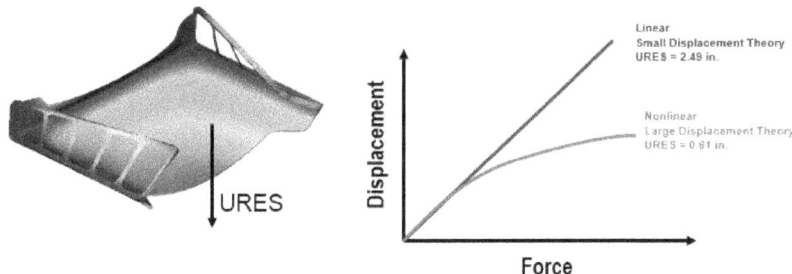

Linear
Small Displacement Theory
URES = 2.49 in.

Nonlinear
Large Displacement Theory
URES = 0.81 in.

Snap-thru and Buckling

Other common geometric nonlinear situations involve snap-thru and buckling problems, often referred to as bi-stable or multi-stable systems. An example of snap-thru buckling is an upward/convex dome or arch that under a sufficient load buckles into a concave shape and then becomes stable once again.

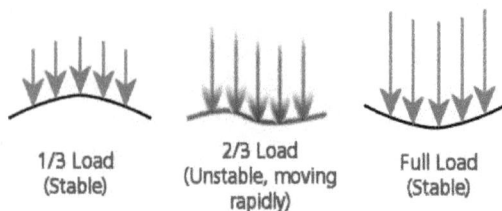

| 1/3 Load (Stable) | 2/3 Load (Unstable, moving rapidly) | Full Load (Stable) |

Many snap-thru problems behave nearly linearly until the point where a small amount of additional load causes a large amount of deflection, after which a secondary stable position is reached. Capturing this snap-thru, or bifurcation point is a very difficult numerical problem. Once buckling or snap-thru has been identified as an issue, a designer can take advantage of the knowledge that FEA solvers may fail in an attempt to model snap-thru, and use the solver failure itself to determine at what load buckling is likely to occur. In other words, when the structure becomes geometrically unstable, the solution convergence will become difficult to achieve. The analyst can infer the point of geometric instability by observing when the solution begins to diverge.

Large Strain

The large strain effect is nearly always coupled with a nonlinear material model as it involves gross plastic deformation of parts. Cold heading, rubber seal compression, and metal forming are good examples of large strain response.

Material Nonlinearity

There can be a significant difference between the linear and nonlinear material responses. For any material besides steel, reviewing the stress-strain curves is the best way to understand the nonlinearity of the problem. Even if you use a linear material model, knowing the nonlinearity model is important when interpreting results.

Simplified models of stress-strain curves are shown below:

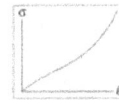

| Linear | Nonlinear Elastic | Plastic | Hyperelastic (Elastomers) |

For example, if you are analyzing a part made of steel and apply a load that pushes it past it's yield strength, you might only care about the linear range for that part, and you would see that as a failure. If you understand that once the material hits its yield it will start work-hardening, you will know that maybe it will yield, but it might not fail completely. It might harden enough to reach a stable equilibrium. You would only be able to see the post yield results if you model it as a bi-linear or multi-linear material.

A linear model can provide valid data for many materials at low strains and can be used for trend comparisons. Consider the following when looking at a nonlinear material:

- A linear analysis can only predict the onset of yielding. Once the limits of the analysis are exceeded, correlation degrades with the complexity of the stress state.

- A nonlinear plasticity analysis can only predict the onset of fracture. The nonlinear material effects can be important when you want to find out what happens past the initial yield of the material.

- Alternatively, non-metal materials like rubber and plastic can show a highly nonlinear stress-strain curve even at low strain values. Therefore, getting a more accurate picture of the stiffness of the material through its strain range is important to accurately predict the stiffness of the overall model.

- Brittle materials such as cast iron have little inelastic deformation before failure, so a linear analysis approach for these types of materials is generally acceptable.

- The majority of materials, including metals, have some amount of ductility. This ductility enables hot-spots to locally yield thus reducing the stresses compared to what a linear analysis would predict.

The metal bracket shown in the following image shows the very different stress distribution between linear and nonlinear materials. The metal has a yield stress of 50ksi. The left image contains the results of a linear material analysis and shows peak stresses well above yield. The nonlinear material analysis on the right shows a much different contour due to the stress redistribution. Peak plastic strain was 1% in the nonlinear material analysis.

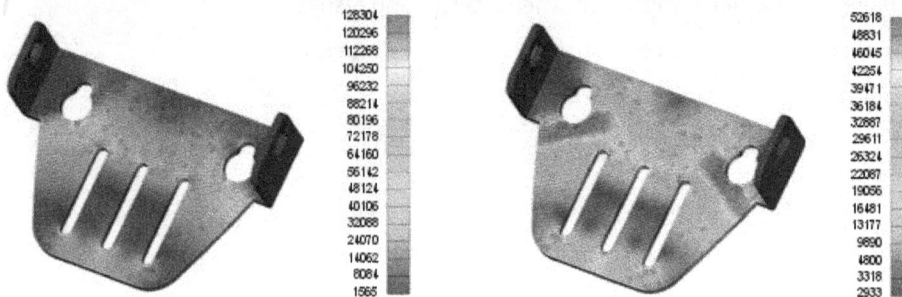

For more information on Nonlinear Materials, refer to *Chapter 7 Nonlinear Materials*.

Boundary Condition Nonlinearity

A model exhibits boundary nonlinearity when the loads, constraints, or load paths change throughout the solution. If the orientation, distribution, or magnitude of applied loads or the load path changes as loading is increased, a nonlinear model may be required. The most common boundary nonlinearities are:

- Contact
- Follower forces

The following sections introduce and describe these properties in more details.

Contact

As previously discussed, contact conditions are used to model boundary conditions that define the interaction between parts or different surfaces on the same part. Surface contacts are generally regarded as nonlinear. However, a new trend has emerged lately that enables a contact analysis to run in a linear solution in some FEA applications. In deciding between a linear and nonlinear contact analysis, it is best to ask these questions:

- Are there large movements in the model or any of the other nonlinear effects mentioned above?
- Is there significant sliding between contact bodies in the model? Is the contact solution path-dependent (for instance a snap-fit)?
- Are detailed contact stresses required in the model?

If the answer is yes to any of the three questions above, it is generally recommended to run a nonlinear solution to get the best accuracy.

The two models below show two examples of when to use linear contact versus nonlinear. The trailer hitch model on the left, while consisting of 6 parts in an assembly can be run as a linear contact solution since all the parts are initially in contact and the displacements are small. The rivet model on the right, however, needs a nonlinear solution due to the large displacements involved and the need for a nonlinear plastic material model.

For more information on Surface Contacts refer to *Chapter 4 Surface Contacts*.

Follower Forces

The follower forces effect means that the direction of the forces moves with the deformation or movement of the part. Pressure loads are a perfect example of follower forces since they always act normal to a surface. As a part deforms, follower forces will adjust the direction of the loads to ensure they stay normal to the surface. Thus, a nonlinear effect can be assumed.

The cantilevered rectangular beam shown below is loaded with a tip pressure load of 100psi, and three analyses are performed with different large displacement settings (using the LGDISP parameter in Autodesk Nastran In-CAD).

100.

Shown below are the results of the three runs. The first image shows the unrealistic "growth" that occurs when large displacement effects are toggled off (LGDISP=OFF). The second image shows the results of large displacements toggled on, but follower forces toggled off (LGDISP=2). The final image uses large displacement effects with follower forces and is the most accurate (LGDISP=ON).

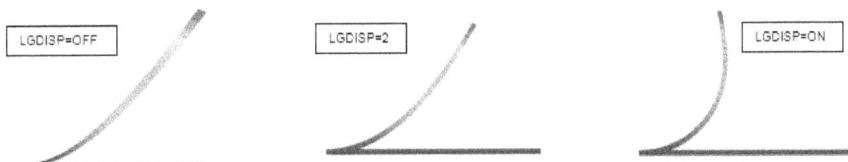

LGDISP=OFF   LGDISP=2   LGDISP=ON

General Guidelines

The following guidelines should be followed when building a nonlinear finite element analysis model:

- Run the analysis as a linear static solution first and ensure that the results are as expected. If not, consider your analysis setup. After this consider a nonlinear analysis if the material yield stress is exceeded, large displacements are observed, or significant relative motion (sliding or separation) occurs along the contacting surfaces.

- Keep the model size small. Simplify the geometry as much as possible before meshing (unnecessary fillets, holes, etc. should be removed). Identify areas of symmetry, cut the model at these planes, and apply symmetry boundary conditions. Using symmetry will not only reduce the model size considerably, but the symmetry constraints will help to stabilize the model preventing rigid body movement.

- Ensure a good quality mesh. The convergence of a nonlinear analysis can be affected by poor quality elements. Perform distortion checks to ensure that there are no severely distorted elements.

- Only apply nonlinear materials in the areas of the model (faces, surfaces, or different models) where you expect nonlinear or plastic behavior. This will help to speed up the analysis and can improve the convergence rate.

- If surface contact is being used, split up the contact areas into specific regions where you expect contact to occur. Using broad or general surfaces will cause a large number of contact elements to be generated, resulting in an increase in the analysis time.

Lesson: Creating a Nonlinear Static Analysis

Overview

This lesson discusses the options that enable you to create a new analysis in your model or edit an existing one to a nonlinear static analysis. You will also learn about the output options available for customizing the results, and how to review the result plots.

Objectives

After completing this lesson, you will be able to:

- Create a new nonlinear static analysis.
- Display a nonlinear static analysis' result plot, incremental plots, and XY plot results.

Creating a New Analysis

By default, when a model is initially opened in Autodesk Nastran In-CAD, a Linear Static analysis is created. To create any other type of analysis, for example a Nonlinear Static analysis, you can use either of the following methods:

- Edit the existing analysis and change its type and settings, as required. To edit an existing analysis, right-click on the analysis name in the Model Tree and select Edit.

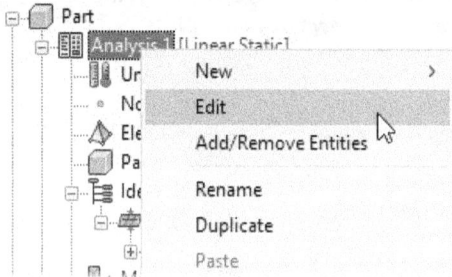

> If a comparison analysis is required, consider using the Duplicate option on the shortcut menu to create a copy of an existing analysis and then edit it to change the type. For example, this can be used when you want both a Linear Static and NonLinear Static analysis for comparison and you don't want to have to keep redefining them to compare results.

- Create a new analysis type with the required settings. To create a new analysis, right-click on the model node at the top of the Model Tree and select New.

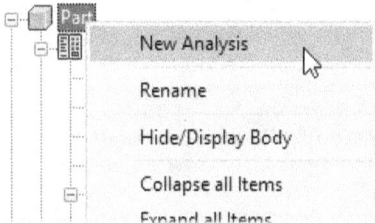

When editing an existing analysis or creating a new one, the Analysis dialog box displays.

The most commonly used settings in the Analysis dialog box are described below. For more information on the Analysis dialog box and its options, refer to Autodesk Nastran In-CAD Help and search for "New Analysis".

- **Type:** Enables you to specify the type of analysis to be created in the model. Autodesk Nastran In-CAD supports the analysis types shown in the following image.
- **Units:** Defines the unit system for the model. By default, the analysis uses the unit system defined for the CAD model. The available units systems that can be selected include the CAD Model, SI, Modified SI, English, and CG.

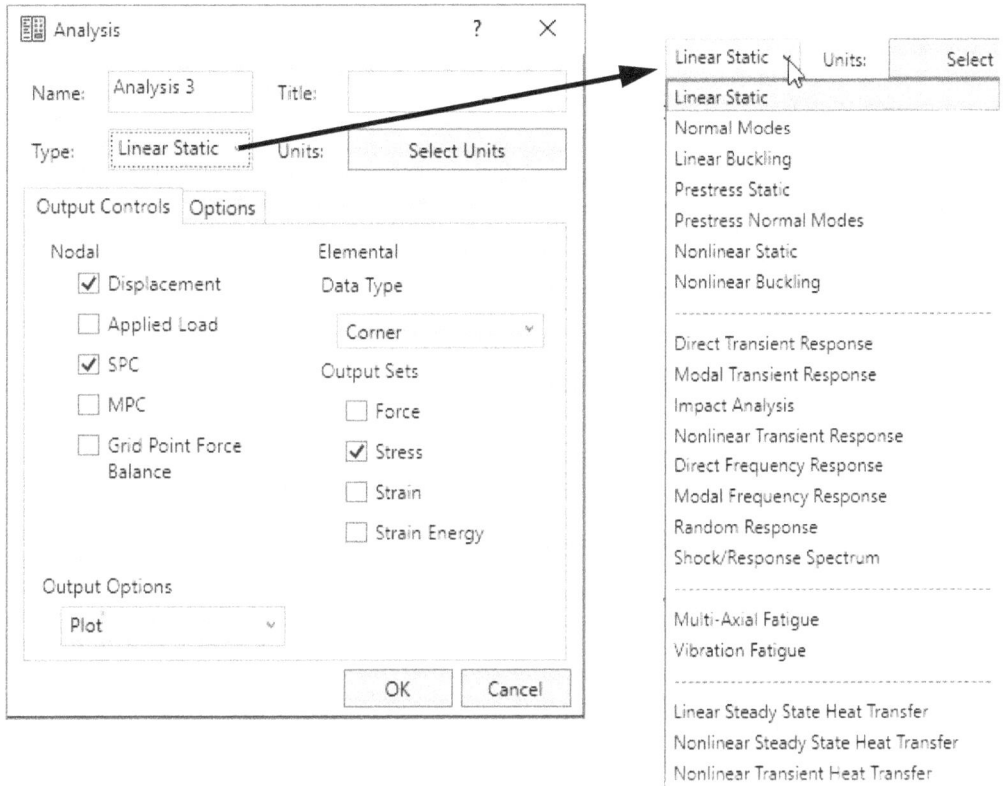

The following tabs provide additional settings for controlling the analysis. The specific options that are available are dependent on the type of analysis that is chosen.

- **Output Controls tab**: Defines the Nodal, Elemental, and Output Set information that will be included in the analysis report.

- **Options tab**: Provides additional options for defining an analysis. The available options vary depending on the analysis type.

  - The Contact Type options are available for all analysis types and enable you to control the default setting for generating Automatic contacts. You can specify the contact type and the maximum distance between contacting entities at which automatic contacts can be generated (tolerance).

  - For the Nonlinear Static, Nonlinear Buckling, and Transient Response analysis types, you can also enable/disable the Large Displacements parameter. This parameter is toggled on by default, which assumes that large displacement, follower force effects, and varying stiffness will be included.

- **Model State tab**: (Assemblies only) Sets a Design View or Level of Detail that exists in the model as the version of the model to be analyzed.

  Note: The default value of these settings is based on the view that was currently active in the modeling environment.

Creating a New Nonlinear Static Analysis

To create a nonlinear static analysis you must either create a new analysis or edit an existing analysis and change the type of analysis to Nonlinear Static. Additionally, you must consider the following:

- Ensure that a required idealization exists or is created that contains any nonlinear material properties specifically required for the nonlinear analysis.
- Assign the required contacts, constraints, and loads.
- To generate and store the intermediate results that are calculated throughout the analysis, you must set the required Nonlinear Options. For nonlinear static analyses, you must enable the option globally and locally for each subcase. To access the global options, right-click on the analysis name, select Nonlinear Options and enable the Generate Intermediate Results option. For each subcase, you must also specify that the intermediate results be generated by right-clicking Nonlinear Setup and selecting Edit. In the Nonlinear Setup dialog box, set the Intermediate Output option to On.

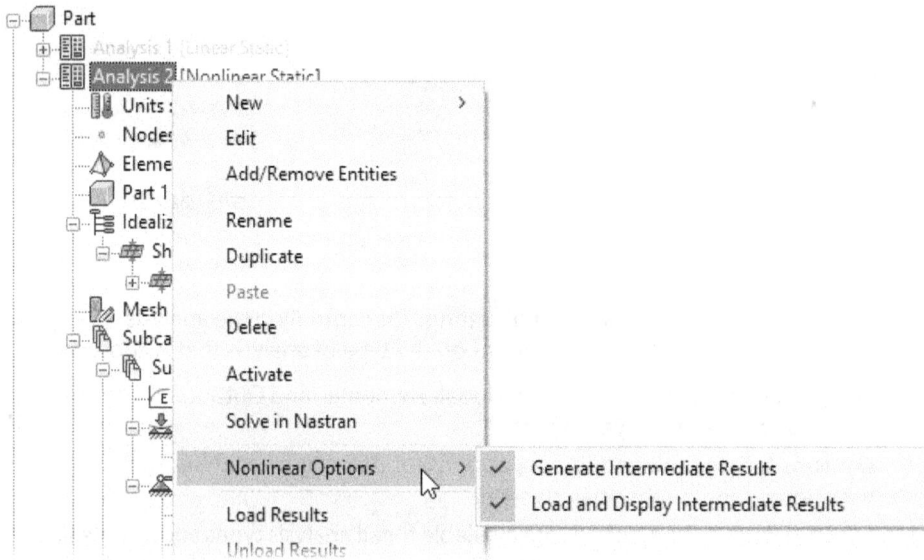

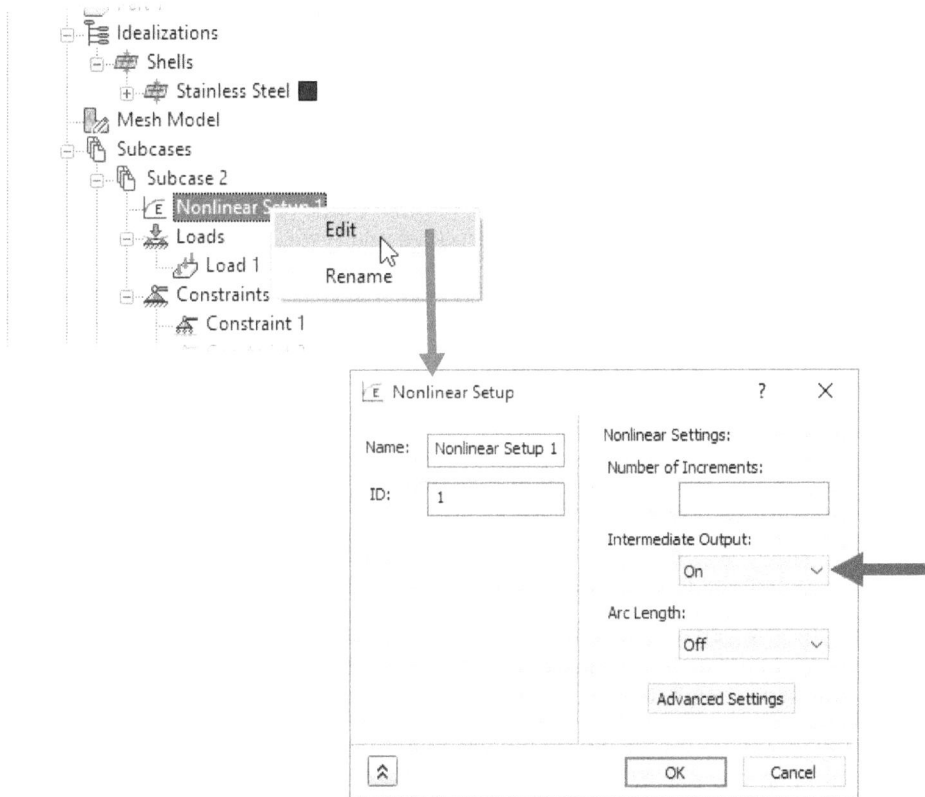

- **Generate Intermediate Results**: When this option is checked, the solver generates .FNO files for each increment that can be loaded while the analysis is being run. When the analysis is completed, these intermediate .FNO files are compiled into one.
- **Load and Display Intermediate Results**: This option works in conjunction with Generate Intermediate Results and thus, is only available when that option is checked. The incremental results are automatically loaded into the tree under Subcases and can be viewed until the next increment has been solved.

■ Nonlinear settings can be customized using the Nonlinear Setup node that gets created in the subcase of a nonlinear static analysis. As previously mentioned, to access the setup options, right-click on Nonlinear Setup and select Edit (as shown above). In the Nonlinear Setup dialog box, select the options as required. In general, the default values that are set in this dialog box provide you with the required settings; however, the options can be changed as required. For example, the default number of increments can be changed from 10. A larger number of increments is required to capture changes that are occurring rapidly and to facilitate convergence where nonlinear effects are compounded (nonlinear material behavior, large displacements, changing contact, and/or geometric instability).

> For more information on the options on the Nonlinear Setup dialog box, refer to Autodesk Nastran In-CAD Help and search for "Nonlinear Setup".

Procedure: To Create a new Nonlinear Static Analysis

1. Right-click on the Part or Assembly node at the top of the Model Tree and select New.

2. Enter the name for the new analysis.

3. Select Nonlinear Static in the Type drop-down list.

4. (Optional) By default, the unit system for the model is set to that of the CAD model. Click Select Units and select an alternative unit system, if required.

5. Define the required options in the Output Controls tab to define the information that will be output to the analysis report when it is run.

6. Define the options in the Options tab:

   - Set the Contact type that should be used by default when generating Automatic contacts.
   - Set the tolerance value between contacting entities at which automatic contacts are to be created.
   - When assuming large displacement in the model, set the Large Displacement parameter to On. Otherwise set the value to Off.

7. If analyzing an assembly, on the Model State tab, verify the Design View or Level of Detail to define the model configuration that is being analyzed. Change the configurations, if required.

8. Click OK to create the new nonlinear analysis.

9. Right-click on the Nonlinear Setup node in the analysis subcase and select Edit. Define the Nonlinear Setup properties, as required.

10. Assign an existing idealization from the Model sub-tree or create a new one, as required.

11. Assign contacts and/or constraints to the model, as required.

12. Assign loads to the model, as required.

Alternatively, you can edit an existing analysis by right-clicking the analysis name in the Model Tree and select Edit.

Nonlinear Static Analysis Plot Results

When a linear static analysis is run, four default plot templates are included that enable you to easily activate them and view the plot results. For a nonlinear static analysis, there are no default plot templates included. When the analysis is run, the results are stored; however, you must use the Plot dialog box to visually display the results.

To access the Plot dialog box:

- Right-click on the Results node and select Edit.
- Double-click on the Results node.
- In the Results panel on the ribbon, click (Options).

Using the Plot dialog box you can perform the following tasks:

- Use the Result Data drop-down list in the Contour Options tab to select the general type of data to plot, such as Displacement or Stress.
- Use the Type drop-down list in the Contour Options tab to select the specific data result to plot, such as SOLID VON MISES STRESS.
- Customize the remaining options as required, based on the result plot that is being created.

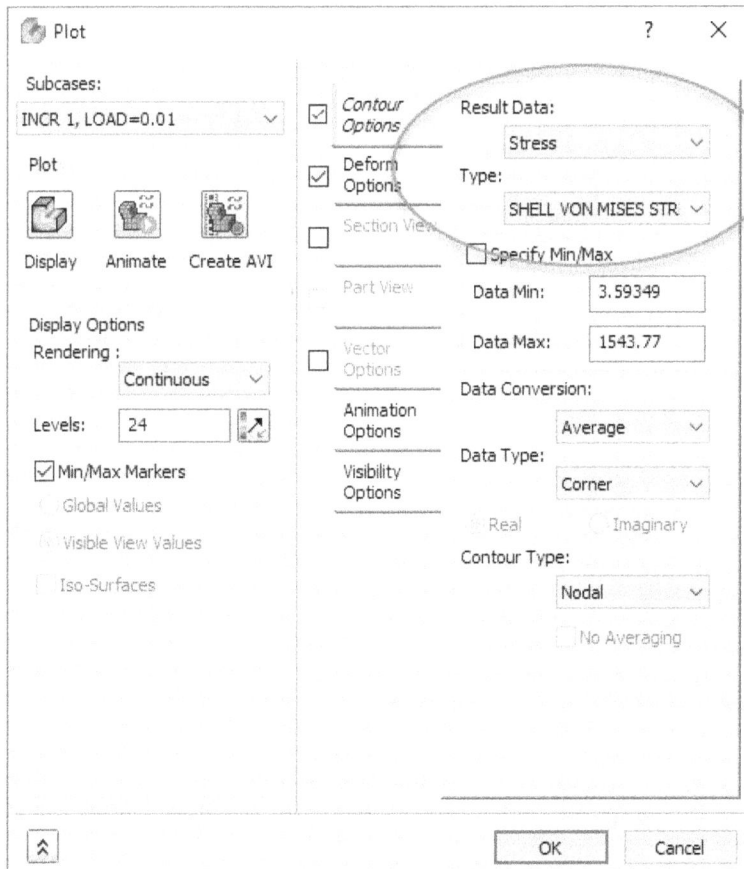

Consider the following tips when viewing results:

- Once customized, click (Display) to visually show the results in the graphics window. With this option enabled, you can continue to make changes to the options in the Plot dialog box, and the plot results will update in the graphics window. Alternatively, click (Animate) or (Create AVI) to display or save an animation of the results plot, respectively.
- To clear the display of the mesh (element edges), select the Visibility Options tab in the Plot dialog box and toggle off the Element Edges option. You can also toggle off the Mesh in the Display panel on the ribbon.
- A result plot cannot be saved for reuse in a nonlinear analysis; however, the last specified settings are saved in the Plot dialog box.
- If the intermediate results were generated for the nonlinear static analysis you can display the intermediate results using either of the following methods.

  - In the Results panel, when the (Contour) or (Deformed) options are enabled, you can select the increment to view using the drop-down list.

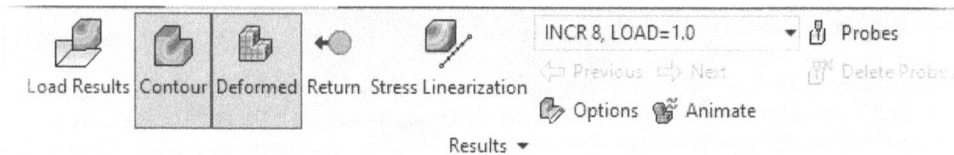

  - In the Results panel, you can also use the ⇐ and ⇒ buttons to progress through the display of each increment.
  - In the Plot dialog box you can select the increment to display in the Subcases drop-down list.

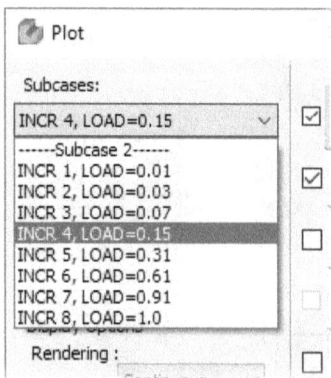

> For more information on Plot dialog box and its options, refer to the *Visualizing Result Plots* lesson in Chapter 3 or to Autodesk Nastran In-CAD Help and search for "Plot Templates".

Nonlinear Static Analysis XY Plot

When a nonlinear static analysis is run, a number of XY plots are generated by default to help you analyze the results.

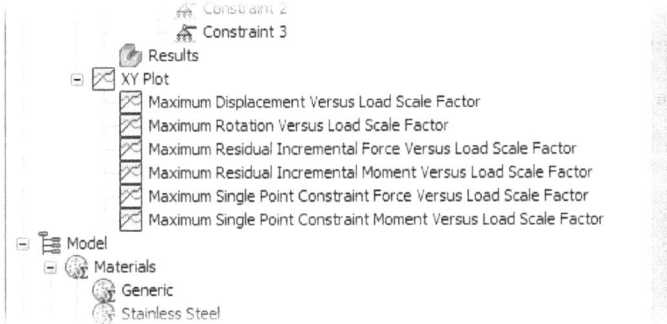

To review any of the plots, double-click on the plot name or right-click on the plot name and select Show XY Plot. The XY Plot dialog box opens displaying the plot. In the following image, the Maximum Displacement Versus Load Scale Factor plot is shown. The options in the left pane of the dialog box enables you to customize the display of the plot.

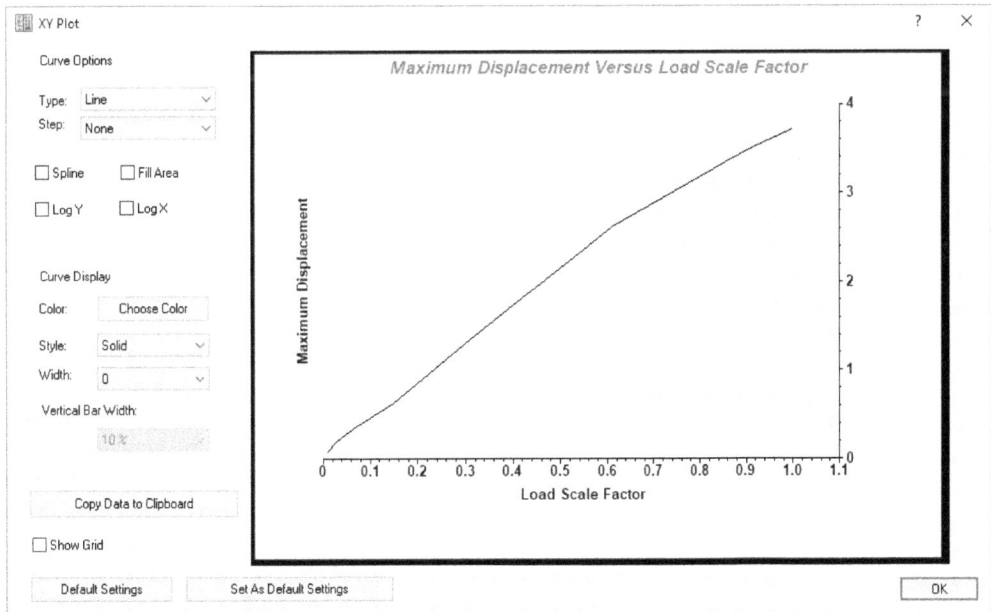

For more information on XY Plot dialog box, its options, and how to create a new XY Plot, refer to the *Visualizing XY Plot Results* lesson in Chapter 3 or to Autodesk Nastran In-CAD Help and search for "Results XY Plotting".

Exercise: Flat Walled Tank

In this exercise, you will conduct a nonlinear static analysis to explore the phenomenon of stress stiffening. The model that will be analyzed is a flat walled tank that is 48 inches x 48 inches x 96 inches tall; however, only a quarter of the model will be analyzed because symmetry is assumed. The walls of the tank are flat and are subject to pressure loading which may lead to large deformation effects. You will also run a linear static analysis on this model to compare the results.

Prepare the Model for use in Nastran In-CAD

1. Open the file *C:\Autodesk Nastran InCAD 2019 Essentials Exercise Files\Flat_Walled_Tank\Flat Walled Tank.ipt*.

    This model is a quarter of the actual tank, created as a single solid volume. You will not use the CAD solid body to create solid elements. Instead, two adjacent sides and the bottom face will be used to create shell elements representing the two half-walls and the quarter-bottom of the partial tank analysis model. Also, note the feature called Split1. This is how the liquid fill height of the tank is identified. You will assume a fill height of 84 inches. The "wetted" faces of the tank walls, which experience the pressure load, are colored purple.

    Note: The quarter-tank could have also been created in the CAD modeling environment as a surface model consisting only of the two side wall surfaces (split at the water fill level) and the bottom surface. As an alternative to this approach, this exercise will show how you can also create shell elements along the surfaces of solid models.

2. Activate the Autodesk Nastran In-CAD environment.

Assign a New Idealization

In this task, you will create a new idealization and assign it to the model for use during the analysis.

1. In the Prepare panel, click 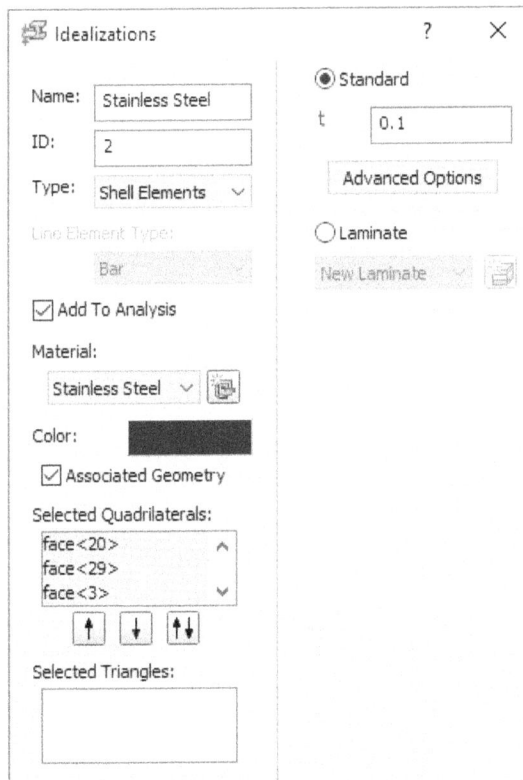 (Idealizations) to open the Idealizations dialog box.

2. Enter **Stainless Steel** as the name of the new idealization.

3. Ensure that Shell Elements is selected as the Type of element for the idealization.

4. Create a new material and select Stainless Steel as the material from the Autodesk Material Library. Click OK.

5. On the Idealizations dialog box, enter **0.1** as the thickness (t) value.

6. In the Idealizations dialog box, select Associated Geometry and select the five surfaces shown below.

7. Ensure that Add to Analysis is selected, change the color to dark purple, and click OK to close the Idealizations dialog box. The new idealization has been assigned for use in the analysis and displays under the Idealizations>Shells node.

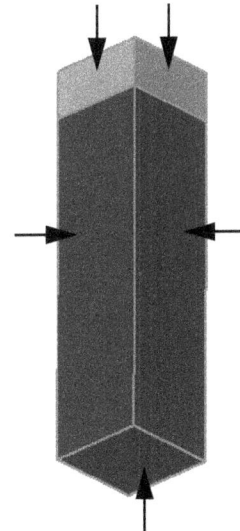

Select the 5 faces shown to be assigned the new idealization.

8. Remove Solid 1 from the Idealizations>Solids node in the analysis.

Mesh the Tank

In this task, you will change the mesh settings globally for the entire model and mesh it.

1. In the Analysis 1 sub-tree, right-click on Mesh Model, and click Edit.

2. Enter **3** as the new Element Size value.

3. Change the Element Order option to Linear using its drop-down list.

4. Click Generate Mesh to update the mesh.

5. Click OK to close the Mesh Settings dialog box. Ensure that all 5 faces are meshed. If not, edit the idealization and add the missing face(s).

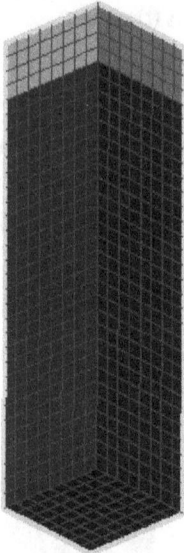

Constrain the Model

In this task, you will constrain the model to take into account the symmetry assumption that is being used to analyze 1/4 of the tank. Additionally, you will add a constraint that prevents movement in the Y direction for the bottom of the tank.

1. In the Setup panel, click ⛰ (Constraints) to open the Constraints dialog box.

2. In the Degrees of Freedom section of the dialog box, select X (X Symmetry) to preselect the degrees of freedom that are to be assigned to a reference edge.

3. In the Subcases section of the dialog box, confirm that Subcase 1 is selected to automatically add the constraint to Subcase 1.

4. If not already defined, set the display color for the constraint to cyan.

5. Select the three edges of the tank, as shown below, as the references for the constraint.

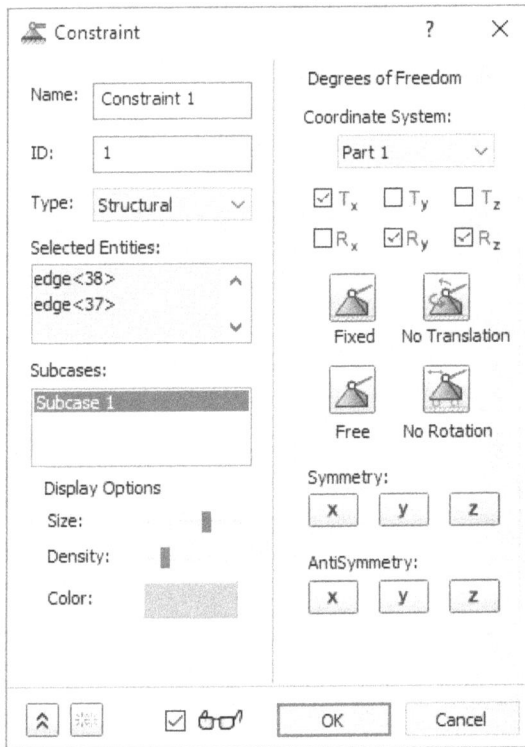

Select the three edges as the reference for the constraint.

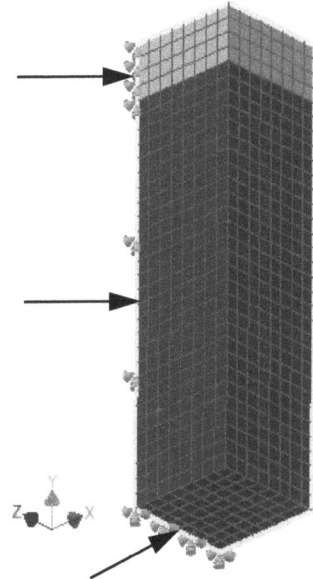

6. Select ☐ 👓 (Preview) at the bottom of the dialog box to show the constraint on the model.

7. Modify the density and size of the constraint's display, as required.

8. Click OK to complete the constraint.

9. Add an additional constraint to the model using the following options. This constrains the other edges of the model.

    ■ In the Symmetry section, click ⌊ z ⌋. Choosing this option sets the constraint in the Tz, Rx, and Ry directions.
    ■ Select the three edges that lie on the symmetry plane.
    ■ Select Preview to show the constraint on the model.
    ■ Modify the density and size of the constraint's display, as required.
    ■ Click OK.

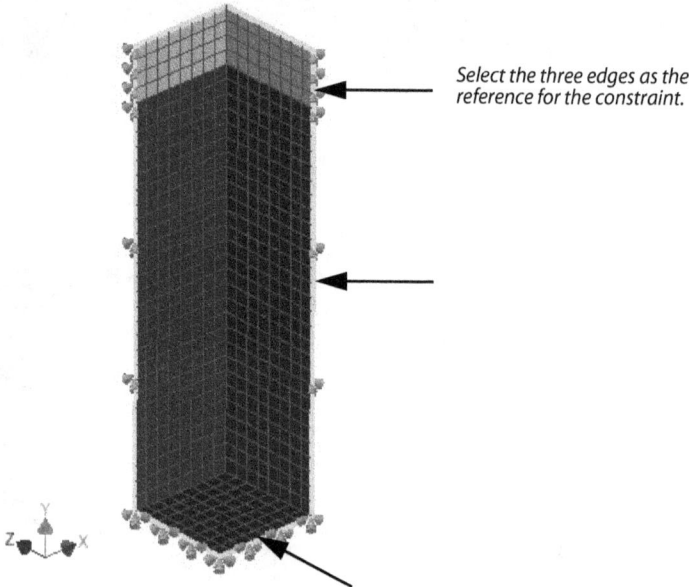

Select the three edges as the reference for the constraint.

10. Add an additional constraint to the model using the following options. This constrains the bottom of the tank.

    ■ Click ⌊⚒⌋ (Free) to clear all the degrees of freedom and then select Ty. This constrains translation in the y-direction.
    ■ Select the bottom surface of the tank to assign the constraint to.
    ■ Select Preview to show the constraint on the model.
    ■ Modify the density and size of the constraint's display, as required.
    ■ Click OK.

    The three constraints are added to the analysis as shown below.

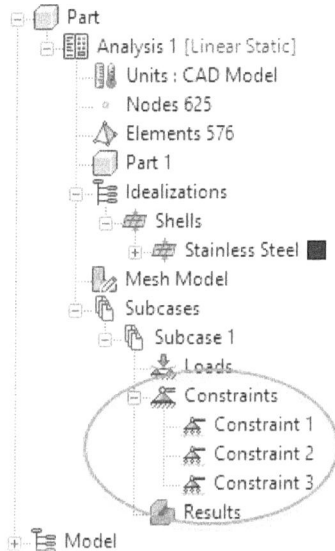

Load the Model

In this task, you will add a pressure load to the model to analyze liquid filling the tank to a height of 84 in. The following calculation was done to determine the pressure at the bottom of the tank.

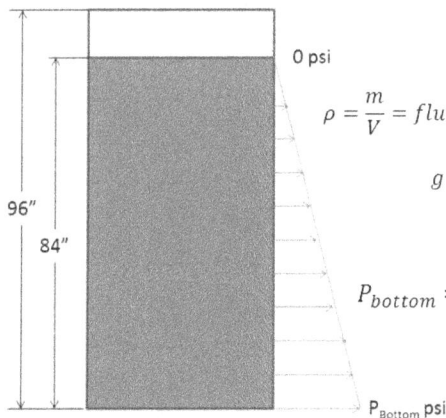

$$P_{static\ fluid} = \rho g h$$

$$\rho = \frac{m}{V} = fluid\ density = 1000\frac{kg}{m^3} = 9.343E - 5\frac{lbsec^2}{in^4}$$

$$g = acceleration\ of\ gravity = 386.4\frac{in}{sec^2}$$

$$h = depth\ of\ fluid = 84\ in$$

$$P_{bottom} = 9.343E - 5 * 386.4 * 84 = 3.032\ psi$$

1. In the Setup panel, click to open the Load dialog box. Select Pressure as the load type.

2. Select the three wetted surfaces of the tank, as shown below. Note that the constraint display has been temporarily toggled off for clarity in this image.

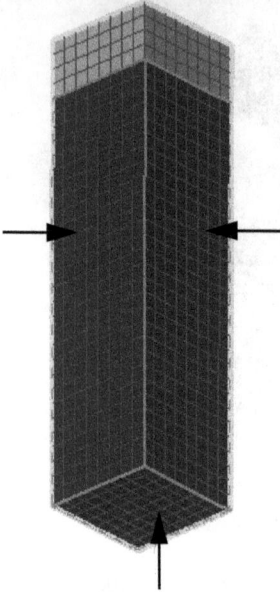

Select the 3 wetted faces shown to be assigned the new pressure load.

3. Assign the load to Subcase 1.

4. Enter a Magnitude of **-1** psi.

5. Click Advanced Options >> to expand the dialog box so that the Variable Load Definition is visible.

6. Select Variable Load Definition and ensure that the Interpolation Method is set to Linear.

7. Select the two vertices in the order shown (from top down). Click Add. Note that the constraint display has been temporarily toggled off for clarity in this image.

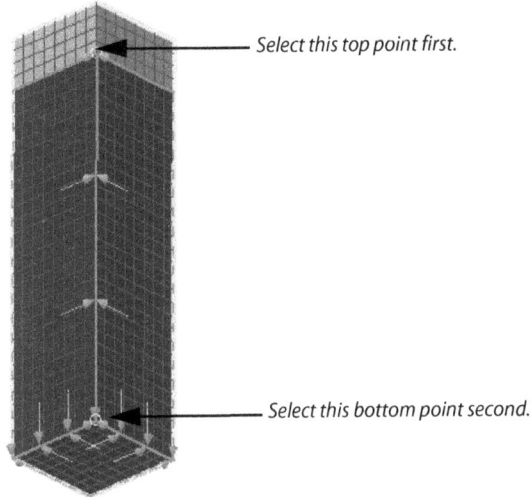

Select this top point first.

Select this bottom point second.

8. Double-click in the Scalar column, and enter **0** in row 1, and **3.032** in row 2.

X	Y	Z	Scalar
48.000...	84.00...	48.00...	0
48.000...	0.000...	48.00...	3.032

9. Select ☐ 👓 (Preview) at the bottom of the dialog box to show the load on the model.

10. To see the varying load more clearly, move the Density slider. Note the variable load from top to bottom and the load on the bottom, as shown below.

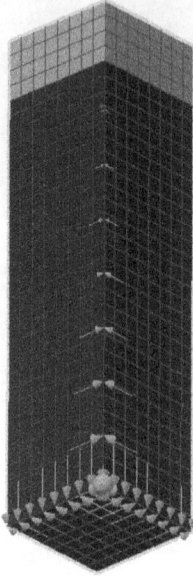

11. Click OK to complete the load definition.

Run the Analysis and Review the Results

In this task, you will run the analysis and then analyze the displacement and stress result plots.

1. Run the analysis.

2. Display the Displacement results plot. The maximum displacement is 8.22 in.

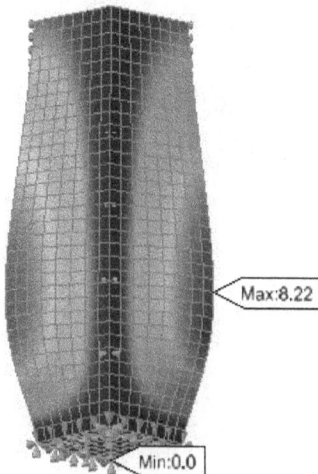

3. Display the von Mises results plot. The maximum stress is approximately 1.57 E$^+$05 psi. By default, the von Mises result reports values for the Top surface of the shell element.

4. Right-click on the von Mises results plot in the Mode Tree and select Edit. In the Contour Options tab, select SHELL MAX VON MISES STRESS BOTTOM/TOP in the Type drop-down list to view the max surface stresses on either the top or bottom. Click

    ![icon] in the Plot section to display the result, if it does not automatically update. The difference between the Top and Bottom stresses for a shell element can be quite significant, so it is recommended to check both.

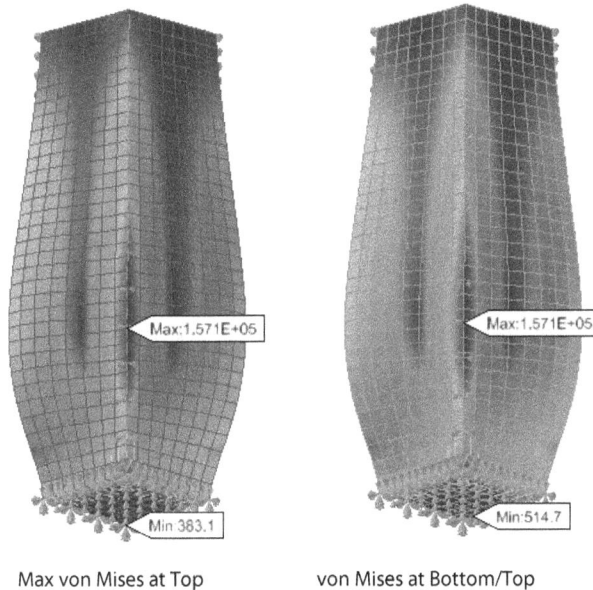

Max von Mises at Top   von Mises at Bottom/Top

5. Close the Plot dialog box. Double-click on the von Mises node in the Model Tree to clear its contour plot display in the graphics window.

Run a Nonlinear Static Analysis & Review the Results

By default, when a model is initially opened in the Nastran In-CAD environment, a Linear Static analysis is created. In this task, you will create a similar nonlinear analysis and compare the results. The linear static analysis shows that there are large deformations in the tank and suggests that linear static will not provide for an accurate analysis. Using a nonlinear static analysis, you will see how the iterative method of analysis improves the results.

1. Right-click on the Part node at the top of the Model Tree and select New Analysis.

2. In the Analysis dialog box:

    ▪ Maintain the default name.
    ▪ Select Nonlinear Static from the Type drop-down list.
    ▪ Maintain the remaining default options on the Output Controls tab.
    ▪ On the Options tab, ensure that Large Displacement is set to On.
    ▪ Click OK.

Analysis	? ✕

Name: Analysis 2   Title: [   ]

Type: Nonlinear Static ▾   Units: [Select Units]

Output Controls | Options

Nodal
  ☑ Displacement
  ☐ Applied Load
  ☑ SPC
  ☐ MPC
  ☐ Grid Point Force Balance

Elemental
Data Type
  [Corner ▾]
Output Sets
  ☐ Force
  ☑ Stress
  ☐ Strain

Output Options
  [Plot ▾]

[OK] [Cancel]

3. Define the analysis:

    ▪ Drag and drop the Stainless Steel idealization to the Idealizations node in the new analysis.
    ▪ Drag and drop the three constraints to the Constraints node in the new analysis.
    ▪ Drag and drop the load to the Loads node in the new analysis.

    Hint: As an alternative to dragging and dropping the constraints and loads you can edit the subcase and assign them using the Subcase dialog box.

4. Edit the global mesh settings for the new analysis, as follows:

    ▪ Enter **3** as the new Element Size value.
    ▪ Change the Element Order option to Linear using its drop-down list.
    ▪ Click Generate Mesh to update the mesh.

5. Run the analysis. Click OK when the analysis is complete.

6. Nonlinear Static analyzes do not have predefined analysis plot templates generated. To display the Displacement results plot, right-click on Results in the Analysis 2 sub-tree and select Edit. The Plot dialog box opens.

7. On the Contour Options tab, ensure that its check box is selected. In the Results Data drop-down list, select Displacement to create a displacement plot. Ensure that TOTAL is selected in the Type drop-down list to create the plot showing the total displacement.

8. Click ⬚ (Display) in the Plot section to display the result plot in the graphics window. You can continue to customize the display and it will update as you make changes.

9. Select the Deform Options tab.

10. Set the Deformation Scale to Actual and enter **1.0** as the Value. The deformation plot updates automatically. This result seems more like a realistic representation of deformation.

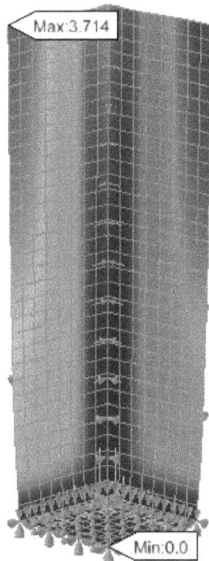

11. To display the von Mises stress results, select the Contour Options tab. In the Result Data drop-down list, select Stress and select SHELL VON MISES STRESS in the Type

drop-down list. If the results don't automatically update, select ⬚ (Display). Keep in mind that the default Type is TOP.

12. In the Type drop-down list, select SHELL VON MISES STRESS BOTTOM/TOP to find the max stress.

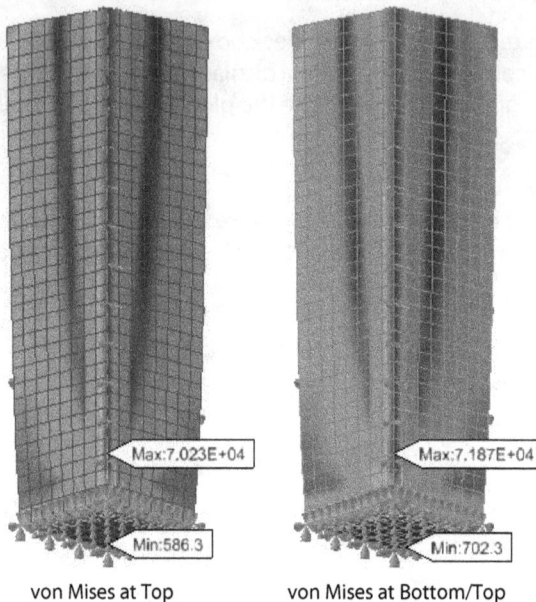

von Mises at Top   von Mises at Bottom/Top

13. Select the Subcases drop-down list in the Plot dialog box. Note that only the INCR 8, LOAD=1.0 result is listed. This is because by default, the intermediate results were not stored for this nonlinear static analysis.

14. Click OK to close the Plot dialog box.

15. To enable the creation of intermediate results, complete the following:

- Right-click on Analysis 2, select Nonlinear Options, and ensure that the Generate Intermediate Results option is enabled. This is the global setting.

- Right-click Nonlinear Setup 1 in the subcase for Analysis 2 and select Edit. In the Nonlinear Setup dialog box, set the Intermediate Output option to On. Click OK.

16. Run the analysis. Click OK when the analysis is complete.

17. In the Results panel on the ribbon, click (Contour), if the von mises stress results are not already showing. In the Results panel, expand the list of incremental results drop-down list and ensure that the INCR 1, LOAD=0.1 result is selected. This enables you to selectively chose an increment to view.

18. In the Results panel, select (Next) to advance the display to the next increment. Continue to display the increments using the arrows.

19. In the Results panel, click ⬛ (Contour) to clear its display. Note that if the

⬛ (Deformed) option remains selected in the Results panel, the deformed geometry remains displayed. Select it again to clear it, if not already cleared.

20. In the XY Plot node for the analysis, double-click on the Maximum Displacement Versus Load Scale Factor plot. Review the plot and close the dialog box. Multiple plots are created for the analysis. Review the other plots as required.

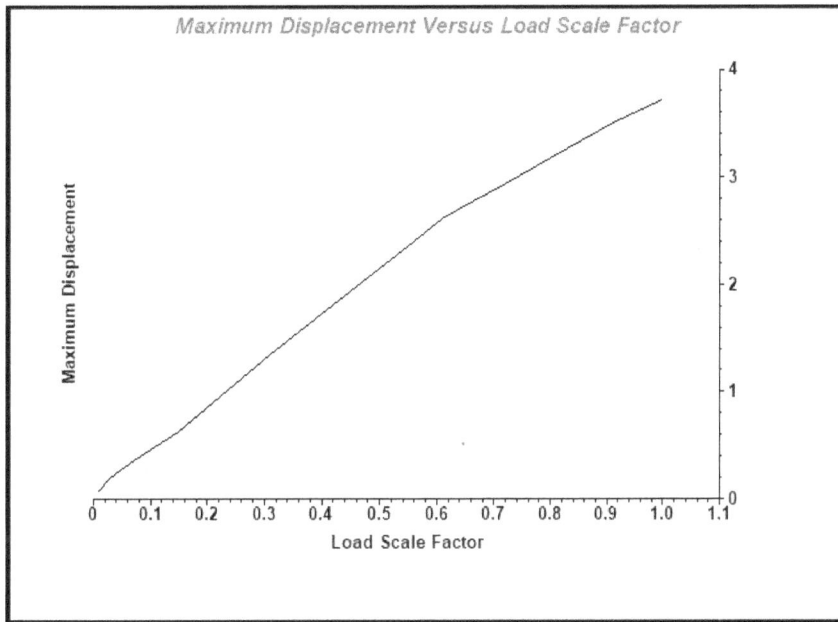

21. Save the model.

Nonlinear Materials

The goal in this chapter is to discuss nonlinear materials and how they differ in properties from linear materials. The chapter begins with a a discussion on the behaviors of nonlinear materials and then explains which nonlinear material properties can be assigned for use in an Autodesk® Nastran® In-CAD analysis.

Objectives

After completing this chapter, you will be able to:

- Describe how the behaviors of linear and nonlinear materials differ.
- List the nonlinear material types that can be created in Autodesk Nastran In-CAD.
- Assign nonlinear material properties to a material being used in an analysis.

Lesson: Working with Nonlinear Materials

Overview

This lesson discusses the properties that can be used to define nonlinear materials for an Autodesk Nastran In-CAD analysis and how they are assigned to the materials used in an idealization.

Objectives

After completing this lesson, you will be able to:

- Describe how the behaviors of linear and nonlinear materials differ.
- List the nonlinear material types that can be created in Autodesk Nastran In-CAD.
- Assign nonlinear material properties to a material being used in an analysis.

Basics of Nonlinear Materials

In a linear material model, the stress-strain relationship must be linear with a slope of E, Young's Modulus (Hooke's law):

$\sigma = E^*\varepsilon$

Material nonlinearity is a concern whenever the response at the operating loads causes strain levels in a material beyond the portion of the stress-strain curve that can reasonably be approximated as linear. Many materials have curves that deviate small amounts from linear for large amounts of strain so that, with all the other uncertainty in the model, there would be little value in a nonlinear material model. On the other hand, many curves deviate from linear almost immediately to such a degree that only the roughest trend studies can be made with a linear approximation.

The constant of proportionality in a linear material model is Young's Modulus. This represents the slope of the linear portion of the stress-strain curve (see image below). For highly nonlinear materials, this modulus may only be applicable at very low strains.

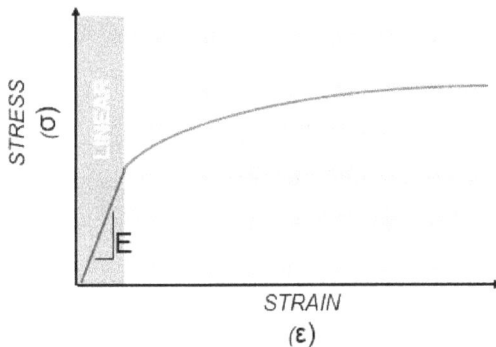

Nonlinear material models of common engineering materials are defined by specifying their stress-strain curves. Most stress-strain curves represent only the tensile response. When a material has the same response in tension and compression, it is said to be symmetric. Cast iron is a good example of an asymmetric stress-strain behavior as it is stronger in compression than tension.

Types of Nonlinear Materials

There are several types of material nonlinearity that might be present in a structural analysis:

- Nonlinear elastic
- Bi-linear elasto-plastic
- Multi-linear plastic
- Hyperelastic
- Viscoelastic

Simplified models of stress-strain curves are shown below:

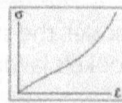

| Linear | Nonlinear Elastic | Plastic | Hyperelastic (Elastomers) |

A nonlinear material model can be defined as nonlinear elastic where the part returns to a zero strain state when the load is removed, or elasto-plastic where permanent strain begins to accumulate after reaching the yield strength of the material.

Additionally, an elasto-plastic stress-strain curve can be input as bi-linear, where only an elastic modulus and a plasticity or hardening modulus are entered. It can also be defined as a multi-linear stress-stress curve where the true nonlinearity of the plastic range can be captured with a series of points.

Autodesk Nastran In-CAD enables the definition of two other nonlinear material models, hyperelastic, for rubber and other elastomeric materials, and viscoelastic, for time-dependent response such as creep. Each of these nonlinear material models requires more detailed knowledge of their behavior as it is not quite like common structural materials.

Stress-Strain Curves

As you can see in the image below, nylon, aluminum and cast iron are materials with 75% of their working range in the nonlinear state. They require the use of an FEA program like Autodesk Nastran In-CAD to calculate the structural response to operating loads.

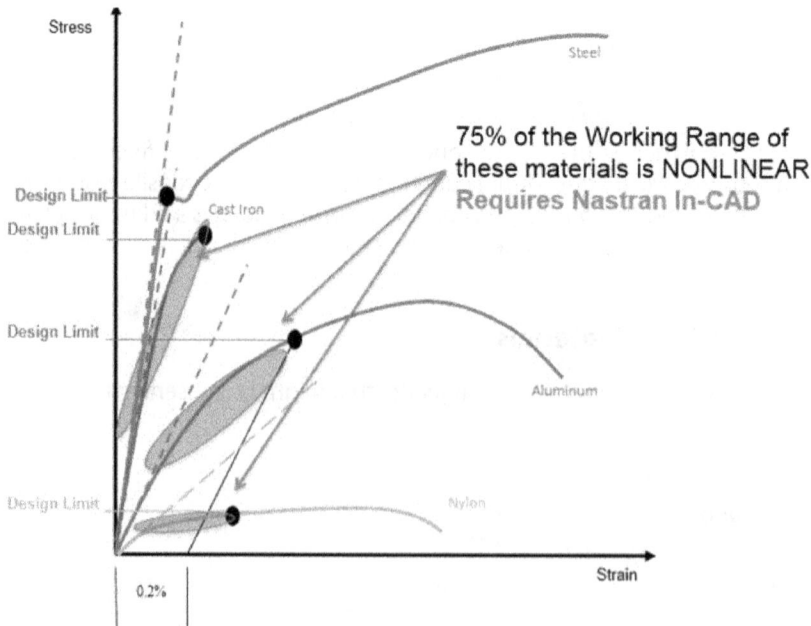

Stress-strain curves for metals are typically measured in tension or compression tests. The tensile test for metals is ASTM E8 and enables multiple strain rates and material temperatures. The graphs below show stress-strain curves for 4340 Steel and 2024 Aluminum. You can see that the steel curves show a consistent slope, or Young's Modulus until yield. The aluminum curve shows the variation in stress-strain response as different material orientations are examined. The curve also shows that 2024-T3 is asymmetric in that its tensile and compressive responses differ.

Note: Both these curves were extracted from Mil Handbook 5H, a publicly available resource with a lot of good material reference data.

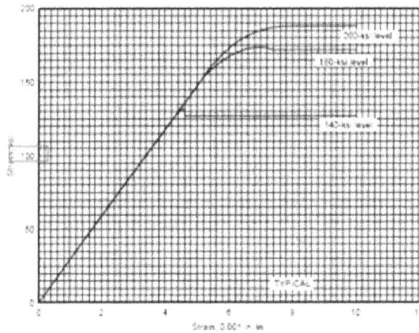

AISI 4340 Steel @ Room Temp
140, 180, 200 ksi yield strengths
MIL-HDBK-5H
1 December 1998

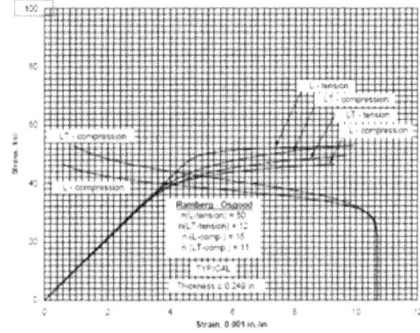

Al 2024-T3 @ Room Temp
Tensile & Compressive Curves
L (Longitudinal) and LT (Long Transverse) refer to grain direction
MIL-HDBK-5H
1 December 1998

These curves below for Noryl, a GE Plastics PPO, were measured using ASTM D638, the standard tensile test for plastics. The curve on the left shows how the stress-strain relationship in plastics can vary with injection molding flow direction. The curves on the right show how the same material can have differing stress-strain responses at different strain, or loading, rates and temperatures.

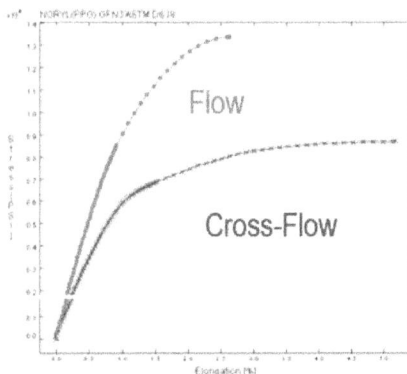

Noryl (PPO) Tensile Curves
Variations with Flow Orientation
GE Plastics

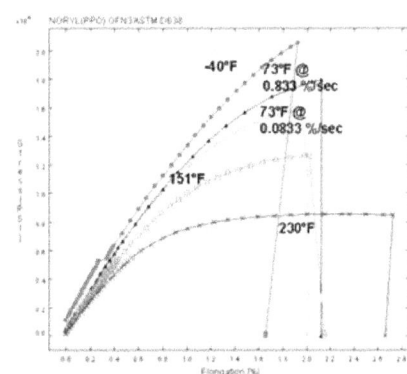

Noryl (PPO) Tensile Curves
Variations with Temperature and Strain Rate
GE Plastics

From these brief examples, you can see how quickly a nonlinear material investigation can get very complex. Therefore, it is recommend that you get the most applicable stress-strain data for the material that you are using or considering to determine if material nonlinearity is even an issue for the strain levels you are operating in. This level can be determined from an initial linear material analysis. If you decide that a nonlinear material model is required, try to find the curve that best represents your expected environment. Then, if required, bracket the results with 2-3 different curves to see how sensitive the response of interest is to this nonlinearity. If there is a difference and you cannot decide which material model is most correct, choose conservatively or back up your analysis with test data.

When post-processing results of a nonlinear material model, it is important to understand how the material yields on an element basis. Internal to each element are Gauss points where stresses and/or strains are calculated. For a nonlinear material, Nastran In-CAD does a table lookup on the stress-strain curve for each Gauss point stress, then it reports an average of all Gauss points (which is the center stress) and extrapolates the Gauss point values to the corners.

If an element undergoes a pure axial load, all Gauss points will yield at the same time, so the center stress will match the input stress-strain curve exactly. In the bending case, the outer Gauss points yield first then the inner points. This means the average center stress may not match the input stress-strain curve exactly during abrupt changes of slope on the input curve. This is because some Gauss points are on one point of the curve and the others are on another. If there is a large difference between the input stress-strain curve and the output stress results, a refined mesh is recommended.

The two images below show the stress-strain curves for two different mesh densities. You can see how a finer mesh follows the input stress-strain curve more accurately.

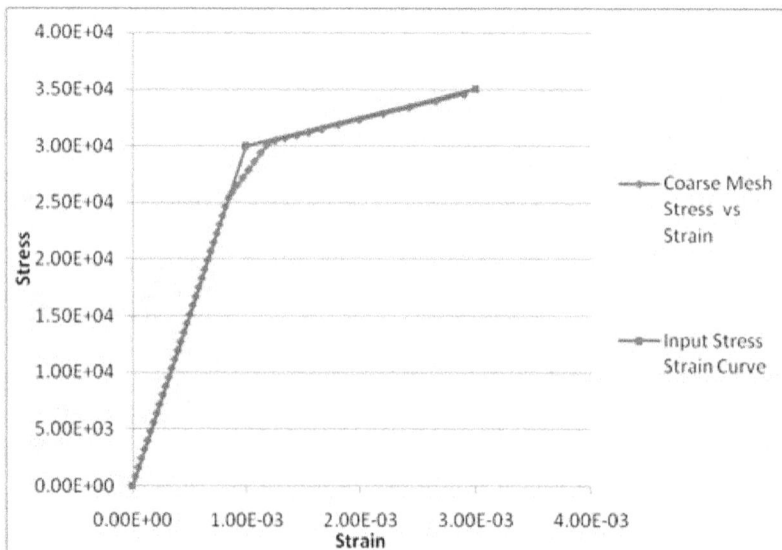

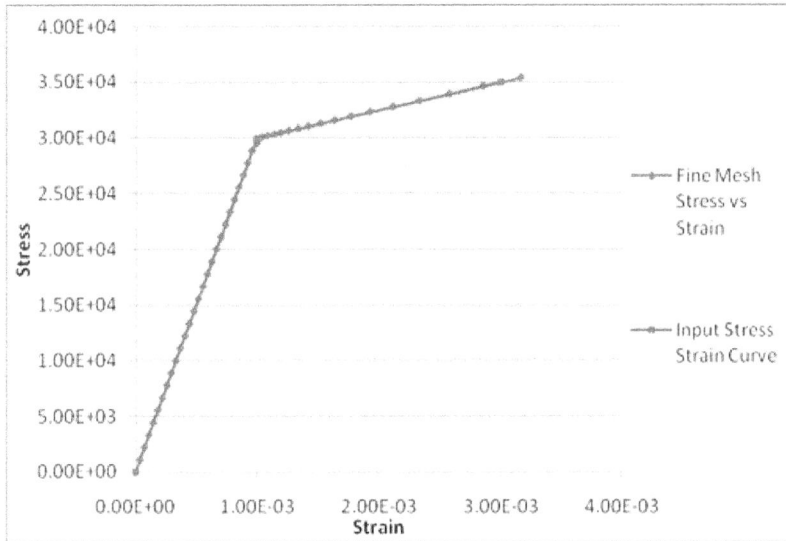

It is also important to note that since the corner stresses are extrapolated from the Gauss points, their stress values can often exceed the stress values on the stress-strain curve. If there is a large difference between the center stress values and the corner stresses, it is recommended to refine the mesh to get a more accurate representation of the yielding that is occurring.

Setting Nonlinear Material Properties

When assigning material nonlinear properties, the Nonlinear Material Data dialog box is used. At the top of this dialog box, you can select the type of nonlinear material that is to be created and the dialog box updates to provide you with the required options. For example, in the following image, the Nonlinear Elastic option has been selected and its options are now available.

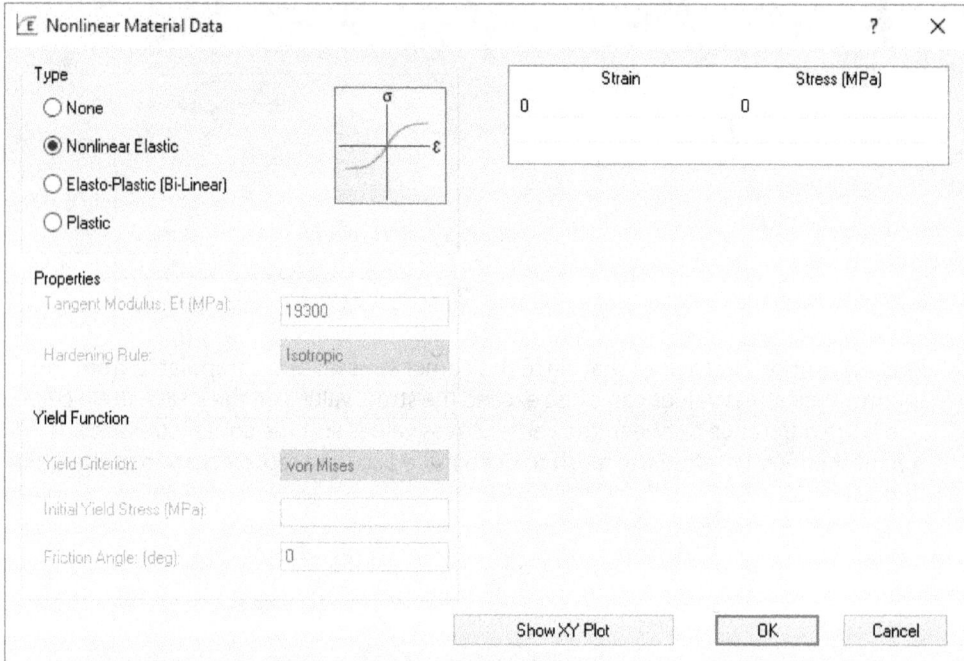

Nonlinear Elastic Materials

Nonlinear Elastic materials spring back elastically. There is no permanent deformation created when the material goes plastic (e.g. rubber). The stress vs. strain data must be true stress vs. true strain. The slope between any two points must not be negative.

- Nonlinear Elastic materials require that you enter the full stress-strain data in the form of a table to define the material's nonlinear elastic behavior.
- Values can be entered for both the first and the third quadrant i.e., tension and compression, passing through (0, 0). If the values for compression are not given, it will be assumed to be identical to tension values and the first row has to be (0, 0).
- You can input the table values by double-clicking the fields and entering or copying values.
- Click Show XY Plot to review the plot once the values are entered.

The following example shows the values that were entered in the table and the resulting Stress vs. Strain plot for the nonlinear elastic material.

Strain	Stress (MPa)
-0.0085	-55000
-0.0055	-52500
-0.004	-50000
-0.002	-30000
0	0
0.002	30000
0.004	40000
0.006	42500
0.008	45000

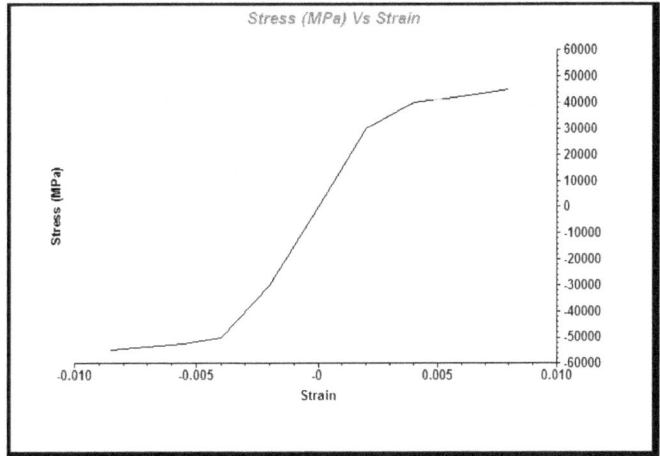

Elasto-Plastic (Bi-Linear) Materials

For this material type, the plastic region can be defined by a Plasticity Modulus (H). The plasticity modulus is in turn related to the Tangent Modulus (E_T) and Young's Modulus (E) as follows:

$$H = \frac{E_T}{1 - E_T/E}$$

By default, the value of Tangent Modulus (E_T) is set to 10% of the Young's Modulus. Thus, the default values ensure a 10% slope for the linear plastic part of the material's stress-strain curve. Autodesk Nastran In-CAD calculates the stress values by linearly extrapolating outside the table and linearly interpolating inside the table based on the last two end points of the curve.

Plastic Materials

For materials where plastic behavior is being assumed, the stress-strain values have to be entered in a similar way to the Nonlinear Elastic option. These values must be defined in the first quadrant. The first two sets of points are filled in automatically so that the slope of the line connecting the two points is always equal to the Young's Modulus value of the material. Hence, based on the Initial Yield Stress value, the amount of plastic strain percentage in the table is adjusted to maintain this relationship. These first two points cannot be deleted or modified. In terms of the remaining options for this material type, it is similar to Elasto-Plastic but does not use a Tangent Modulus.

The following options apply to both Elasto-Plastic and Plastic options.

- The available Hardening Rules options include:
  - Isotropic
  - Kinematic
  - Isotropic + Kinematic

When isotropic hardening is assumed, the material work-hardens and becomes stronger in all directions. For a simple 1D (one-dimensional) stress-strain case, if the direction of strain is reversed, the maximum stress reached (in the tensile work-hardened state) must be achieved in the opposite (compressive) direction before yielding will resume.

When kinematic hardening is assumed, yielding the material in a particular direction shifts the stress threshold at which yielding will occur for different load directions. For a simple 1D example, the difference between the tensile maximum stress and the compressive yield strength (after reversal of the load) is two times the original yield strength.

Consider the images below, which quantify the difference between the two hardening models for a simple 1D case. For both graphs, if the part is taken beyond the yield stress in tension, it begins to deform plastically and it work hardens and becomes stronger. If the part is taken to a maximum stress (point A) and the load is released, the part unloads along the dashed line. If the part is loaded again in tension, no additional plastic deformation occurs until the stress reaches point A again. However, if the part is unloaded and then put into compression, it compresses elastically along the dashed line until it reaches point B, and then it yields in compression. The difference between the two hardening models is the stress value of the compressive yield point (B).

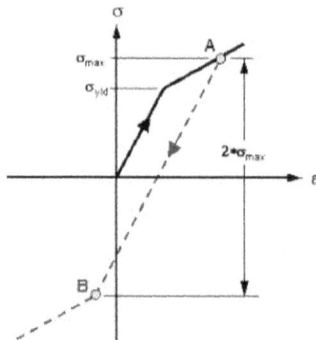

Isometric Hardening

The change in stress from point A to point B is twice the maximum stress obtained.

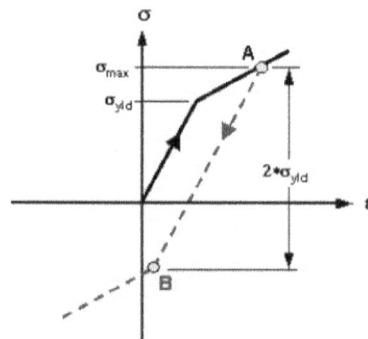

Kinematic Hardening

The change in stress from point A to point B is twice the initial yield stress.

(Cont.)	Consider an example where the material yield strength = 36 ksi. The material is yielded in tension, resulting in work hardening to a stress level of 40 ksi.

> - For the isotropic hardening model, if the load is reversed, a compressive stress of -40ksi (point B in the Isometric Hardening graph, the inverse of the tensile yield strength after work hardening) must be reached before yielding occurs in compression. Once work hardening occurs, the yield point extends in all directions (regardless of the sign/direction of the stress). This method is recommended for one-way bending.
> - For the kinematic hardening model, if the load is reversed, yielding resumes at a compressive stress of -32 ksi [point B in the Kinematic Hardening graph, max stress with work hardening - 2 * original yield strength, or 40 ksi - (2 * 36 ksi)]. This method is recommended when stress reversals occur (two-way bending).
>
> The Isotropic + Kinematic hardening rule averages the isotropic hardening and kinematic hardening models.
>
> For more information on this topic, refer to the following recommended texts.
>
> - Mechanical Engineering Design (5th Edition), Joseph Shigley & Charles Mischke, McGraw Hill 1989 (Chapter 5 - Materials)
> - Failure of Materials in Mechanical Design (2nd Edition), Jack A. Collins, John Wiley & Sons 1993 (Chapter 6.6: Distortion Energy Theory (Huber-Von Mises-Hencky Theory)

- The available Yield Criterion options include the following options. Modify the Initial Yield Stress values, as required, to accurately define the material.

  - **von Mises**: This is most widely used for ductile materials. It requires an Initial Yield Stress value.

  - **Tresca**: Also applicable to ductile materials, but it is more conservative than von Mises. It requires an Initial Yield Stress value.

  - **Mohr-Coulomb**: This theory is applicable to frictional materials like soil and concrete. It requires a 2*Cohesion value, in units of stress and a Friction Angle value, 0<F<45 in degrees.

  - **Drucker-Prager:** This is an approximation to the Mohr-Coulomb theory, it is a modification to the von Mises theory. It is also applicable to frictional materials like soil and concrete. It requires a 2*Cohesion value, in units of stress, and a Friction Angle value, 0<F<45 in degrees.

Procedure: To Create a new Nonlinear Material

1. In the Material dialog box select Nonlinear in the Analysis Specific Data section.

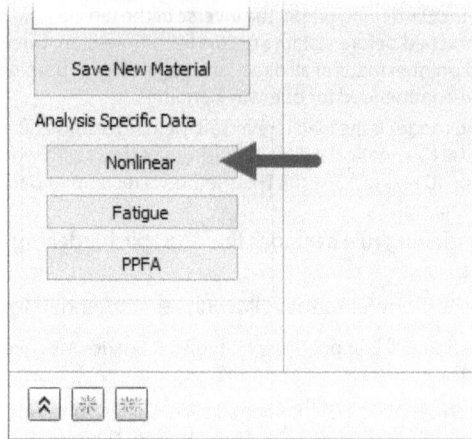

2. Select the Type of nonlinear material that is to be defined. Based on the type selected, the Nonlinear Material Data dialog box will update with the required fields.

3. Define the options and table values as required, to define the nonlinear material properties. When entering table data for the Nonlinear Elastic and Plastic types select each cell and enter or copy a value from a table.

    ▪ Ensure that the Initial Yield Stress (MPa) value is changed from its default value to match that of the material being used.

    ▪ For Elasto-Plastic (Bi-Linear) ensure that the Tangent Modulus, Et (MPa) is changed from its default value (10% of E) to that of the material being used (assuming you have material data that is more accurate than the 0.1 E assumption).

4. Click Show XY plot to review the plot of the material's stress/strain values. This is only available for the Nonlinear Elastic and Plastic types.

5. Click OK to close the Nonlinear Material Data dialog box.

Guidelines for Working with Nonlinear Materials

The following guidelines should be followed when building a nonlinear finite element analysis model with nonlinear materials:

- When performing an analysis that will have large amounts of strain but where permanent deformation is not expected, it is recommended to use a nonlinear elastic material.

- Check that the slope of your stress-strain curve (in the linear region) matches the Young's Modulus of the material.

- Stress-strain data should be taken from a true stress-strain curve, not an engineering stress-strain curve. A true stress-strain curve takes into account the "necking" or reduction of cross-sectional area during a standard axial pull test. If the slope of the stress-strain curve is very "flat" (or negative) you may get a non-positive definite error during the analysis. If acceptable, remove the flat area on the stress-strain curve and re-run the analysis. If you must use a flat or negative slope stress-strain curve you can try and force a solution by turning SOLUTIONERROR=ON and FACTDIAG=0. Also, try setting NLMATSFACT to 0.1 – 0.5. These parameters can be set in the Parameters dialog box, under Solution Processor Parameters (select the Advanced Settings checkbox first).

- When using a nonlinear plastic material, it is recommended to use a stress-strain curve instead of the Bi-Linear method. The Bi-Linear method essentially creates a stress-strain curve with two different slopes. This abrupt change in the elastic modulus makes it more difficult to converge on a solution. In addition, a stress-strain curve more faithfully represents the true behavior of the material. The Bi-Linear method is a rougher approximation.

> For more information on the options for the Nonlinear Materials refer to Autodesk Nastran In-CAD Help and search for "Nonlinear Material".

Exercise: Flexural Test Fixture

In this exercise, you will duplicate the three-point bending test required in ASTM D638 for plastic material flexural testing. The analysis will feature a section of polymer (acrylonitrile butadiene styrene) subjected to a uniform stress (uniaxial tension test) in a test fixture. You will setup a nonlinear material model and will intentionally over-deform the beam into the apparent nonlinear and post-yield range of the material. Finally, you will unload the test bar to look for permanent deformation. To reduce simulation time, you will use quarter symmetry of the model.

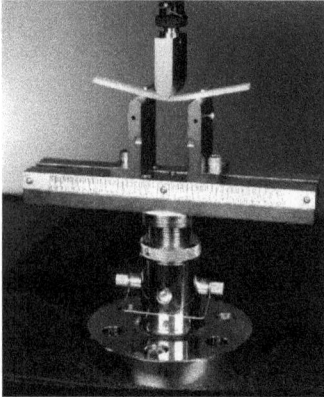

It is important to note that some polymers behave differently in tension and compression. In such materials, the Flexural Modulus = Average Modulus. Nonlinearities cause stress redistribution during bending, meaning that linear calculations are no longer valid.

Prepare the Model for use in Nastran In-CAD

1. Open the file *C:\Autodesk Nastran InCAD 2019 Essentials Exercise Files\Flex_Test_Fixture\Flex Test.iam*. This assembly was modeled as 1/4 of the test fixture.

2. Activate the Autodesk Nastran In-CAD environment.

Setup a Nonlinear Static Analysis

In this task, you will edit the default linear static analysis and change it to a Nonlinear Static.

1. Right-click on Analysis 1 [Linear Static] node at the top of the Analysis sub-tree and select Edit.

2. In the Analysis dialog box:

    -   Maintain the default name.
    -   Select Nonlinear Static from the Type drop-down list.
    -   On the Output Controls tab, ensure that both Stress and Strain are selected in the Output Sets section. Because stress-strain curves for plastic materials often have shallow slopes in the plastic region, it is preferable to view results in terms of strain.
    -   On the Options tab, ensure that Large Displacement is set to On.
    -   On the Model State tab, note that both a Design View and Level of Detail can be selected for analysis. Maintain the respective Default and Master options for these views.

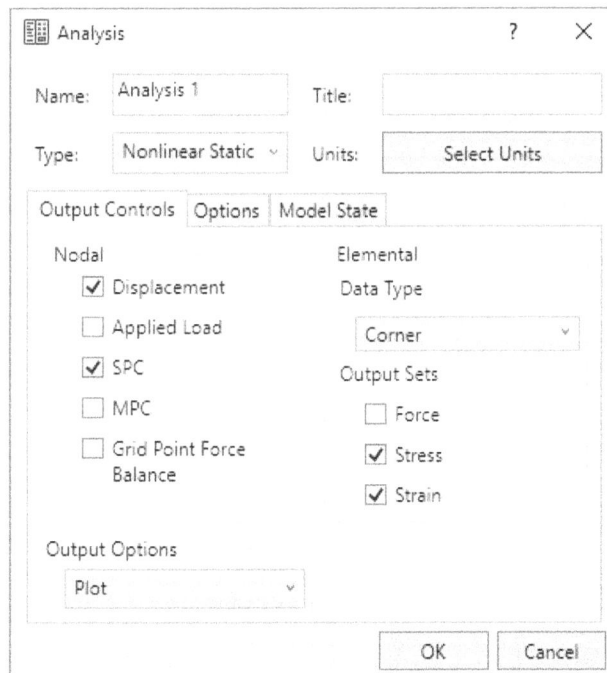

3. Click OK.

Assign new Idealizations to the Assembly Components

In this task, you will create a new idealization that uses Alloy Steel and assign it to the load pin and support pin. Additionally, you will create a second idealization that uses a nonlinear ABS material to assign to the test piece. For this exercise, you will assume the yield strength at the point on the curve where the slope of the stress/strain curve is 0.

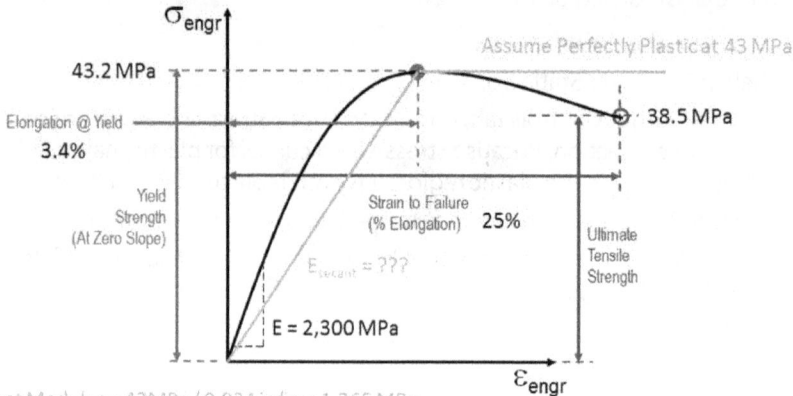

Secant Modulus = 43MPa / 0.034 in/in = 1,265 MPa

1. Create a new idealization using the following settings and add it to the analysis:

    - Enter **Alloy Steel** as the name of the new idealization.
    - Ensure that Solid Elements is selected as the Type of element.
    - Create a new material and select Alloy Steel as the material from the Autodesk Material Library.
    - In the Idealizations dialog box, select Associated Geometry and select the two pins shown below.

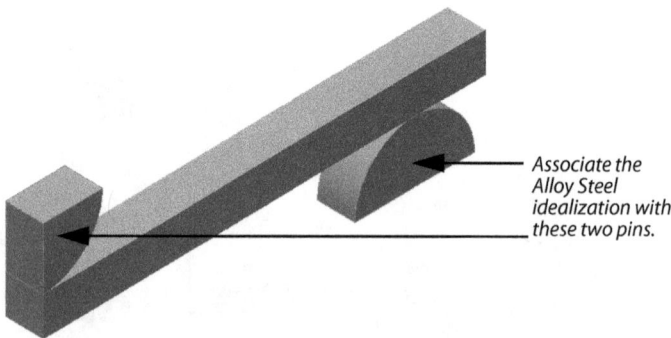

Associate the Alloy Steel idealization with these two pins.

    - Click ⬢ (New) to create the idealization and keep the dialog box open to create another.

2. The next idealization that is required uses a nonlinear material. Use the following settings and add it to the analysis:

    ▪ Enter **ABS Plastic** as the name of the new idealization.
    ▪ Ensure that Solid Elements is selected as the Type of element.
    ▪ Create a new material and select **Acrylonitrile Butadiene Styrene** as the material from the Autodesk Material Library.
    ▪ Enter **1265** MPa as the new value of E.

3. In the Analysis Specific Data section, select Nonlinear. Define the settings as follows:

    ▪ On the Nonlinear Material Data dialog box, set the Type to Plastic.
    ▪ Ensure the Hardening Rule is set to Isotropic.
    ▪ Enter **43 MPa** as the Initial Yield Stress.
    ▪ In the table, double-click in the Strain column in the third row (not counting the column header - currently this row is blank), and enter 0.5. (This is 50%.)
    ▪ Double-click in the adjacent Stress cell, and enter **43**.

4. Click Show XY Plot. The XY Plot displays.

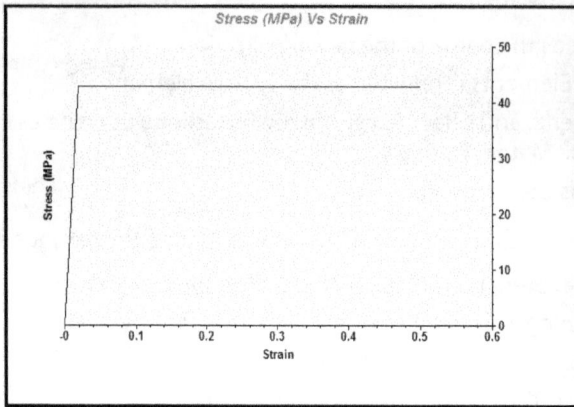

5. Click OK in the XY Plot, Nonlinear Material Data, and Material dialog boxes.

6. In the Idealizations dialog box, select Associated Geometry and select the test piece in the assembly (Test Sample). Click OK.

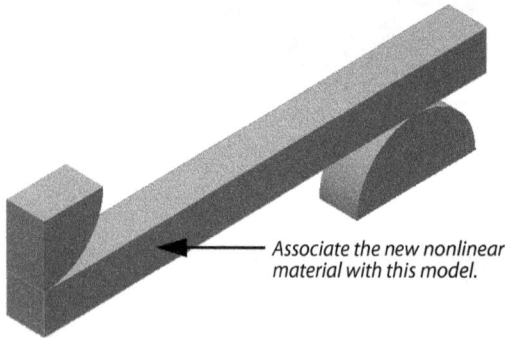

Associate the new nonlinear material with this model.

7. Remove Solid 1 from the analysis.

Constrain & Load the Model

In this task, you will constrain the model to take into account the symmetry assumption that is being used to analyze 1/4 of the test fixture. You will also add two constraints to the pins. One constraint will fix the support pin to remove all degrees of freedom and the second will be added to the movable pin that enables a pushing load (enforced motion) in the Z direction only. To complete this task, a pushing and gravity load will be added.

1. Create a constraint that defines the Y-axis symmetry using the following settings:

   - In the Degrees of Freedom section of the dialog box, select [y] (Y Symmetry) to preselect the degrees of freedom that are to be assigned to a reference face. Only the Ty, Rx, and Rz degrees of freedom should be selected.
   - Assign the constraint to Subcase1.
   - Select the three faces of the test fixture, as shown below, as the reference faces.
   - Select Preview to show the constraint on the model.
   - Modify the density of the constraint's display, as required.
   - Click [✳] (New) to create the constraint and keep the Constraint dialog box open to create another.

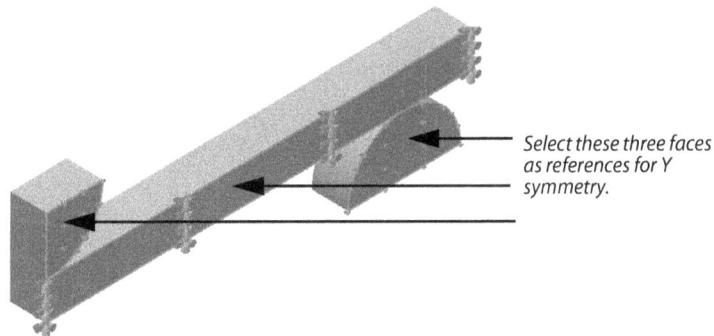

Select these three faces as references for Y symmetry.

2. Create a constraint that defines the X-axis symmetry using the following settings:

- In the Degrees of Freedom section of the dialog box, select ⬚ˣ (X Symmetry) to preselect the degrees of freedom that are to be assigned to a reference face. Only the Tx, Ry, and Rz degrees of freedom should be selected.
- Assign the constraint to Subcase1.
- Select the two faces of the test fixture, as shown below, as the reference faces for the constraint.
- Select Preview to show the constraint on the model.
- Modify the density of the constraint's display, as required.

- Click ✳ (New) to create the constraint and begin the creation of a third constraint.

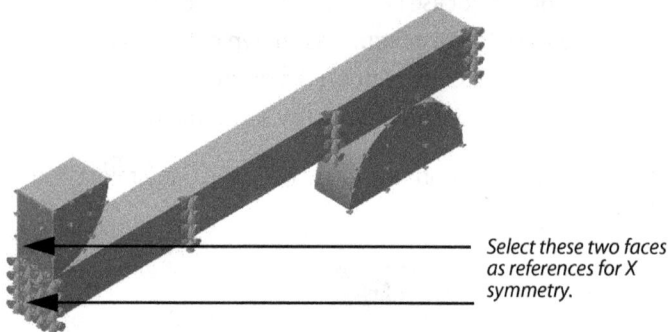

Select these two faces as references for X symmetry.

3. Create a constraint that fixes the support pin using the following settings:

- In the Degrees of Freedom section of the dialog box, select 📐 (Fixed) to preselect the degrees of freedom that are to be assigned to a reference face. All degrees of freedom should be selected.
- Assign the constraint to Subcase1.
- Select the face of the test fixture, as shown below, as the reference face for the constraint.
- Select Preview to show the constraint on the model.
- Modify the density of the constraint's display, as required.

Click ✳ (New) to create the constraint and begin the creation of a fourth constraint.

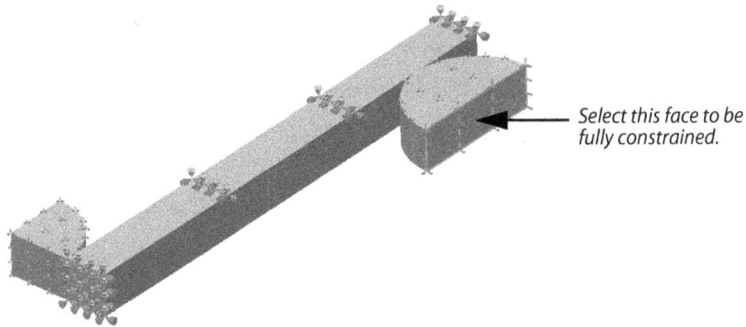

Select this face to be fully constrained.

4. Create a constraint in the Z-direction using the following settings:

   - In the Degrees of Freedom section, deactivate all checkboxes except the Tz direction.
   - Assign the constraint to Subcase1.
   - Select the face of the test fixture, as shown below, as the reference face for the constraint.
   - Select Preview to show the constraint on the model.
   - Modify the density of the constraint's display, as required.
   - Click OK.

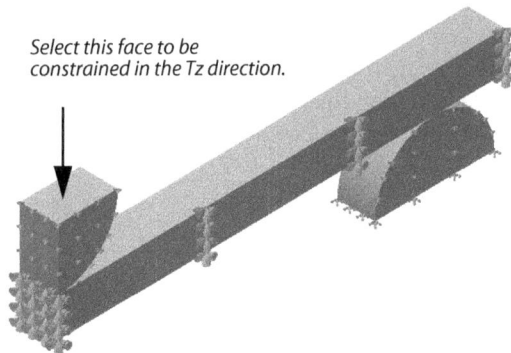

Select this face to be constrained in the Tz direction.

Note: To load the pin, it pushes the center of the beam through a defined displacement. This enforced displacement is defined using a combination of this constraint and a pushing load that we will add in the next step.

5. Create a load using the following settings:

- Set the Type of load as Enforced Motion.
- Set the Sub Type of load as Displacement.
- Enter **-35** as the Tz value.
- Assign the constraint to Subcase1.
- Select the face of the test fixture, as shown below, as the reference face for the load.
- Select Preview to show the load on the model.
- Modify the density of the load's display, as required.
- Click ⊞ (New) to create the load and begin the creation of a new load.

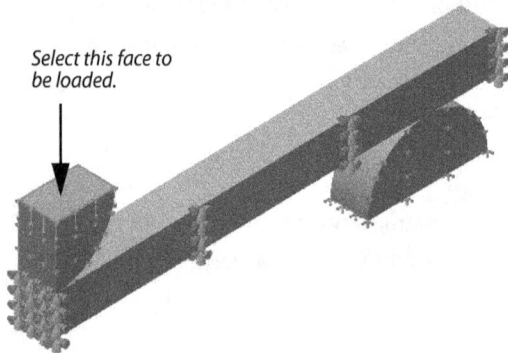

Select this face to be loaded.

6. Create a load to represent gravity using the following settings. This is assigned to keep the test piece against the fixed pin during release and to stabilize the solution when the test piece is not tightly held between the pins.

- Set the Type of load as Gravity.
- Enter **-9807** as the Fz value.
- Assign the load to Subcase1.
- Select Preview to show the load on the model. Only a G is displayed in the graphics window indicating this load.
- Click OK.

Assign Contacts to the Model

In this task, you will use the Automatic option to detect contacts and assign them to the analysis. Additionally, you will change the default Bonded contact type so that movement is permitted.

1. In the Contacts panel, click ☁ (Automatic) to launch automatic contact creation.

2. Expand the newly created Surface Contacts node. Two contacts have been identified and were automatically created between the Test Sample and Pin components.

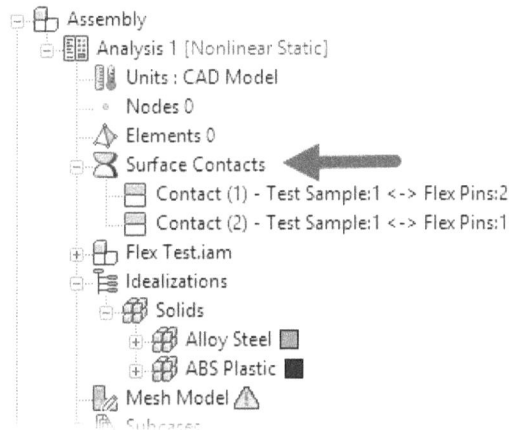

3. The default contact type for both contacts is Bonded. For this assembly, some movement is to be permitted. Select Contact (1) in the Surface Contacts node, right-click and select Edit.

4. In the Surface Contact dialog, select Separation in the Contact Type drop-down list.

5. Enter **20** as the Max Activation Distance value. Click OK.

6. Edit Contact (2) using the same settings.

    Note: The icon associated with both contacts now indicates that there is separation.

Mesh the Model

In this task, you will globally mesh the model and add local mesh control between the contacting faces.

1. In the Analysis 1 sub-tree, right-click on Mesh Model, and click Edit to open the Mesh Settings dialog box. The current settings are the default values that were assigned when the analysis was created.

2. In the Mesh Settings dialog box, make the following changes:

    - Enter **5** as the Element Size.
    - Set the Element Order option to Linear.
    - Clear the selection of the Continuous Meshing option.
    - Click Generate Mesh.
    - Click OK to close the Mesh Settings dialog box.

3. In the Analysis 1 sub-tree, right-click on Mesh Model, and click Add Mesh Control.

4. In the Mesh Control dialog box make the following changes:

    - Enter **2** as the Face Data Element Size.
    - Click in the Selected Faces box, and select the four faces that are in contact with one another, as shown below.
    - Click OK.

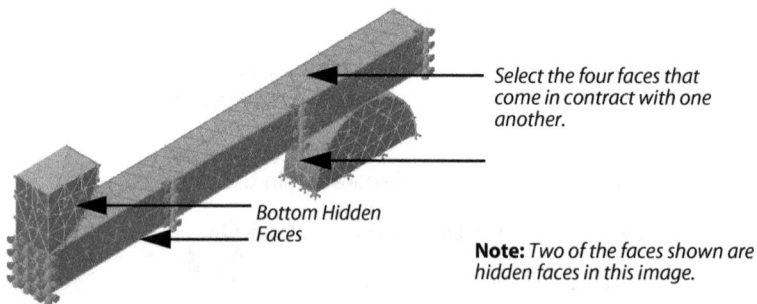

Select the four faces that come in contract with one another.

Bottom Hidden Faces

Note: *Two of the faces shown are hidden faces in this image.*

5. Right-click on the Mesh Model node and select Generate Mesh to update the mesh with the new mesh control.

Define an Additional Subcase in the Analysis

In this task, you create an additional subcase to represent the "released" state of the test fixture. This subcase will have all the existing constraints but a different load.

1. Right-click on Subcases, and click New. Enter **Release** as the new name for the subcase.

2. Select the four constraints to be automatically added to the new subcase.

3. Select the gravity load (Load 2) to be automatically added to the new subcase and click OK.

4. Right-click on the Loads node in the Release subcase and select New.

5. Create the new load using the following settings:

    - Set the Type of load as Enforced Motion.
    - Set the Sub Type of load as Displacement.
    - Enter **0** as the Tz value.
    - Assign the load to Release.
    - Select the face of the test fixture, as shown below, as the references for the load.
    - Click OK.

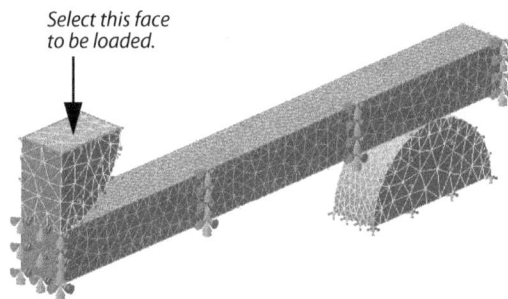

Select this face to be loaded.

Define the Nonlinear Setup Options for the Subcases

In this task, you will define the nonlinear setup options for these two subcases.

1. Right-click on the Nonlinear Setup 1 node in Subcase 1and click Edit.

2. On the Nonlinear Setup dialog box, set the Intermediate Output option to On.

3. Enter **20** as the Number of Increments that should be calculated.

    Note: A finer calculation increment is helpful when trying to capture large displacements, surface contact, and nonlinear material behavior.

4. Click OK.

5. Edit the Nonlinear Setup options for the Release subcase in the same way so that a finer calculation increment is used (Number of Increments = 20) and the intermediate output is generated and stored during the analysis.

6. Right-click on Analysis 1 in the Model Tree and select Nonlinear Options. Ensure that the Generate Intermediate Results is also set in this location.

Run the Analysis & View the Results

In this task, you will run the analysis and review the results.

1. Run the analysis. Click OK when the analysis is complete. Subcases 1 and 2 will solve for 20 load steps each. Subcase 2 will use the results from Subcase 1 as its initial conditions.

    Note: The analysis will likely take approximately 15 minutes to complete. Optionally, to continue with this exercise, you can open the file *C:\Autodesk Nastran InCAD 2019 Essentials Exercise Files\Flex_Test_Fixture\Completed\Flex Test2.iam*, right-click on the Results node and select Load. This will load the *11znwbzda.FNO* results file from the *...\Flex_Test_Fixture\Completed\Flex Test2\InCAD\FEA* directory.

2. Nonlinear Static analyzes do not have predefined analysis plot templates generated. To Display the Displacement results plot, right-click on Results in the Analysis 1 sub-tree and select Edit. The Plot dialog box opens.

3. Set the following options in the Plot dialog box to view the Displacement results:

    - In the subcases drop-down list, select INCR 20, LOAD = 1.0.
    - Select Displacement from the Result Data drop-down list.
    - Select TOTAL from the Type drop-down list.
    - On the Deform Options tab, change the Deformation Scale to Actual and maintain the 1.0 value.
    - Select the Visibility Options tab, and click Hide All.

4. Click ![Display icon] (Display) in the Plot section to display the result plot in the graphics window. Change the orientation of the model to Bottom using the ViewCube. As expected, this value is approximately the push value of 35.

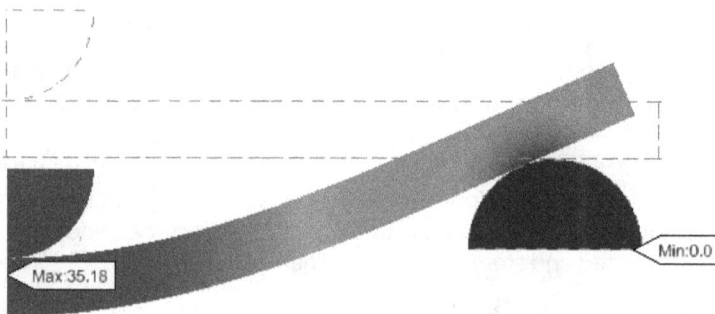

5. In the Contour Options tab, select Strain from the Result Data drop-down list and

    SOLID VON MISES STRAIN from the Type drop-down list. Toggle ⬚ (Display) if the
    result plot does not update.

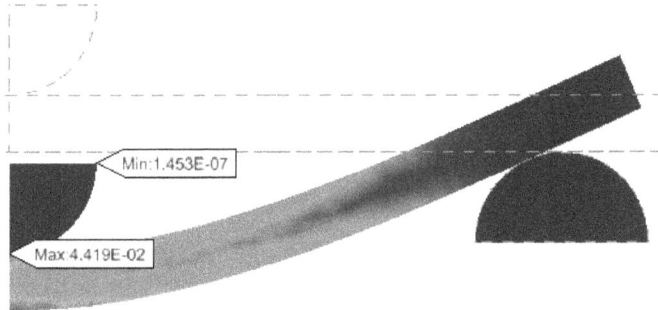

6. In the Contour Options tab, select Stress from the Result Data drop-down list and

    SOLID VON MISES STRESS from the Type drop-down list. Toggle ⬚ (Display) if the
    result plot does not update. Based on the displayed increment, you can see that the
    max stress has been reached. To determine the point at which the model yields, you
    can display previous increments to locate the point.

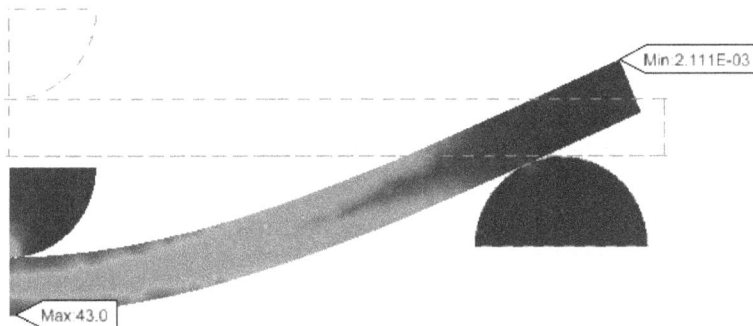

7. Review INCR 15 and INCR 16 in the initial subcase. The yield stress (43 Mpa) is reached
    between these increments or between 75 and 80% of load.

8. Change the subcase to INCR 20, LOAD=2.0.

   ▪ Display the Solid Von Mises Stress result. This plot shows the residual stress in the test piece due to the local yielding of the part.

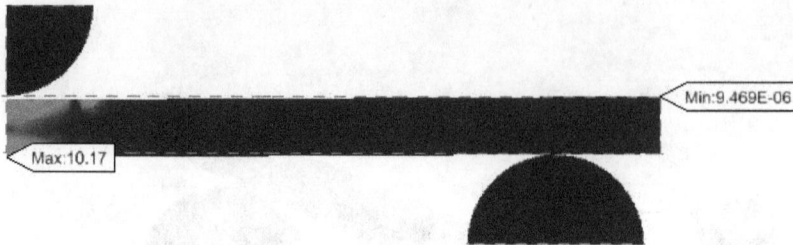

   Min:9.469E-06

   Max:10.17

   ▪ Display the total Displacement result. This plot shows the residual deformation after the test piece has been released, and it clearly indicates that permanent deformation of the material has occurred.

   Min:0.0

   Max:0.8373

9. Click OK to close the Plot dialog box.

10. Right-click on the Results node for the analysis and select Multiset Animation Settings. This enables you to customize settings so that you can display a multiset animation.

11. Click the Contour Options tab. Select Strain from the Result Data drop-down list and SOLID VON MISES STRAIN from the Type drop-down list.

12. Click the Deform Options tab. Set the vector option to Displacement and the Type to Total. Change the Deformation Scale to Actual, and specify a Value of 1.0.

13. Click the Animation Options tab and change the Mode to Half.

14. In the Output Set section, set the Start Set option to INCR 1, LOAD = 0.05 and the End Set option to INCR 20, LOAD = 2.0.

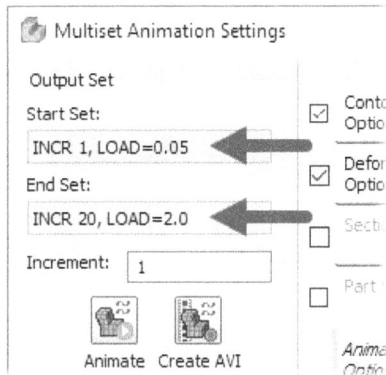

15. Click the Visibility Options tab and hide all options.

16. In the Output Set section, click (Animate) to view an animation of the analysis.

Select (Animate) a second time to stop the animation. Click OK to close the dialog box.

Determine the Force Required to Bend the Beam

In this task, you will find the total force to bend the beam.

1. Right-click on the push constraint (Constraint 4 if the constraints were created in the order described in this exercise.) from Subcase 1, and select SPC Summation.

2. Select INCR 20, LOAD = 1.0 as the Subcase in the drop-down list.

3. Note the Total Force is reported. The total force is the highest for this increment. You can verify this by checking some of the other increments.

4. Close the dialog box.

5. Save the model.

> SPC Summation enables you to do single point constraint (SPC) force and moment summation for a single point constraint output. For more information on SPC Summation, refer to Autodesk Nastran In-CAD Help and search for "SPC Summation".

Nonlinear Transient Response Analysis

The goal in this chapter is to learn about nonlinear transient response analyzes in the Autodesk® Nastran® In-CAD environment. This analysis type is commonly used when the effects of inertia, damping, and transient loading are significant. You will learn to create a nonlinear transient response analysis, run it, and review Results plots and XY Plots.

Objectives

After completing this chapter, you will be able to:

- Create a new nonlinear transient response analysis.
- Define Damping in a nonlinear transient response analysis.
- Define the Nonlinear and Dynamics Setup options required in a nonlinear transient response analysis.
- Display the Results plot and XY Plot results for a nonlinear transient response analysis.

Lesson: Creating a Nonlinear Transient Response Analysis

Overview

This lesson discusses how you can create a new nonlinear transient response analysis in a model. It also discusses the settings in this analysis, which differ from those of the analysis types previously discussed in the learning guide. You will also learn to define damping, nonlinear settings, and time step settings that are used in a nonlinear transient response analysis.

Objectives

After completing this lesson, you will be able to:

- Create a new nonlinear transient response analysis.
- Define damping in a nonlinear transient response analysis.
- Define the Nonlinear and Timestep Setup options required in a nonlinear transient response analysis.
- Display the Results plot and XY Plot results for a nonlinear transient response analysis.

Basics of Nonlinear Response Analysis

If the effects of inertia, damping, and transient loading are significant, a nonlinear transient response analysis should be used. Additionally, "quasi-static" models that undergo buckling or other unstable loading conditions will often converge better in a nonlinear transient response analysis due to the inertia effects keeping the model stable.

Consider the following when preparing for a nonlinear transient response analysis:

- In most situations, it is recommended to perform a hand calculation to find the velocity at impact and then, start the two models near each other. This approach will net shorter analysis times and better fidelity than starting the two bodies at a physical distance (i.e., as in a drop test). A good method for calculating the small separation distance is to use the following equation. This separation distance will enable the solution of 2 time steps before impact. Additional time steps can be made smaller, if required.

    d = v * (2*dt)

    where:

    d = separation distance

    v = velocity

    dt = time increment

- When pre/post-impact behavior is required, using multiple subcases is a good way to fine-tune the analysis such that detailed time stepping can be used during impact, and a much coarser time-step can be used after impact.

- It is important to understand the linear response characteristics of the structure to get some idea of what the actual nonlinear frequencies and mode shapes are going to be. Find the mode that you consider to be the "dominate" response of the structure during/ after impact. Often times, the dominate load is the first mode of the structure. It can never be an exact representation, but the frequency can provide a starting point for several key input parameters:

    - Frequency range of interest - The frequency of the dominant mode.

    - Size of time step - Calculated using 1/f, and then assuming 100 data points per cycle would net: dt = 1/ (100*f).

    - Duration of analysis - Largely depends upon the velocity of the impact, the size of the model, and the flexibility of the model. A good estimate is to run the analysis for 2-5 cycles.

Creating a New Nonlinear Transient Response Analysis

To create a nonlinear transient response analysis you must either create a new analysis or edit an existing analysis and change the type of analysis to Nonlinear Transient Response. You can also select any additional options in the Analysis dialog box to define the output controls, options, and model state (Design View or Level of Detail to be analyzed).

When a nonlinear transient response analysis is created the Autodesk Nastran Model Tree displays as shown in the following image.

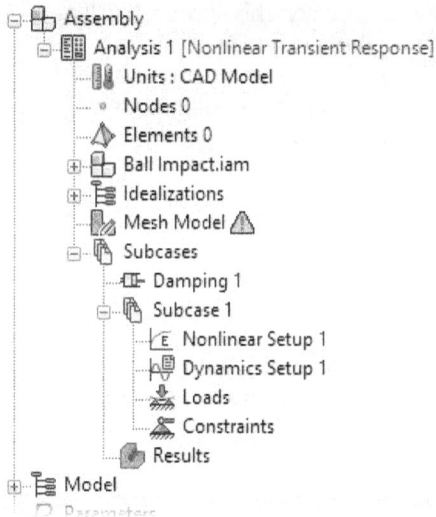

Additionally you must consider the following:

- Ensure that a required idealization exists or is created that contains any material properties that are specifically required for the analysis.
- Assign any constraints and loads required for the analysis.
- Assign any required surface contacts, as required, to fully describe the model being analyzed.
- Setup damping.
- Set the Nonlinear options that define the analysis.
- Set the Dynamics options that define the timesteps for the analysis.

A nonlinear transient response analysis requires both nonlinear and dynamic (timestep) setup steps. Damping is also included and must be assigned. The following describes these:

Nonlinear Setup

Nonlinear settings can be customized using the Nonlinear Setup node that gets created in the subcase of a nonlinear transient response analysis. To access the setup options, right-click on the Nonlinear Setup node in the Analysis subcase and select Edit. These are advanced overrides and typically do not need to be changed unless a model has trouble converging, and you are comfortable with the changes that are being made.

For more information on the options on the Nonlinear Setup dialog box, refer to Autodesk Nastran In-CAD Help and search for "Nonlinear Setup".

Dynamic Setup

Dynamics settings can be customized using the Dynamics Setup node that gets created in the subcase of a nonlinear transient response analysis. To access the setup options, right-click on the Dynamics Setup node in the analysis subcase and select Edit. The settings in the Dynamics Setup dialog box enable you to define the time steps that will be used through the analysis. The time interval can be set for a subcase, and any additional subcases can have unique settings that continue from the previous subcase.

The specific options that are available are described as follows:

- **Name**: Names the time step for the dynamics setup.
- **ID**: The ID of the property is automatically updated by Autodesk Nastran In-CAD.
- **Interval Listing**: Automatically generates an interval listing based on the interval setup.
- **Interval Setup**: Defines the steps that will be analyzed.
  - **Cycle Dependent**: Defines which option will be calculated based on the values of the other two fields. The options include Time Step(s), Number of Timesteps, and Duration(s). For example, if Duration is selected as the Cycle Dependent option, it is automatically calculated based on the Time Step(s) x Number of Timesteps, instead of manually entering the value.
  - **Time Step (s)**: Sets the duration of the time step.
  - **Number of Timesteps**: Sets the number of timesteps to be performed for the interval.
  - **Duration (s)**: Sets the duration of the interval.
  - **Skip Factor (for output)**: Limits the number of output sets. Using a skip factor of 2 will give you 1 output set for every two time steps.

Damping Setup

An important consideration to having a stable nonlinear transient response (NLTR) solution is to provide damping in the model. A note of caution when using damping in an NLTR solution is that, for models where the velocity/inertia is the main driver of the analysis, damping can have a significant effect on the acceleration/velocity/displacement of the model. To create damping, right-click on Damping in the Autodesk Nastran Model tree and select Edit to open the Damping dialog box.

The Damping dialog box contains the following options for defining Damping. Depending on the type of damping the options are available or not. For nonlinear transient analysis, you can enable Structural Damping or Rayleigh Damping:

- **Structural Damping**: Applies structural based damping. Select the checkbox adjacent to its title to enable it. By default, this option is enabled.
  - **Damping Value, G (%)**: This is a global structural damping setting. Enter the damping value.
  - **Dominant Frequency, W3 (Hz)**: This is a global structural damping setting. Enter the frequency of interest for the conversion of element structural damping into equivalent viscous damping.
  - **Dominant Frequency, W4 (Hz)**: This is a material structural damping setting. Enter the frequency of interest for the conversion of element structural damping into equivalent viscous damping. It will use the damping specified in your material property and give you the flexibility to apply different damping values to different areas/materials of the model.

- **Rayleigh Damping**: Represents the special case where you choose to form the damping matrix from a linear combination of mass and stiffness matrices.
  - **Mass Proportional, ALPHA**: Applies mass based damping to the analysis.
  - **Stiffness Proportional, BETA**: Applies stiffness based damping to analysis.

Creating the Nonlinear Transient Response Analysis

Use the following procedure to create a nonlinear transient response analysis.

Procedure: To Create a new Nonlinear Transient Response Analysis

1. Right-click on the Part or Assembly node at the top of the Autodesk Nastan Model Tree and select New.

2. Enter the name for the new analysis.

3. Select Nonlinear Transient Response in the Type drop-down list.

4. (Optional) By default, the unit system for the model is set to that of the CAD model. Click Select Units and select an alternative unit system, if required.

5. Define the required options in the Output Controls tab to define the information that will be output to the analysis report when it is run. For example, for a nonlinear transient response analysis, you might also want to include the Velocity and Acceleration options, which are included in the Nodal section for impact type solutions.

6. In the Options tab:

    - Set the Contact type that should be used by default when generating Automatic contacts.
    - Set the tolerance value between contacting entities at which automatic contacts are created.
    - When assuming large displacement in the model, set the Large Displacement parameter to On. Otherwise set its value to Off. Toggling it off can help improve solving time if large displacement is not expected.

7. If analyzing an assembly, on the Model State tab, select a Design View or Level of Detail to define the model configuration that is being analyzed.

8. Click OK to create the new nonlinear transient response analysis.

9. Define damping.

10. Set the Nonlinear and Dynamic setup options.

11. Assign an existing idealization from the Model sub-tree or create a new one, as required.

12. Assign contacts and/or constraints to the model, as required.

13. Assign loads to the model, as required.

14. Add any additional subcases, as required. Multiple subcases can be used to control the time step size for multiple calculation intervals.

Alternatively, you can edit an existing analysis by right-clicking the analysis name in the Autodesk Nastran Model Tree and select Edit and redefine all the options, as required, to change the current analysis to a nonlinear transient response analysis.

Nonlinear Transient Response Analysis Plot Results

For a nonlinear transient response analysis, there are no default plot templates. When the analysis is run, the results are stored; however, you must use the Plot dialog box to visually display the results.

To access the Plot dialog box:

- Right-click on the Results node and select Edit.
- Double-click on the Results node.
- In the Results panel on the ribbon, click (Options).

Using the Plot dialog box you can perform the following tasks:

- Use the Result Data drop-down list in the Contour Options tab to select the general type of data to plot, such as Displacement or Stress.
- Use the Type drop-down list in the Contour Options tab to select the specific data result to plot, such as SOLID VON MISES STRESS.
- Customize the remaining options as required, based on the result plot that is being created.

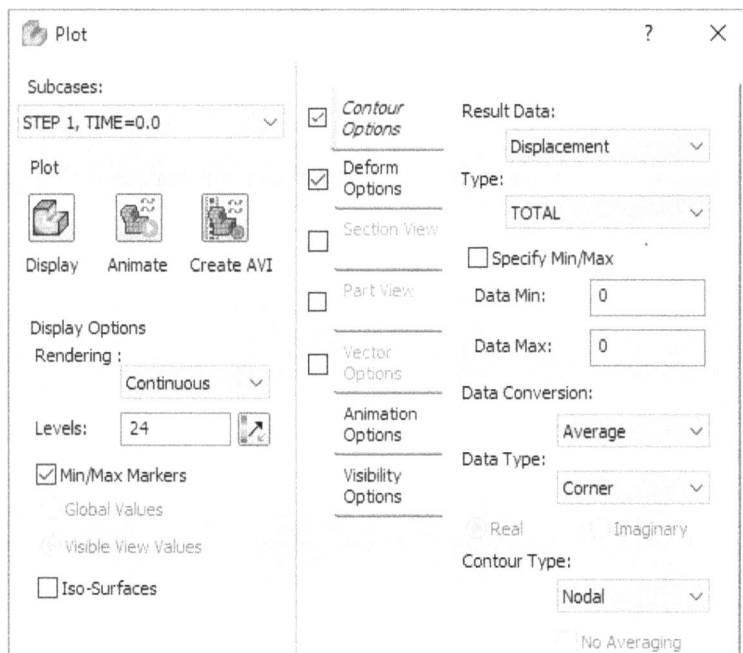

Consider the following tips when viewing results:

- Once the type of report is defined using the Result Data and Type drop-down lists, click (Display) to visually show the results in the graphics window. With this option enabled, you can continue to make changes to the options in the Plot dialog box and the plot results will update in the graphics window. Alternatively, click (Animate) or (Create AVI) to display or save an animation of the results plot.

- To clear the display of the mesh (element edges), select the Visibility Options tab in the Plot dialog box and toggle off the Element Edges option. You can also toggle off the Mesh in the Display panel on the ribbon.

- A result plot cannot be saved for reuse in a nonlinear analysis.

- If the intermediate results were generated for the nonlinear transient response analysis, you can display the intermediate results using either of the following methods.

  - In the Results panel, when the (Contour) or (Deformed) options are enabled, you can select the increment to view using the drop-down list

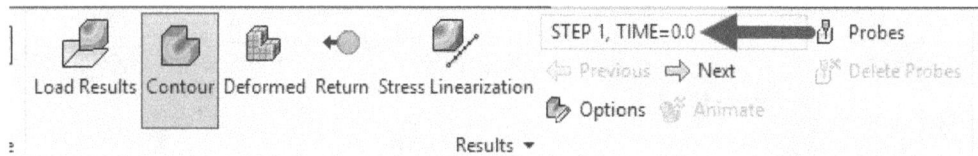

  - In the Results panel, you can also use the ⇐ and ⇒ buttons to progress through the display of each increment.

  - In the Plot dialog box you, can also select the increment to display in the Subcases drop-down list. Note that the increments for each subcase are listed.

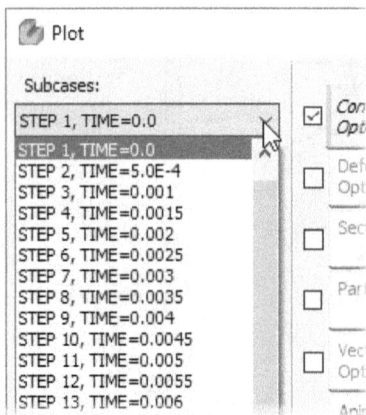

> For more information on the Plot dialog box and its options, refer to the *Visualizing Result Plots* in lesson Chapter 3 or to Autodesk Nastran In-CAD Help and search for "Plot Templates".

Nonlinear Transient Response Analysis XY Plot

When a nonlinear transient response analysis is run, a number of XY plots are generated by default to help you analyze the results.

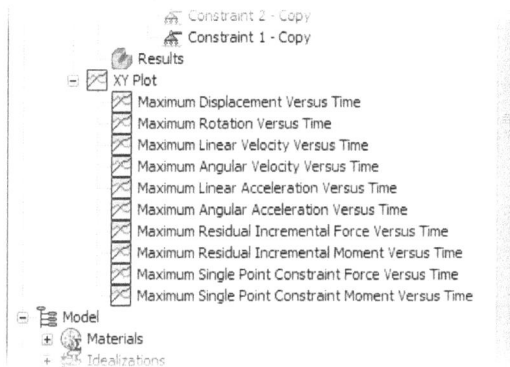

To review any of the plots, double-click on the plot name or right-click on the plot name and select Show XY Plot. The XY Plot dialog box opens displaying the plot. The Maximum Displacement Versus Time plot is shown in the following image. The options in the left pane in the dialog box enables you to customize the display of the plot.

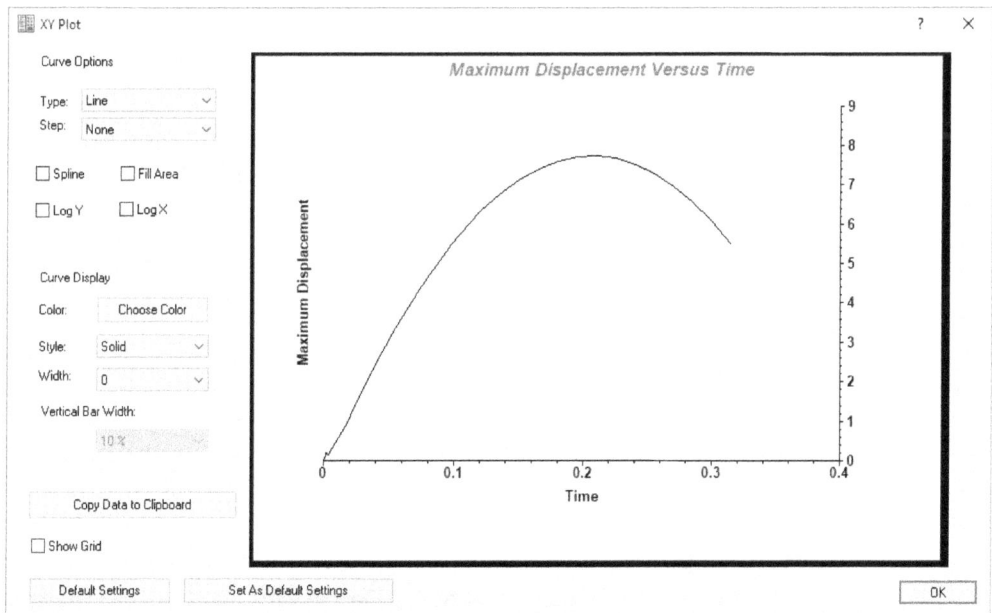

> For more information on XY Plot dialog box, its options, and how to create a new XY Plot, refer to the *Visualizing XY Plot Results* lesson in Chapter 3 or to Autodesk Nastran In-CAD Help and search for "Results XY Plotting".

Exercise: Ball Impact

In this exercise, we will simulate a ball dropping from 12 inches onto a steel plate and rebounding back up into the air. This is an example of a nonlinear transient analysis. It requires both dynamic and nonlinear setup steps. Autodesk Nastran In-CAD solves both domains essentially simultaneously.

Prepare the Model for use in Nastran In-CAD

1. Open the file *C:\Autodesk Nastran InCAD 2019 Essentials Exercise Files\Ball_Impact\Ball Impact.iam*.

2. Rotate the model to the Front view. Note that the ball is assembled at a small distance (.06 in) from the top of the plate. Even through the ball is being dropped from 12 inches, it is placed in this location for solution efficiency. During loading, a velocity will be assigned to the ball to accurately describe falling from a more substantial height.

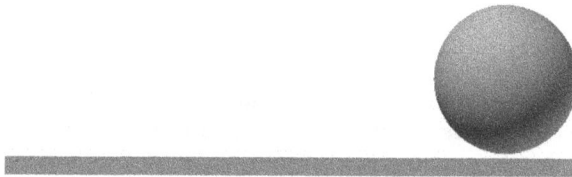

3. Activate the Autodesk Nastran In-CAD environment.

Setup a Nonlinear Transient Response Analysis

By default, when a model is initially opened in the Nastran In-CAD environment, a Linear Static analysis is created. In this task, you will edit this analysis and change it to a Nonlinear Transient Response Analysis.

1. Right-click on Analysis 1 [Linear Static] node at the top of the Analysis sub-tree and select Edit.

2. In the Analysis dialog box:

- Maintain the default name.
- Select Nonlinear Transient Response from the Type drop-down list.
- Enable the Velocity and Acceleration options in the Nodal section on the Output Controls tab.
- Maintain the remaining default options.
- Select the Options tab, ensure that Large Displacement is set to On.
- On the Model State tab, note that both a Design View and Level of Detail can be selected for analysis because this is an assembly design. Maintain the respective Default and Master options for these views.

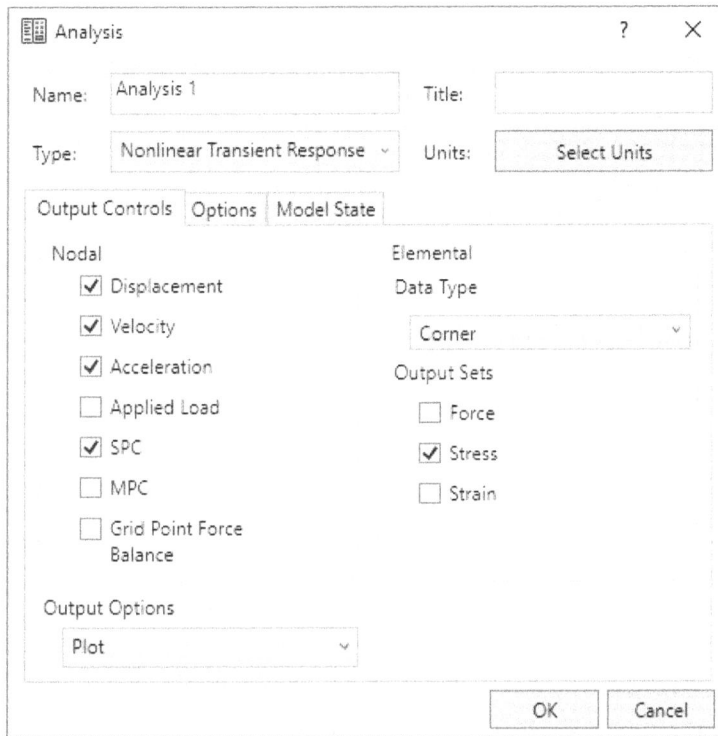

3. Click OK.

Assign a new Idealization

In this task, you will edit the default idealization and change the material that it assigns to the model during the analysis.

1. Right-click on the Solid 1 idealization in the Analysis sub-tree and click Edit. This avoids deleting the Solid 1 idealization and creating a new one.

2. Enter **Alloy Steel** as the new name for the idealization.

3. Ensure that Solid Elements is selected as the Type of element.

4. Create a new material and select Alloy Steel as the material from the Autodesk Material Library.

5. Ensure that the new material is assigned to the Solid1 Idealization. Click OK.

6. Change the color to green, if not already set.

7. In the Idealizations dialog box, select Associated Geometry and select the two models in the assembly (Ball and Plate).

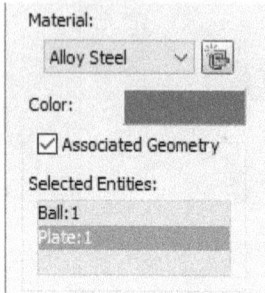

8. Click OK to close the Idealizations dialog box. The edited Solid 1 idealization has been updated and renamed in the analysis.

Constrain the Plate and Ball Components

In this task, you will constrain the plate on one end to remove all degrees of freedom. Additionally you will add a constraint that ensures the ball does not bounce sideways as a result of element face angles. Although not required for the analysis, it ensures that we get the response in the expected direction.

1. Add a constraint for the plate using the following settings:

   - Remove all degrees of freedom in the model by selecting all of the options or by selecting (Fixed).
   - Automatically add the constraint to Subcase 1 in the analysis.
   - Select the end face shown below as the placement reference.
   - If not already defined, set the display color for the constraint to cyan.
   - Select Preview to show the constraint on the model.
   - Modify the density of the constraint's display, as required.
   - Click OK.

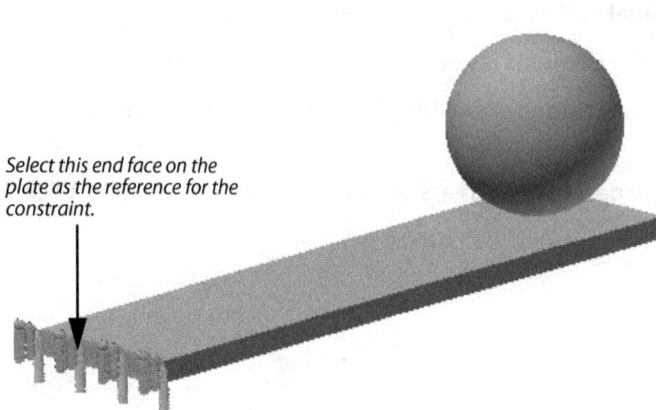

Select this end face on the plate as the reference for the constraint.

2. Add a constraint for the ball using the following settings:

- Ensure that only the Tz degree of freedom checkbox is enabled. Clear the selection of the other 5 options (Tx, Ty, Rx, Ry, and Rz). This constraint prevents the ball from falling off the sides of the plate.
- Automatically add the constraint to Subcase 1 in the analysis.
- Select the two edges shown below as the placement references.
- If not already defined, set the display color for the constraint to cyan.
- Select Preview to show the constraint on the model.
- Modify the density of the constraint's display, as required.
- Click OK.

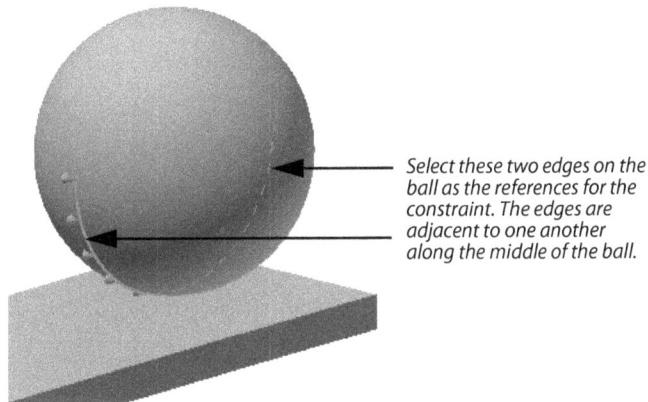

Select these two edges on the ball as the references for the constraint. The edges are adjacent to one another along the middle of the ball.

Load the Model

In this task, you will add an Initial Condition load to include a velocity value for the ball falling from 12 inches to its current position. The following calculation was done to determine the velocity at its assembled position. You will assume that the difference in velocity from the assembled (initial) position to the actual contact is negligible.

V = SQRT(2 x G x d) = SQRT(2 x 386.4 x 12) = 96.3 in/s

You will assign an initial velocity to the ball of 96.3 in/s, which is the velocity the ball would reach after dropping 12 inches. The other consideration is to determine roughly how long it will take the ball to traverse the distance in the model (0.06 inches) at a velocity of 96.3 in/s.

T = d/V = 0.06 / 96.3 = 0.0006 s

1. Add a load for the initial velocity of the ball using the following settings:

   - Select Initial Condition as the load Type.
   - Select Velocity as the Sub Type.
   - Select the solid ball as the reference.

     Hint: To easily select the ball, hover over one of its surfaces (but don't click it). When the Select Other menu displays, expand it and select Solid1.

   - Enter **-96.3** for the Vy magnitude.
   - Select Preview to show the load on the model.
   - Modify the density of the load's display, as required.
   - Click OK.

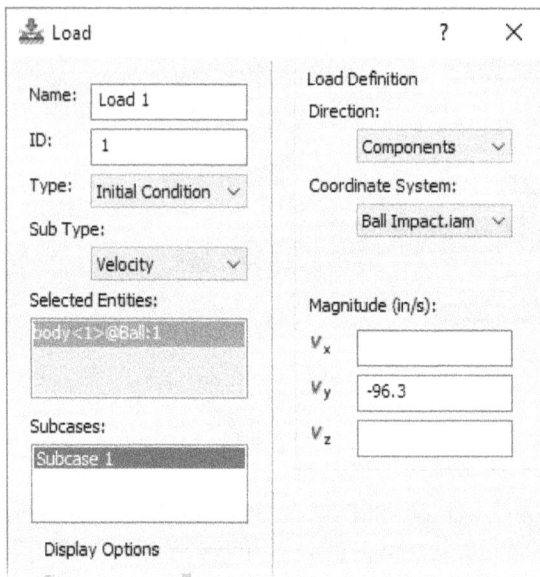

2. Add a load to enable gravity using the following settings:

   - Select Gravity as the load Type.
   - Enter **-386.4** for the Fy magnitude.
   - Select Preview to show the load on the model. The gravity vector displays in the lower right corner of the graphics window.
   - Click OK.

   This is the only load that persists throughout the analysis. The initial condition only applies at the beginning of the analysis.

Define Contacts in the Model

In this task, you will use the Manual option to define a contact been the two components.

1. In the Contacts panel, click ⬚ (Manual) to create a surface contact.

2. Click in the Master Entity field, and select the flat surface of the plate that comes in contact with the ball.

3. Click in the Slave Entity field, and select the four bottom surfaces of the ball.

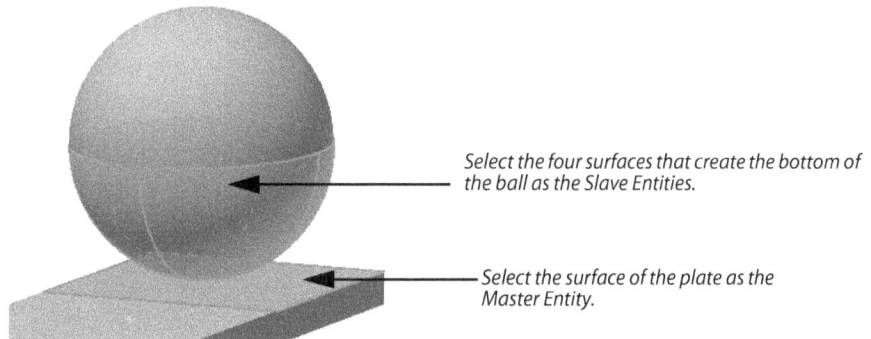

Select the four surfaces that create the bottom of the ball as the Slave Entities.

Select the surface of the plate as the Master Entity.

4. Ensure that Separation is set as the Contact Type.

5. Enter **0.1** as the Max Activation Distance. Click OK.

   Note: The icon associated with Surface Contact (1) indicates that there is separation.

Define Damping in the Model

In this task, you will edit the default damping that gets added for nonlinear transient response analyzes. You will choose the first bending mode as the Dominant Frequency.

1. In the Analysis sub-tree, right-click on Damping 1 in the Subcases node and select Edit.

2. Ensure that Structural Damping is enabled as the type of damping.

3. In the Structural Damping area, enter **4** as the Damping Value, G.

4. Enter **129.97** as the Dominant Frequency, W3.

5. Click OK to complete the changes to Damping 1.

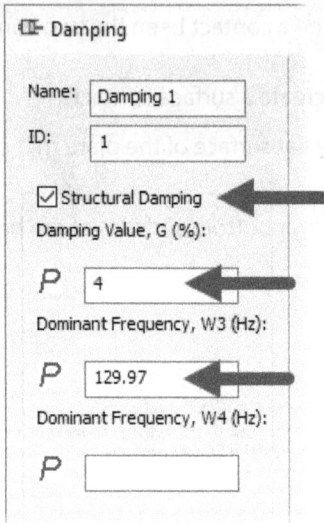

Define the Subcases in the Analysis

In this task, you create a second subcase to control the time step size. The first subcase will capture the descent and impact of the ball. The second subcase will be created with a larger time step to capture the motion of the ball as it rebounds off of the plate.

1. Right-click on Subcase 1, and click Rename. Enter **SmallSteps** as the new name for the subcase.

2. Right-click on the Nonlinear Setup 1 node in the SmallSteps subcase and click Edit.

3. On the Nonlinear Transient Parameters dialog box, select AUTO as the Stiffness update method. Click OK.

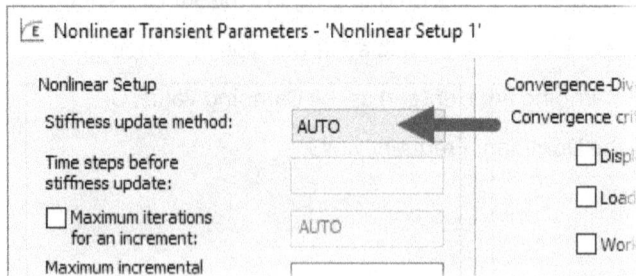

4. Right-click on Dynamics Setup 1, and click Edit.

5. Ensure that the Cycle Dependent option is set to Duration (s).

6. Enter **0.0005** as the Time Step (s).

7. Enter **16** as the Number of Timesteps. Click OK.

8. Right-click on the SmallSteps subcase and click Duplicate.

9. Right-click on the new SmallSteps - Copy subcase and select Rename. Enter **BigSteps** as the new name.

10. Right-click on the Initial Condition load (Load 1 - Copy) in the BigSteps subcase and select Remove. Only the effect of gravity will be analyzed in this subcase.

11. Right-click on Dynamics Setup 2, and click Edit. Make the following changes:

    - Ensure that the Cycle Dependent option is set to Duration (s).
    - Enter **0.015** as the Time Step
    - Enter **20** as the Number of Timesteps.

12. Click OK. Two subcases are now listed and defined in the analysis.

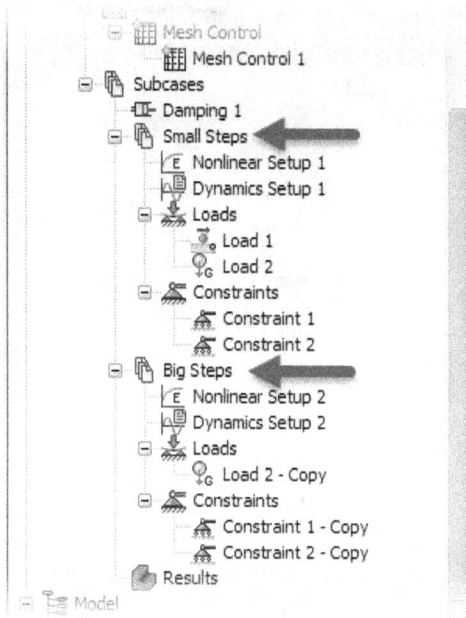

Tip: When the subcase was duplicated, copies of the loads and constraints were made. You can replace the loads and constraints with the same ones used in the original subcase to ensure that if changes are made to their properties, they are incorporated in both subcases.

Mesh the Model and Run the Analysis

In this task, you will globally mesh the model, assign local mesh settings for the contacting faces, and run the analysis.

1. In the Analysis 1 sub-tree, right-click on Mesh Model, and click Edit to open the Mesh Settings dialog box. The current settings are the default values that were assigned when the analysis was created.

2. In the Mesh Settings dialog box make the following changes:

  - Enter **0.2** as the Element Size.
  - Set the Element Order option to Linear.
  - Clear the selection of the Continuous Meshing option.

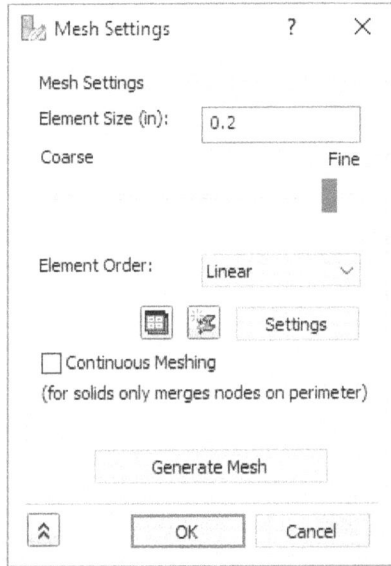

3. Click Generate Mesh to generate the mesh. Click OK to close the Mesh dialog box.

4. In the Analysis 1 sub-tree, right-click on Mesh Model, and click Add Mesh Control.

5. Enter **0.1** as the new Element Size value for the Face Data.

6. Select the four bottom surfaces of the ball and the split face on the end of the beam. Note that the constraint, load, and global meshing display has been temporarily toggled off for clarity in this image.

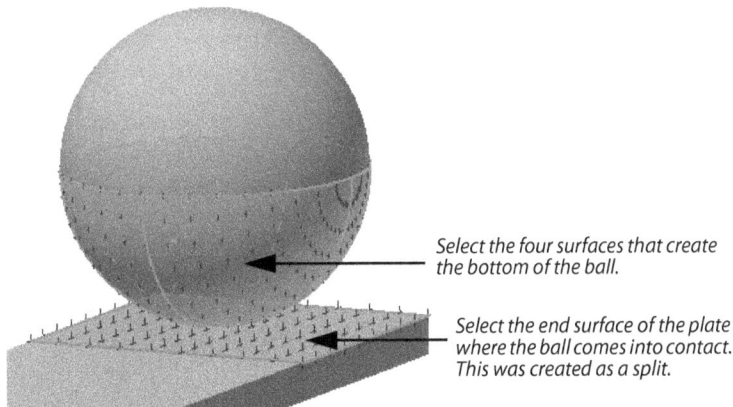

Select the four surfaces that create the bottom of the ball.

Select the end surface of the plate where the ball comes into contact. This was created as a split.

7. Click OK.

8. Right-click on the Mesh Model node and select Generate Mesh to update the mesh.

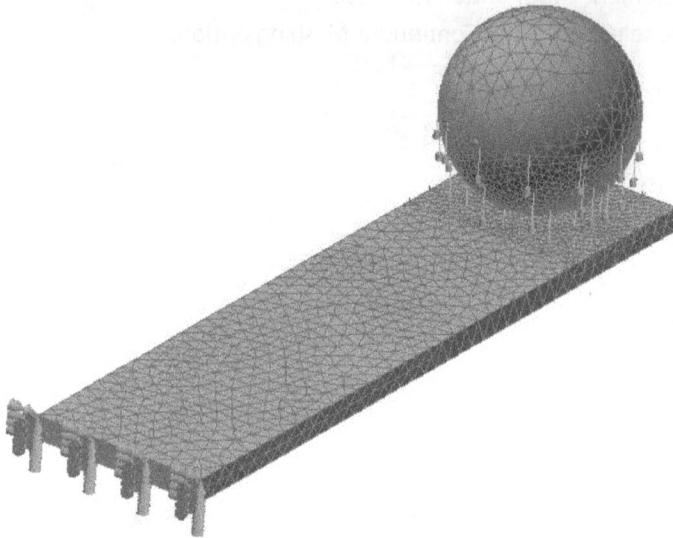

9. To enable the creation of intermediate results for this type of analysis, only the global setting must be set. Right-click on Analysis 1, select Nonlinear Options and ensure that the Generate Intermediate Results option is enabled.

10. Run the analysis. Click OK when the analysis is complete.

Note: During the solution, the default displacement scale will make it look like the ball is passing through the plate. Disregard this effect. When viewing with the Actual displacement option, you will see that the ball does not penetrate the plate. You must wait until the solution is complete to change the plot settings. The analysis may take over 10 minutes to complete. Optionally, to continue with this exercise, you can open the file *C:\Autodesk Nastran InCAD 2019 Essentials Exercise Files\Ball_Impact\Completed\ Ball Impact2.iam*, activate the Nastran In-CAD environment, right-click on the Results node and select Load. This loads the *...\Completed\Ball Impact2\InCAD\FEA\ nsn4dbhcr.FNO* results file. Note: You must be running 2019.1 to open and use this file.

11. Right-click on the XY Plot node and select New. In the XY Plot dialog box, define the plot as follows:

- Enter **Nodal Y Displacement of Ball** as the Name of the new XY Plot.

Activate the ID field in the Entity to Plot section and then select the node shown below. Reorient the model to the Front view.

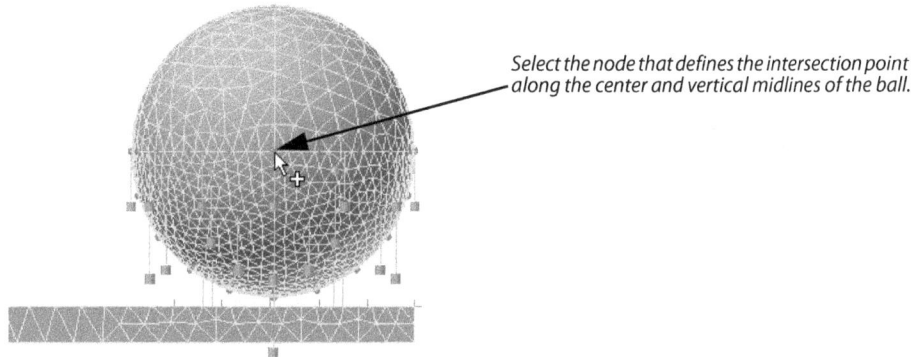

Select the node that defines the intersection point along the center and vertical midlines of the ball.

- Ensure that the Start Set and End Set options in the X-Axis: Output Sets are set to show the full range.
- Select TY in the Component drop-down list for the Y-Axis: Output Sets section. This ensures that the plot shows only the Y displacement of the Ball.
- Click Show XY Plot.
- Select Line+Symbol in the Type drop-down list. This enables you to show the plotted points. Hover the cursor over the points to obtain an accurate X and Y value.

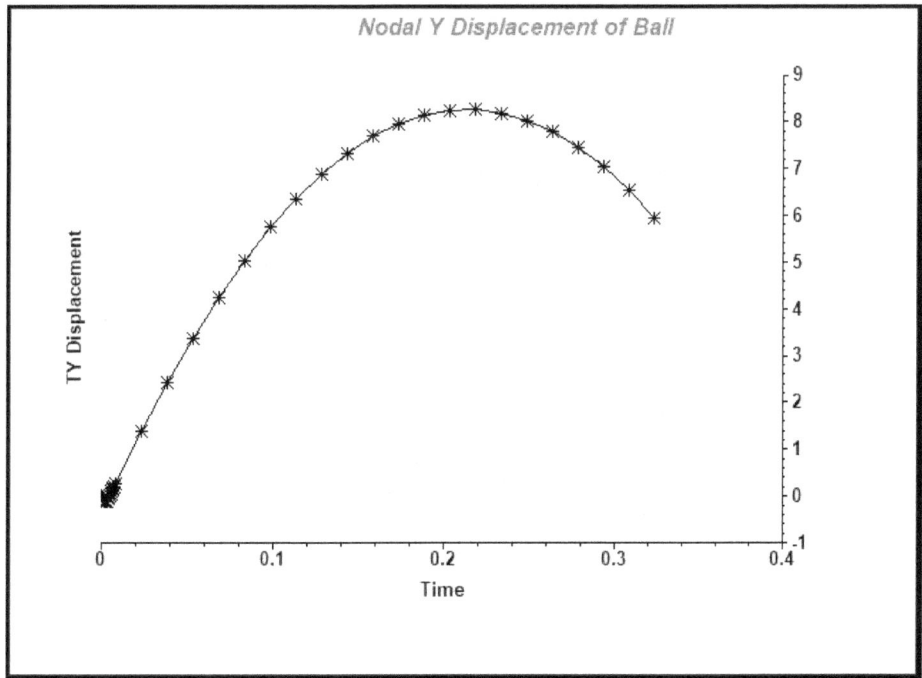

Note that in this plot, the ball initially falls 0.06in and then it comes in contact with the plate. The ball is then pushed upward to about 8.25in.

12. Click OK to close the XY Plot dialog box and click Save to save the newly created plot to the Model Tree.

13. Click Close to close the XY Plot dialog box.

14. Right-click on the Results node for the analysis and select Multiset Animation Settings. This enables you to customize settings so that you can display a multiset animation.

15. Click the Deform Options tab. Set the Vector to Displacement, and the Type to Total. Change the Deformation Scale to Actual, and specify a Value of 1.0.

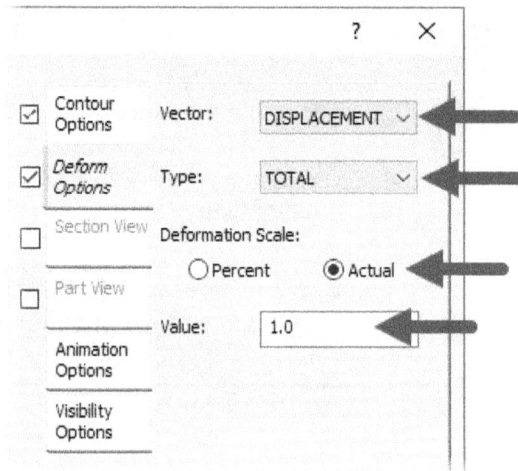

16. In the Output Set section, set the Start Set option to STEP 1, and the End Set option to STEP 22 of the BigSteps subcase.

17. Click the Animation Options tab. Set the Mode option to Half.

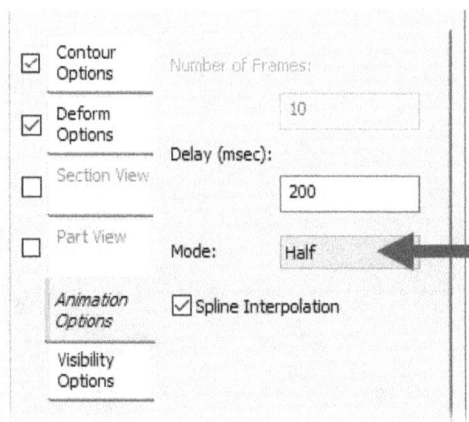

18. In the Output Set section, click ⊞ (Animate) to view an animation of the analysis. Select ⊞ (Animate) a second time to stop the animation.

19. Continue to view any of the results, as required, using the Plot dialog box, the predefined XY Plots or new ones, or the Results panel on the ribbon.

20. Save the model.

Normal Modes Analysis

The goal in this chapter is to create and view the results of a Normal Modes analysis. In preparation for this lesson, an introduction is provided on the general topic of dynamic analysis. Dynamic analysis enables the study of kinetic behavior in a model. In the Autodesk® Nastran® In-CAD software, the Normal Modes analysis type determines the natural vibration frequencies of a model based on the assigned idealizations, constraints, and loads.

Objectives

After completing this chapter, you will be able to:

- Describe the differences between static and dynamic analysis types and which dynamic analysis types Autodesk Nastran In-CAD supports.
- Create a new Normal Modes analysis.
- Display the modal result plot and XY plot results from a Normal Modes analysis.

Lesson: Basics of a Dynamic Analysis

Overview

Dynamic analysis enables for the study of models that have kinetic behavior. This lesson introduces and discusses the basics of dynamic analysis and which dynamic analysis types are supported in the Autodesk Nastran In-CAD.

Objectives

After completing this lesson, you will be able to:

- Describe the differences between static and dynamic analysis types and which dynamic analysis types Autodesk Nastran In-CAD supports.

Introduction to Dynamic Analysis

Dynamics can be thought of as the kinetic behavior of an object. That is, if an object is moving, it is involved in a dynamic activity. However, from an analytical point of view, moving objects can usually be divided into two classes:

- Those where the object is moving through space as a rigid body (called kinematics).
- Those where the body itself is deforming (called dynamics).

Further, the relative magnitude of the motion or deformation must to be considered as well. If the object is moving very slowly, it could still be considered a static problem for any arbitrarily short period of time.

A further refinement to the definition of dynamics would relate to the loading and motion. If the rate of loading is such that it is roughly equal to the object's natural frequency, the response will be dynamic. That is, the loading will interact with the system's natural frequencies. At slow loading rates, the natural frequencies are not excited and the model can be considered static. In the dynamic range, the loading will excite certain natural frequencies which will change the response from strictly static. At higher frequencies, the system will not have time to respond to the excitation, and the excitation will have little effect on the system.

The dynamic response of a structure is impacted by:

- Mass (weight)
- Stiffness
- Distribution of mass

Types of Dynamic Problems

There are several types of problems that are analyzed with finite elements that are dynamic in nature. These include the following:

Modal or Natural Frequency Analysis

Any non-rigid system will have one or more natural vibration frequencies. A modal or natural frequency analysis (also known as normal modes or eigenvalue analysis) will find these frequencies and the corresponding mode shapes (eigenvectors).

Examples of such systems include structures (buildings, bridges, towers), bodies (support brackets, housings), and shafts.

The benefits of this type of analysis are:

- Avoiding operating speeds or frequencies that would produce a resonant response (that is, excess vibration).
- Understanding excited modes.
- Controlling mode shapes at specific frequencies.

The modal analysis will output:

- Natural frequencies (Hertz)
- Mode shapes (non-dimensional)

For Autodesk Nastran In-CAD this type of problem is analyzed using the Normal Modes or Prestress Normal Modes analysis types. For more information, refer to the *Creating a Normal Modes Analysis* lesson.

Frequency Response Analysis

If a system is known to be dynamic, a frequency (harmonic) response analysis will calculate the response of the system to a series of enforced sinusoidal loads or acceleration. If the load is assumed to continue indefinitely, the solution to these problems can be found in closed form, resulting in a series of static-like results at a series of excitation frequencies.

Examples of enforced sinusoidal loads (oscillatory excitation) include rotating machinery, unbalanced tires, and helicopter blades.

The benefits of this type of analysis are:

- Determine required damping.
- Avoid damage from fatigue or cyclic loading.
- Understand magnitude of displacements.

The frequency response analysis will output:

- User-defined output frequencies (for example stress and displacement at frequencies)
- No phase content or load reversal
- Peak response

For Autodesk Nastran In-CAD, this type of problem is analyzed using the Direct Frequency Response or Modal Frequency Response analysis types. For more information, refer to *Chapter 10 Frequency Response Analysis*.

Transient Response Analysis

If the loading is not periodic, it may be required to load the model in the time domain. In this case, the model is solved at a series of time steps that trace the response of the system over time. A transient analysis does this, using the solution at each time step as the initial condition for the next time step.

Examples of structures subjected to transient events would be buildings, bridges, towers, and bodies like housings and support brackets.

The benefits of a transient response analysis are:

- True dynamics response with phase content.
- System response or vulnerability to drop or impact.

The transient response analysis will output:

- User-defined time steps (for example stress due to impact and settle time)
- Control solution accuracy and results insight

For Autodesk Nastran In-CAD, this type of problem is analyzed using the Direct Transient Response, Modal Transient Response, or Nonlinear Transient Response analysis types. For more information, refer to *Chapter 11 Transient Response Analyzes*.

Random Response Analysis

If the actual excitation of a structure is unknown, but the loading can be roughly quantified as a power spectrum, you can do a random analysis. A random analysis is run after a frequency response analysis, and the responses at the different frequencies are combined into a single result based on the relative magnitude of the spectrum at different frequencies. The result is a single set of results, incorporating the contributions of all the different excitation values.

Example of structures subjected to random events would be electronics mounted on moving vehicles.

The benefits of a random response analysis are:

- System response or vulnerability due to multiple frequency vibrations.

The random response analysis will output:

- The RMS results. which is the area under the response power spectrum.

For Autodesk Nastran In-CAD, this type of problem is analyzed using the Random Response analysis type. For more information, refer to Chapter 12.

Shock/Response Spectrum Analysis

A response spectrum analysis is similar to a random analysis in that the actual loads are unknown. In a spectral response solution, the peak accelerations at different frequencies are specified, instead of a power density. But like the random analysis, the results at different natural frequencies are combined to produce a single result.

Examples of structures subjected to shock/response spectrum events would be seismic activity, pyrotechnic activity, explosive activities, or sudden impacts.

The benefits of a Shock/Response Spectrum analysis are:

- Reduced solve time as compared to transient response.
- System response or vulnerability to sudden, highly energetic events.

The Shock/Response Spectrum analysis will output:

- Peak stress, deflection, forces, velocity, and acceleration results

For Autodesk Nastran In-CAD, this type of problem is analyzed using the Random Response analysis type. For more information, refer to Chapter 13.

> Impact Analysis, and Nonlinear Buckling are additional types of dynamic analyses that can be performed in Autodesk Nastran In-CAD. These are not covered in this learning guide.

Lesson: Creating a Normal Modes Analysis

Overview

In this lesson, you will learn about the dynamic analysis type called Normal Modes available in the Autodesk Nastran In-CAD software. The Normal Modes analysis type enables the study of modal or natural frequency response in a model. You will learn to create and setup the model for this type of analysis, run the analysis, and review the mode results.

Objectives

After completing this lesson, you will be able to:

- Create a new Normal Modes analysis.
- Display the modal result plot and XY plot results from a Normal Modes analysis.

Modal or Natural Frequency Static Analysis

A modal or natural frequency analysis (also known as Normal Modes or Eigenvalue analysis) forms the basis of several other dynamic analyses, including the modal approach formulations. In Autodesk Nastran In-CAD, the Normal Modes and Prestress Normal Modes analysis types can be used for this type of analysis. The results of these analyses reveal the dynamic characteristics of the model, including whether or not you really have a dynamic system. For this reason, analysts often run a Normal Modes analysis first to examine if there are any natural frequencies within a given range. Structures that are excited at or near their natural frequencies will often respond by failing under smaller loading conditions.

These analyses produce mode shape and natural frequency results. Note that the output mode shape is an eigenvector with the maximum value set to 1.0. Thus, the resulting deformations are scaled such that the largest deformation in the structure is 1.0 and is not representative of the scale of the deformations expected during actual vibrations.

Rigid Body Modes

Normal Modes analysis can include constraints, but its not a requirement. Models that run without constraints should have their first 6 vibration frequencies at almost 0 Hz since these are "free" (or rigid-body) modes. Partially constrained models have less than 6 "free" modes. If your model is attached to a rigid structure it is recommended you add a constraint for this attachment. Modal analyses are usually divided into two types based on the constraints:

- If the model is unconstrained (such as a rocket or aircraft in flight), it is referred to as a free-free analysis, after the corresponding beam representation, i.e. a beam analyzed this way would be free at both ends. When a modal analysis is run on a free-free system, there will be six zero-frequency rigid body modes (or mechanism modes) found in addition to the elastic modes. These modes represent the free translation and rotation of the system in the six directions of motion and will be extracted as modes one through six. Mode seven is then refereed to as the first flexible mode and will not be a zero energy mode. It is always a good model check to run an unconstrained modal analysis to assure that you are finding these modes. This way, you'll know that the model is not internally constrained accidentally. Some systems really are unconstrained, and unlike a static analysis, a modal analysis can be run successfully on a free-free structure.
- The other type of modal analysis is a constrained system. In this case, there should be no zero-frequency modes. If any are found, it is an indication that some portion of the model is free to move in a rigid body manner. This type of motion is usually referred to as a mechanism. And while a modal analysis can solve this type of problem, a static analysis will fail. For this reason, a modal analysis is often used as a debugging tool for a static analysis that has failed. Once the source of the zero frequency mode is identified, it can be constrained and a static analysis successfully run.

Mechanism modes occur in an insufficiently constrained structure where a portion of the structure displaces as a rigid body. An example would be a flat plate on a hinge or a ball joint. A mechanism mode can also occur when two parts of a structure are not connected properly. A common example of this is a bar connected to a solid element.

Rigid body and mechanism modes are indicated by zero or near zero frequency eigenvalues. For most structures near zero should be on the order of 1.0E-3 Hz or less and may be negative.

Creating a New Normal Modes Analysis

To create a normal modes analysis you must either create a new analysis or edit an existing analysis and change the type of analysis to Normal Modes. You can also select any additional options in the Analysis dialog box to define the output controls, options, and model state (Design View or Level of Detail to be analyzed).

When a normal modes analysis is created the Model Tree displays as shown in the following image.

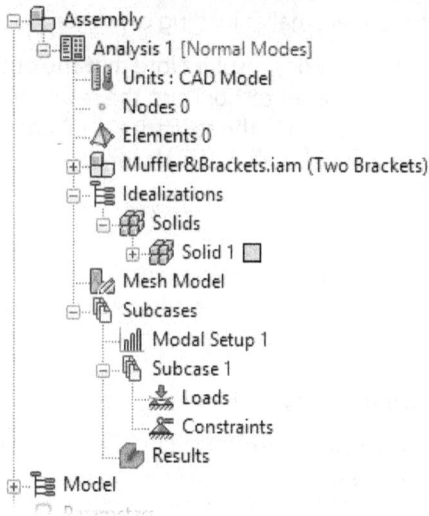

```
Assembly
    Analysis 1 [Normal Modes]
        Units : CAD Model
        Nodes 0
        Elements 0
        Muffler&Brackets.iam (Two Brackets)
        Idealizations
            Solids
                Solid 1
        Mesh Model
        Subcases
            Modal Setup 1
            Subcase 1
                Loads
                Constraints
        Results
Model
```

Additionally you must consider the following:

- Ensure that the required idealizations exists or is created and contains any material properties that are specifically required for the analysis.
- Assign any constraints that are required for the analysis.
- Assign loads that are required for the prestress normal modes analysis. Loads are not evaluated for a normal modes analysis
- Assign any required Surface Contacts, as required to fully describe the model being analyzed.
- Set the Modal Setup options that define the analysis.

A normal modes analysis requires that you set modal settings, as described below. The damping is assumed to be zero for this analysis type.

Modal Setup

Modal settings can be customized using the Modal Setup 1 node that gets created in the subcase of a Normal Modes analysis. To access the setup options, right-click on the Modal Setup node in the analysis subcase and select Edit.

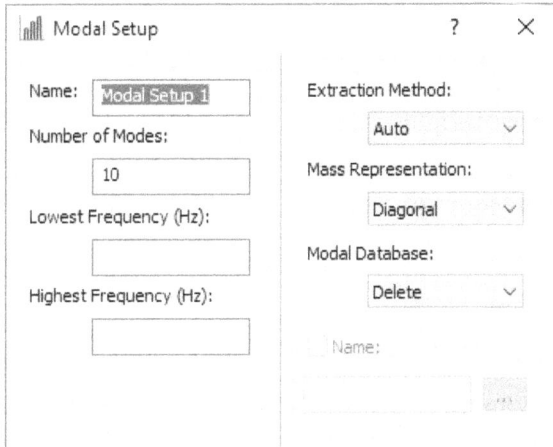

The Modal Setup dialog box contains the following options:

- **Name**: Sets the name for modal setup.
- **Number of Modes**: Sets the specified number of natural frequencies and mode shapes the solver will find. This is set at 10 as the default value.
- **Lowest/Highest Frequency**: Sets the lowest and highest frequency in the range to be analyzed for natural frequencies and mode shapes. This can be used as an alternative to defining the number of modes to be analyzed.
- **Extraction Method**: Defines the extraction method to be used.
    - **Auto**: Picks the best method based on the RAM directive setting (Parameters-Memory Management Directives) and model size.
    - **Subspace Iteration**: Uses the subspace eigensolver.
    - **Lanczos Iteration**: Uses the high performance PCGLSS block Lanczos eigensolver. This eigensolver is recommended for large problems and will generally be faster than the subspace eigensolver.
- **Mass Representation**: Defines the mass representation model that will be used.
    - **Diagonal**: Requests the generation of diagonal mass matrices. Diagonal, or lumped, mass matrices contain uncoupled, translational components of mass.
    - **Coupled**: Requests the generation of coupled mass matrices for elements with coupled mass capability. Coupled mass matrices contain translational components of mass with coupling between the components. This option may be more accurate than lumped diagonal mass.
    - **Element Type Default**: Will use the coupled mass formulation when rigid elements are specified in the model.

- **Modal Database**: Controls the storage and retrieval of modal data such as eigenvalues and eigenvectors used in dynamic response analysis. You have 4 options:
  - **Delete**: The default value will purge all modal data when the program terminates normally.
  - **Store**: The modal database is stored in a single file with the name you specify by selecting the browse option and a .MDB file extension.
  - **Fetch**: The database specified by the browse option is retrieved and the eigenvalue extraction phase is skipped.
  - **Update**: The modal database will be retrieved and stored.

Procedure: To Create a new Normal Modes Analysis

1. Right-click on the Part or Assembly node at the top of the Model Tree and select New.

2. Enter the name for the new analysis.

3. Select Normal Modes in the Type drop-down list.

4. (Optional) By default, the unit system for the model is set to that of the CAD model. Click Select Units and select an alternative unit system, if required.

5. Define the required options in the Output Controls tab to define the information that will be output to the analysis report when it is run.

6. Define the options in the Options tab:
   - Set the Contact type that should be used by default when generating Automatic contacts.
   - Set the tolerance value between contacting entities at which automatic contacts are created.

7. If analyzing an assembly, on the Model State tab, select a Design View or Level of Detail to define the model configuration that is being analyzed.

8. Click OK to create the new Normal Modes analysis.

9. Right-click on the Modal Setup node in the analysis subcase and select Edit. Define the Modal Setup properties, as required.

10. Assign an existing idealization from the Model sub-tree or create a new one, as required.

11. Assign contacts and/or constraints to the model, as required.

Alternatively, you can edit an existing analysis, by right-clicking the analysis name in the Model Tree and select Edit.

Normal Modes Analysis Plot Results

When a normal modes analysis is run, there are no default plot templates included. You must use the Plot dialog box to visually display the results.

To access the Plot dialog box:

- Right-click on the Results node and select Edit.
- Double-click on the Results node.
- In the Results panel on the ribbon, click ![icon] (Options).

Using the Plot dialog box you can select the type of result to be displayed using the Result Data drop-down list and customize the options, as required.

Using the Plot dialog box, you can perform the following tasks:

- Use the Result Data drop-down list in the Contour Options tab to select the general type of data to plot, such as Displacement or Stress.
- Use the Type drop-down list in the Contour Options tab to select the specific data result to plot, such as SOLID VON MISES STRESS.
- Customize the remaining options as required, based on the result plot being created.

Consider the following tips when viewing results:

- Select the subcase Mode to view using the subcases drop-down list.
- Displacement is the commonly used result for a Normal Modes Analysis.

- Once customized, click (Display) to visually show the results in the graphics window. With this option enabled, you can continue to make changes to the options in the Plot dialog box and the plot results will update in the graphics window. Alternatively, click (Animate) or (Create AVI) to display or save an animation of the results plot.
- To clear the display of the mesh (element edges), select the Visibility Options tab in the Plot dialog box and toggle off the Element Edges option. You can also toggle off the Mesh in the Display panel on the ribbon.
- A result plot cannot be saved for reuse in a normal modes analysis.
- For the mode results you can display each using either of the following methods.

  - In the Results panel, when the (Contour) or (Deformed) options are enabled, you can select the mode that is to viewed in the drop-down list to display it.

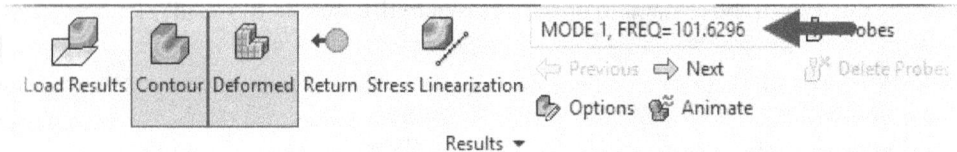

  - In the Results panel, you can also use the ⇐ and ⇒ buttons to progress through the display of each mode.
  - In the Plot dialog box you can also select the mode to display in the Subcases drop-down list.

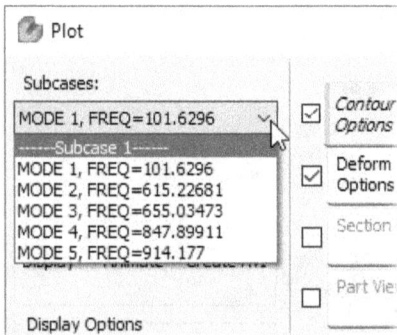

> For more information on Plot dialog box and its options, refer to the *Visualizing Result Plots* lesson in Chapter 3 or to Autodesk Nastran In-CAD Help and search for "Plot Templates".

Normal Modes Analysis XY Plot

When a normal mode analysis is run, a number of XY plots are generated by default to help you analyze the results.

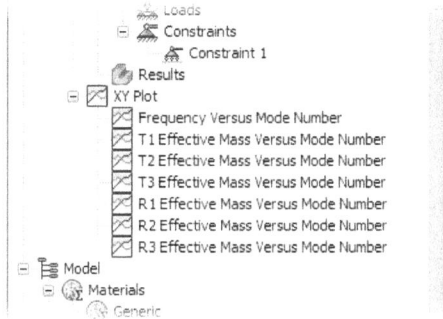

To review any of the plots, double-click on the plot name or right-click on the plot name and select Show XY Plot. The XY Plot dialog box opens displaying the plot. The Frequency Versus Mode Number plot is shown in the following image. The options in the left pane in the dialog box enables you to customize the display of the plot.

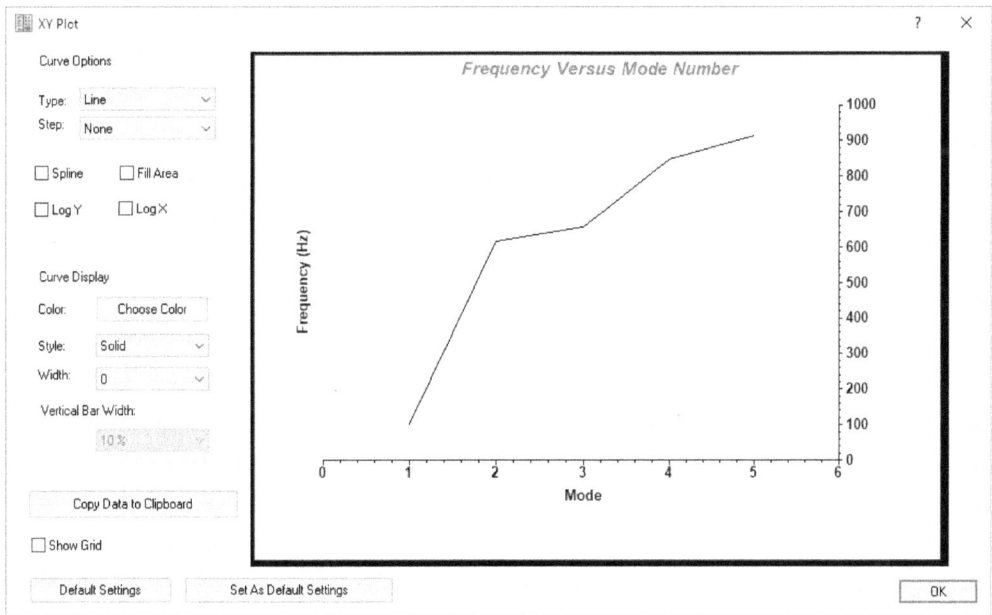

> For more information on XY Plot dialog box, its options, and how to create a new XY Plot, refer to the *Visualizing XY Plot Results* lesson in Chapter 3 or to Autodesk Nastran In-CAD Help and search for "Results XY Plotting".

Exercise: Muffler I - Determining Natural Frequencies

Automotive mufflers for on-road applications are subject to road load vibration. Testing in actual conditions, however, is time consuming and expensive. Simulation is an effective tool for exploring a product's response to published road vibration loading. It is a critical part of the design process for evaluating design variations and for identifying a final design candidate that warrants physical testing. In this exercise, you will set up a normal modes (modal) analysis. You will compare the modes to known road excitation per MIL-STD-810G. In a subsequent exercise, you will make design improvements to reduce sensitivity to frequencies of higher energy.

Prepare the Model for use in Nastran In-CAD

1.   Open the file *C:\Autodesk Nastran InCAD 2019 Essentials Exercise Files\Muffler_Modal_Analysis\ Muffler&Brakets.iam*.

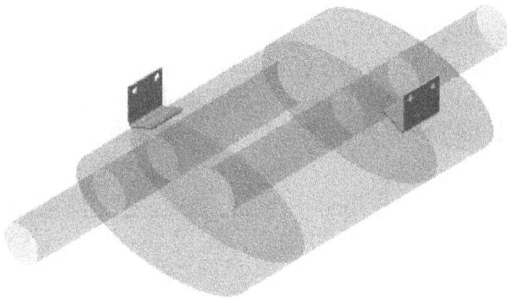

2.   In the Model Browser, expand the Representations node and the Level of Detail node. Note that the currently active Level of Detail (LOD) is called Two Brackets. This is the LOD that will be analyzed.

3.   Activate the Autodesk Nastran In-CAD environment.

Change the Analysis Type and Set the Modal Options

In this task, you will change the default Linear Static analysis type to a Normal Modes analysis. This will enable you to analyze the system's natural frequencies. Additionally you will set the modal setup options that are required for this type of analysis.

1.   Right-click on Analysis 1 and select Edit.

2.   Select Normal Modes in the Type drop-down list.

3.   Maintain the options on the Output Controls and Options tab.

4.   Select the Model State tab. In the Level of Detail drop-down list, select Two Brackets as the LOD to be analyzed. Click OK.

5. In the Subcases node, right-click on Modal Setup 1 and select Edit. Set the following options in the Modal Setup dialog box:

- Delete the value (10) in the Number of Modes field.
- Set the Lowest Frequency to 10.
- Set the Highest Frequency to 1000.

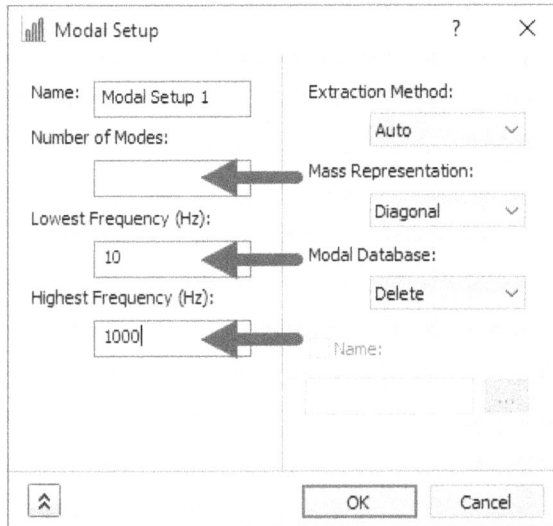

6. Click OK.

Assign new Idealizations

In this task, you will create new idealizations and assign them to the components in the assembly for use during the analysis. Multiple idealizations are used with the different components to enable flexibility when making changes in a subsequent exercise.

1. Create a new idealization using the following settings and add it to the analysis:

    - Enter **Outer Shell** as the name of the new idealization.
    - Ensure that Shell Elements is selected as the Type of element.
    - Enter **0.033** as the thickness (t) value.
    - Create a new material and select Alloy Steel as the material from the Autodesk Material Library. Click OK.
    - In the Idealizations dialog box, select Associated Geometry and select the three elliptical surfaces that create the outer muffler shell.
    - Change the color of the idealization to blue.
    - At the bottom of the Idealizations dialog box, click ▦ (Create Duplicate). This saves the new idealization and prepares the dialog box to create another.

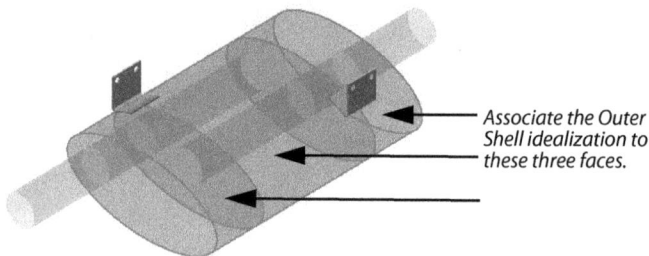

Associate the Outer Shell idealization to these three faces.

2. A copy of the previously created idealization was created. Use the following settings and add this new idealization to the analysis:

    - Enter **Tubes** as the name for the new idealization.
    - Right-click in the Selected Quadrilaterals section and select Clear All.
    - Ensure that the Associated Geometry option remains selected and select the six cylindrical surfaces that create the tubes. (You will have to hover over the surfaces and expand the Select Other menu to select the correct surfaces from the list.)
    - Once created, click ▦ (Create Duplicate) again.

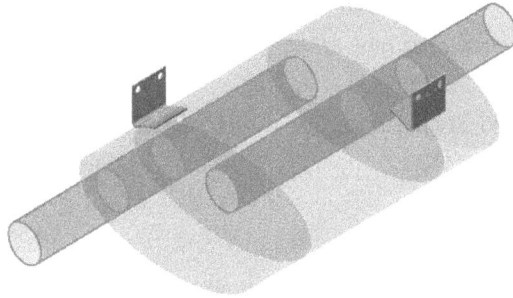

Associate the Tubes idealization to the six segments of the tubes that are in the model.

3. Use the following settings and add another idealization to the analysis:

- Enter **Endcaps** as the name for the new idealization.
- Right-click in the Selected Quadrilaterals section and select Clear All.
- Ensure that the Associated Geometry option remains selected and select the four planar surfaces that create the end caps and bulkheads. (You will have to hover over the surfaces and expand the Select Other menu to select the correct surfaces from the list.)
- Once created, click ▦ (Create Duplicate) again.

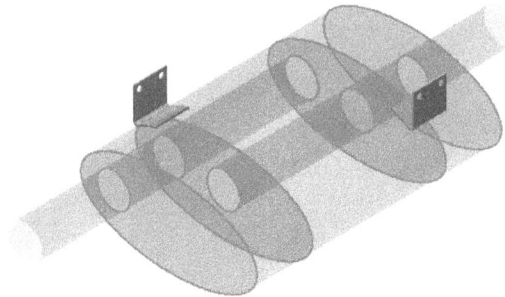

Associate the Endcaps idealization to the two endcaps and two bulkhead faces.

4. Use the following settings and add another idealization to the analayis:

   - Enter **Mounts** as the name for the new idealization.
   - Change the Type to Solid Elements.
   - Ensure that the Associated Geometry option is selected and select the brackets.
   - Click OK.

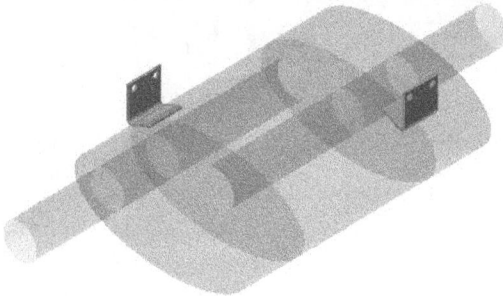

Associate the Mounts idealization to the two brackets.

5. Remove Solid 1 from the Idealizations node. There should be four idealizations assigned to the analysis.

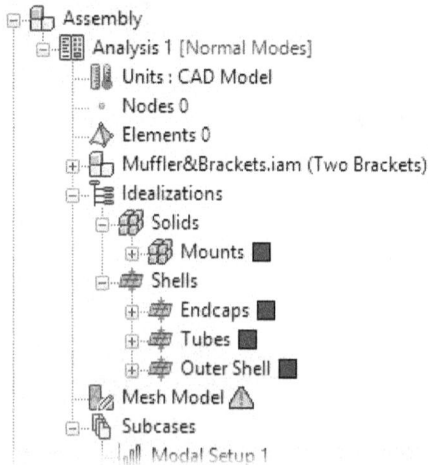

Constrain the Model & Define Contacts

In this task, you will constrain the model and manually define contacts between the outer shell of the muffler and the supporting brackets.

1. Create a constraint that fixes the brackets using the following settings:

   - In the Degrees of Freedom section of the dialog box, select (Fixed) to preselect the degrees of freedom that are to be assigned to a reference face. All degrees of freedom should be selected.
   - Assign the constraint to Subcase1.
   - Select the two inside faces of the holes in the bracket, as shown below, as the references for the constraint. Also select the two inside faces on the other bracket to assign the constraint to a total of four holes.
   - Select Preview to show the constraint on the model.
   - Modify the density of the constraint's display, as required.
   - Click OK.

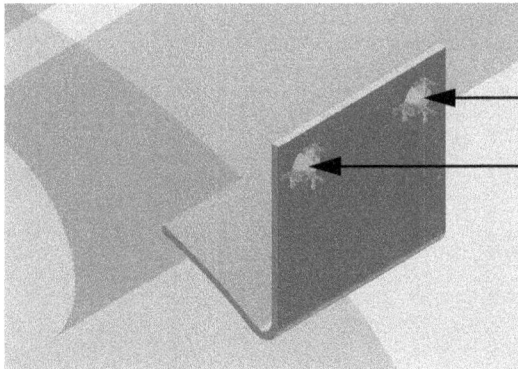

Select the two inside hole faces on each bracket to be fully constrained. There should be a total of four holes on two brackets selected.

2. In the Contacts panel, select ⬚ (Manual). Define the settings in the Surface Contact dialog box as follows:

- Set the Contact Type to Offset Bonded.
- Enter **0.2** as the Max Activation Distance.
- Click in the Master Entity field, and select the bottom face of the bracket. (You will have to hover over the surface and expand the Select Other menu to select the correct surface from the list.)
- Click in the Slave Entity field and select the two adjacent faces of the muffler.

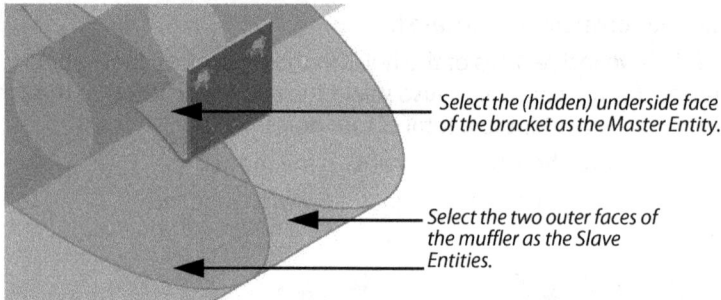

Select the (hidden) underside face of the bracket as the Master Entity.

Select the two outer faces of the muffler as the Slave Entities.

3. Click ![Create Duplicate icon] (Create Duplicate) to duplicate the surface contact. Using the Surface Contact dialog box, define the Master and Slave Entities to define contacts for a second bracket. To clear the current selections that are listed in the fields, right-click and select Clear All. Reselect the references, as required.

4. Click OK. Once completed you should have 2 Offset Bonded contacts.

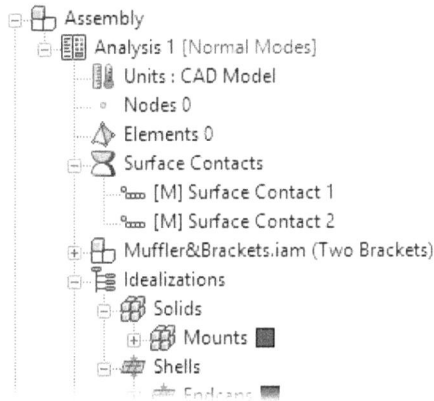

Mesh the Model

In this task, you will change the mesh settings globally for the entire model and mesh it.

1. In the Analysis 1 sub-tree, right-click on Mesh Model, and click Edit.

2. Enter **.25** as the new Element Size value.

3. Change the Element Order option to Linear using its drop-down list.

4. Click Generate Mesh to update the mesh.

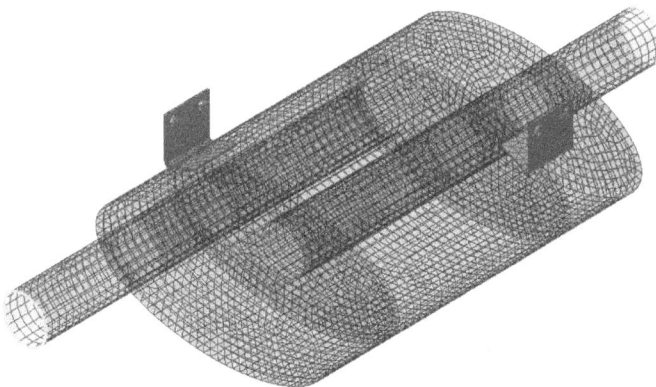

5. Click OK to close the Mesh Settings dialog box.

Run the Analysis and Review the Results

In this task, you will run the analysis and then analyze the displacement and stress result plots.

1. Run the analysis.

2. Normal Modes analyzes do not have predefined analysis plot templates generated. To display a results plot, right-click on Results in the Analysis 1 sub-tree and select Edit. The Plot dialog box opens.

3. Expand the subcases drop-down list. The normal frequencies for the model are listed. These are between the range that was specified (10-1000 Hz) in the Modal Setup.

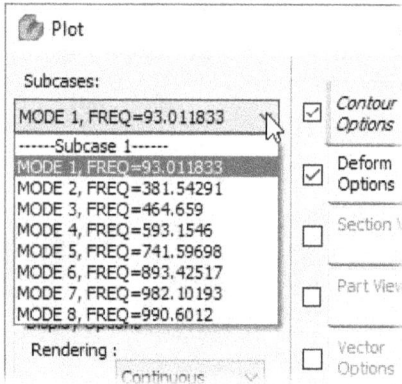

Based on vibration energy plots from MIL-STD-810G, frequencies between 5 and 60 are high energy. We don't have modes in this range so this is of no concern. The next area of concern is between 90-450. In the following image, the first four modes have been added to the plot.

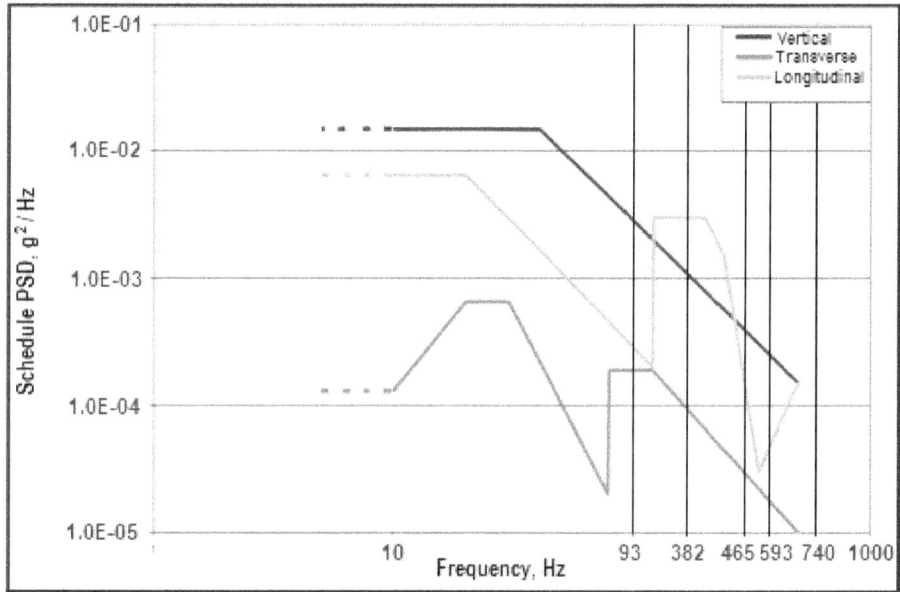

4. Set the following options in the Plot dialog box to view the Displacement results:

   - In the subcases drop-down list, select the first mode (Mode 1).
   - Select Displacement from the Result Data drop-down list and Total from the Type drop-down list on the Contour Options tab.
   - Select the Deform Options tab and set the Deformation Scale as 10% (Percent).
   - Select the Visibility Options tab and click Hide All.

5. Click (Animate) in the Plot section to display the animation for Mode 1 in the graphics window.

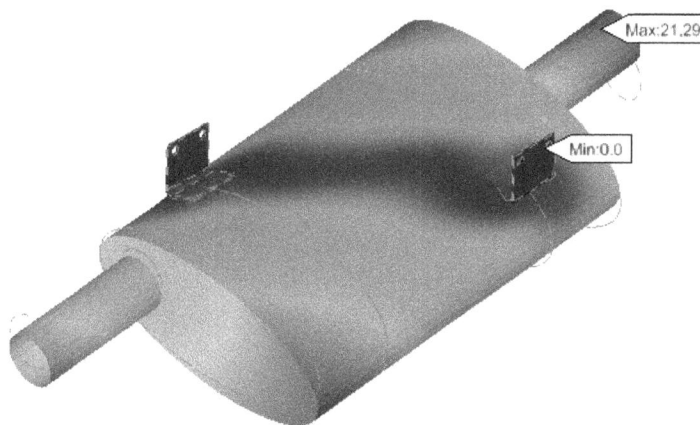

6. View the animation for Mode 2. This is the other mode that is within the range where you should be concerned. This mode has high input energy in longitudinal direction causing the input tube, baffles and end caps to move in the same direction. A section view of the animation would be more useful.

7. To add a section view, select the checkbox adjacent to the Section View tab in the Plot dialog box. This enables the use of a section view. If this remains unchecked the options will not be available.

8. In the Section View tab, click ⬛ (Right Plane). Enter 180 in the Y Rotation field to flip the viewing direction. Click ⬛ (Animate).

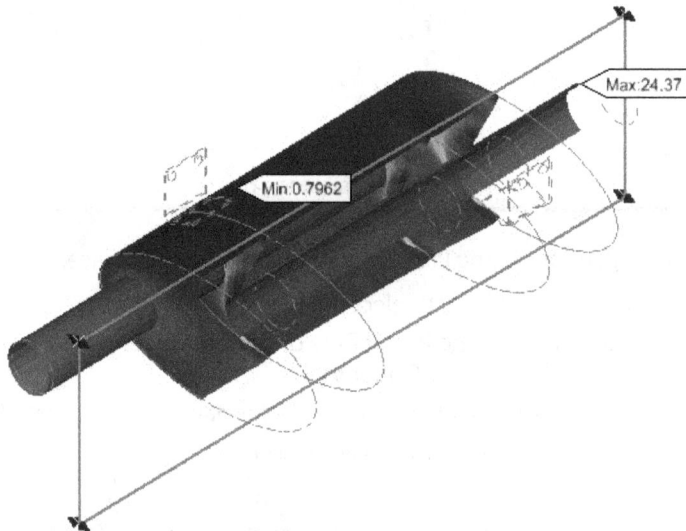

9. Continue to view any additional modes, as required.

10. Save the model. This model will be used in the next exercise, or you can open a model that has been provided for you.

Exercise: Muffler II - Modal Avoidance

In the previous exercise, you saw that there were normal modes (natural frequencies) that corresponded to higher energy road load inputs. Ideally, the muffler should not excite at those frequencies. If you can modify the design to push the questionable modes out of the peak energy portions of the curve, you will minimize the chance that vibration-related fatigue will occur. The process of moving modes to avoid high energy or excitation frequencies is called modal avoidance. In this exercise, you will modify the model to avoid these frequencies and rerun the analysis to verify the results

Prepare the Model for use in Nastran In-CAD

1. Open the file *C:\Autodesk Nastran InCAD 2019 Essentials Exercise Files\Muffler_Modal_Analysis\ Muffler&Brakets.iam*, if not already open. If you did not complete the previous exercise, open the file *C:\Autodesk Nastran InCAD 2019 Essentials Exercise Files\Muffler_Modal_Analysis\ Completed\ Muffler&Brakets2.iam*.

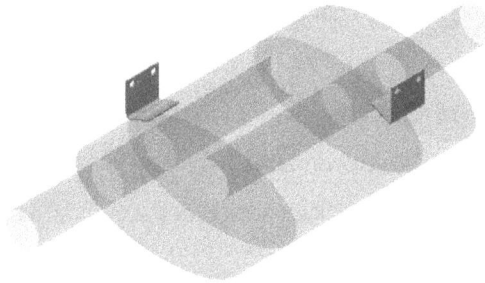

2. Activate the Autodesk Nastran In-CAD environment.

Change the Endcap/Bulkhead Thickness for Strain Calculations

The 380 Hz mode is very near the drop off region in the road load longitudinal curve. Pushing this mode up 20 to 25% could reduce its sensitivity to this frequency. You will change the "t" value in the shell idealization to change the thickness used to perform strain calculations and shift these modes.

1. Right-click on the Endcaps idealization and select Edit. Enter **0.062** as the new thickness (t) value. Click OK.

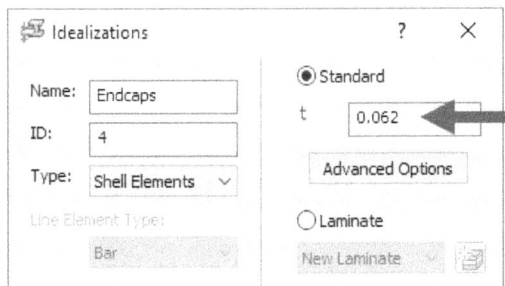

Thicken the Mounting Brackets

The approximate 95 Hz mode is close to the drop off in the road load transverse curve. Increased material thickness on a small part like this will have a minor cost impact. In this task, you will return to the Inventor modeling environment to make changes to the model.

1. In the Exit panel on the ribbon, click Finish Autodesk Nastran In-CAD to return to the modeling environment.

2. Select the Model tab in the browser for the assembly design. Select the Modeling option at the top of the browser to display the list of features in the model.

3. Right-click on the Thicken1 feature in the Muffler Mount:2 component and select Edit Feature.

4. Enter a Distance of **0.1**, and click OK.

5. Double-click on the Muffler&Brackets.iam (Two Brackets) node at the top of the Model Browser to activate the top-level assembly. The same Muffler Mount.ipt component is used multiple times so you don't have to change the thickness in multiple locations.

Update the Mesh

In this task, you will update the mesh to reflect the changes to the models.

1. Activate the Autodesk Nastran In-CAD environment.

2. Right-click on the Mesh Model node and click Generate Mesh to update the mesh.

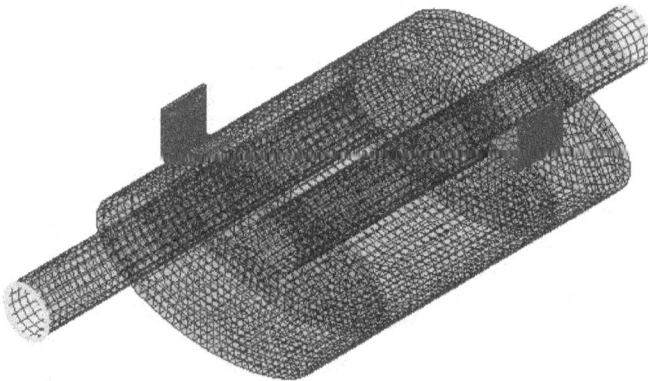

Run the Analysis and Review the Results

In this task, you will run the analysis and then analyze the displacement plots for the modes of interest.

1. Run the analysis.

2. Open the Plot dialog box and review the subcases drop-down list. The frequencies for each mode are listed.

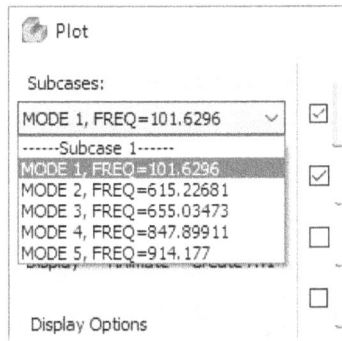

3. Set the following options in the Plot dialog box to view the Displacement results:

    ▪ In the subcases drop-down list, select the first mode (Mode 1).

    ▪ Select Displacement from the Result Data drop-down list and Total from the Type drop-down list on the Contour Options tab.

    ▪ Select the Deform Options tab and set the Deformation Scale as 10% (Percent).

    ▪ Select the Visibility Options tab and click Hide All.

4. Click (Animate) in the Plot section to display the animation in the graphics window.

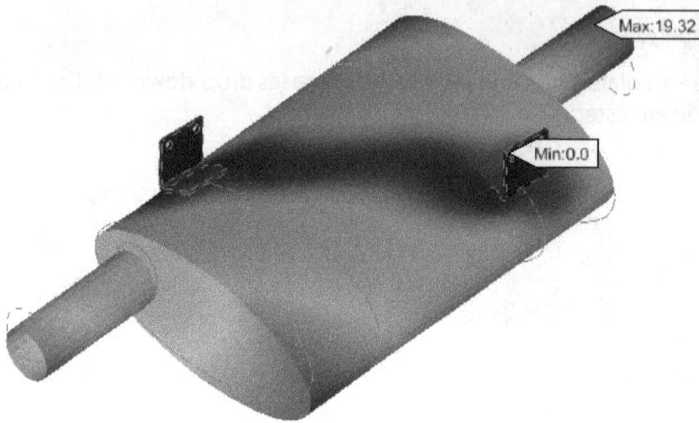

The changes made to the model did not significantly impact the 100 Hz mode. This rotational movement occurred because the bulkheads were centered on the brackets. Additional modeling changes should be considered in this model to prevent this natural frequency. If time permits, consider making additional changes and rerun the analysis.

5. Save the model and close it.

Frequency Response Analysis

Frequency response analysis solves for the steady state response (amplitudes and phase angles of displacements, velocities, accelerations, forces, stresses, and strains) of structures subjected to sinusoidal (harmonic) loading. Examples of oscillatory excitation include rotating machinery, unbalanced tires, and propeller blades. Unlike transient response, where the excitation is explicitly defined in the time domain, in frequency response, it is defined in the frequency domain. Applied loads are specified as a function of frequency. The goal in this chapter is to learn about both the direct and modal frequency response analysis types available in the Autodesk® Nastran® In-CAD software.

Objectives

After completing this chapter, you will be able to:

- Create a new direct and modal frequency response analysis.
- Define damping in both a direct and modal frequency response analysis.
- Define the Dynamic Setup options in both a direct and modal frequency response analysis.
- Define the Modal Setup options in a modal frequency response analysis.
- Display the Result plot and XY Plot results for a direct and modal frequency response analysis.

Lesson: Creating a Frequency Response Analysis

Overview

This lesson discusses the direct and modal frequency response analysis types available in the Autodesk Nastran In-CAD software. The frequency response analysis enables you to analyze a model's response to steady-state oscillatory excitation that is defined in the frequency domain. You will learn to setup, run, and review the results of these analysis types.

Objectives

After completing this lesson, you will be able to:

- Create a new direct and modal frequency response analysis.
- Define damping in both a direct and modal frequency response analysis.
- Define the Dynamic Setup options in both a direct and modal frequency response analysis.
- Define the Modal Setup options in a modal frequency response analysis.
- Display the Result plot and XY Plot results for a direct and modal frequency response analysis.

Basics of a Frequency Response Analysis

The frequency response analysis is used to compute structural response to steady-state oscillatory excitation. In frequency response analysis, the excitation is explicitly defined in the frequency domain. Excitations can be in the form of applied forces and enforced motions (displacements, velocities, or accelerations).

There are two types of frequency response analysis:

- **Direct Frequency Response Analysis**: The structural response is computed at discrete excitation frequencies by solving a set of coupled matrix equations using complex algebra. The direct method may be more efficient for models where high-frequency excitation requires the extraction of a large number of modes.

- **Modal Frequency Response Analysis**: An alternative method to compute frequency response. It uses the mode shapes of the structure to uncouple the equations of motion (when no damping or only modal damping is used) and, depending on the number of modes computed and retained, reduces the problem size. Both of these factors tend to make modal frequency response analysis computationally more efficient than direct frequency response analysis. It is used for large models where a large number of solution frequencies are specified. This method replaces the physical degrees of freedom (DOF) with a reduced number of modal degrees of freedom. Fewer degrees of freedom mean a faster solution. Because modal frequency response analysis uses the mode shapes of a structure, modal frequency response analysis is a natural extension of normal modes analysis.

Damping in Frequency Response Analysis

An important thing to ensure you have a stable solution is to provide damping in the model. Any real structure will dissipate energy (mainly through friction), therefore damping is an important component of reality in a dynamic solution. Generally, damping would be ignored for non-transient events (such as wind loading, or crowd loading), but would be important for transient events (like an earthquake loading or bomb blast). Damping is also important for frequency response analysis.

The following table describes how some of the different damping terms affect the different solutions.

Analysis Type	Damping Elements	Structural Damping	Modal Damping	Raleigh Damping
Direct Frequency Response	Normal	Normal	Ignored	Forced Coupled Solution
Modal Frequency Response	Forced Coupled Solution	Normal	Normal	Forced Coupled Solution

If possible, it is recommended to use damping that corresponds to the Normal entries on the above table. Those combinations will yield the fastest run times.

Creating a Frequency Response Analysis

To create a direct or modal frequency response analysis you must either create a new analysis or edit an existing analysis and change the type of analysis to Direct Frequency Response or Modal Frequency Response, respectively. You can also select any additional options in the Analysis dialog box to define the output controls, options, and model state (Design View or Level of Detail to be analyzed).

When a direct or modal frequency response analysis is created the Autodesk Nastran Model Tree displays as shown in the following image. The direct and modal frequency response analyzes require dynamic setup steps, and in the case of a modal frequency response analysis, a modal setup is also required. Damping can also be set for both analysis types. Only a single Damping setting exists in the subcases.

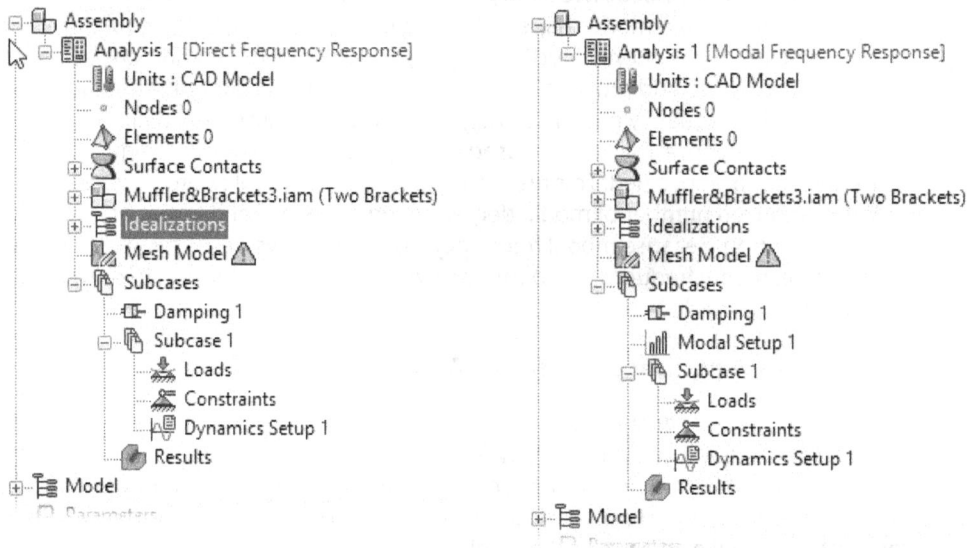

Additionally you must consider the following:

- Ensure that a required idealizations exists or is created that contains any material properties that are specifically required for the analysis.
- Assign any constraints and loads that are required for the analysis.
- Assign any required surface contacts, as required, to fully describe the model being analyzed.
- Setup damping.
- Setup the Modal Setup options (Modal Frequency Response analysis only).
- Set the Dynamics options that define the frequencies for the analysis.

Damping Setup

Damping settings can be assigned for both Modal and Direct Frequency Response analysis types. To access the setup options, right-click on the Damping Setup node in the analysis subcase and select Edit.

The Damping dialog box contains the following options for defining Damping. Depending on the type of damping, these options might be available or not. For frequency response analysis, you can enable Structural Damping, Rayleigh Damping, or Modal Damping (Modal Frequency Response only):

- **Structural Damping**: Applies structural based damping to transient analysis. Select the checkbox adjacent to its title to enable it. By default, this option is enabled.
    - **Damping Value, G (%)**: This is a global structural damping setting. Enter the damping value.
    - **Dominant Frequency, W3 (Hz)**: This is a global structural damping setting. Enter the frequency of interest for the conversion of element structural damping into equivalent viscous damping.
    - **Dominant Frequency, W4 (Hz)**: This is a material structural damping setting. Enter the frequency of interest for the conversion of element structural damping into equivalent viscous damping. It will use the damping specified in your material property and give you the flexibility to apply different damping values to different areas/materials of the model.

- **Rayleigh Damping**: Represents the special case where you choose to form the damping matrix from a linear combination of mass and stiffness matrices.
  - **Mass Proportional, ALPHA**: Applies mass based damping to the analysis.
  - **Stiffness Proportional, BETA**: Applies stiffness based damping to analysis.

- **Modal Damping**: Applies modal based damping to modal frequency response analysis.
  - **Type**: Enables you to define the model damping as constant or variable.
  - **Damping Definition**: Enables you to define the units for the damping value. You can choose from percentage of critical damping (C/C0), amplification or quality factor (1/(2C/C0), or in the units of g (2C/C0).
  - **Damping Value(%)**: For constant modal damping, enter the damping value.
  - **Use Table**: For variable modal damping, use these options to define the damping versus frequency curve.

For more information on the Damping dialog box, refer to Autodesk Nastran In-CAD Help and search for "Damping".

Modal Setup

Modal settings can be customized using the Modal Setup node that gets created in the subcase of a Modal Frequency Response analysis. To access the setup options, right-click on the Modal Setup node in the analysis subcase and select Edit.

The Modal Setup dialog box contains the same options that are used for a Normal Modes analysis that was previously discussed. For more information on the Modal Setup dialog box and its options, refer to the *Creating a Normal Modes Analysis* lesson in Chapter 9 or to Autodesk Nastran In-CAD Help and search for "Modal Setup".

Dynamics Setup

Dynamics settings can be customized using the Dynamics Setup node that gets created in the subcase of a direct or modal frequency response analysis. It enables you to define the frequency limits and the number of points that will be examined during the analysis. To access the setup options, right-click on the Dynamics Setup node in the analysis subcase and select Edit.

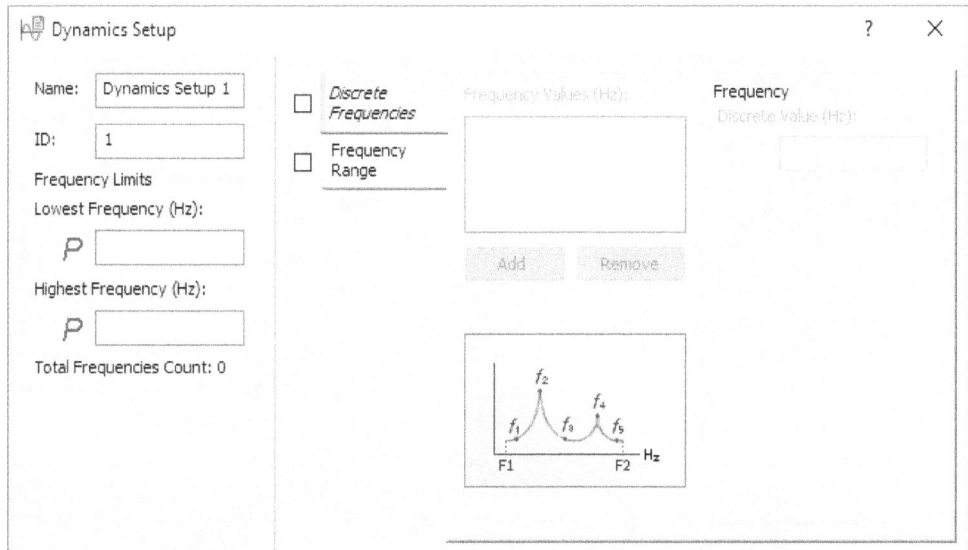

Dynamics Setup dialog box for a Direct Frequency Response Analysis

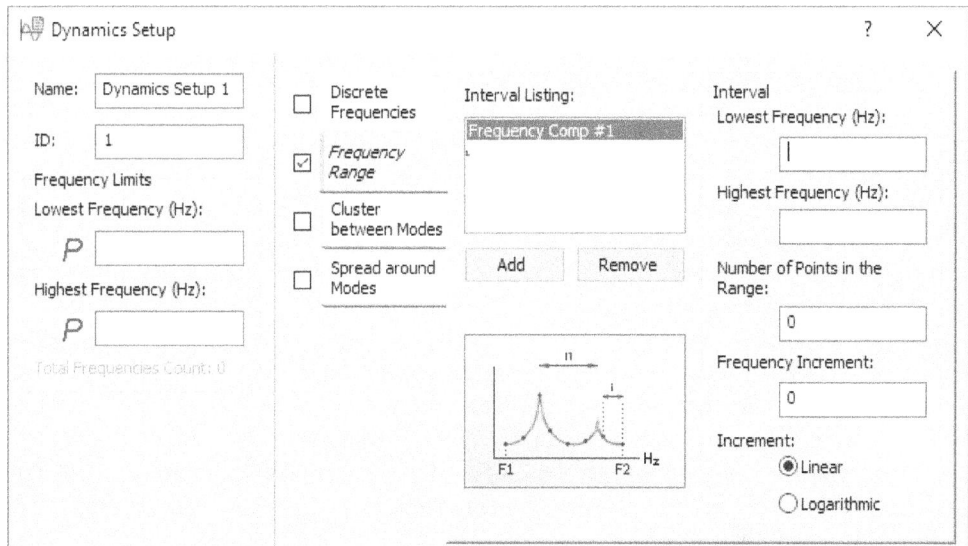

Dynamics Setup dialog box for a Modal Frequency Response Analysis

The specific options available are described as follows:

- **Name**: Assigns a name to the dynamic setup.
- **ID**: The ID of the property is automatically updated by Autodesk Nastran In-CAD.
- **Frequency Limits**:
  - **Lowest Frequency (Hz)**: For a Direct Frequency Response analysis, this sets the lowest frequency in the frequency range of interest. In a Modal Frequency Response solution, Lowest Frequency uses the parameter LFREQ in the Bulk Data file. This cuts off any frequencies below this number.
  - **Highest Frequency (Hz)**: For a Direct Frequency Response analysis, this sets the highest frequency in the frequency range. In a Modal Frequency Response analysis, Highest Frequency uses the parameter HFREQ in the Bulk Data file. This cuts off any frequencies above this number.
    - Note: The P symbol adjacent to the Lowest and Highest Frequency values denotes that this is written out as a parameter.
  - **Total Frequencies Count**: Identifies the total count of frequencies that will be calculated. This is based on lowest and highest frequency values, along with the number of points and frequency increments that are set on the Frequency Range tab. This is only available for the Direct Frequency Response analysis type.

As an alternative, or in conjunction with, when entering the frequency limits, you can use the tabs on the right-hand side of the dialog box to specifically define the frequencies that should be analyzed. To define a tabs' values and have the values be used during an analysis, ensure that the checkbox adjacent to the tab name is selected. Consider using the following tabs:

- **Discrete Frequencies tab**: Enables discrete frequencies to be specified by adding them to the list. Enter a value and click Add to include in the list of frequencies being analyzed. Use Remove to remove frequencies from the list.
- **Frequency Range tab**: Enables the entry of a range of frequencies (lowest and highest), the number of points that should be created in the range, and the frequency increment. Additionally you can define whether the increment is linear or logarithmic. If logarithmic the frequency increment cannot be defined.
- **Cluster between Modes tab**: (Modal Frequency Response analysis only) Enables the entry of a range of frequencies (lowest and highest), the number of points that should be created between modes, and the Bias Factor. Additionally you can define whether the increment is linear or logarithmic.
  - The Bias Factor defines how the points are located. A value of 1 indicates evenly spaced points, and a value greater than 1.0 will bias the points toward the ends of the set and a value less than 1.0 will bias the points toward the center of set. As an example, a set is defined as flowest -> fw1 then fw1 -> fw2 and fwn ->fhighest.
- **Spread around Modes tab**: (Modal Frequency Response analysis only) Enables the entry of a range of frequencies (lowest and highest), the number of points spread per mode, and the Percentage Spread.
  - The Percentage Spread defines a percent of +/- on each side of a natural frequency.

For more information on the Dynamics Setup dialog box and its options, refer to Autodesk Nastran In-CAD Help and search for "Dynamics Setup".

Procedure: To Create a new (Direct or Modal) Frequency Response Analysis

1. Right-click on the Part or Assembly node at the top of the Model Tree and select New.

2. Enter the name for the new analysis.

3. Select either the Direct Frequency Response or Modal Frequency Response analysis types in the Type drop-down list.

4. (Optional) By default the unit system for the model is set to that of the CAD model. Click Select Units and select an alternative unit system, if required.

5. Define the required options in the Output Controls tab to define the information that will be output to the analysis report when it is run. For example for a direct or modal frequency response analysis you might also want to include the Velocity and Acceleration options that are included in the Nodal section.

6. In the Options tab:
    - Set the Contact type that should be used by default when generating Automatic contacts.
    - Set the tolerance value between contacting entities at which automatic contacts are created.

7. If analyzing an assembly, on the Model State tab, select a Design View or Level of Detail to define the model configuration that is being analyzed.

8. Click OK to create the new analysis.

9. Right-click on the Damping node in the analysis subcase and select Edit. Define the Damping properties, as required.

10. Right-click on the Modal Setup node in the analysis subcase and select Edit. Define the Modal Setup properties, as required. (Available for Model Frequency Response only)

11. Right-click on the Dynamics Setup node in the analysis subcase and select Edit. Define the time step properties, as required.

12. Assign an existing idealization from the Model sub-tree or create a new one, as required.

13. Assign contacts and/or constraints to the model, as required.

14. Assign loads to the model, as required.

15. Add any additional subcases, as required. Multiple subcases can be used to control different excitation conditions.

Alternatively, you can edit an existing analysis by right-clicking the analysis name in the Model Tree and select Edit.

Direct or Modal Frequency Response Analysis Plot Results

When a direct or modal frequency response analysis is run, there are no default plot templates included. You must use the Plot dialog box to visually display the results. To access the Plot dialog box, right-click on the Results node and select Edit. You can customize the Plot dialog box, as required, to create the required plot for the analysis.

> For more information on Plot dialog box and its options, refer to the *Visualizing Result Plots* lesson in Chapter 3 or to Autodesk Nastran In-CAD Help and search for "Plot Templates".

Direct or Modal Frequency Response Analysis XY Plot

When a direct or modal frequency response analysis is run, a number of XY plots are generated by default to help you analyze the results.

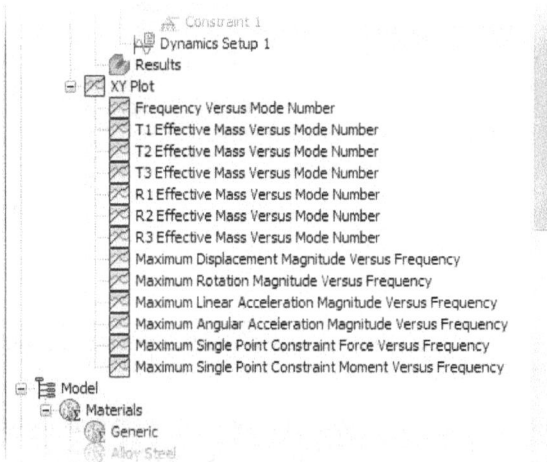

To review any of the plots, double-click on the plot name or right-click on the plot name and select Show XY Plot. The XY Plot dialog box opens displaying the plot. Additional XY plots can be created, as required, to further review the results.

> For more information on XY Plot dialog box, its options, and how to create a new XY Plot, refer to the *Visualizing XY Plot Results* lesson in Chapter 3 or to Autodesk Nastran In-CAD Help and search for "Results XY Plotting".

Exercise: Muffler III - Frequency Response

In this exercise, you will perform a modal frequency response analysis simulation on the muffler model. The frequency response analysis will be used to compute structural response to steady-state oscillatory excitation. The design changes that were made in the Modal Avoidance exercise will be used in this exercise.

Prepare the Model for use in Nastran In-CAD

1.   Open the file *C:\Autodesk Nastran InCAD 2019 Essentials Exercise Files\Muffler_Frequency_ Response\Muffler&Brakets3.iam.*

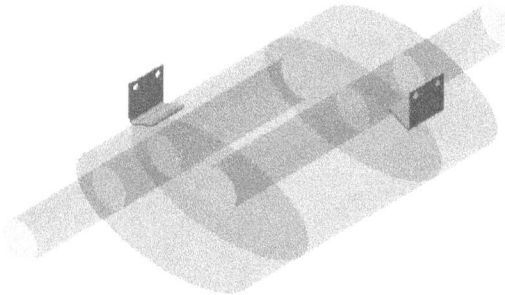

2.   Activate the Autodesk Nastran In-CAD environment. The Normal Modes analysis has been provided in this model. All of the same idealizations, surface contacts, and constraints that were assigned in the previous chapter, will be used in this exercise to create the Frequency Response analysis.

Setup a new Modal Frequency Response Analysis

In this task, you will create a new modal frequency response analysis in the model to further analyze its design changes.

1.   Right-click on Analysis 1 and select Edit.

2.   Select Modal Frequency Response in the Type drop-down list.

3.   In the Output Controls tab, select Acceleration in the Nodal section.

4.   Select the Model State tab and ensure that the Two Brackets Level of Detail is selected for analysis.

5.   Maintain the remaining defaults in the Analysis dialog box. Click OK.

6. In the Subcases node, right-click on Damping 1 and select Edit. Set the following options in the Damping dialog box:
   - Clear the Structural Damping checkbox.
   - Enter **2** as the Damping Value (%) for Modal Damping.
   - Click OK.

7. In the Subcases node, right-click on Modal Setup 1 and select Edit. Verify that the following options in the Modal Setup dialog box are set:
   - The Lowest Frequency is set to 10.
   - The Highest Frequency is set to 1000.
   - Click OK.

Create the Load

In this task, you will load the model using a value of 386 in/s^2. This values is equal to the standard acceleration due to gravity (1G).

1. Create a load using the following settings:

    - Set the Type of load as Enforced Motion.
    - Set the Sub Type of load as Acceleration.
    - Enter **386.4** as the a_y value.
    - Assign the load to Subcase1.
    - Select the inner cylindrical surfaces of each hole on the two brackets, as the references for the load (four surfaces in total). The surfaces are shown below for one of the brackets.
    - Select Preview to show the load on the model.
    - Modify the density and size of the load's display, as required.
    - Click OK.

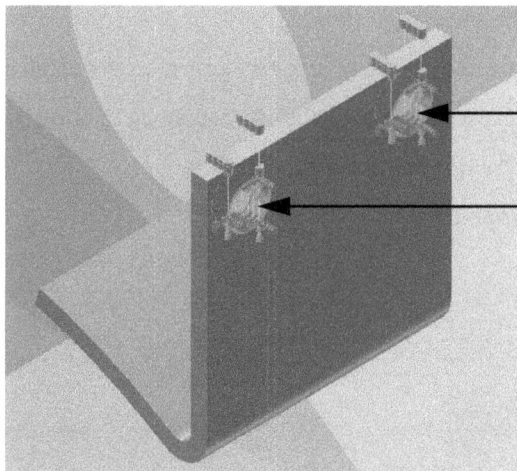

Select the inner cylindrical surfaces of each hole on the two brackets

Define the Dynamic Setup Options for the Analysis

In this task, you will define the dynamic setup options for the subcase.

1. Right-click on the Dynamics Setup 1 node in Subcase 1and click Edit.

2. On the Dynamics Setup dialog box, select the checkbox adjacent to the Frequency Range tab to enable it.

3. Enter **60** as the Lowest Frequency value.

4. Enter **1000** Hz as the Highest Frequency value.

5. Enter **20** as the Number of Points in the Range value.

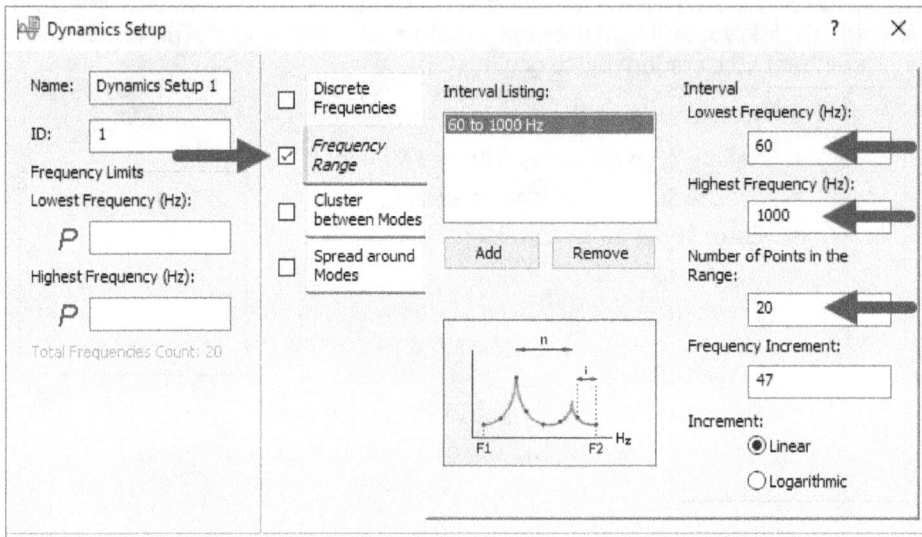

6. Select the checkbox adjacent to the Spread around Modes tab to enable it.

7. Set the Lowest Frequency to **60** Hz and the Highest Frequency to **1000** Hz.

8. Enter **10** as the Number of Points Spread per Mode value.

9. Enter **5** as the Percentage Spread value.

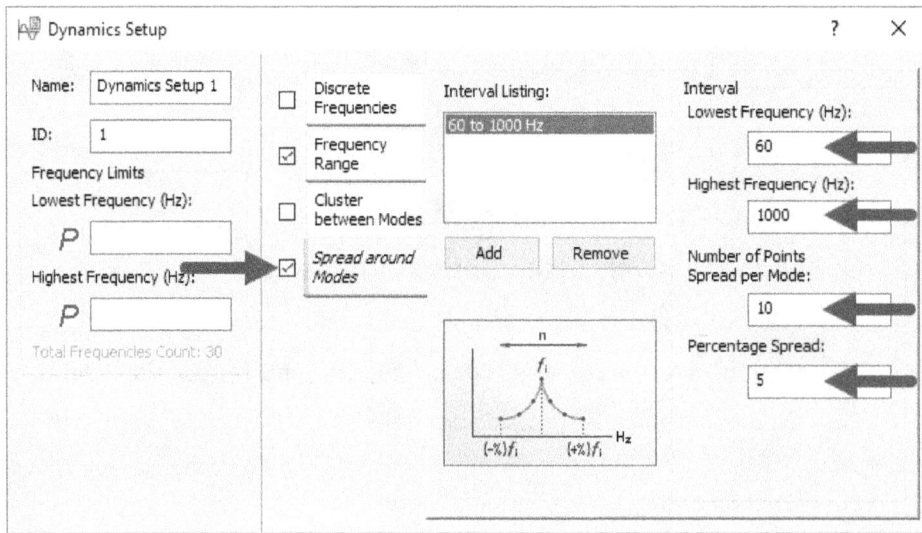

10. Click OK.

Run the Analysis and Review the Results

In this task, you will run the analysis and then analyze the displacement and stress result plots.

1. Run the analysis. Ensure that the mesh is updated prior to running the analysis.

2. In the XY Plot node for the analysis, right-click on Maximum Displacement Magnitude Versus Frequency and click Show XY Plot. To customize the XY Plot's display, set the following options:

   - Select Line+Symbol in the Type drop-down list.
   - The peak displacements occur at 60Hz, 100 Hz, and 914Hz. These are the frequencies where the structure will be excited the most.

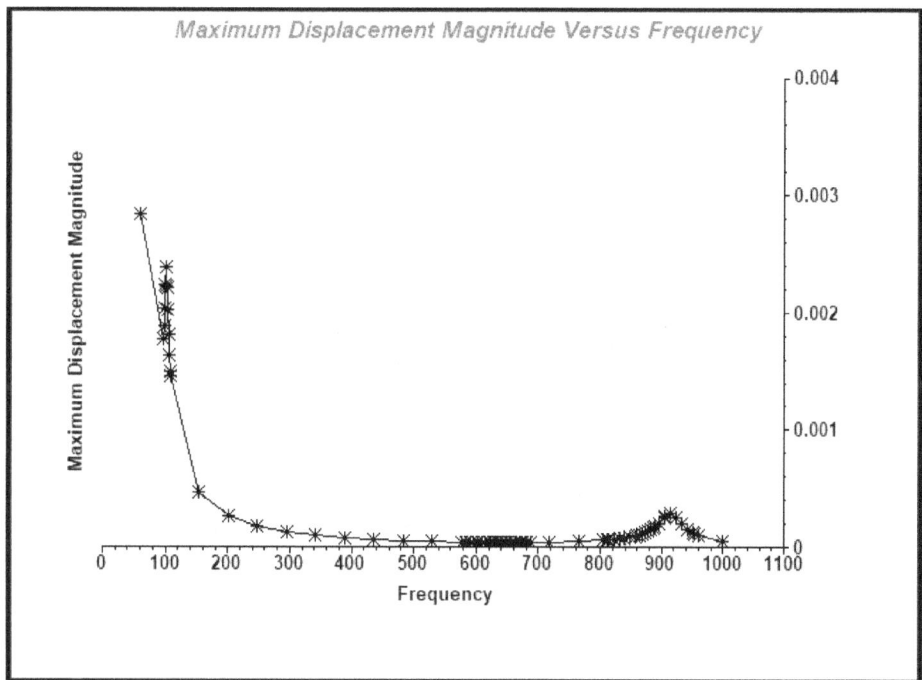

Note: The max displacements were found by copying the data to the clipboard and reviewing the values in a spreadsheet file. You can also hover the cursor over the datapoints on the graph. A pop-up tool tip indicates the horizontal (frequency) and vertical (displacement) values at the point.

3. Click OK to close the dialog box

4. In the XY Plot node for the analysis, double-click on Maximum Linear Acceleration Magnitude Versus Frequency. This can be used as an alternative method for displaying the plot. To customize the XY Plot's display, set the following options:

- Select Line+Symbol in the Type drop-down list.
- The latter two frequencies where we previously saw displacement peaks, also show maximum acceleration.

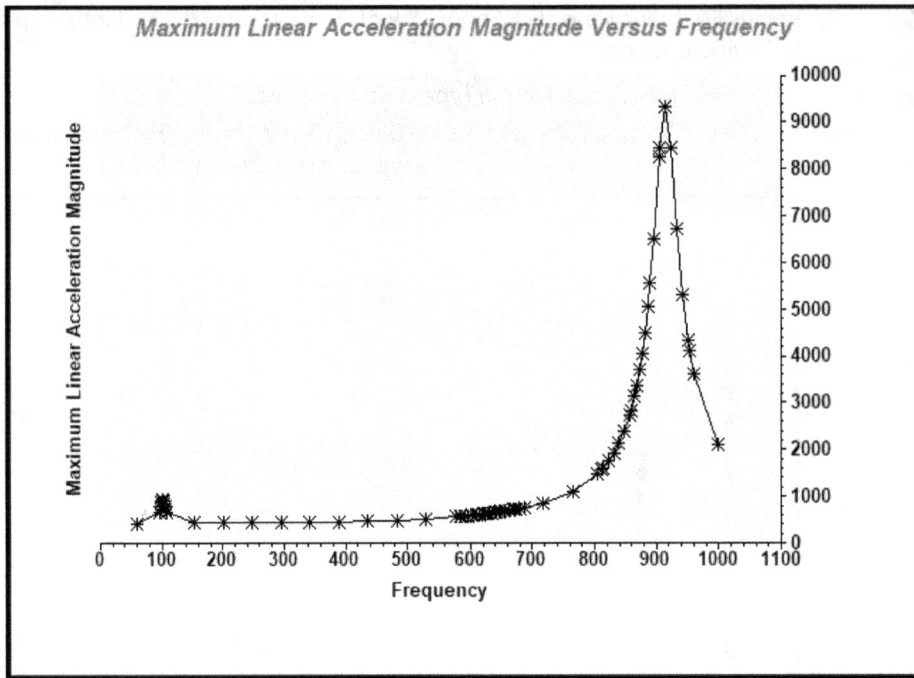

Maximum Linear Acceleration Magnitude Versus Frequency

5. Click OK to close the dialog box

6. To display a results plot, right-click on Results in the Analysis 1 sub-tree and select Edit. To view the stress results, set the following options in the Plot dialog box:

- In the subcases drop-down list, ensure that STEP 6, FREQ=100.6133.
- Select SHELL VON MISES STRESS from the Result Data drop-down list on the Contour Options tab.
- Click (Animate) in the Plot section to display the animation of this step in the graphics window.

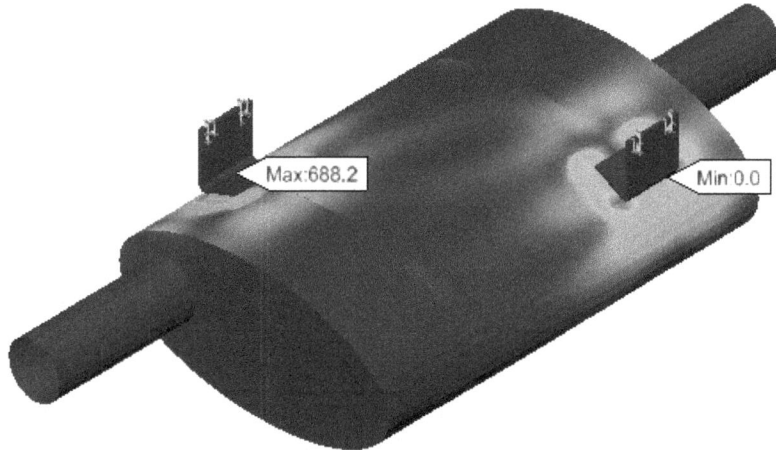

7. Repeat this to review any other critical frequencies. For example, the 914 Hz frequency step.

8. Save the model.

In this exercise, we incorporated road load inputs to shake the muffler to see how much stress is expected, since we still had natural frequencies in the operating range of the curve. From the resultant stress levels, we can determine if a fatigue study is required.

Transient Response Analyzes

Problems in structural dynamics can be divided into two broad areas. In one, the objective is to determine natural frequencies of vibration and the corresponding mode shapes. In the other, the objective is to determine how the structure behaves with time, under an applied set of loads. In this chapter, you will examine the latter, which is termed transient response analysis. In transient response analysis, the applied loading and damping are not necessarily zero and loading can vary with time. Loading can be in the form of applied forces, acceleration, and enforced motions. Available grid point output includes: displacements, velocities, accelerations, and loading at each output time step. Available element output includes: energy, forces, and stresses at each output time step. The goal in this chapter is to learn about the direct and modal transient response analysis types available in the Autodesk® Nastran® In-CAD software.

Objectives

After completing this chapter, you will be able to:

- Create a new direct and modal transient response analysis.
- Define damping in a direct and a modal transient response analysis.
- Define the Modal Setup options in a modal transient response analysis.
- Define the Dynamic Setup options in a direct and a modal transient response analysis.
- Display the Result plot and XY Plot results for Direct and Modal Transient Response analyzes.

Lesson: Creating Direct & Modal Transient Response Analysis

Overview

This lesson discusses the direct and modal transient response analysis types available in the Autodesk Nastran In-CAD software. Transient response analysis is the most general method for computing forced dynamic response and analyzes how a structure behaves to time-varying excitation for an applied force or enforced motion. You will learn to setup, run, and review the results of these analysis types.

Objectives

After completing this lesson, you will be able to:

- Create a new direct and modal transient response analysis.
- Define damping in a direct and a modal transient response analysis.
- Define the Modal Setup options in a modal transient response analysis.
- Define the Dynamic Setup options in a direct and a modal transient response analysis.
- Display the Result plot and XY Plot results for a direct and modal transient response analysis.

Basics of a Transient Response Analysis

Transient response analysis is the most general method for computing forced dynamic response. The purpose of a transient response analysis is to determine the behavior of a structure subjected to time-varying excitation. The transient excitation is explicitly defined in the time domain. The loads applied to the structure are known at each instant in time. Loads can be in the form of applied forces and enforced motions. The results obtained from a transient response analysis are typically displacements, velocities, and accelerations of grid points, and forces and stresses in elements, at each output time step.

Depending upon the structure and the nature of the loading, two different numerical methods can be used for a transient response analysis:

- **Direct Transient Response Analysis**: Calculates the response of a system to a load over time. The load applied to the system can vary over time or simply be an initial condition that is permitted to evolve over time. This method is more efficient for models where high-frequency excitation require the extraction of a large number of modes. Also, if structural damping is used, the direct method should be used.

- **Modal Transient Response Analysis**: An alternative technique available for dynamics that uses the mode shapes of the structure, reduces the solution degrees of freedom, and can significantly impact the run time. This approach replaces the physical degrees of freedom with a reduced number of modal degrees of freedom. Fewer degrees of freedom mean a faster solution. This can be a big time saver for transient models with a large number of time steps. Because modal transient response analysis uses the mode shapes of a structure, this analysis is a natural extension of normal modes analysis.

Creating a Transient Response Analysis

To create a direct or modal transient response analysis, you must either create a new analysis or edit an existing analysis and change the type of analysis to Direct Transient Response or Modal Transient Response. You can also select any additional options in the Analysis dialog box to define the output controls, options, and model state (Design View or Level of Detail to be analyzed).

Once created, the Autodesk Nastran Model Tree displays as shown below, listing the nodes which are required for the analysis type.

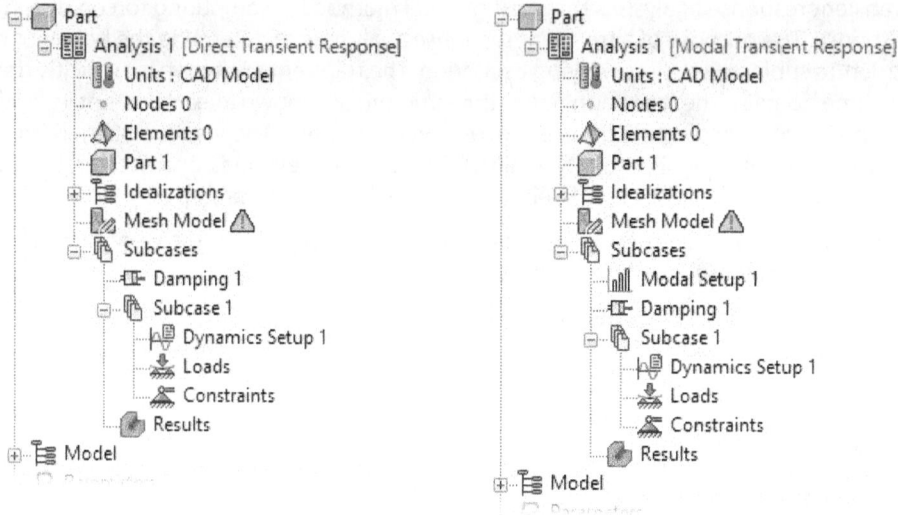

Additionally, you must consider the following:

- Ensure that a required idealization exists or is created that contains any material properties that are specifically required for the analysis.
- Assign any constraints and loads that are required for the analysis.
- Assign any required surface contacts, as required, to fully describe the model being analyzed.
- Setup damping.
- Setup the Modal Setup options (Modal Transient Response analysis only).
- Set the Dynamics options that define the time steps for the analysis.

The transient response analyzes require damping and dynamic (timestep) setups. For a modal transient response analysis, the Modal setup must also be defined. The following describes these items in the analysis.

Damping Setup

Damping settings can be assigned for both Modal and Direct Transient Response analysis types. To access the setup options, right-click on the Damping Setup node in the analysis subcase and select Edit. The damping options that are available are the same as those in a frequency response analysis that was previously discussed.

The following table describes how some of the different damping terms affect the various solutions.

Analysis Type	Damping Elements	Structural Damping	Modal Damping	Raleigh Damping
Direct Transient Response	Normal	Converted to Equivalent Viscous	Ignored	Normal
Modal Transient Response	Forced Coupled Solution	Converted to Equivalent Viscous - Force Coupled Solution	Normal	Normal

If possible, it is recommended to use damping that corresponds to the Normal entries on the above table. Those combinations will yield the fastest run times.

For more information on the Damping dialog box and its options, refer to the *Creating a Frequency Response Analysis* lesson covered in Chapter 10 or to Autodesk Nastran In-CAD Help and search for "Damping".

Modal Setup

For a modal transient response analysis, modal settings must be specified to define the modes that will be analyzed. To access the setup options, right-click on the Modal Setup node in the analysis subcase and select Edit.

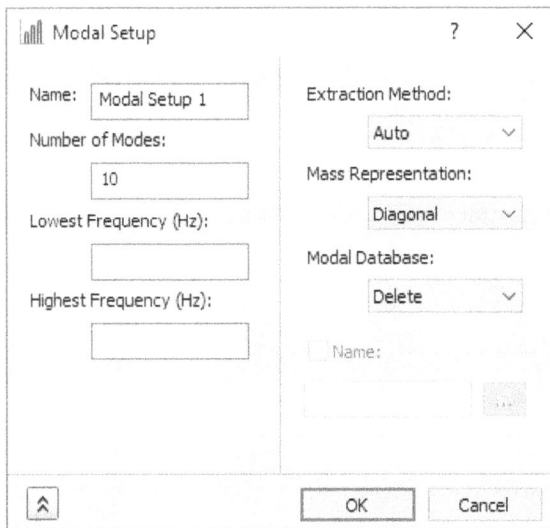

The Modal Setup dialog box contains the same options that are used for a normal modes analysis that was previously discussed. For more information on the Modal Setup dialog box and its options, refer to the *Creating a Normal Modes Analysis* lesson in Chapter 9 or to Autodesk Nastran In-CAD Help and search for "Modal Setup".

Dynamics Setup

Dynamics settings can be customized using the Dynamics Setup node that gets created in the subcase of a direct or modal transient response analysis. The dynamics setup for a direct or modal transient response analysis is the same as that for a nonlinear transient response analysis. It enables you to define the time intervals that will be used during the analysis. To access the setup options, right-click on the Dynamics Setup node in the analysis subcase and select Edit. The time interval can be set for a subcase and any additional subcases can have unique settings that continue from the previous subcase.

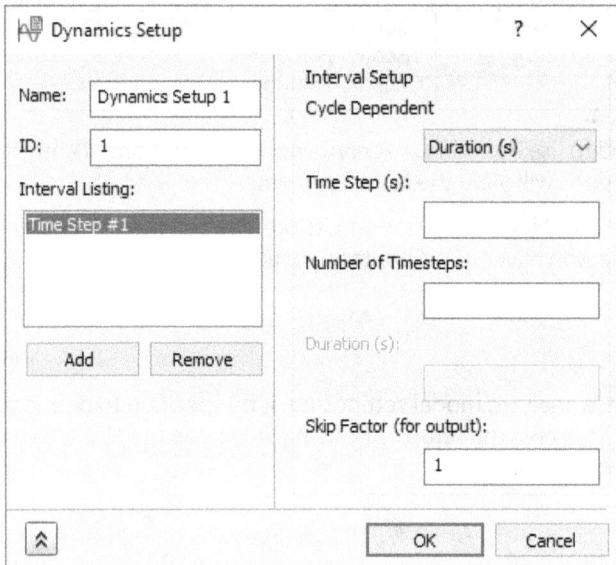

For more information on the Time Step dialog box and its options, refer to the *Creating a Nonlinear Transient Response Analysis* lesson in Chapter 8 or to Autodesk Nastran In-CAD Help and search for "Dynamics Setup".

Procedure: To Create a new (Direct or Modal) Transient Response Analysis

1. Right-click on the Part or Assembly node at the top of the Model Tree and select New.

2. Enter the name for the new analysis.

3. Select either the Direct Transient Response or Modal Transient Response analysis types in the Type drop-down list.

4. (Optional) By default, the unit system for the model is set to that of the CAD model. Click Select Units and select an alternative unit system, if required.

5. Select the required options in the Output Controls tab to define the information that will be output to the analysis report when it is run. For example, for a direct or modal transient response analysis you might also want to include the Velocity and Acceleration options in the Nodal section of the dialog box.

6. In the Options tab:

    - Set the Contact type that should be used by default when generating Automatic contacts.
    - Set the tolerance value between contacting entities at which automatic contacts are created.

7. If analyzing an assembly, on the Model State tab, select a Design View or Level of Detail to define the model configuration that is being analyzed.

8. Click OK to create the new analysis.

9. Right-click on the Damping node in the analysis subcase and select Edit. Define the Damping properties, as required.

10. Right-click on the Modal Setup node in the analysis subcase and select Edit. Define the Modal Setup properties, as required.

11. Right-click on the Dynamics Setup node in the analysis subcase and select Edit. Define the time step properties, as required.

12. Assign an existing idealization from the Model sub-tree or create a new one, as required.

13. Assign contacts and/or constraints to the model, as required.

14. Assign loads to the model, as required.

15. Add any additional subcases, as required. Multiple subcases can be used to control the time step size for multiple calculation intervals.

Alternatively, you can edit an existing analysis by right-clicking the analysis name in the Autodesk Nastran Model Tree and select Edit.

Direct or Modal Transient Response Analysis Plot Results

Similar to the nonlinear transient response analysis, there are no default plot templates included. You must use the Plot dialog box to visually display the results. To access the Plot dialog box, right-click on the Results node and select Edit. You can customize the Plot dialog box, as required, to create the required plot for analysis.

> For more information on Plot dialog box and its options, refer to the *Visualizing Result Plots* lesson in Chapter 3 or to Autodesk Nastran In-CAD Help and search for "Plot Templates".

Direct or Modal Transient Response Analysis XY Plot

When a direct or modal transient response analysis is run, a number of XY plots are generated by default to help you analyze the results.

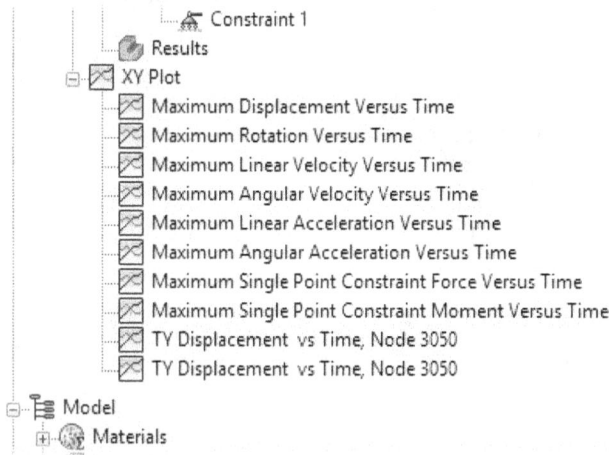

To review any of the plots, double-click on the plot name or right-click on the plot name and select Show XY Plot. The XY Plot dialog box opens displaying the plot. Additional XY plots can be created, as required, to further review the results.

> For more information on XY Plot dialog box, its options, and how to create a new XY Plot, refer to the *Visualizing XY Plot Results* lesson in Chapter 3 or to Autodesk Nastran In-CAD Help and search for "Results XY Plotting".

Exercise: Wing

In this exercise, you will perform a Direct Transient Response analysis on a model of an airplane wing. You will use shell elements and the direct transient response analysis type to calculate the response of the wing to a load over time. The load will be an applied force to an edge at the end of the wing and a Load Scale Factor table will be used to define the transient loading. To complete the exercise, you will review the displacement plots and XY plots at steps throughout the analysis.

Prepare the Model for use in Nastran In-CAD

1. Open the file *C:\Autodesk Nastran InCAD 2019 Essentials Exercise Files\Wing\Wing.ipt*.

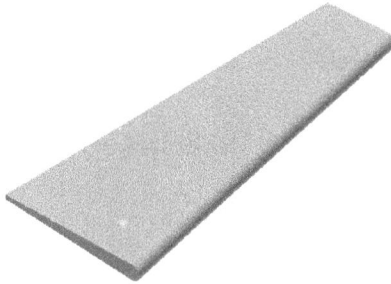

2. Activate the Autodesk Nastran In-CAD environment.

Setup a new Direct Transient Response Analysis

In this task, you will create a new Direct Transient Response analysis in the model to analyze the response of the wing to a load over time.

1. Right-click on Analysis 1 and select Edit.

2. Select Direct Transient Response in the Type drop-down list.

3. In the Output Controls tab, select Velocity and Acceleration in the Nodal section.

4. Maintain the remaining defaults in the Analysis dialog box. Click OK.

Assign a new Idealization for the Wing

In this task, you will create a new idealization and assign it to the model for use during the analysis. The material that is used in the idealization will be selected from the Nastran materials library.

1. Create a new idealization using the following settings and add it to the analysis:

    - Enter **Wing - Aluminum 7075 HTW** as the name of the new idealization.
    - Ensure that Shell Elements is selected as the Type of element.
    - Enter **0.1** as the thickness (t) value.

2. Select ▣ (New Material) and in the Material dialog box, click Select Material.

3. In the Material DB dialog box, select Load Database. The Open dialog box displays the *C:\Program Files\Autodesk\Nastran In-CAD 2019\In-CAD\Materials* folder. This is the default location of the Nastran materials library.

4. Select ADSK_materials.nasmat and click Open to load the library.

5. Expand the Aluminum Alloys category and select Aluminum 7075 Heat Treated (T6) Wrought. Click OK. The Material dialog box populates with its values. Click OK.

6. Change the color of the idealization to blue.

7. Click OK in the Idealizations dialog box.

8. Remove Solid 1 idealization from the analysis.

Define the Subcase for the analysis

In this task, you will define the Damping, Dynamic Setup, Loads, and Constraints for the subcase.

1. In the Subcases node, right-click on Damping 1 and select Edit. Set the following options in the Damping dialog box:

    ▪ Ensure the Structural Damping checkbox is selected.

    ▪ Enter **10** as the Damping Value, G (%) value.

    ▪ Enter **7.861** as the Dominant Frequency, W3(Hz) value. Previously, a modal analysis was performed to determine the dominant frequency for this model. This is typically the first natural frequency.

    ▪ Click OK.

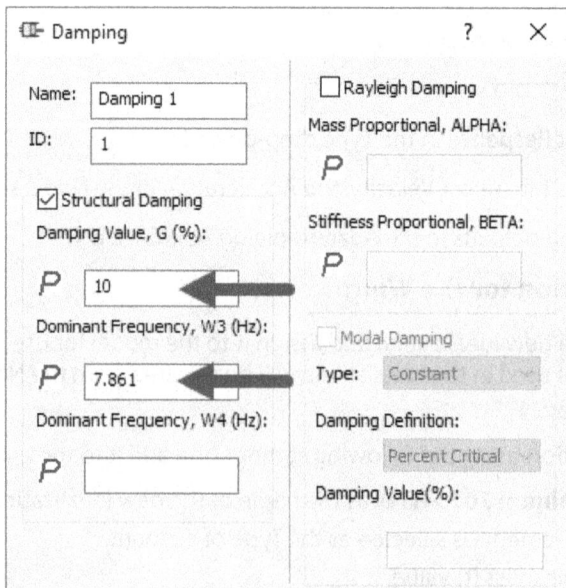

2. In the Subcases node, right-click on Dynamics Setup 1 and select Edit. Set the following options in the Time Step dialog box:

    ▪ Enter **0.005** as the Time Step(s) value.
    ▪ Enter **60** as the Number of Timesteps value.
    ▪ Click OK.

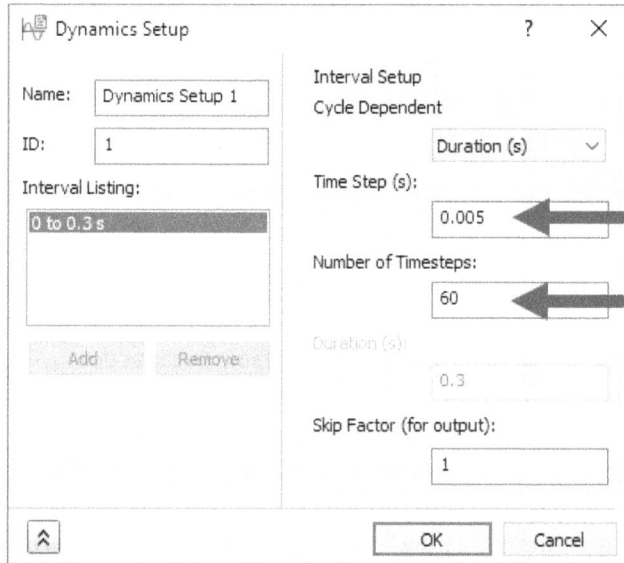

3. Create a constraint using the following settings:

    ▪ Ensure that all degrees of freedom are selected by selecting ⬚ (Fixed) or ensuring that all checkboxes are selected.
    ▪ Select the planar face on the wider end of the wing to assign the constraint to.
    ▪ Preview the constraint and change the density as required to show the constraint.
    ▪ Click OK.

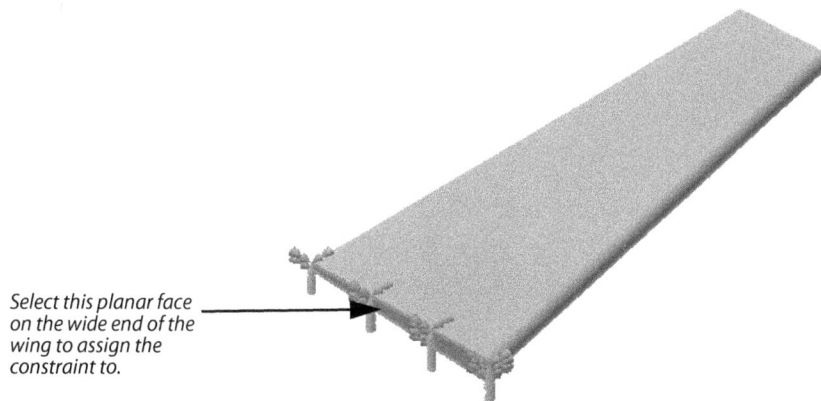

Select this planar face on the wide end of the wing to assign the constraint to.

4. Create a load using the following settings:

- Enter **Shear Load** as the name of the load.
- Ensure the Type of load is set to Force.
- Assign the load to Subcase1.
- Select the edge of the wing, as shown below. The edge is on the narrow end.

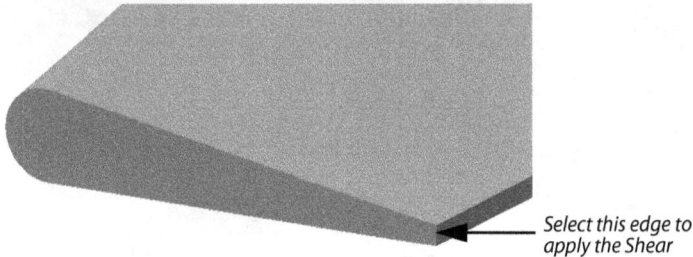

Select this edge to
apply the Shear

- Enter **1000** as the Fy value.

- Select ![icon](Define New Table) in the Transient Table Data section.

- Enter **vs. Time** as the new name of the table.

- Select Load Scale Factor vs. Time from the Type drop-down list.

- Open the file *C:\Autodesk Nastran InCAD 2019 Essentials Exercise Files\Wing\Loading Table Data.xls.*

- Copy the data from the table (row 2-23). Click in the first empty cell in the Time column and paste the data into the table. Alternatively, you can enter the values into the table.

- Click OK. The icon for the table has changed () indicating a table has been assigned.

- Preview the load and change the density as required to show the load.

- Click OK.

Mesh the model and Run the Analysis

In this task, you will modify the global mesh setting for the model and run the analysis.

1. Right-click on the Mesh Model node and select Edit. Enter **2.0** as the Element Size value for the global mesh. Generate the mesh and click OK.

2. Run the analysis.

Analyze the Results

In this task, you will review the analysis results to show the displacement contour plot and a von Mises contour plot for a specific step in the analysis. You will also view the multiset animation for all the steps, and create an XY Plot for two points on the model.

1. Set the following options in the Plot dialog box to view the Displacement results:

   - In the subcases drop-down list, select STEP 40, Time=0.195.
   - Ensure the Contour Options and Deform Options tabs are active.
   - Select DISPLACEMENT from the Result Data drop-down list and TOTAL from the Type drop-down list on the Contour Options tab.
   - Review the Deform Options tab and note that the results are scaled by 10%.
   - Display the results.

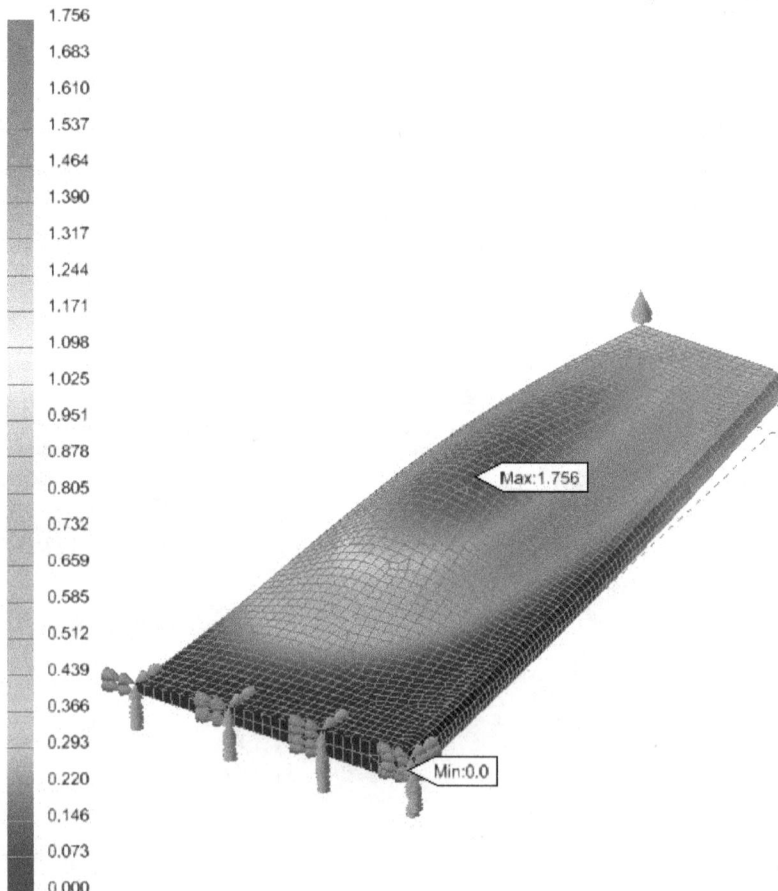

CONTOUR: DISPLACEMENT (in) (TOTAL)
DEFORMED TOTAL: (MIN   =0, MAX=1.75633)
OUTPUT SET: STEP 40, TIME=0.195

2. Set the following options in the Plot dialog box to view the Displacement results:

- In the subcases drop-down list, ensure that STEP 40, Time=0.195 is still selected.
- Select Stress in the Result Data drop-down list and SHELL MAX VON MISES STRESS BOTTOM/TOP from the Type drop-down list on the Contour Options tab. This result contour shows the maximum von Mises stress value regardless of whether it occurs at the top or bottom surface of the shell elements.
- Display the results if they don't automatically update.

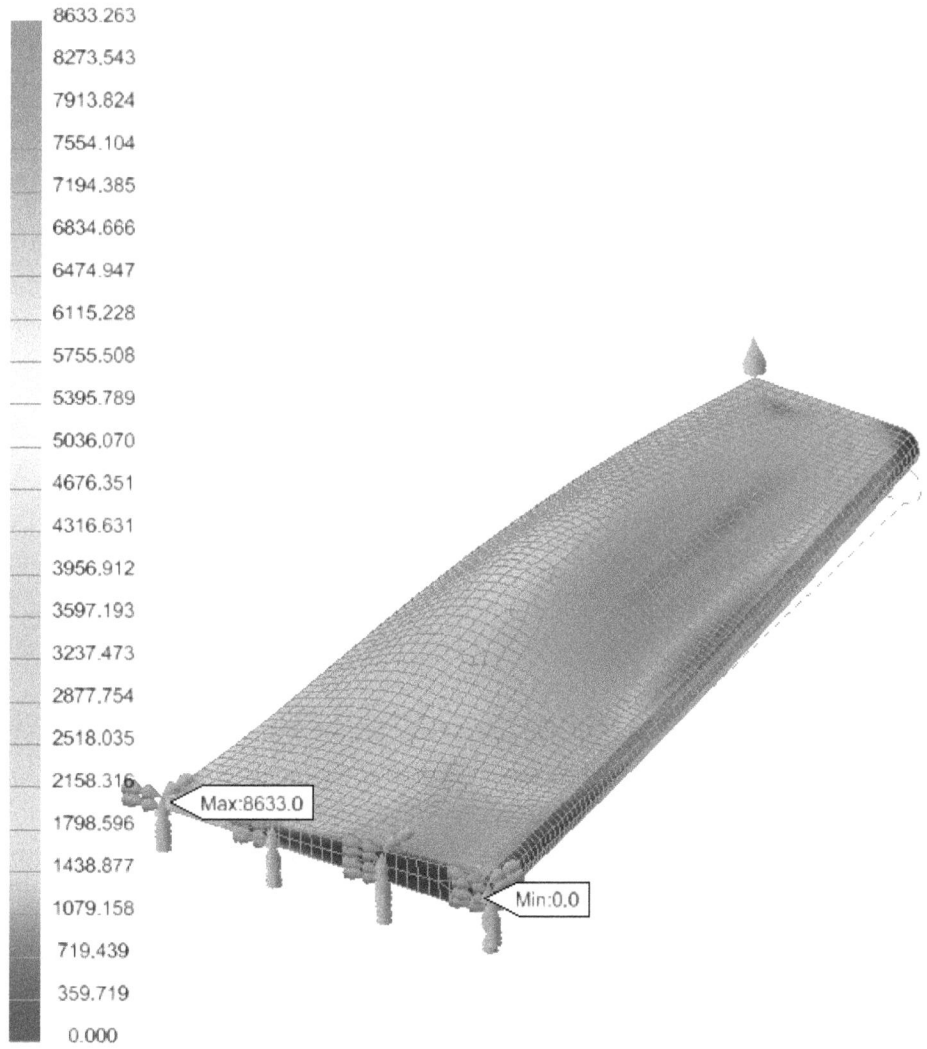

CONTOUR: SHELL MAX VON MISES STRESS BOTTOM/TOP (psi) (TOP)
DEFORMED TOTAL: (MIN   =0, MAX=1.75633)
OUTPUT SET: STEP 40, TIME=0.195

3. Close the Plot dialog box and clear the display of the results from the model.

4. Right-click on the Results node for the analysis and select Multiset Animation Settings. Set the following options in the Multiset Animation Settings dialog box:

   - Ensure the Start Set drop-down list has STEP 1, Time=0.0 selected.
   - In the End Set drop-down list, select STEP 62, Time=0.305.
   - Select Half as the Mode option in the Animation Options tab.
   - Animate the results.

5. Click Cancel to close the dialog box and stop the animation when finished viewing it.

6. Right-click on Nodes at the top of the Autodesk Nastran Model Tree and select Query Display. This will enable you to look at the information on individual nodes by moving the cursor over them. Hover the cursor over the node where the load is displayed. Write down the Node ID; it will be used in the next step to create an XY Plot of that particular node's displacement.

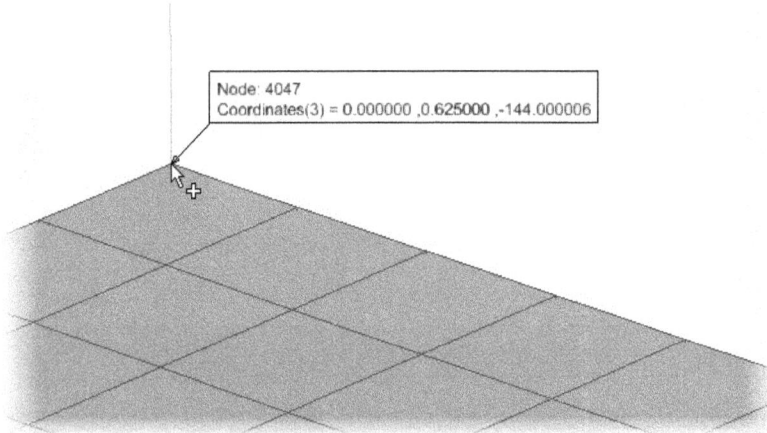

Node: 4047
Coordinates(3) = 0.000000 ,0.625000 ,-144.000006

7. Right-click on XY Plot and select New. Set the following options in the XY dialog box:

   - Select Node in the General section as the entity to plot.
   - Enter the node number from your model (e.g. 4047) in the ID field.
   - For the X-Axis Outset Sets, ensure that the start and end fields include the entire range of steps (Start Set = STEP 1, TIME=0.0 and End Set = STEP 62, TIME=0.305).
   - For the Y-Axis Output Sets, ensure that DISPLACEMENT is selected in the Result Data drop-down list and that TOTAL is selected as the Component option.
   - Show the XY Plot.

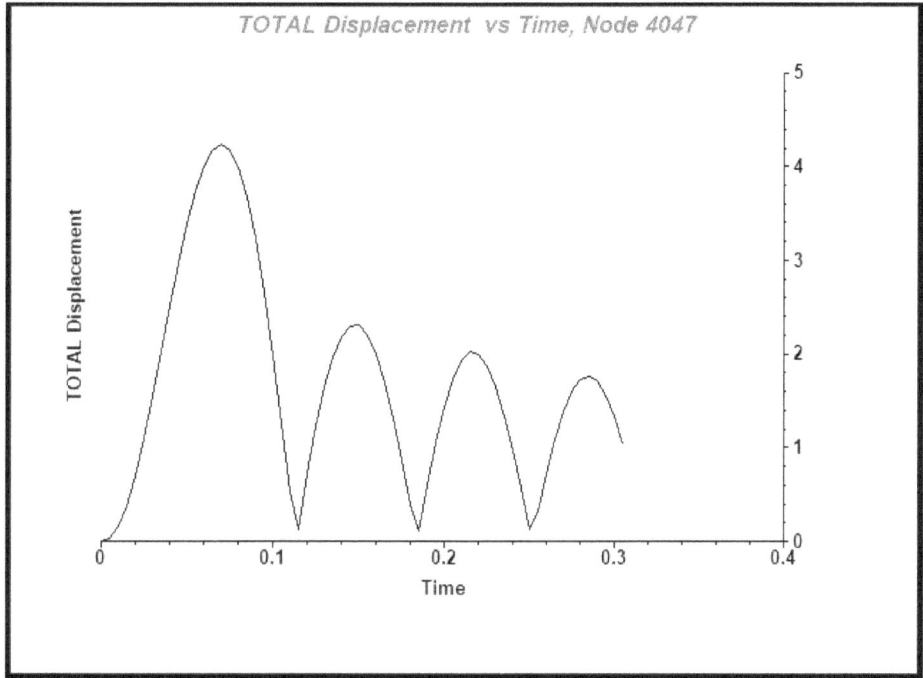

TOTAL Displacement vs Time, Node 4047

8. Click OK on the XY Plot dialog box to close the plot display.

9. In the XY Plot dialog box, click in the ID field to activate it and then select a node in the middle of the center span of the wing to change the node that is being plotted.

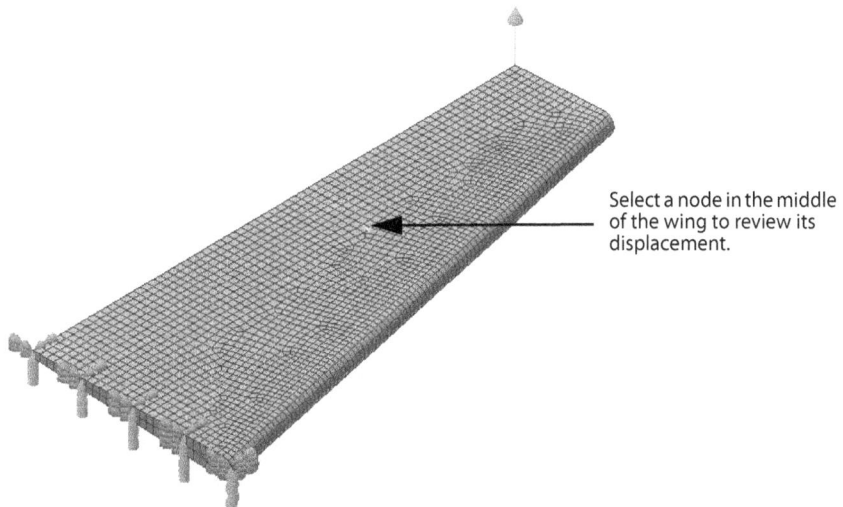

Select a node in the middle of the wing to review its displacement.

10. Change the following options in the XY dialog box:
    - Set Ty as the Component option in its drop-down list to display the translation in the Y direction.
    - Show the XY Plot.

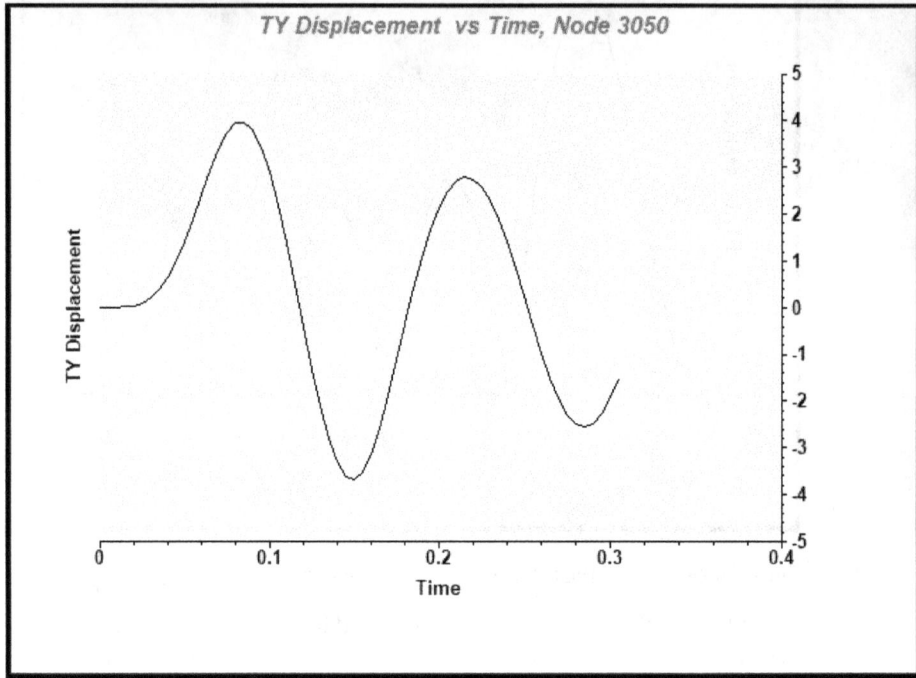

TY Displacement vs Time, Node 3050

11. Close the XY Plot dialog boxes.
12. Save the model.

Random Response Analysis

The goal in this chapter is to learn about random response analyses in the Autodesk® Nastran® In-CAD environment. Random analysis is a statistical analysis that provides a peak response magnitude within a certain percentage certainty based on a random vibration signal/load. With random loading, the precise magnitudes are unknown and a statistical representation of the load is incorporated into the analysis with the use of power spectral density (PSD) data. You will learn to create a random response analysis, run the analysis, and review Results plots and XY Plots.

Objectives

After completing this chapter, you will be able to:

- Create a new random response analysis.
- Define damping in a random response analysis.
- Set the range and number of modes included in the response using the Modal Setup.
- Set the power spectral density (PSD) data and the frequency range of study for the analysis using the Dynamics setup.
- Display the Results plot and XY Plot results for a random response analysis.

Lesson: Creating a Random Response Analysis

Overview

This lesson discusses how you can create a new random response analysis in a model. It discusses the settings that are required for this analysis and specifically covers those settings that have not been previously discussed in other analysis types that have previously been discussed in this learning guide (i.e. power spectral density (PSD) data in the Dynamics Setup). To complete the lesson you will learn which results are automatically generated with a random response analysis and how to review other results.

Objectives

After completing this lesson, you will be able to:

- Understand the basics of power spectral density (PSD) data.
- Create a new random response analysis.
- Define damping in a random response analysis.
- Set the range and/or number of modes included in the response using the Modal Setup.
- Set the power spectral density (PSD) data and the frequency range of study for the analysis using the Dynamics setup.
- Display the Results plot and XY Plot results for a random response analysis.

Basics of Random Response Analysis

A Random Response analysis, also known as a random vibration analysis, is a linear-dynamic analysis method that is based on probability. It is used to predict the likely effect on a structure when subjected to vibration loads that are random (non-deterministic) in nature. Because the loads vary by frequency, phase shift, and magnitude, there is no way to know exactly what the peak response will be. The response therefore is based on a statistical representation of where the most vibrational energy exists along a range of frequencies known as a Power Spectral Density. Examples of where this type of analysis is used are for electrical components in a car subjected to vibrations from the engine or road, turbulence, or acoustic pressure.

During a random response analysis in Nastran In-CAD, the random portion of the analysis is run as a post-process to a frequency response analysis. During the frequency response solution the model is solved for response to a unit excitation over the range of frequencies. The resulting output is used to generate a transfer function (ratio of the output to the input) that is coupled with the defined power spectral density (PSD) load to generate a single set of results. This single set of results incorporates the contributions of all the different excitation values. Results can be viewed for each frequency step, the PSD scaled frequency at each step, and the root mean square peak response (RMS). In addition, an NPX or number of positive crossings output is returned for the statistical number of cycles per unit time of the RMS results.

- The RMS values are the areas under the resultant PSD plots. We can plot as contours for stress etc. They are factored by 3 to give 3s (99.7%) probability that the peak response will not exceed the calculated response. The results calculated by default are 1s (68%) certainty.

- The PSD plots show response compared to the input PSD. Important frequencies can be identified and verified with this plot.

- Number of positive crossings is a statistical calculation that predicts how many zero crossings will occur per unit time of response. That is, how many times the vibration will change from negative to positive. This is also known as the apparent frequency and gives cycle count for fatigue.

- The cumulative RMS plot is another way to identify which frequencies contribute the most.

> Autocorrelation is an indication of the degree of randomness of a response. The signal is multiplied by itself with different phase shifts. If a signal is non-random (e.g., sine function, square wave, etc.), then a broad correlation is seen, and distinct and regular peaks become evident. If a signal is highly random, then the autocorrelation output is very 'peaky', and large irregular peaks will occur randomly.

Power Spectral Density (PSD) Data

Power spectral density data is a statistical representation of the load time history. It is used in a random response analysis to roughly quantify the random loading of the structure.

The following provides a general description of how the power spectral density data is generated. Consider the following typical signal. The loading mean is 0.0, and the signal is an acceleration measured in gs.

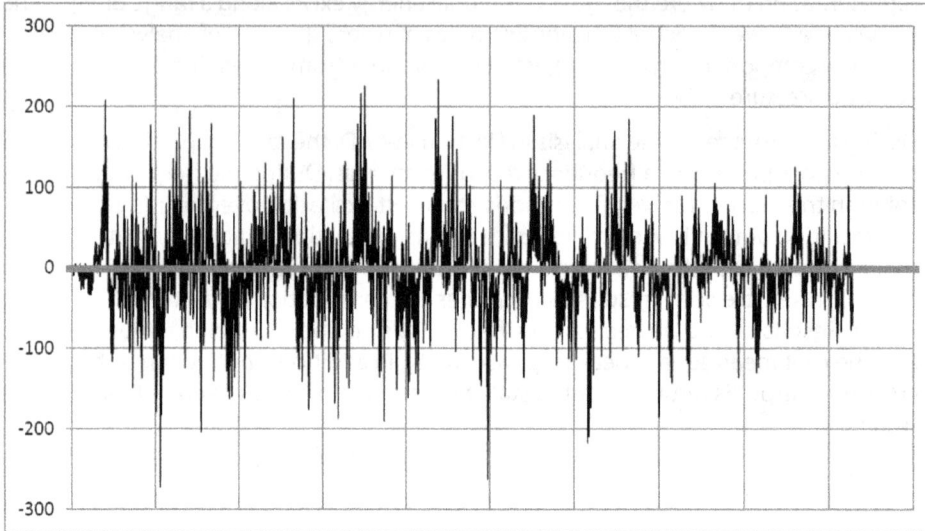

If the signal is squared at all times (G²), the signal become positive and the mean is no longer zero.

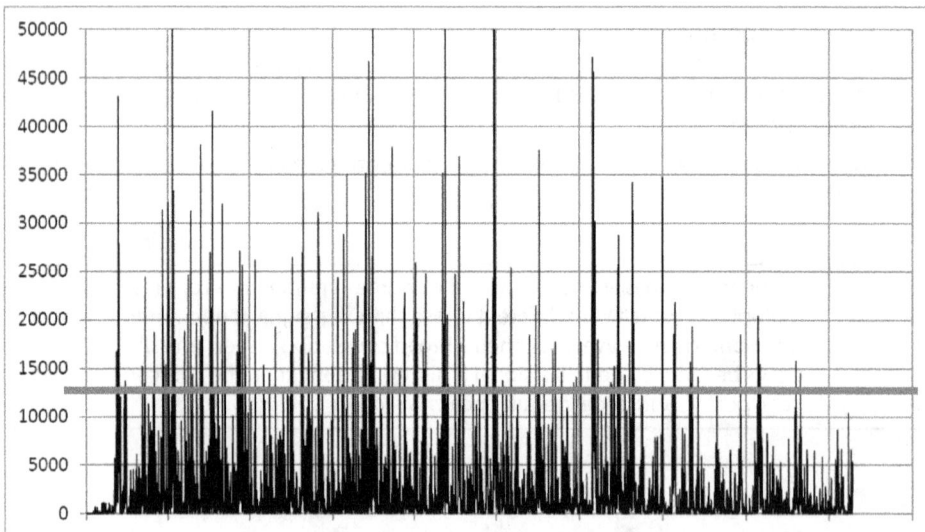

Statistically, the Square Root of the Mean Square Value (RMS) is equal to the standard deviation s of a normal distribution. One standard deviation s of the RMS value of the signal is the value that has a 68.3% chance of occurring. "3s" gives a probability of 99.73% chance of occurring. We now have a measure of the mean amplitude of the signal as its RMS value.

To further characterize the signal a filter can be applied to the original signal to eliminate all frequencies above, f1. This is done by squaring the signal and finding the mean square again. The same plot has been recreated, but it is now missing some high frequency content.

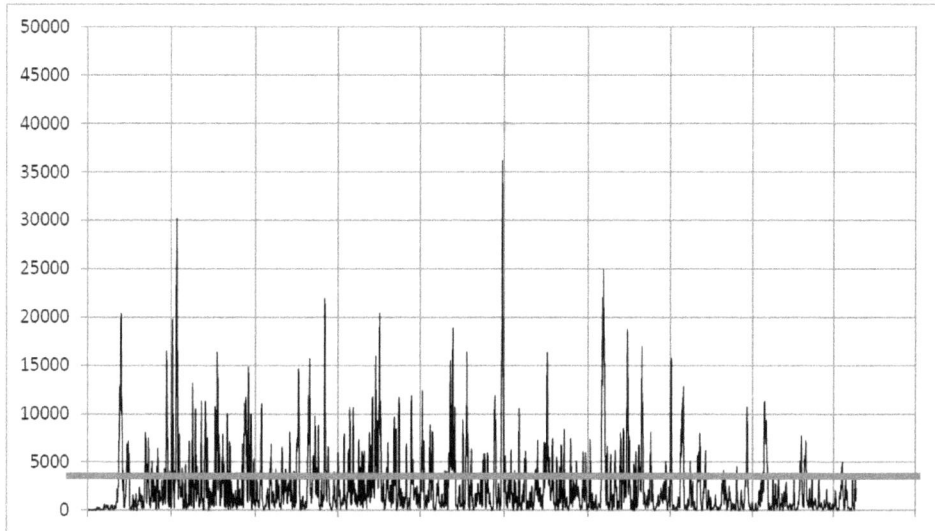

The new mean square is necessarily below the mean square of the unfiltered signal. Continue to apply a reducing upper limit on f. As each frequency range is cut off, the Mean Square value will be decreasing.

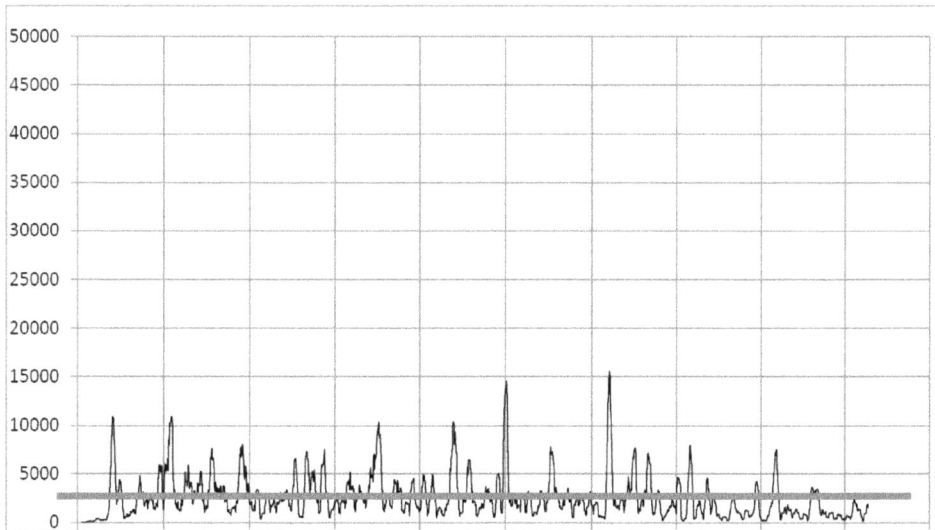

The variation of Mean Square with fi can be plotted (CRMS plot). It shows the frequency content of the random signal. In this example, the Mean Square value jumps considerably between f3 and f2. Note that the Total Mean Square value represents the unfiltered signal.

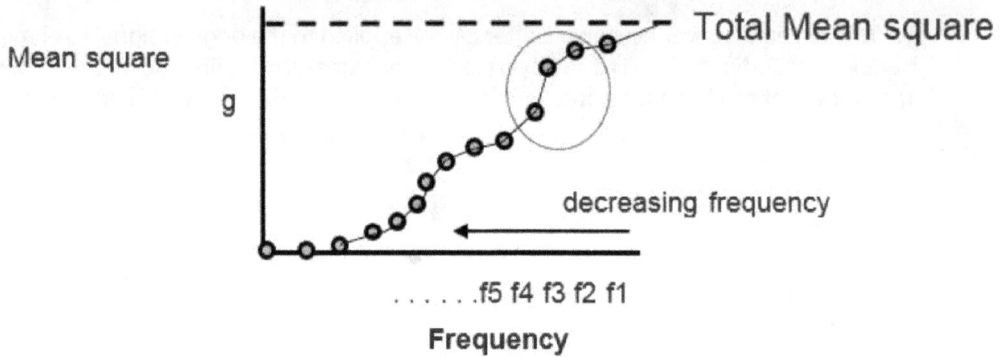

The final step to generate the Power Spectral Density (PSD) is to find the gradient by taking the derivative of the CRMS plot. It shows the frequency content of the random signal, more directly than the CMRS. Like the CRMS plot, the G2/Hz value jumps considerably between f3 and f2. The square root of the area under the curve is the RMS value of the signal. This type of plot is used as input to a random analysis, as it statistically describes the variation of the magnitude of the signal with frequency. Typically, a series of tests are run and PSD plots are generated for each. These are then combined under an envelope such that the PSD of any of the test signals will fall under the enveloped value. This envelope is what is commonly input to Nastran for a random analysis.

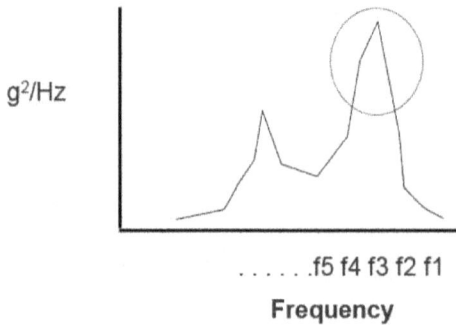

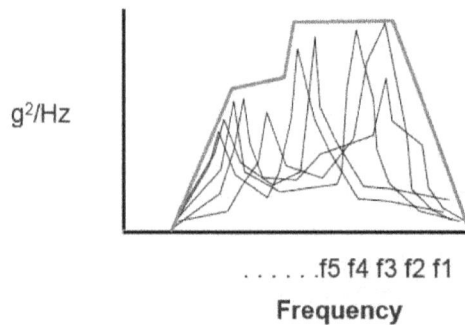

Creating a Random Response Analysis

To create a random response analysis, you must either create a new analysis or edit an existing analysis and change the type of analysis to Random Response. You can also select any additional options in the Analysis dialog box to define the output controls, options, and model state (Design View or Level of Detail in assembly designs) to be analyzed. For random response analysis the Dynamic Options section on the Output Controls tab is uniquely available and enables you to define the output options.

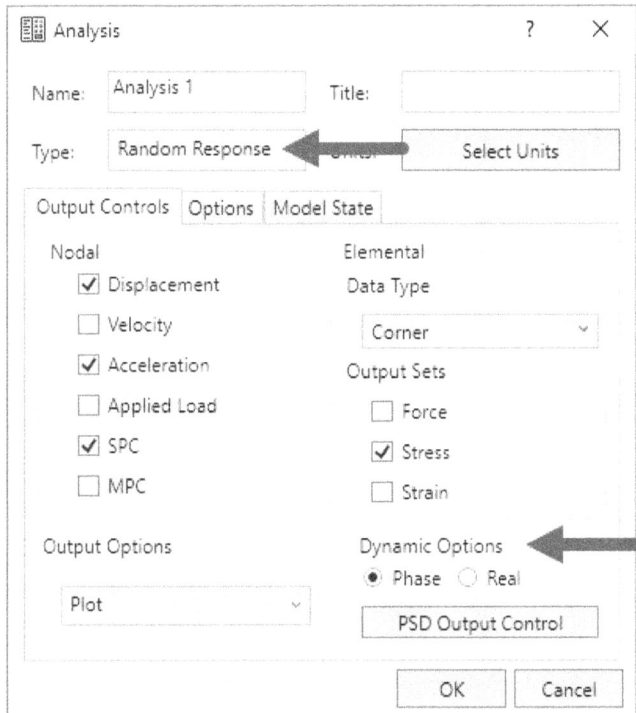

- **Dynamic Options**
  - **Phase**: This option will display as a choice for Magnitude and Phase output.
  - **Real**: This option will display as a choice for Real and Imaginary output.
  - **PSD Output Control**: This button enables you to define nodal and elemental output requests.

When a random response analysis is created the Autodesk Nastran Model Tree displays as shown in the following image.

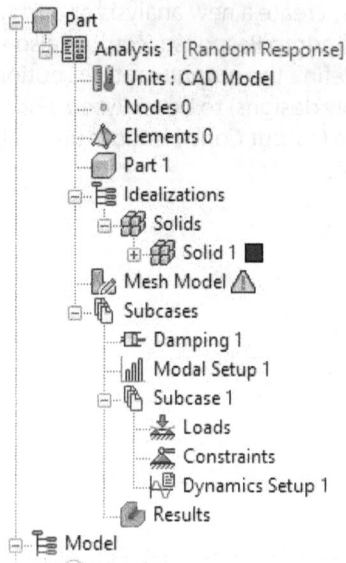

```
Part
  Analysis 1 [Random Response]
    Units : CAD Model
    Nodes 0
    Elements 0
    Part 1
    Idealizations
      Solids
        Solid 1 ■
    Mesh Model ⚠
    Subcases
      Damping 1
      Modal Setup 1
      Subcase 1
        Loads
        Constraints
        Dynamics Setup 1
      Results
Model
```

A random response analysis requires damping, modal, and dynamic (Power Spectrum Density Curve definition) setup steps. Additionally you must consider the following:

- Ensure that a required idealization exists or is created that contains any material properties that are specifically required for the analysis.
- Assign any surface contacts, as required, to fully describe the model being analyzed.
- Assign any required structural constraints, loads, connections.

The following describes the settings that are required in a random response analysis.

Damping Setup

The Damping setup must be defined for a random response analysis. To create damping, right-click on Damping in the Autodesk Nastran Model tree and select Edit to open the Damping dialog box. Similar to a frequency response analysis, when defining damping for a random response analysis Structural, Rayleigh, or Modal damping can be applied. In general for random response analysis, if loading is using a Gravity load, then modal damping is most commonly used. However if enforced motion is the load used, then that modal damping will be changed by the solver to structural damping and the % may not match the modal damping values. Structural damping can also be applied manually at the peak response frequency.

> For more information on Damping and its options, refer to the *Creating a New Normal Modes Analysis* lesson in Chapter 9, or to Autodesk Nastran In-CAD Help and search for "Damping Setup".

Modal Setup

A random response analysis is run as a post-process to a modal analysis. The modal setup determines the number of modes and the frequency range that will be used in the initial process of the overall analysis. Modal settings are customized using the Modal Setup node that gets created in the subcase of a random response analysis. To access the setup options, right-click on the Modal Setup node in the analysis subcase and select Edit.

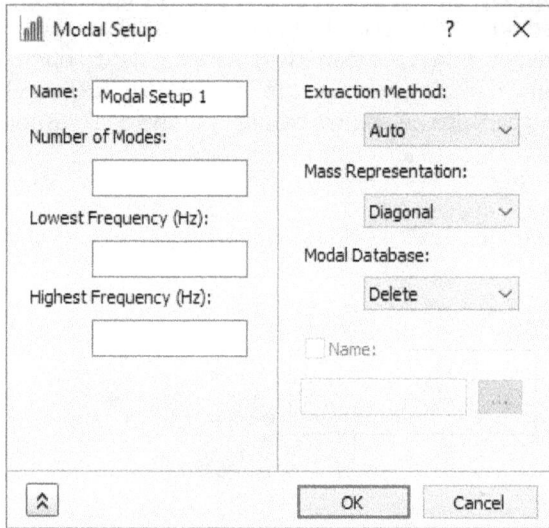

The Modal Setup dialog box contains the same options that are used for a Normal Modes, Frequency Response, and Transient Response analysis that were previously discussed. Defining these settings enables you to define the number of modes and the frequency range that will be reported on for the results and prevents you from having to run a separate normal modes analysis prior to the random response spectrum analysis. For more information on the Modal Setup dialog box and its options, refer to the *Creating a Normal Modes Analysis* lesson in Chapter 9 or to Autodesk Nastran In-CAD Help and search for "Modal Setup".

Dynamic Setup

The dynamic settings can be customized using the Dynamics Setup node that gets created in the subcase of a random response analysis. Similar to direct or modal frequency response analyses, the options enable you to define the frequency limits and the number of points that will be examined during the analysis. Unlike direct or modal frequency response analysis, for a random response analysis, a power spectrum density curve is also required in the dynamics setup. This is done in the Random Analysis Options area and enables you to create/assign the power spectrum density curve table(s) for the analysis. Multiple curves (tables) can be setup and used for different scenarios. The data for these tables is generally obtained from physical testing using shaker-tables or even accelerometer data collected from field use/field testing. To access the setup options, right-click on the Dynamics Setup node in the analysis subcase and select Edit.

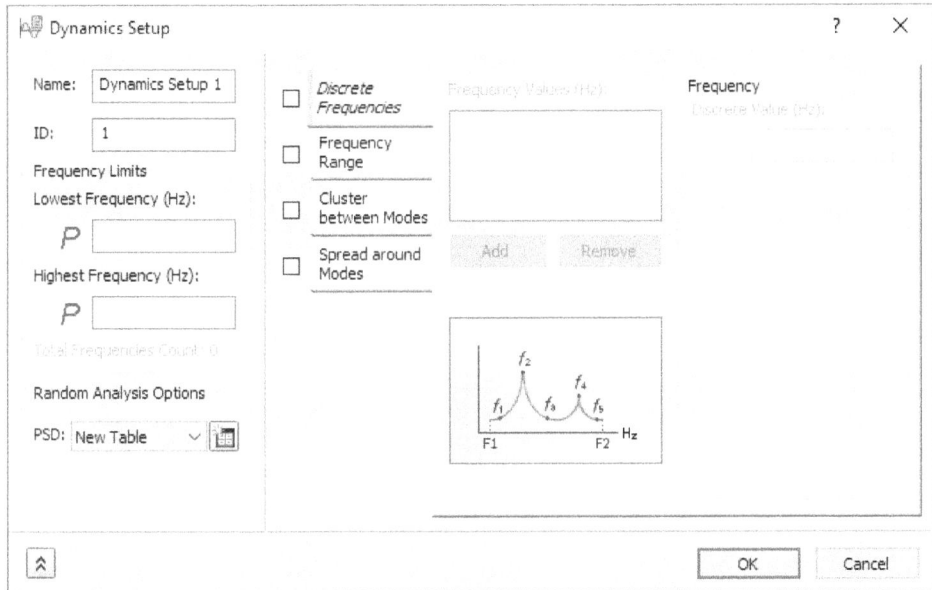

Use the following procedure to create a power spectrum density curve table.

Procedure: To Create a new Power Spectrum Density Curve Table

1. Select New Table in the Table Data drop-down list, if not already active.

2. Select ▦ (Define New Table). The Table Data dialog box opens to define the spectrum curve table.

3. Enter a name for the spectrum curve table and accept the default ID value that is automatically assigned by Autodesk Nastran In-CAD.

4. Select the Type of spectrum curve table:

    - **PSD (Acceleration) vs. Frequency**: Used for measuring linear acceleration of points in response to a range of frequencies.
    - **PSD (Force) vs. Frequency**: Used for measuring linear acceleration of points in response to a range of frequencies.

5. Define the spectrum curve data:

    - Manually enter the Frequency data (Hz) in column 1.
    - Manually enter the power spectrum density (PSD) data in column 2. Ensure that you are entering the data as per the type defined (i.e., acceleration or force values for each frequency value).
    - Copy and paste data from an external table.

6. Use the Log X and Log Y options in the Data Interpolation area to interpolate the data values in the table in logarithmic scale. (This is a Recommended setting.)

7.   (Optional) Use the Sort Data option to reorder the data by frequency. Once reordered it cannot be undone.

8.   (Optional) Use the Data Show XY Plot option to review the entered data in an XY plot. You can use the standard options in the XY Plot dialog box to customize the plot.

9.   Click OK to create the power spectrum density (PSD) table that will be used for the analysis.

10. Ensure that the new table is displayed as the selection in PSD field to use it in the analysis.

To delete a power spectrum density table from the analysis, expand the Tables node in the Model sub-tree to list all the tables that have been created in the file. Right-click on a table name and select to permanently remove it from the file. Note: Tables can not be deleted from within the Dynamics Setup.

Loads & Constraints for Random Response Analyses

A random response analysis requires a load. In general, the load can be added as an enforced motion load with a sub-type of Acceleration. It is applied to determine the direction of the PSD load. The magnitude must be 1 unit of the PSD base unit (if the PSD is in G^2/Hz, then the acceleration load must be 1G or 386.4 in/s^2).

Structural constraints, connectors, and contacts can be added to a random response analysis similar to how they were previously discussed for linear static analysis.

Creating the Random Response Analysis

Use the following procedure to create a random response analysis.

Procedure: Create a new Random Response Analysis

1. Right-click on the Part or Assembly node at the top of the Autodesk Nastran Model Tree and select New.

2. Enter the name for the new analysis.

3. Select Random Response in the Type drop-down list.

4. (Optional) By default, the unit system for the model is set to that of the CAD model. Click Select Units and select an alternative unit system, if required.

5. Define the required options in the Output Controls tab to define the information that will be output to the analysis report when it is run.

   - For a random analysis, you might also want to include the Acceleration.
   - In the Dynamic Options area, select the required options. Select Phase for magnitude and phase outputs or Real for real and imaginary output. Select the PSD Output Control options to define nodal and elemental output requests.

6. In the Options tab:

   - Set the Contact type that should be used by default when generating Automatic contacts.
   - Set the tolerance value between contacting entities at which automatic contacts are created.

7. If analyzing an assembly, on the Model State tab, select a Design View or Level of Detail to define the model configuration that is being analyzed.

8. Click OK to create the new random response analysis.

9. Assign an existing idealization from the Model sub-tree or create a new one, as required.

10. Define the Damping setup.

11. Define the Modal setup.

12. Set the Dynamic setup options for the random response analysis which includes the power spectrum density curve.

13. Assign contacts, connectors, constraints, and loads to the model, as required.

14. Mesh the model.

15. Run the analysis.

Alternatively, you can edit an existing analysis by right-clicking the analysis name in the Autodesk Nastran Model Tree and select Edit and modify the selected options, as required, to change the current analysis to a random response analysis.

Random Response Analysis Plot Results

Similar to a normal modes analysis, there are no default plot templates included. You must use the Plot dialog box to visually display the results.

To access the Plot dialog box:

- Right-click on the Results node and select Edit.
- Double-click on the Results node.
- In the Results panel on the ribbon, click 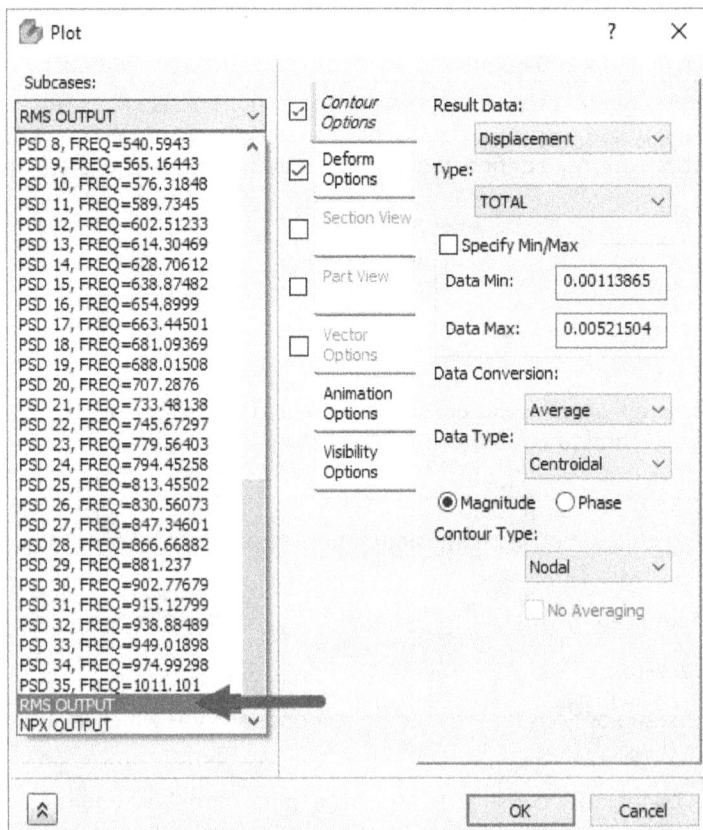 (Options).

Using the Plot dialog box you can select the type of result to be displayed using the Result Data drop-down list and customize the options, as required. For Random Response analysis the RMS Output is generally the most important result. This option is selected at the bottom of the Subcases drop-down list and the result data can be set to display Displacement.

> For more information on Plot dialog box and its options, refer to the *Visualizing Result Plots* lesson in Chapter 3, *Normal Modes Analysis Plot Results* in Chapter 9, or open Autodesk Nastran In-CAD Help and search for "Plot Templates".

Random Response Analysis XY Plot

When a random response analysis is run, a number of XY plots are generated by default to help you analyze the results.

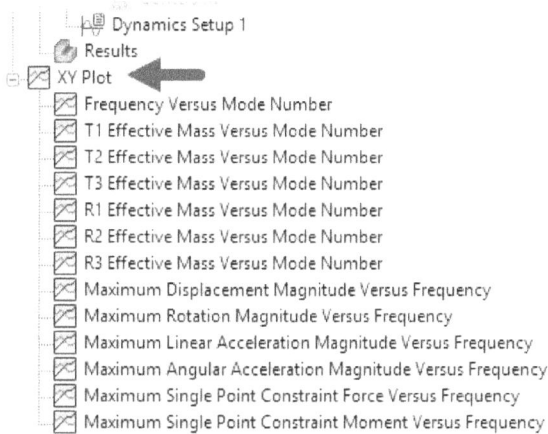

To review any of the plots, double-click on the plot name or right-click on the plot name and select Show XY Plot. The XY Plot dialog box opens displaying the plot. The options in the left pane in the dialog box enables you to customize the display of the plot. For a random response analysis the Maximum Displacement Magnitude Versus Frequency plot is commonly reviewed and customized as follows. It identifies the peak magnitude and the mode in which it occurs.

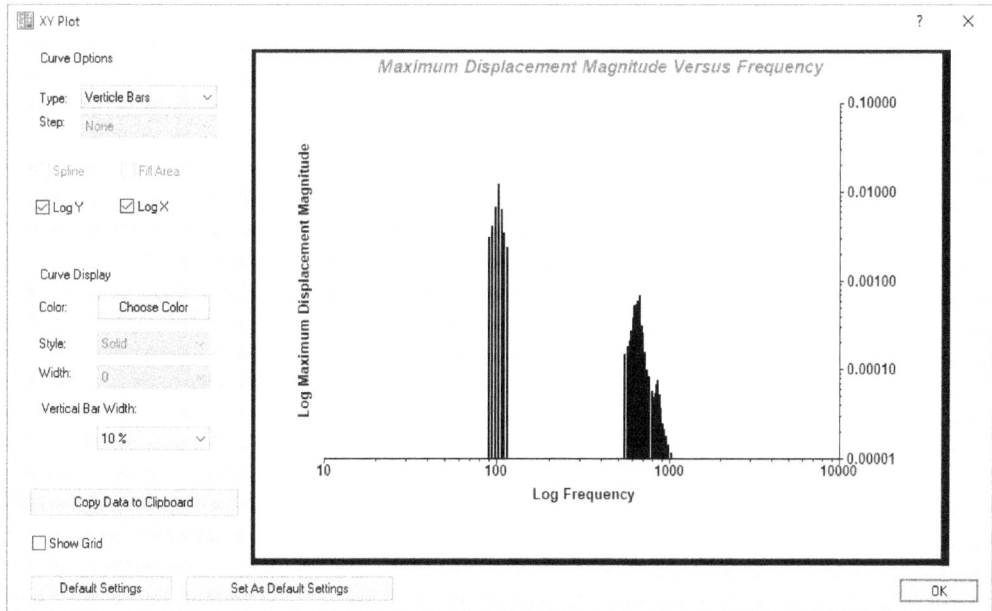

New XY plots can be created as needed by right-clicking on the XY Plot node and selecting New. Using the options in the XY Plot dialog box you can customize the plot.

> For more information on XY Plot dialog box, its options, and how to create a new XY Plot, refer to the *Visualizing XY Plot Results* lesson in Chapter 3 or open Autodesk Nastran In-CAD Help and search for "Results XY Plotting".

Exercise: Muffler IV - Random Response

In this exercise, you will perform a random response analysis simulation on the muffler model. This analysis will be used to predict the response of a muffler assembly subjected to a continuous excitation. The design changes that were made to the model in the Modal Avoidance exercise earlier in this learning guide will be used in this exercise.

Prepare the Model for use in Nastran In-CAD

1. Open the file *C:\Autodesk Nastran InCAD 2019 Essentials Exercise Files\ Muffler_Random_Response\Muffler&Brakets4.iam*.

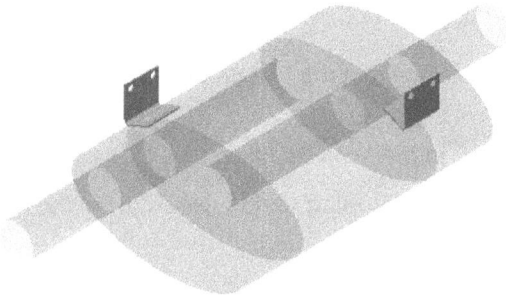

2. Activate the Autodesk Nastran In-CAD environment. The Normal Modes analysis that was previously conducted has been provided in this model. All of the same idealizations, surface contacts, and constraints that were assigned in the previous chapter, will be used in this exercise to create the Random Response analysis.

3. Load the results that were previously generated. Right-click the Results node and select Edit. The modal frequencies are listed in the Plot dialog box. The modes exist in the 0 to 1000Hz frequency band.

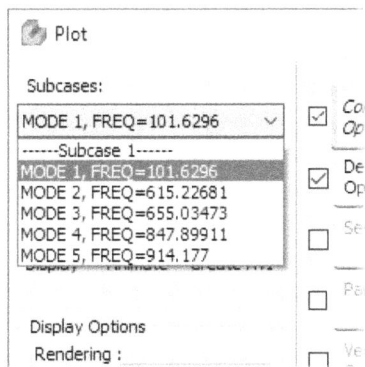

Set up a new Random Response Analysis

In this task, you will edit the existing Normal Modes analysis to conduct a random response analysis. Note: As part of the new random response analysis, a normal modes analysis is automatically conducted.

1. Right-click on Analysis 1 and select Edit.

2. Select Random Response in the Type drop-down list.

3. In the Output Controls tab, select Acceleration in the Nodal section.

4. In the Dynamic Options area, ensure the Phase is selected in order to see your peak magnitude. The default options for the PSD Output Control options will be maintained.

5. Select the Model State tab and ensure that the Two Brackets Level of Detail is selected for analysis.

6. Maintain the remaining defaults in the Analysis dialog box. Click OK.

7. In the Subcases node, right-click on Damping 1 and select Edit. Set the following options in the Damping dialog box:

    -   Enable the Structural Damping checkbox.
    -   Enter **5** as the Damping Value G (%).
    -   Enter **101.63** as the Dominant Frequency, W3 (Hz)
    -   Clear the selection of the Model Damping option, if enabled.
    -   Click OK.

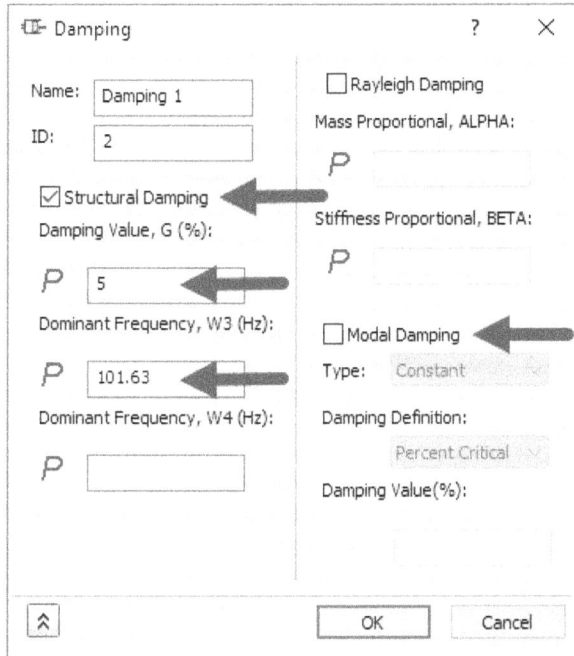

8. In the Subcases node, right-click on Modal Setup 1 and select Edit. Verify that the following options in the Modal Setup dialog box are set:

- The Lowest Frequency is set to 10.
- The Highest Frequency is set to 1000.
- Click OK.

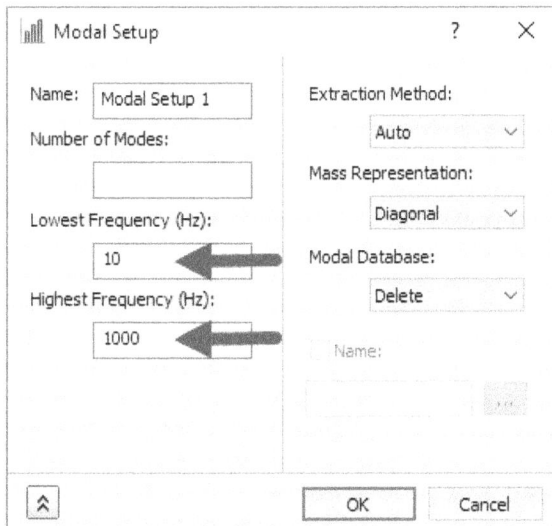

Review the Constraints and Create the Load

In this task, you will review the existing constraints on each of the brackets and setup the loads.

1. In SubCase1, right-click on Constraint 1 and select Edit. Notice that the four cylindrical faces of the brackets were selected as constrained entities to prevent translation and rotation.

2. Right-click in the Select Entities area and select Clear All. With this area active select the four work points at the centers of all the holes.

3. For this random response analysis the constrained entities should be the points at the centers of each hole and rotation will be permitted in the x direction to treat the constraint as a pin constraint. In the Degrees of Freedom area, ensure that all but the Rx option is selected. Click OK.

4. For clarity in reference selection, right-click on Constraint1 in the Constraints node and clear the selection of the Display option to remove its symbols from the display.

5. In the Prepare panel, click 🔧 (Connectors). The Connector dialog box opens.

   Tip: Connectors cannot be directly added through the Analysis node until the first connector is created and is added to the analysis.

6. In the Connector dialog box, select Rigid Body from the Type drop-down list.

7. Ensure that the Rigid Body Type is set to Rigid.

8. Ensure that all the degrees or freedom options are selected.

9. Select in the Dependent Entities section to activate it (turns blue) and select the cylindrical face of one of the holes in the Muffler Mount model. Note: The mesh has been turned off for clarity in the image.

---

10. Ensure that Select Point is selected in the Independent Vertex/Point area and select inside its selection field to activate it. Select the Work Point at the center of the same hole as the independent point.

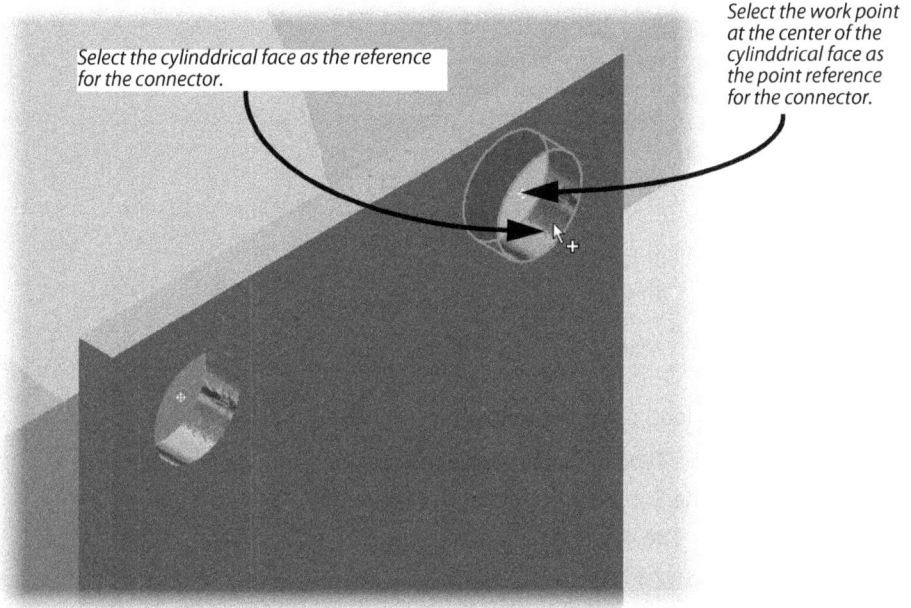

Select the cylinddrical face as the reference for the connector.

Select the work point at the center of the cylinddrical face as the point reference for the connector.

11. Ensure that the Add to Analysis option is selected so that the connector is added directly to the Analysis sub-tree when it is created. Click OK.

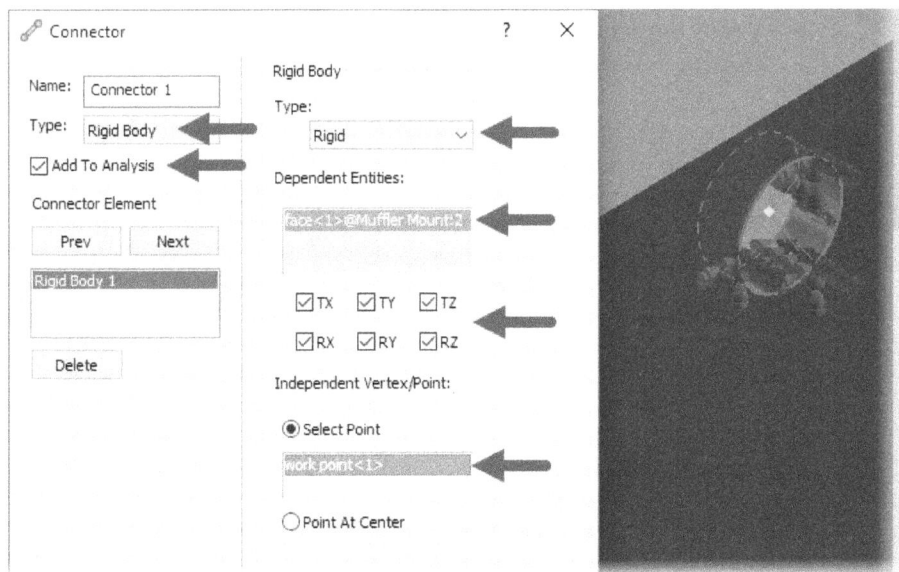

12. Create three additional Rigid Body Connectors on the other three holes. The four connectors are listed in the Connectors node in the Analysis node. Tip: Consider creating all connectors at once using the Next option in the Connector Element area. In this situation only a single Connector item is listed in the analysis.

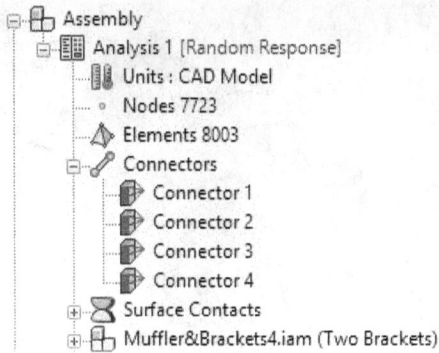

```
Assembly
  Analysis 1 [Random Response]
    Units : CAD Model
    Nodes 7723
    Elements 8003
    Connectors
      Connector 1
      Connector 2
      Connector 3
      Connector 4
    Surface Contacts
    Muffler&Brackets4.iam (Two Brackets)
```

13. Create a load using the following settings:

- Set the Type of load as Enforced Motion.
- Set the Sub Type of load as Acceleration.
- Enter **386.4** as the a_x value.
- Assign the load to Subcase1.
- Select the workpoints at the center of each of the holes on the two brackets, as the references for the load (four points in total). The work point are shown below for one of the brackets.
- Select Preview to show the load on the model.
- Modify the density and size of the load's display, as required.
- Click OK.

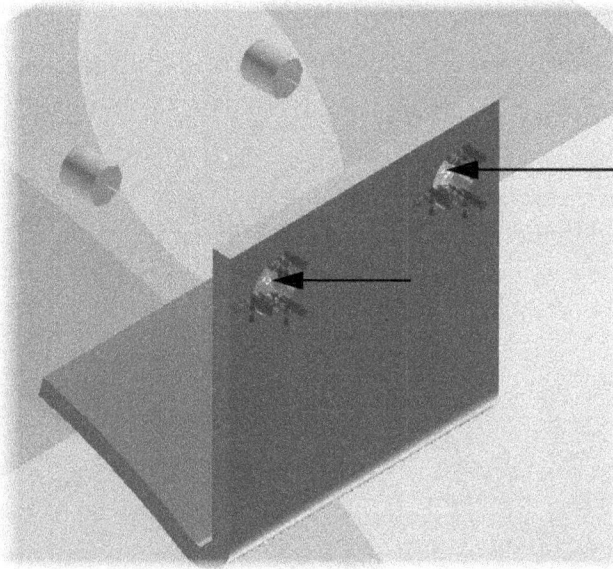

Select the workpoint at the center of each hole on the two brackets

Define the Dynamic Setup Options for the Analysis

In this task, you will define the dynamic setup options for the subcase.

1. Right-click on the Dynamics Setup 1 node in Subcase 1and click Edit.

2. In the Random Analysis Options area, select ⬛ to create a new Power Spectral Density curve.

3. Enter PSD Data as the name of the table.

4. In the Type drop-down list, select PSD (Acceleration) vs. Frequency as the Power Spectral Density curve type.

5. Enter the following data in the first three rows for the Frequency and PSD columns.

6. Enable the LogX and LogY options in the Data Interpolation area. Click OK to complete the table.

7. Select the checkbox adjacent to the Spread around Modes tab to enable it.

8. Define the Interval options as follows:

   - Enter **10** as the Lowest Frequency value.
   - Enter **1000** as the Highest Frequency value.
   - Enter **7** as the Number of Points Spread per Mode value.
   - Enter **12** as the Percentage Spread value.

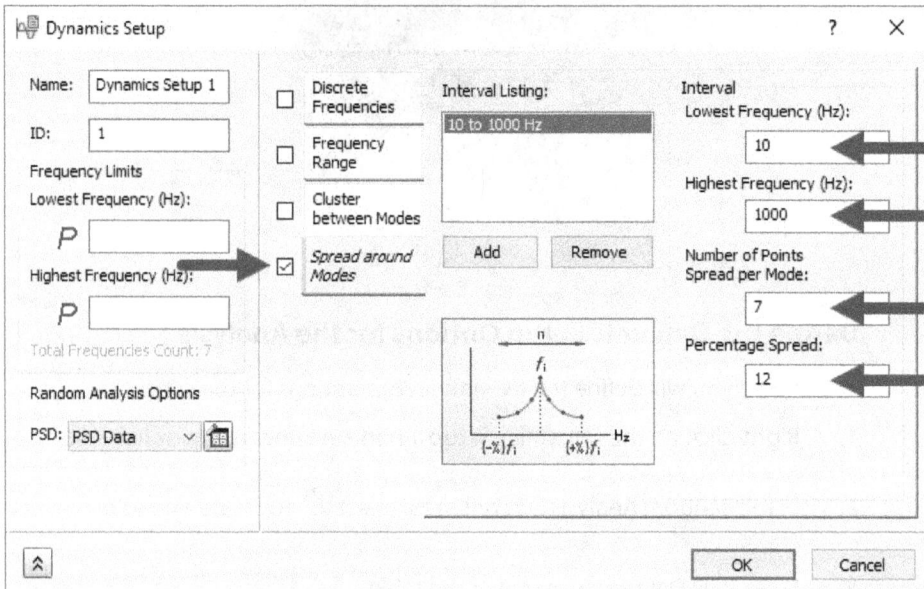

9. Click OK to complete the Dynamics setup.

Run the Analysis and Review the Results

In this task, you will run the analysis and then review the RMS displacement results. Note: For a random response analysis you may want to consider turning the FREQRESPSLTOUT and RANDRESPSLTOUT parameters off to prevent all the results being calculated except RMS and NPX.

1. Run the analysis. Ensure that the mesh is updated prior to running the analysis.

2. Right-click the Results node and select Edit to open the Plot dialog box.

3. Expand the Subcases drop-down list and scroll down to the bottom of the list. Select RMS output.

4. Select Displacement in the Results Data drop-down list. Display the result if not already displayed. The max displacement is .005215in. Click OK to close the Plot dialog box.

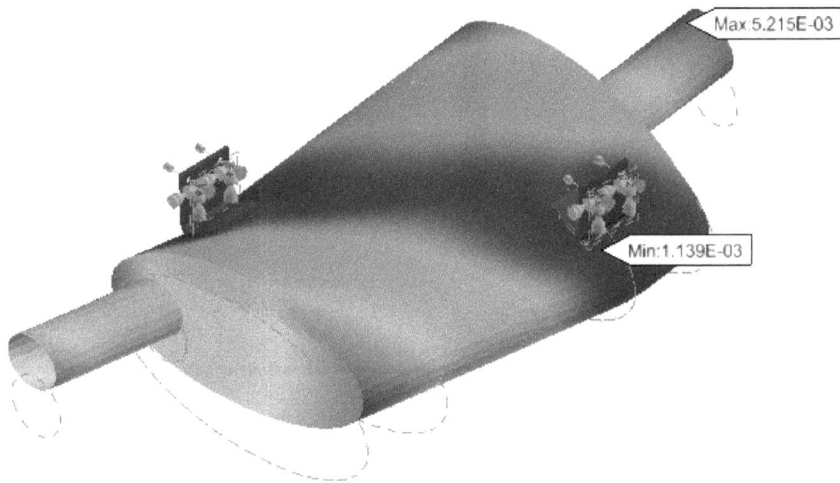

5. In the XY Plot node, right-click on the Maximum Displacement Magnitude Versus Frequency plot and select Show XY Plot.

6. To customize the XY Plot's display, set the following options:

   ▪ Select Vertical Bars as the Curve Option type.
   ▪ Select LogY and LogX.
   ▪ The peak displacement occurs at the first mode (101Hz).

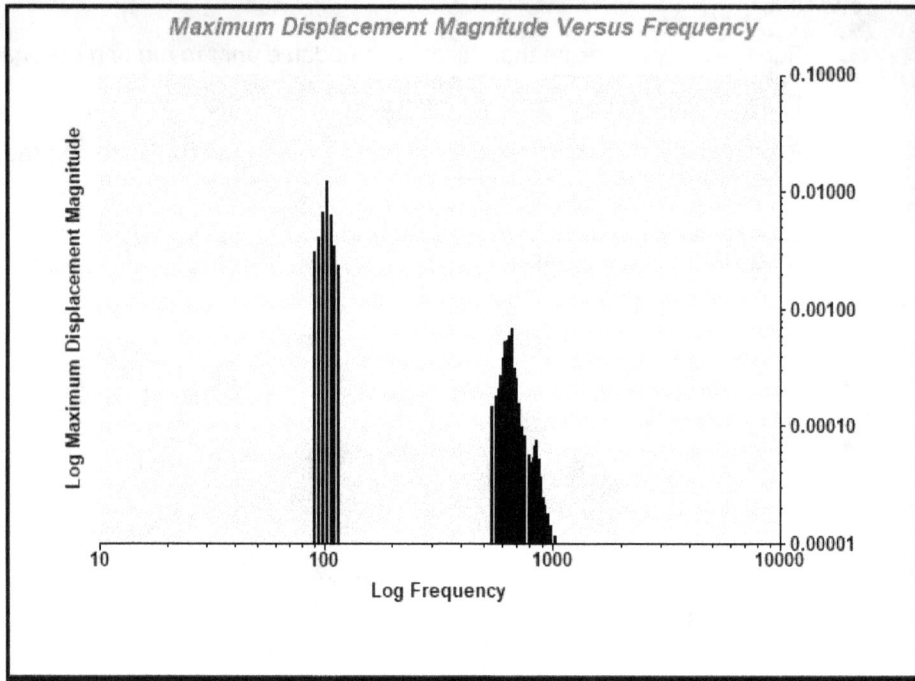

Maximum Displacement Magnitude Versus Frequency

7. Click OK to close the XY Plot dialog box

8. Save the model.

Autodesk

Shock/Response Spectrum Analysis

The goal in this chapter is to learn about shock/response spectrum analyses in the Autodesk® Nastran® In-CAD environment. Similar to a random response analysis, the precise transient load magnitudes used are undefined in the shock/response spectrum analysis. In a random response analysis, however, a power spectral density is used to define load magnitude for a confluence of persistent vibrational loads. For shock response spectrum analysis, the peak responses due to a finite duration shock load are defined at multiple frequencies along a response spectrum. You will learn to create a shock/response spectrum analyses, run it, and review Results plots and XY Plots.

Objectives

After completing this chapter, you will be able to:

- Create a new shock/response spectrum analysis.
- Define Damping in a shock/response spectrum analysis.
- Set the range and/or number of modes included in the response summation using the Modal Setup.
- Set the response spectrum for the analysis using the Dynamics setup.
- Create a Response Spectrum constraint to define the excitation location and loading direction.
- Display the Results plot and XY Plot results for a shock/response spectrum analysis.

Lesson: Creating a Shock/Response Spectrum Analysis

Overview

This lesson discusses how you can create a new shock/response spectrum analysis in a model. It discusses the settings that are required for this analysis and specifically covers those settings that have not been previously discussed in other analysis types that have previously been discussed in this learning guide (i.e. spectrum definition and response spectrum constraints). To complete the lesson you will learn which results are automatically generated with a shock/response spectrum analysis.

Objectives

After completing this lesson, you will be able to:

- Create a new shock/response spectrum analysis.
- Define Damping in a shock/response spectrum analysis.
- Set the range and/or number of modes included in the response summation using the Modal Setup.
- Set the response spectrum for the analysis using the Dynamics setup.
- Create a Response Spectrum constraint to define the excitation location and loading direction.
- Display the Results plot and XY Plot results for a shock/response spectrum analysis.

Basics of Shock/Response Spectrum Analysis

A Shock/Response Spectrum analysis, also known as a response-spectrum analysis or RSA, is a linear-dynamic analysis method. It is used to predict the likely effect of a structure when subjected to shock responses (i.e., seismic events, impact events, or explosive and pyrotechnic events). This type of analysis if useful as an analysis method to predict results when a non-dynamic structure is subjected to a dynamic response.

Response spectrum analysis can be divided into two categories.

- The creation of a response spectrum from a transient load.
- The application of a response spectrum to predict analysis results. This evaluates the peak time-independent response from a shock load.

Response Spectrum

Response spectrum data is usually generated from previously recorded data (i.e. shock acceleration data from an impact test, seismic data, explosive and pyrotechnic data). To create response spectrum data, a multi-DOF model is setup that consists of multiple independently vibrating bodies (oscillators), each tuned to a different frequency. The model is then subjected to a transient load. Based on the peak response on an oscillator of a particular natural frequency, the acceleration magnitude vs frequency can be quantified for the response spectrum.

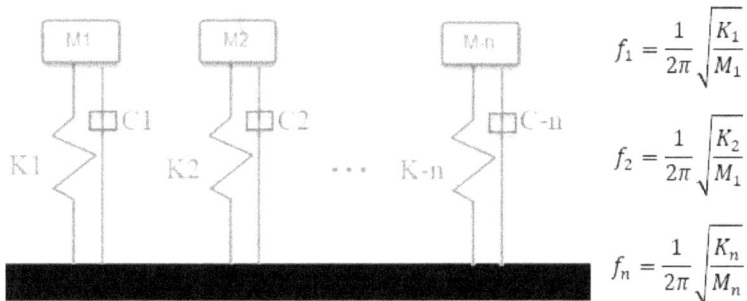

$$f_1 = \frac{1}{2\pi}\sqrt{\frac{K_1}{M_1}}$$

$$f_2 = \frac{1}{2\pi}\sqrt{\frac{K_2}{M_1}}$$

$$f_n = \frac{1}{2\pi}\sqrt{\frac{K_n}{M_n}}$$

Spectrum Creation Theory

Common summation methods are used on the individual modal results to calculate the overall response. These methods include SRSS (square root of the sum of the squares) and NRL (a Naval Research Lab modification of the SRSS method), ABS (Absolute), or CQC (Complete Quadratic Combination). With these, only the peak responses are considered for each mode, and the phasing caused by the different frequencies are ignored. The resulting displacement of a node is the response of that node to each mode.

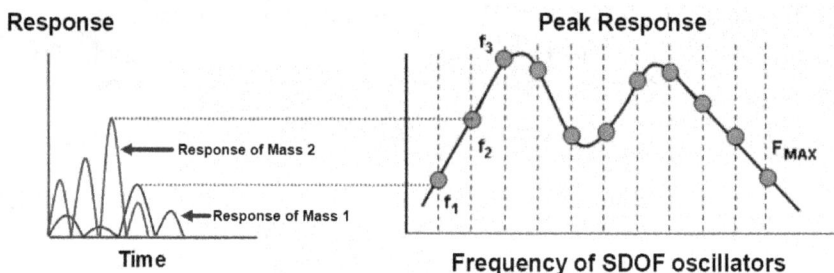

In theory, if time were run out long enough, eventually all the modes would combine constructively, resulting in a peak response that was the absolute sum of the individual responses. However, response spectrum analysis is often used for transient shock events in systems with damping. In that situation, the responses of the individual modes will die out over time, with the higher frequencies dying out faster. As a result, as time progresses, the sums will generally get smaller and smaller. Thus a summation that takes an SRSS sum of the peaks will usually suffice to represent the maximum responses that would ever be seen.

Another concept in the summation is that modes with small scale factors or small modal effective masses will contribute very little to the net response. As a result, it is often possible to create a summation from a smaller number of important modes that is almost identical to a full summation of all modes. Most SRSS techniques exploit this by allowing the extraction of a limited number of modes and summing only the contributions of those relatively low frequency modes. The technique can be further improved by limiting the summation to only to modes with a significant contribution of modal mass. Thus is it often possible to obtain almost identical results from a run with a small number of modes and that with a large number, provided all of the important modes have been included in the smaller case.

Consider the following images. The first image shows the raw transient input data that was used to excite the oscillators. This data is not directly used in a shock/response spectrum analysis. Complex mathematical equations are then incorporated into the process to convert raw transient data into the response spectrum data. The second image is the response magnitude of each oscillator that has a particular natural frequency. It shows the resulting response magnitude vs. frequency data (response spectrum plot) that can be used by Autodesk Nastran In-CAD.

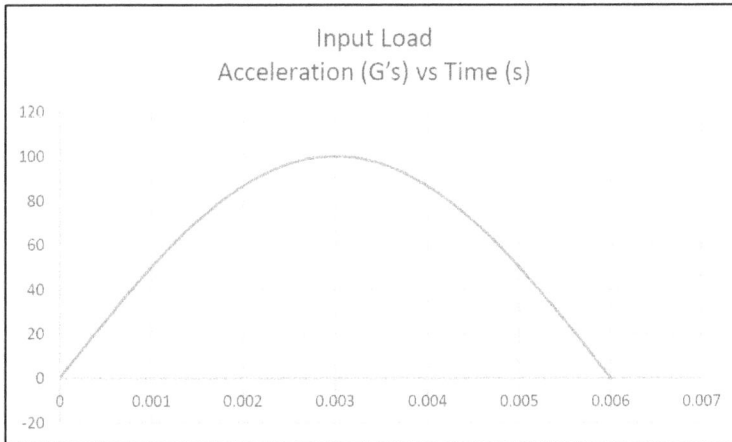

Input Load
Acceleration (G's) vs Time (s)

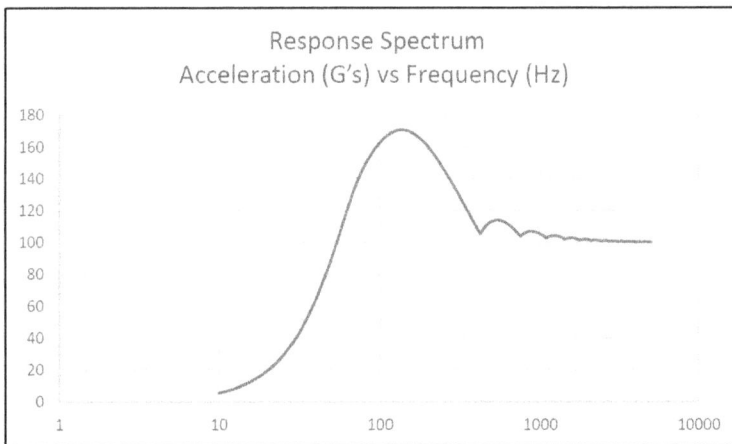

Response Spectrum
Acceleration (G's) vs Frequency (Hz)

Autodesk Nastran In-CAD enables you to enter the data for peak responses for Displacement vs. Frequency, Velocity vs. Frequency, and Acceleration vs. Frequency.

Using the Response Spectrum to Predict Results

In many cases, what people describe as spectral response problems are really referring to the use of a resource spectrum instead of the creation of a spectrum. A shock/response spectrum analysis in Autodesk Nastran In-CAD is no different. Once the response spectrum data is generated it is used in the dynamics setup for the analysis to predict the results. The following topics in this chapter describe how to setup a shock/response spectrum analysis

In the following image, a seven-story building is shown modeled as a series of beam elements with the results of a shock/response spectrum analysis displayed.

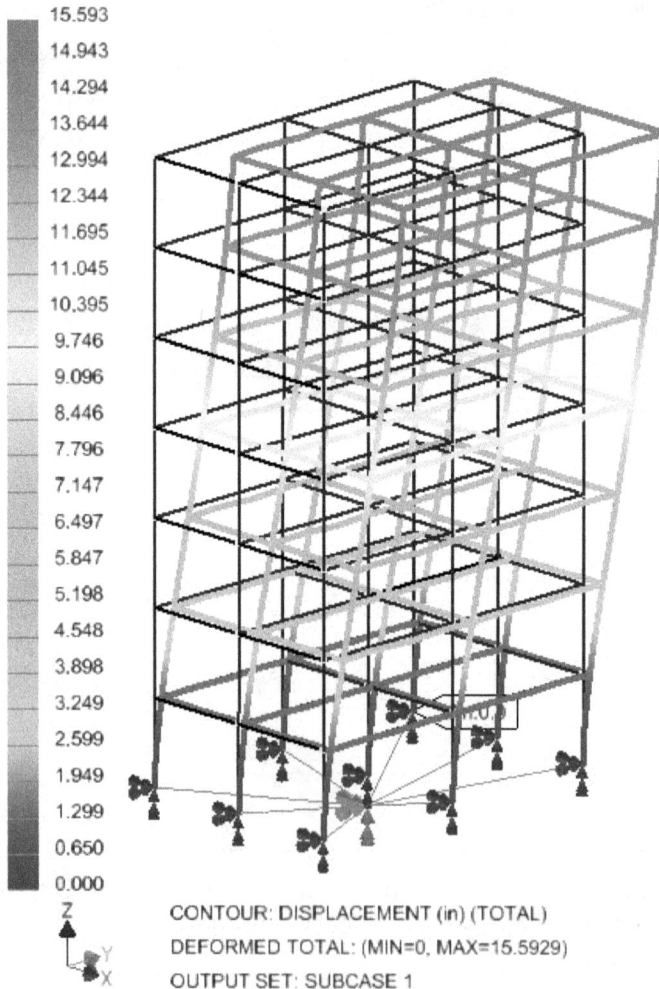

CONTOUR: DISPLACEMENT (in) (TOTAL)
DEFORMED TOTAL: (MIN=0, MAX=15.5929)
OUTPUT SET: SUBCASE 1

Creating a Shock/Response Spectrum Analysis

To create a shock/response spectrum analysis you must either create a new analysis or edit an existing analysis and change the type of analysis to Shock/Response Spectrum. You can also select any additional options in the Analysis dialog box to define the output controls, options, and model state (Design View or Level of Detail in assembly designs) to be analyzed. For shock/response spectrum analysis the Spectrum Data section on the Options tab is uniquely available and enables you to define spectrum settings that only pertains to this analysis type.

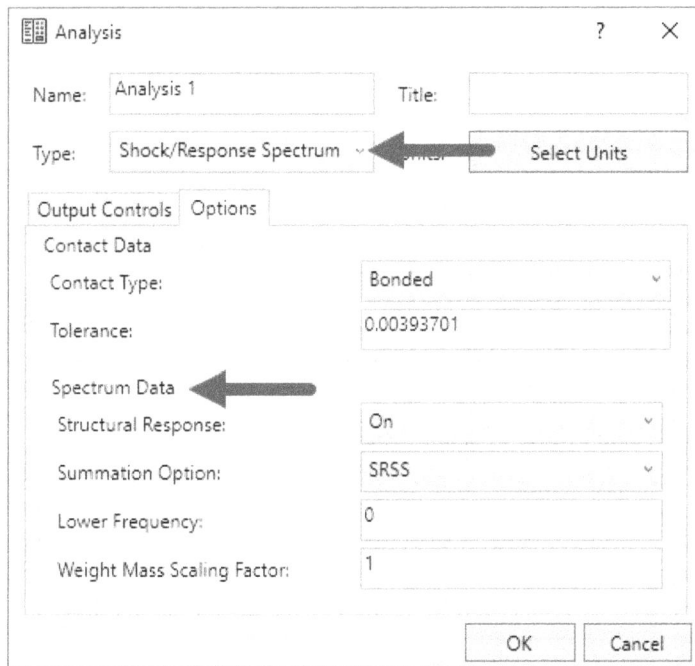

- **Spectrum Data**
  - **Structural Response**: Select On or Off to specify whether the analysis will include structural response.
  - **Summation Option**: Select the method to use for summing responses: Absolute (ABS), Square Root of Summation of Squares (SRSS), Naval Research Lab (NRL), or Complete Quadratic Combination (CQC).
  - **Lower Frequency**: Sets the lowest frequency of modes to be summed during the RSA analysis. Modes found below this frequency will be ignored.
  - **Weight Mass Scaling Factor**: Specify this factor if material density is input in weight units and must be converted to mass units. This is commonly not modified for most analyzes.

When a shock/response spectrum analysis is created the Autodesk Nastran Model Tree displays as shown in the following image.

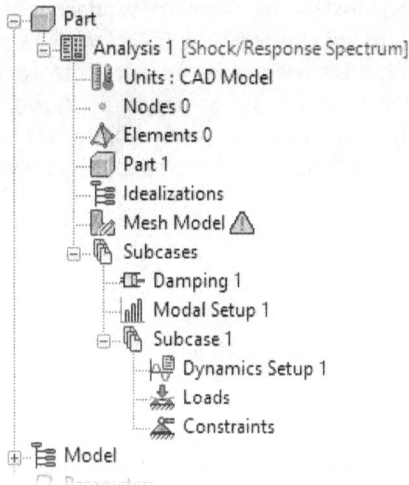

A shock/response spectrum analysis requires damping, modal, and dynamic (spectrum definition) setup steps, as well as the definition of a unique response spectrum constraint type. Additionally you must consider the following:

- Ensure that a required idealization exists or is created that contains any material properties that are specifically required for the analysis.
- Assign any surface contacts, as required, to fully describe the model being analyzed. Note that separation contacts do not work as intended with this type of analysis.
- Assign Rigid Connectors as needed to the model.
- Assign any required structural constraints in addition to a response spectrum constraint.

> Although the Loads node is shown in the Model Tree their application will not affect the results.

The following describes the settings that are required in a shock/response spectrum analysis.

Damping Setup

The Damping setup must be defined for a shock/response spectrum analysis. To create damping, right-click on Damping in the Autodesk Nastran Model tree and select Edit to open the Damping dialog box.

When defining damping for a shock/response spectrum analysis the only type of damping that is available is Modal Damping. Both the Structural and Rayleigh Damping settings are not applicable. Modal Damping is the damping value that is assigned at every natural frequency that is calculated.

- **Modal Damping**
  - **Type**: Enables you to define the model damping as constant or variable.
  - **Damping Definition**: Enables you to define the units for the damping value. You can choose from percentage of critical damping (C/C0), amplification or quality factor (1/(2C/C0), or in the units of g (2C/C0).
  - **Damping Value(%)**: For constant modal damping, enter the damping value.
  - **Use Table**: For variable modal damping, use these options to define the damping versus frequency curve.

In general for shock/response spectrum analyzes the Percent Critical damping definition is most widely used. For more information on the Damping dialog box, refer to Autodesk Nastran In-CAD Help and search for "Damping".

Modal Setup

A shock/response spectrum analysis is run as a post-process to a modal analysis. The modal setup determines the number of modes and the frequency range that will be used in the initial process of the overall analysis. The number of modes found should be modified to ensure that an adequate effective mass is obtained for the SRS analysis. Modal settings are customized using the Modal Setup node that gets created in the subcase of a Shock/Response Spectrum analysis. To access the setup options, right-click on the Modal Setup node in the analysis subcase and select Edit.

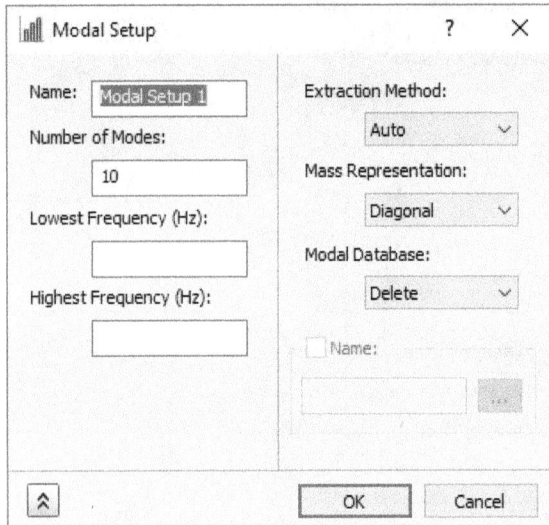

The Modal Setup dialog box contains the same options that are used for a Normal Modes, Frequency Response, and Transient Response analysis that were previously discussed. Defining these settings enables you to define the number of modes and the frequency range that will be reported on for the results and prevents you from having to run a separate normal modes analysis prior to the shock/response spectrum analysis. For more information on the Modal Setup dialog box and its options, refer to the *Creating a Normal Modes Analysis* lesson in Chapter 9 or to Autodesk Nastran In-CAD Help and search for "Modal Setup".

Dynamic Setup

The shock/response spectrum that will be used as the input for the analysis is setup using the subcase's Dynamics Setup node. The settings in the Dynamics Setup dialog box enable you to create and assign the response spectrum table(s) for the analysis. Multiple spectra (tables) can be setup and used for different loading scenarios/damping values. The data for these tables is generally obtained directly from previously recorded data (i.e. shock acceleration data from an impact test, seismic data, explosive and pyrotechnic data). To access the setup options, right-click on the Dynamics Setup node in the analysis subcase and select Edit.

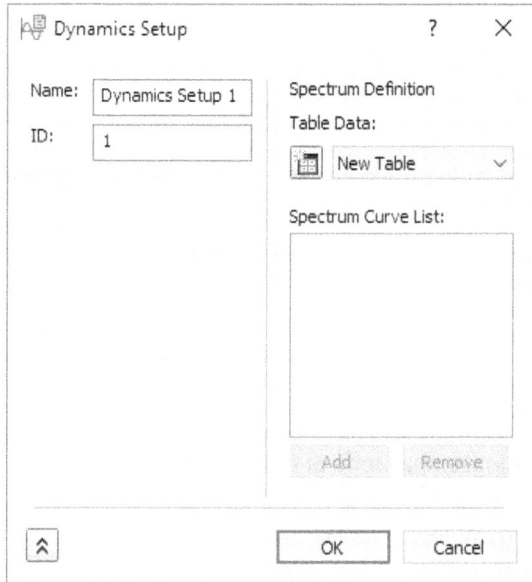

The specific options that are available are described as follows:

- **Name**: Names the dynamics setup.
- **ID**: The ID of the property is automatically updated by Autodesk Nastran In-CAD.
- **Spectrum Definition**: Defines the spectrum table(s) that will be used in the analysis.

  - : Defines or edits a spectrum curve table. With the New Table option selected in the drop-down list the button creates a new table. If a table already exists in the setup you can select its table name in the drop-down list and select the button to edit it.
  - **Spectrum Curve List**: Lists all of the curve spectra that have been added and are being included in the analysis. Note: There can be more tables in the file that are not included in the analysis.
  - **Add**: Adds a newly created table to the Spectrum Curve List so that it will be used in the analysis.
  - **Remove**: Removes the selected table from the Spectrum Curve List so that it is not included in the analysis.

> To delete a response spectrum table from the analysis, expand the Tables node in the Model sub-tree and to list all the tables that have been created in the file. Right-click a table name and select to permanently remove it from the file. Note: tables can not be deleted from within the Dynamics Setup.

Use the following procedure to create a spectrum curve table.

Procedure: To Create a new Spectrum Curve Table

1. Select New Table in the Table Data drop-down list, if not already active.

2. Select ▦ (Define New Table). The Table Data dialog box opens to define the spectrum curve table.

3. Enter a name for the spectrum curve table and accept the default ID value that is automatically assigned by Autodesk Nastran In-CAD.

4. Enter the Damping Value(%) value that corresponds to the table data that will be used.

5. Select the Type of spectrum curve table:

   - **Response Spectrum - Displacement vs. Frequency**: Used for measuring linear displacement of points in response to a range of frequencies.
   - **Response Spectrum - Velocity vs. Frequency**: Used for measuring linear velocity of points in response to a range of frequencies.
   - **Response Spectrum - Acceleration vs. Frequency**: Used for measuring linear acceleration of points in response to a range of frequencies.

6. Define the spectrum curve data:

   - Manually enter the Frequency data (Hz) in column 1.
   - Manually enter the Response Spectrum data in column 2. Ensure that you are entering the data as per the type defined (i.e., displacement, velocity, and acceleration values for each frequency value).
   - Copy and paste data from an external table.

7. (Optional) Use the Sort Data option to reorder the data by frequency. Once reordered it cannot be undone.

8. (Optional) Use the Data Show XY Plot option to review the entered data in an XY plot. You can use the standard options in the XY Plot dialog box to customize the plot.

9. Click OK to create the spectrum curve table.

10. Click Add to add the new table to the Spectrum Curve List to use it in the analysis.

    Note: You must explicitly add the table in the analysis once created. This is required so that you can use multiple tables in the model and then selectively add and remove them for inclusion in the analysis, as needed. To add a previously removed table, select it in the drop-down list and click Add.

11. (Optional) Create additional spectrum curve tables as needed (see step 1).

The Damping Value (%) that is listed in the Table Data dialog box represents the damping ratio that was used in generating the response spectrum data. The Modal damping value should reflect the true damping of the system being analyzed. During analysis, the response-spectrum curve will automatically adjust from the function damping value to that of the actual damping present in the model. For more information on shock response damping, see *Appendix A: Dynamic Analysis Theory*.

Response Spectrum Constraints

When assigning constraints in a shock/response spectrum analysis the default constraint Type is set as Response Spectrum. This is a unique type of constraint that is only used for shock/response spectrum analyzes. It is used to assign the excitation point in the design and set its loading direction. Similar to structural constraints, use the checkboxes in the Degrees of Freedom area is to indicate the translational and/or rotational degrees of freedom that will define the loading direction for the response spectrum.

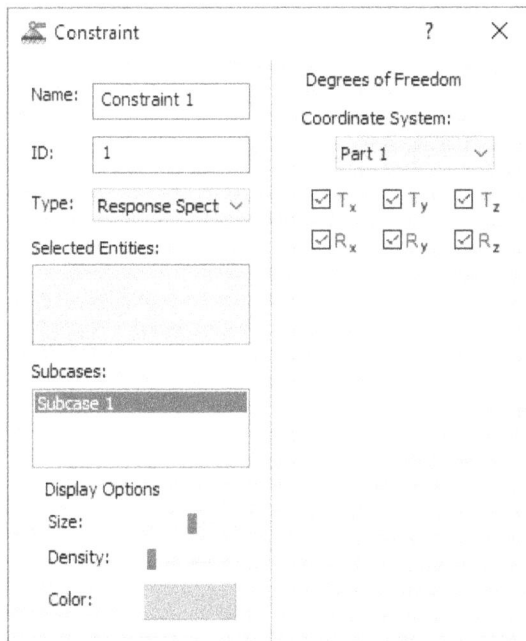

The shock response spectrum table data is used as the excitation values for the assigned constraint along the degree of freedom that was set in the Response Spectrum constraint. Additional Structural constraint should also be assigned to fully constrain the model.

Rigid Connectors

SRS constraints can only by applied to points or vertices; therefore, rigid connectors are required if the shock load will be applied to faces or edges of the model. The spectrum load can be applied directly to the independent point of a rigid connector, which will then transfer the load to the connected faces or edges. Connectors are defined using the Connectors command on the Prepare panel.

Creating the Shock/Response Spectrum Analysis

Use the following procedure to create a shock/response spectrum analysis.

Procedure: Create a new Shock/Response Spectrum Analysis

1. Right-click on the Part or Assembly node at the top of the Autodesk Nastran Model Tree and select New.

2. Enter the name for the new analysis.

3. Select Shock/Response Spectrum in the Type drop-down list.

4. (Optional) By default, the unit system for the model is set to that of the CAD model. Click Select Units and select an alternative unit system, if required.

5. Define the required options in the Output Controls tab to define the information that will be output to the analysis report when it is run. For example, for a shock/response spectrum analysis, you might also want to include the Velocity and Acceleration options, which are included in the Nodal section for impact type solutions.

6. In the Options tab:
   - Set the Contact type that should be used by default when generating Automatic contacts.
   - Set the tolerance value between contacting entities at which automatic contacts are created.
   - Set the Spectrum Data for the analysis.

7. If analyzing an assembly, on the Model State tab, select a Design View or Level of Detail to define the model configuration that is being analyzed.

8. Click OK to create the new shock/response spectrum analysis.

9. Assign an existing idealization from the Model sub-tree or create a new one, as required.

10. Define the Modal setup.

11. Define the Damping setup.

12. Set the Dynamic setup options for the analysis.

13. Add the response spectrum constraint to define the excitation location and loading direction.

14. Assign contacts and/or structural constraints to the model, as required.

15. Run the analysis.

Alternatively, you can edit an existing analysis by right-clicking the analysis name in the Autodesk Nastran Model Tree and select Edit and modify the selected options, as required, to change the current analysis to a shock/response spectrum analysis.

Working with Existing Analysis Results

Unlike other Autodesk Nastran In-CAD analysis types, a shock/response spectrum analysis does not have the Results node listed in the Model Tree until after the analysis is either run or results have been loaded.

- As with all analysis types, in the Solve panel, click ▦ (Run) to run an analysis.
- To load existing Results node you must load them from the .FNO results file.

Procedure: To Load existing Analysis Results from an .FNO file

1. Activate the analysis that is to be loaded.

2. Initiate the Load Results option using one of the following methods:

- On Results panel on the ribbon, click ◺ (Load Results).
- Right-click on the Analysis name at the top of the Autodesk Nastran Model Tree and select Load Results.

3. In the Open dialog box, navigate to and select the *.FNO results file that is to be loaded.

4. The results populate all subcases in the analysis that existed when the analysis was initially run.

> 💡 For more information on working with results, refer to the *Loading Analysis Results* lesson in Chapter 3 or to Autodesk Nastran In-CAD Help and search for "Results".

Shock/Response Analysis Plot Results

Similar to a linear static analysis, there are four default plot templates automatically created for a shock/response spectrum analysis. Once the analysis is run, the default von Mises result will display on the model.

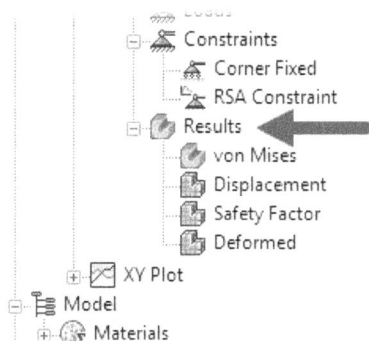

The settings that have been specified for these plot templates are based on generic settings; however, they can be further customized to modify how the plot is displayed or create a new saved plot result.

To access the Plot dialog box:

- Right-click on the Results node and select New or double-click on the Results node to create a new result. Note: An existing result can also be copied to be used to begin the creation of a new result.

- Right-click on any of the existing results and select Edit.

- In the Results panel on the ribbon, click (Options). Using this option one of the existing results is opened for editing. You can rename it to create a new result or edit it as needed.

Using the Plot dialog box you can perform the following tasks:

- Use the Result Data drop-down list in the Contour Options tab to select the general type of data to plot, such as Displacement or Stress.

- Use the Type drop-down list in the Contour Options tab to select the specific data result to plot, such as SOLID VON MISES STRESS.

- Customize the remaining options as required, based on the result plot that is being created.

- Edits made to the plot result are saved with the edited result. To save a new customized result, enter a new unique name in the Name field and click OK. The new result is added to the Results node.

> For more information on the Plot dialog box and its options, refer to the *Visualizing Result Plots* in lesson Chapter 3 or to Autodesk Nastran In-CAD Help and search for "Plot Templates".

Shock/Response Spectrum Analysis XY Plot

When a shock/response spectrum analysis is run, a number of XY plots are generated by default to help you analyze the results.

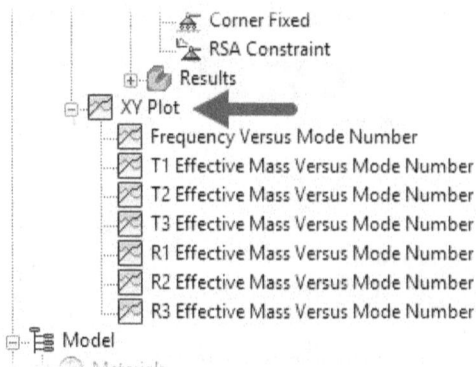

To review any of the plots, double-click on the plot name or right-click on the plot name and select Show XY Plot. The XY Plot dialog box opens displaying the plot. The options in the left pane in the dialog box enables you to customize the display of the plot.

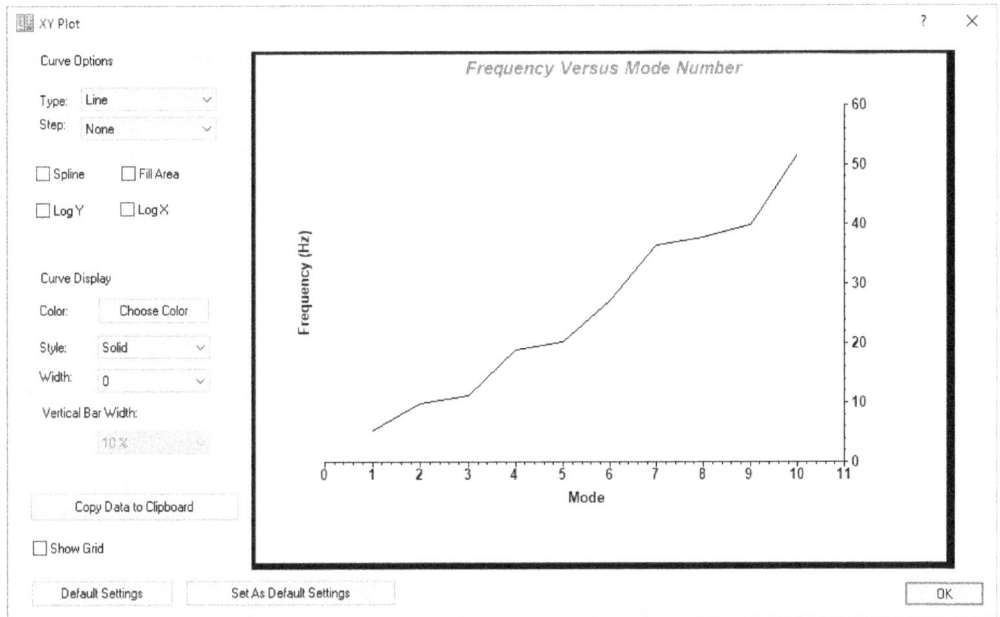

New XY plots can be created as needed by right-clicking on the XY Plot node and selecting New. Using the options in the XY Plot dialog box you can customize the plot.

> For more information on XY Plot dialog box, its options, and how to create a new XY Plot, refer to the *Visualizing XY Plot Results* lesson in Chapter 3 or to Autodesk Nastran In-CAD Help and search for "Results XY Plotting".

Exercise: Multi-Story Building

In this exercise, we will simulate a shock/response spectrum analysis of a office building using beam elements. It requires definition of the modal, damping, and dynamic setup steps. Autodesk Nastran In-CAD will solve the analysis to determine the maximum displacement of the body fixed at the nine base supports.

Prepare the Model for use in Autodesk Nastran In-CAD

1. Open the file *C:\Autodesk Nastran InCAD 2019 Essentials Exercise Files\Building\ 7storybuilding.ipt.*

2. The model consists of a series of 2D and 3D sketches that represent the framework for a seven story office building.

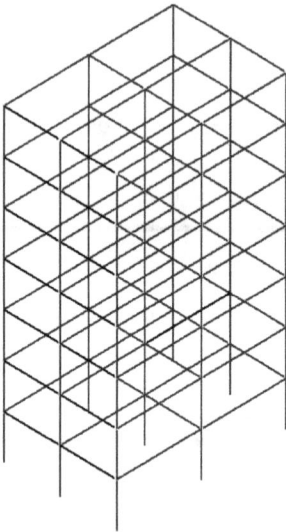

3. In the Model Browser notice Work Point1. This will be used as the independent point reference for a rigid body connector that you will create later in this exercise. Depending on the color scheme in your model it may be difficult to locate the point. Consider right-clicking and selecting 3D Move/Rotate to display the move/rotate triad to help identify where the point is located in the model. Close the toolbar without making changes.

4. Activate the Autodesk Nastran In-CAD environment.

5. Notice in the Model node that seven beam idealizations have been setup for you and a custom material was created and assigned to these beam idealizations.

Set up a Shock/Response Spectrum Analysis

By default, when a model is initially opened in the Nastran In-CAD environment, a Linear Static analysis is created. In this task, you will edit this analysis and change it to a Shock/Response Spectrum Analysis.

1. Right-click on Analysis 1 [Linear Static] node at the top of the Analysis sub-tree and select Edit.

2. In the Analysis dialog box:

    ▪   Maintain the default name.

    ▪   Select Shock/Response Spectrum from the Type drop-down list.

    ▪   Enable the Displacement, Velocity, Acceleration, and Stress options in the Nodal and Elemental sections on the Output Controls tab.

    ▪   Select the Options tab. In the Spectrum Data section, maintain the default options, as shown below.

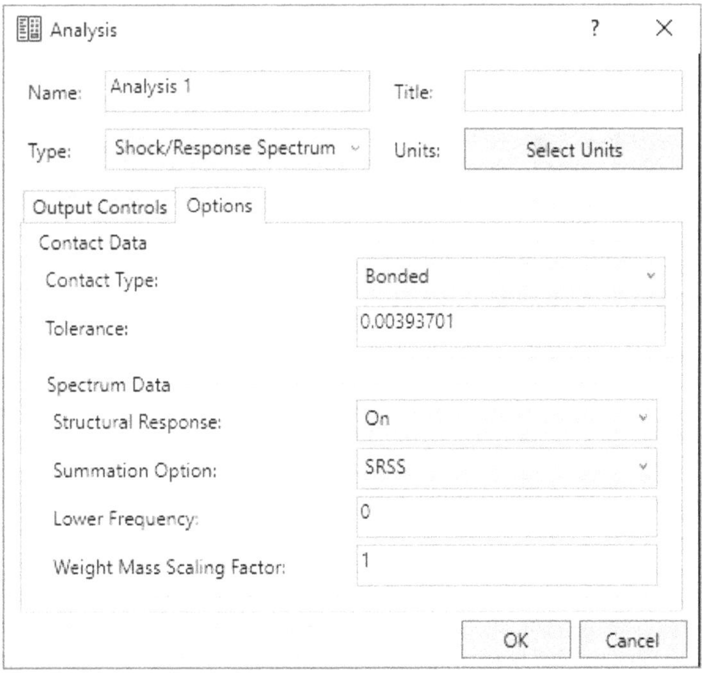

3. Click OK.

Assign the Beam Idealizations

In this task, you will assign the Beam idealizations for use in the shock/response spectrum analysis. These have been created for you by manually defining the beam property information for the various sketched entities. There are seven different idealizations that will be added to the analysis.

1. Expand the Model>Idealizations>Beams nodes in the Model sub-tree.

2. Drag and drop the seven Beam idealizations into the Idealization node for the shock/response spectrum analysis.

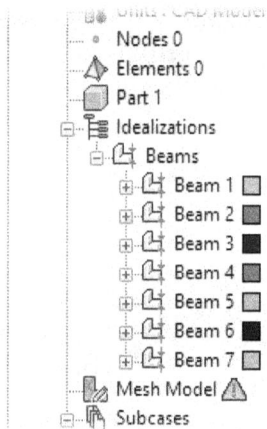

Mesh the Model

In this task, you will globally mesh the model.

1. In the Analysis 1 sub-tree, right-click on Mesh Model, and click Edit to open the Mesh Settings dialog box. The current settings are the default values that were assigned when the analysis was created.

2. In the Mesh Settings dialog box make the following changes:

- Enter **45** as the Element Size.
- Maintain the default Element Order option as Parabolic.
- Clear the Continuous Meshing option.
- Click Generate Mesh to generate the mesh.

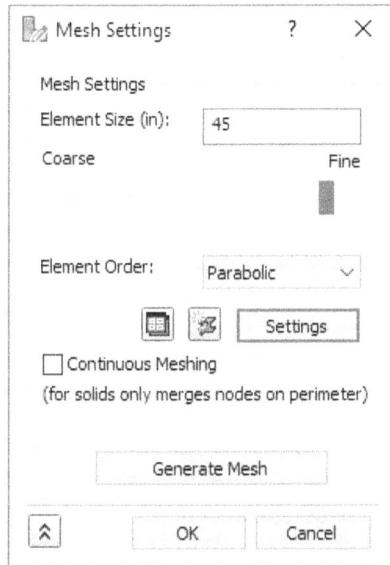

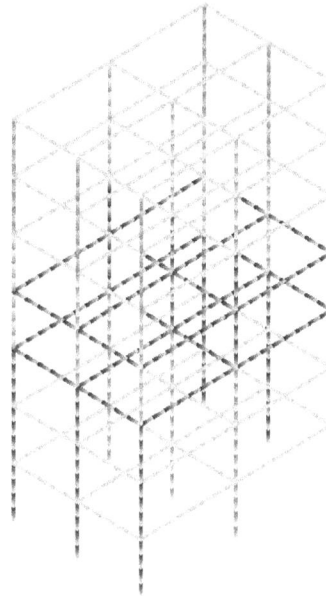

3. Click OK to close the Mesh dialog box.

Add a Rigid Connector to the Model.

In this task, you will add a Rigid Body connector to the model to more accurately represent how the model behaves and how the load is applied.

1. In the Prepare panel, click (Connectors). The Connector dialog box opens.

    Tip: Connectors cannot be directly added through the Analysis node until the first connector is created and is added to the analysis.

2. Enter **RSA Rigid Connector** as the name of the connector.

3. In the Connector dialog box, select Rigid Body from the Type drop-down list.

4. Ensure that the RigidBody Type is set to Rigid.

5. Ensure that Dependent Entities section is active and select the nine endpoints at the bottom of each of the vertical beam elements.

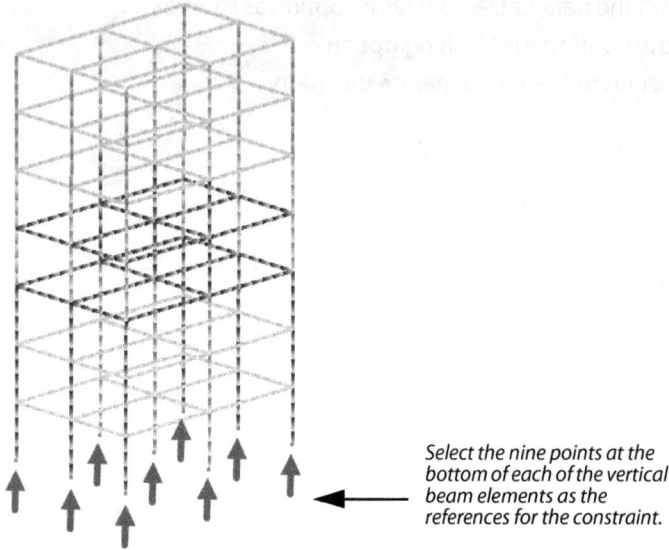

Select the nine points at the bottom of each of the vertical beam elements as the references for the constraint.

6. Ensure that Select Point is selected and its selection field is active. Select Work Point1. This is located below the endpoint of the middle beam. Enable the remaining options as follows.

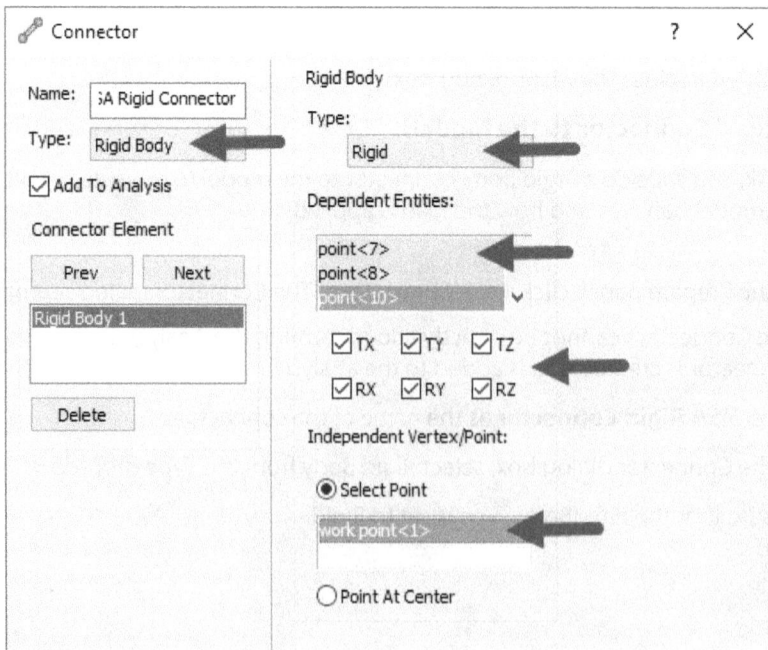

7. Set the color of the connector to red and modify the density of the constraint's display, as required. Click OK. The connector displays as shown in the following image.

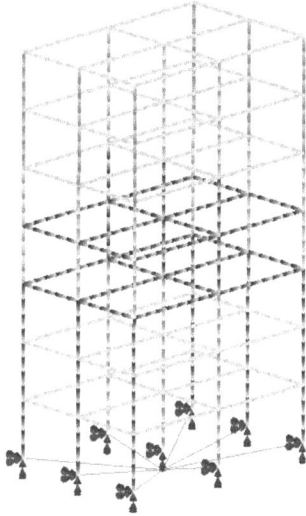

Constrain the Building

In this task, you will constrain the building. This is done to both remove all degrees of freedom and to setup the unique response spectrum constraint that will define the excitation location and direction for the load.

1. Add a structural constraint using the following settings:

    - Enter **Fixed** as the name of the constraint.
    - Change the Type to Structural. By default a Shock/Response Spectrum analysis defaults to the Response Spectrum constraint type.
    - In the Degrees of Freedom section of the dialog box, select ⛰ (Fixed). This presets the degrees of freedom options so that translation and rotation is constrained in all directions.
    - Add the constraint to Subcase 1 in the analysis.
    - Select Work Point1 at the bottom of the middle vertical beam element as the reference for the constraint.
    - If not already defined, set the display color for the constraint to cyan.
    - Select Preview to show the constraint on the model.
    - Modify the density of the constraint's display, as required.
    - Click OK.

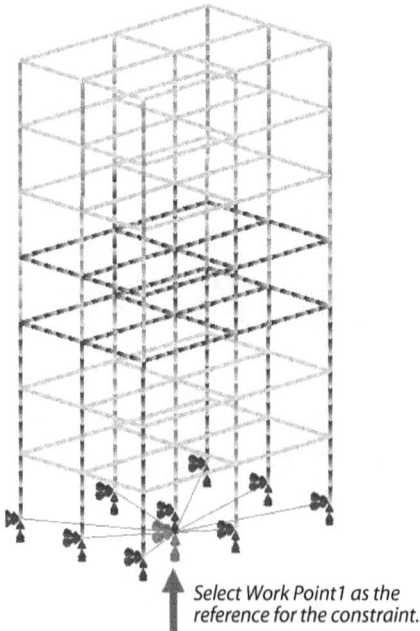

Select Work Point1 as the reference for the constraint.

2. Prior to creating the next constraint, right-click on the Fixed constraint in the Analysis sub-tree and click Display to clear it from the display. Doing this turns off the display of the constraint symbols so that in the next steps you can more easily select the reference.

3. Add a second constraint to the model using the following settings. This constraint uses the Response Spectrum constraint type that is unique for this type of analysis. It enables you to define the excitation point and the loading direction for the analysis.

- Enter **Spectrum XY** as the name of the constraint.
- Ensure the Type is set to Response Spectrum.
- Ensure that the Tx and Ty degree of freedom checkboxes are enabled. Clear the selection of the other 4 options (Tz, Rx, Ry, and Rz). This constraint allows translational motion along the x and y axis and defines how the spectrum data is loading at a 45 degree angle.
- Add the constraint to Subcase 1 in the analysis.
- Select Work Point1 at the bottom of the middle vertical beam element as the reference for the constraint.
- Set the display color for the constraint to green to help identify it.
- Select Preview to show the constraint on the model.
- Modify the density of the constraint's display, as required.
- Click OK.

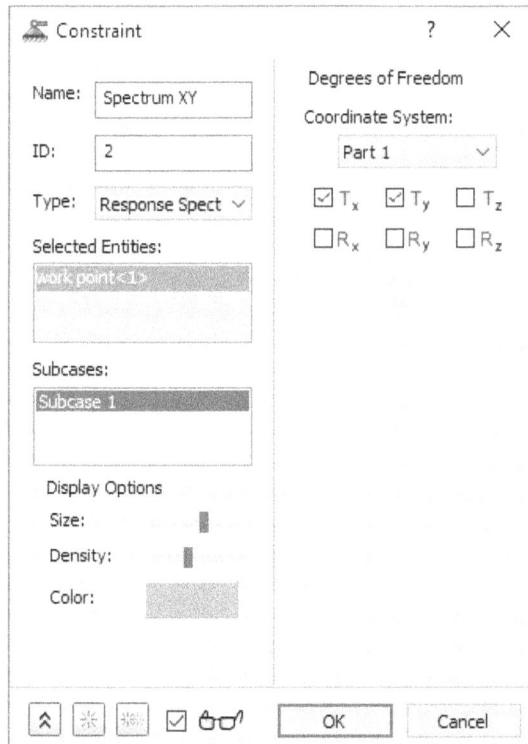

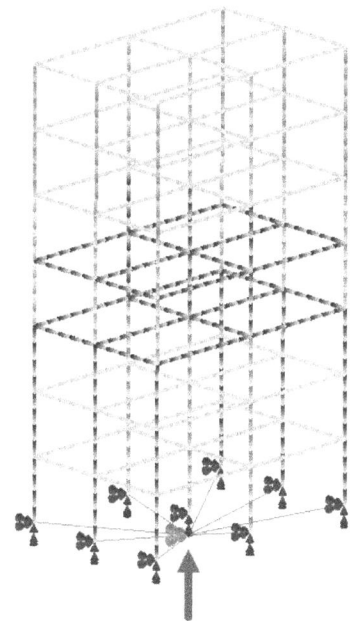

Select the same Work Point1 as the references for the constraint.

4. Return to the Constraints node in the Analysis sub-tree and once again toggle on the display of the Fixed constraint by right-clicking on it and selecting Display. The connector and two constraints should now be visible.

Define Damping in the Model

In this task, you will edit the default Damping setting for the shock/response spectrum analysis.

1. In the Analysis sub-tree, right-click on Damping 1 in the Subcases node and select Edit.

2. Ensure that Modal Damping is enabled. Notice that for a shock/response spectrum analysis this is the only type of damping that can be added.

3. Set the Modal Damping using the following settings:
   - Select Constant as the damping type.
   - Select Percent Critical as the Damping Definition.
   - Enter **2** as the Damping Value (%).
   - Click OK.

Define the Modal Setup in the Model

In this task, you will define the modal settings for the shock/response spectrum analysis. Within a shock/response spectrum analysis a modal analysis is run as the first process to ensure that enough effective mass is included in the range of modes that are included in the summation for the SRS analysis.

1. In the Analysis sub-tree, right-click on Model Setup 1 in the Subcases node and select Edit.

2. Set the Modal Setup using the following settings. Click OK.

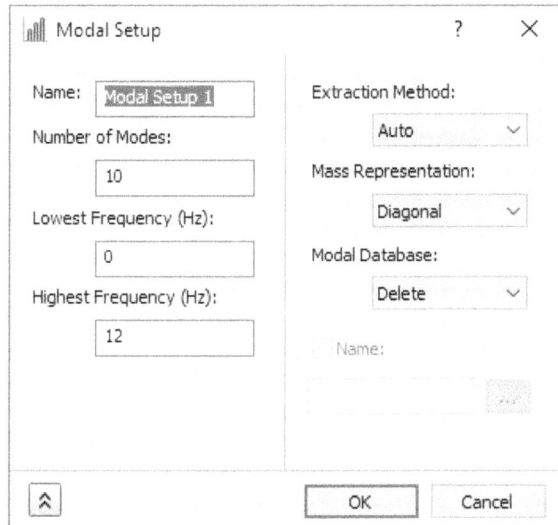

Define the Dynamic Setup Options for the Analysis

In this task, you will define the dynamic setup options for the subcase.

1. Right-click on the Dynamics Setup 1 node in Subcase 1and click Edit.

2. On the Dynamics Setup dialog box, select (define New Table) to create a table that will define the response spectrum for the analysis.

3. In Windows Explorer, open the file *C:\Autodesk Nastran InCAD 2019 Essentials Exercise Files\Building\Building Response Spectrum Dynamics Data.xls*.

4. In the Table Data dialog box, enter **Freq vs Acceleration** as the name of the table.

5. Enter **0** as the Damping Value (%).

6. Select Response Spectrum - Acceleration vs. Frequency as the table type.

7. Return to the .xls file and in the 0% Critical Damping tab. Copy the data in cells A3 through B16. Do not select the text-based column headings.

8. Return to the Table Data dialog box and paste the data into the first cell in the second row (i.e. in the Frequency column). All of the data pastes into the table as shown below.

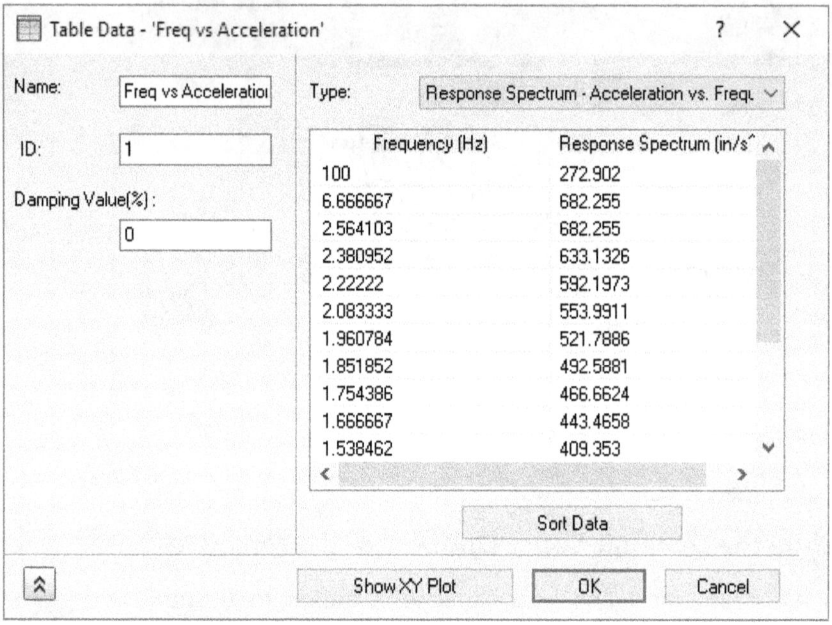

Frequency (Hz)	Response Spectrum (in/s^
100	272.902
6.666667	682.255
2.564103	682.255
2.380952	633.1326
2.22222	592.1973
2.083333	553.9911
1.960784	521.7886
1.851852	492.5881
1.754386	466.6624
1.666667	443.4658
1.538462	409.353

Table Data - 'Freq vs Acceleration'

Name: Freq vs Acceleratior
ID: 1
Damping Value(%) : 0
Type: Response Spectrum - Acceleration vs. Frequ

Sort Data

Show XY Plot   OK   Cancel

9. Click OK to return to the Dynamics Setup dialog box.

10. Click Add to add the newly created table to the Spectrum Curve List so that it will be used in the analysis.

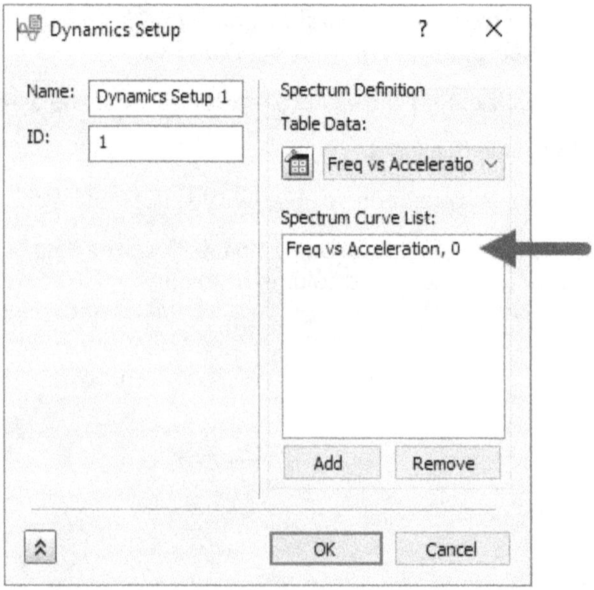

Dynamics Setup

Name: Dynamics Setup 1
ID: 1

Spectrum Definition
Table Data:
Freq vs Acceleratio

Spectrum Curve List:
Freq vs Acceleration, 0

Add   Remove

OK   Cancel

11. Click OK to close the Dynamics Setup dialog box.

Run the Analysis

In this task, you will run the analysis.

1. Run the analysis. Click OK when the analysis is complete.

2. In the Analysis sub-tree, note that in Subcase1 there are now four Result nodes listed. Similar to a Linear Static analysis, these results templates are defined for the Shock/Response Spectrum analysis.

3. To visualize the displacement, right-click on Displacement in the Results node and select Display. The maximum displacement is 15.6in.

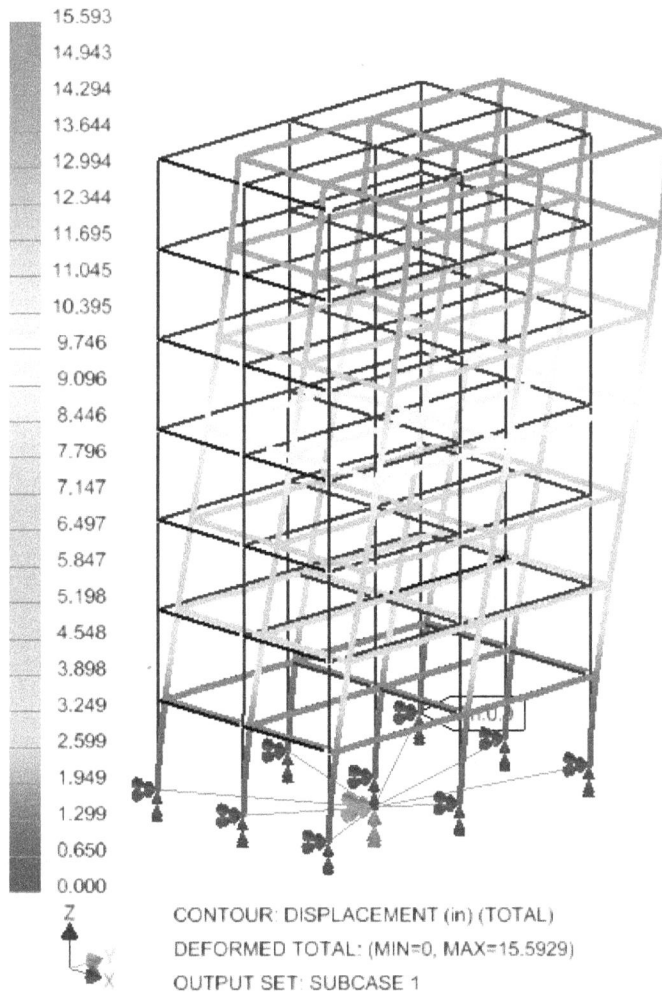

4. Continue to view any of the results, as required, using the Plot dialog box, the predefined XY Plots or new ones, or the Results panel on the ribbon.

5. To visualize the beam equivalent stress, double-click von Mises in the Results node to activate it. Right-click on von Mises in the Results node and select Edit to modify its setting.

   - In the Contour Options tab, ensure that Stress is selected in the Result Data drop-down list and select BEAM EQUIVALENT STRESS in the Type drop-down list.

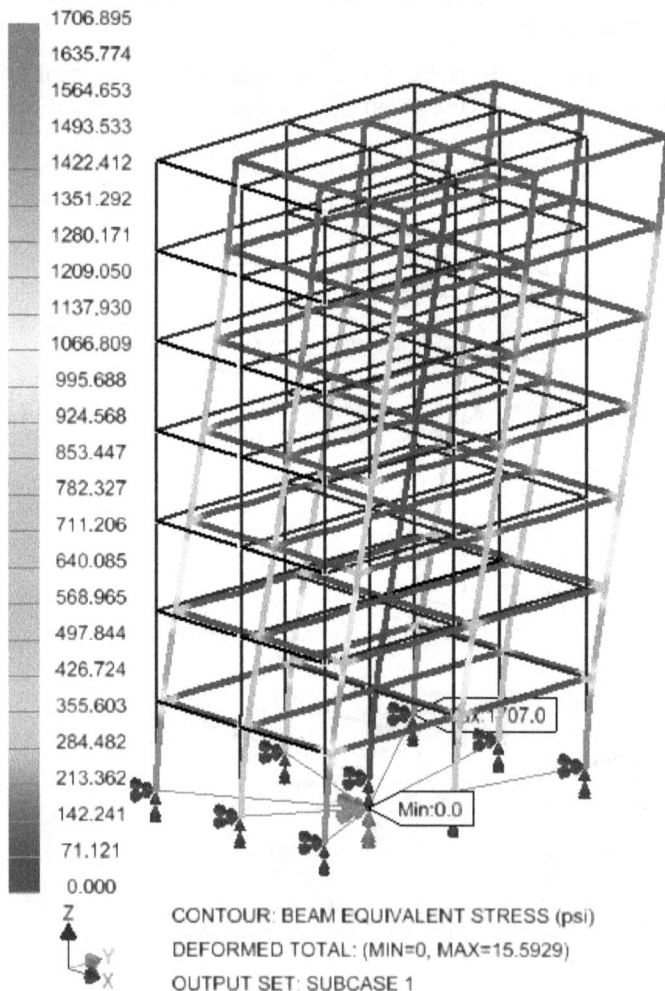

1706.895
1635.774
1564.653
1493.533
1422.412
1351.292
1280.171
1209.050
1137.930
1066.809
995.688
924.568
853.447
782.327
711.206
640.085
568.965
497.844
426.724
355.603
284.482
213.362
142.241
71.121
0.000

Max:1707.0
Min:0.0

CONTOUR: BEAM EQUIVALENT STRESS (psi)
DEFORMED TOTAL: (MIN=0, MAX=15.5929)
OUTPUT SET: SUBCASE 1

This result shows the combined peak stress for the beam elements due to the shock load.

6. Save the model.

Dynamic Analysis Theory

This appendix provides theoretical information on the normal modes, frequency response, and transient response analysis types that are available in the Autodesk® Nastran® In-CAD software.

Normal Modes Analysis Theory

Normal Modes (Eigenvalue) Theory

Consider a dynamic system. In general, the equations of motion can be expressed as a function of the system mass, stiffness, damping and applied loads:

$$[M]\{\ddot{x}(t)\} + [B]\{\dot{x}(t)\} + [K]\{x(t)\} = \{P(t)\}$$

where:

[M] = global mass matrix

[K] = global stiffness matrix

[B] = global damping matrix

{P} = global load vector

Eigenvalues or natural frequencies are found when there is no damping or applied loads. The equations of motion for free vibration can then be written as:

$$[M]\{\ddot{x}(t)\} + [K]\{x(t)\} = 0$$

Assume a sinusoidal vibration, where the displacement can be described by:

$$\{x(t)\} = \{\phi\}e^{i\omega t}$$

Then replace the {x(t)} term with the above and consider that, for a sinusoidal variation, the acceleration is the second derivative of the displacement:

$$\{\ddot{x}(t)\} = -\omega^2 \{\phi\}e^{i\omega t}$$

Thus the equation of motion becomes:

$$(-\omega^2[M] + [K])[\phi]e^{i\omega t} = 0$$

Since $e^{i\omega t}$ is never zero, the equation can be rearranged to the form of a general eigenvalue problem. Autodesk Nastran In-CAD determines the natural frequency by solving the eigenvalue problem:

$$|[K] - \lambda[M]|[\phi] = 0$$

where:

[K] = global linear stiffness matrix

[M] = global mass matrix

λ = the eigenvalue for each mode that yields the natural frequency = ω^2

ϕ = the eigenvector for each mode that represents the natural mode shape

---

The eigenvalue is related to the system's natural frequency:

$$\lambda_i = \omega_i^2$$

where:

ω = the circular frequency (radians per second)

or in Hertz:

$$\omega = 2\pi f$$

where:

f = the cyclic frequency (Hertz)

One solution is trivial (ω = 0), but the other solutions for ω are interesting. ω^2 is called the eigenvalue λ, and each is accompanied by a unique $\{\phi\}$ called the eigenvector.

In solving the above eigenvalue problem, there are as many eigenvalues and corresponding eigenvectors as there are unconstrained degrees of freedom. Often, however, only the lowest natural frequency is of practical interest. This frequency will always be the first mode extracted.

The solution of the eigenvalue problem is difficult and a number of different approaches have been developed over the years. Currently, the Lanczos approach is favored as it is fast, accurate and robust. The Autodesk Nastran In-CAD software also offers the Subspace method. This can be used in those rare cases where Lanczos fails. SUBSPACE is selected using the Nastran directive EXTRACTMETHOD=SUBSPACE in the Parameters dialog box under Program Control Directives (select the Advanced Settings checkbox first). For more details, see the Parameters topic of the User's Guide. The default AUTO setting for this parameter uses Lanczos in most circumstances, but changes to Subspace for some small problems. Note that Autodesk Nastran In-CAD does not recognize the EIGR card available in other Nastrans to use other extraction methods.

Also, while the λ found is the exact eigenvalue, the eigenvectors are arbitrarily scaled. That is, there is no unique magnitude to the vectors. They simply represent a shape. By default Autodesk Nastran In-CAD performs a mass scaling on the vectors. This is done by calculating the generalized mass of the model from the equation:

$$M = [\phi]^T [M][\phi]$$

All of the terms of the vector are then divided by it. This results in a seemingly arbitrary scaling of the vectors, but it has important mathematical properties that can be exploited elsewhere. In addition to mass scaling, Nastran also has max scaling available, where the largest value in the vector will be 1.0. This enables small vectors to be examined manually.

A property of eigenvectors is that they are orthogonal. This means that one eigenvector multiplied by another will produce an identity matrix. An eigenvector vector multiplied by itself will be zero.

$$[\phi]_i[\phi]_i = [0]$$
$$[\phi]_i[\phi]_j = [I]$$

This is another property that is exploited in dynamics solutions.

Direct & Modal Frequency Response Analysis Theory

Direct Frequency Response Theory

A direct frequency response starts with the general equations of motion, but assumes an oscillating load:

$$[M]\ddot{x}(t) + [B]\dot{x}(t) + [K]x(t) = \{P(\omega)\}e^{i\omega t}$$

We can then propose that the solution is also in the form of an oscillating function:

$$x(t) = \{u(\omega)\}e^{i\omega t}$$

$u(\omega)$ is a complex displacement vector. The velocity and acceleration can be found by taking the derivative:

$$\dot{x}(t) = i\omega\{u(\omega)\}e^{i\omega t}$$

$$\ddot{x}(t) = -\omega^2\{u(\omega)\}e^{i\omega t}$$

Substitute this into the equation of motion and divide by the $e^{i\omega t}$ term to get:

$$-\left(\omega^2[M] + i\omega[B] + [K]\right)\{u(\omega)\} = \{P(\omega)\}$$

The frequency ω is a constant in this equation. Therefore, the solution will yield a complex displacement vector u for each frequency that is selected.

In a direct frequency response analysis, this equation is solved repeatedly for each selected frequency. As a result, the solution time is proportional to the number of frequencies that are selected for solution.

Modal Frequency Response Theory

To run a modal frequency response, it is required to transform the physical coordinates to modal coordinates. The natural frequencies and eigenvectors are a good way to do this because of their property of orthogonality. As such, we can replace the physical coordinates u with the modal coordinates. First, a transformation is defined:

$$\{x\} = [\phi]\{\xi(\omega)\}e^{i\omega t}$$

This is substituted into the equations of motion (temporarily ignoring the damping term):

$$-\omega^2[M]\{x\} + [K]\{x\} = \{P(\omega)\}$$

Resulting in the following:

$$-\omega^2[M][\phi]\{\xi(\omega)\} + [K][\phi]\{\xi(\omega)\} = \{P(\omega)\}$$

Now premultiply by $[\phi]^T$:

$$-\omega^2[\phi]^T[M][\phi]\{\xi(\omega)\} + [\phi]^T[K][\phi]\{\xi(\omega)\} = [\phi]^T\{P(\omega)\}$$

These terms are replaced with the uncoupled generalized components that are easily handled:

$[\phi]^T[M][\phi]$ = modal or generalized mass matrix

$[\phi]^T[K][\phi]$ = modal or generalized stiffness matrix

$[\phi]^T\{P(\omega)\}$ = modal load vector

Resulting in an uncoupled series of equations that are easily solved:

$$-\omega^2 m_i\{\xi(\omega)\} - k_i\{\xi(\omega)\} = \{p_i(\omega)\}$$

And once the modal displacements ξ are found, the physical displacements can be found from the sum of the modal displacements:

$$\{x\} = [\phi]\{\xi(\omega)\}e^{i\omega t}$$

This approach will yield the exact same answer as the direct approach, provided that all modal degrees of freedom are included in the transformation. However, the strength of the approach comes about because an answer that is very close to exact can usually be obtained with significantly fewer modal degrees of freedom than there are physical degrees of freedom. With fewer DOF, the solution can proceed much faster. This can be especially efficient for large models and for models with large numbers of frequencies.

Direct & Modal Transient Response Analysis Theory

Direct Transient Response Theory

In direct transient response analysis, the structural response is computed by solving a set of coupled equations using direct numerical integration. The method used is the same as for nonlinear transient response and enables an adaptive time stepping algorithm. We begin with the dynamic equation of motion in matrix form:

$$[M]\{\ddot{x}(t)\} + [B]\{\dot{x}(t)\} + [K]\{x(t)\} = \{P(t)\}$$

The fundamental structural response (displacement) is solved at discrete times, typically at a series of time steps with a constant time increment between them. The solution strategy is called the central finite difference method and is based on finding the displacement, velocity and acceleration at subsequent times, knowing those values at the current and past times. The image below shows a transient integration graph.

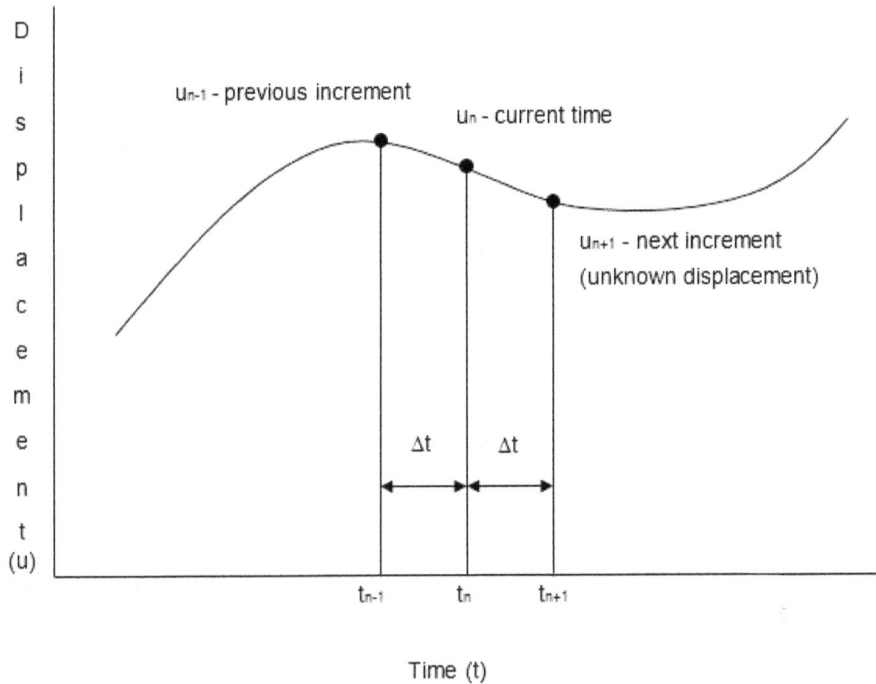

Time (t)

At any time n, we know the displacement, velocity and acceleration. Using this information, there are a number of ways to find the displacement, velocity and acceleration at a subsequent step. For example, if we assume the current velocity remains constant until the next time increment, the subsequent displacement u_{n+1} would simply be the current location plus the velocity times the time increment, $u_n + V\Delta t$. However, if the velocity is not constant, something we cannot assume in a general problem, we have to account for a changing velocity, so that we have an acceleration term in the equation.

This is true if we assume the current acceleration remains constant to the next increment. However, this cannot necessarily be assumed in a general problem. The mean value theorem postulate an acceleration. A_γ is a function of a constant gamma such that the acceleration is a weighted average of the accelerations at n and n+1:

$$A_\gamma = \gamma A_n + (1 - \gamma) A_{n-1}.$$

Newmark was able to show that 0.5 is a good value for gamma, such that:

$$A_\gamma = \frac{1}{2}(A_n + A_{n-1}),$$

and

$$V_{n-1} = V_n + \frac{1}{2}\Delta t(A_n + A_{n-1})$$

Since velocity is the first derivative of displacement, and acceleration the second, they are usually represented in dot notation as their derivatives.

$$\dot{u}_{n-1} = \dot{u}_n + \frac{1}{2}\Delta t(\ddot{u}_n + \ddot{u}_{n-1})$$

However, since the acceleration may vary with time as well, we can propose that the displacement will be corrected by both velocity and acceleration terms thus:

$$u_{n-1} = u_n + \Delta t \dot{u}_n + \frac{1}{2}\Delta t^2 \ddot{u}_\beta$$

The acceleration $\ddot{u}_\beta$ in the above term is calculated like the velocity above, such that:

$$\ddot{u}_\beta = (1 - 2\beta)\ddot{u}_n + 2\beta \ddot{u}_{n-1}.$$

u can then be written in terms of the beta constant:

$$u_{n-1} = u_n + \Delta t \dot{u}_n + \frac{1 - 2\beta}{2}\Delta t^2 \ddot{u}_n + \beta \Delta t^2 \ddot{u}_{n-1}.$$

The beta value in the above equation is called the Newmark-Beta, and can vary between 0 and 1. It is usually used as ¼, which yields the constant average acceleration method, where:

$$u_{n-1} = u_n + \Delta t \dot{u}_n + \frac{1}{4}\Delta t^2 (\ddot{u}_n + \ddot{u}_{n-1})$$

These equations can be manipulated to find expressions for velocity and acceleration at the current time increment, but expressed in terms of the displacement at past and subsequent time intervals:

$$\{\dot{u}_n\} = \frac{1}{2\Delta t}\{u_{n-1} - u_{n-1}\}$$

$$\{\ddot{u}_n\} = \frac{1}{\Delta t^2}\{u_{n-1} - 2u_n + u_{n-1}\}$$

These representations are then substituted into the equations of motion, resulting in the following:

$$\left[\frac{m}{\Delta t^2}\right](u_{n-1} - 2u_n + u_{n-1}) + \left[\frac{b}{2\Delta t}\right](u_{n-1} - u_{n-1}) +$$

$$\left[\frac{k}{3}\right](u_{n-1} + u_n + u_{n-1}) = \frac{1}{3}(P_{n-1} + P_n + P_{n-1})$$

However, since u_{n+1} is the unknown, we need a u_{n+1} value in each expression for the solution. We will represent the displacement at the current time as the average over the adjacent times. Likewise, the load can be averaged over three steps, the difference being that we know P_{n+1} as it is an input value.

Using these average values:

$$u_n = \frac{(u_{n-1} + u_n + u_{n-1})}{3}$$

$$P_n = \frac{(P_{n-1} + P_n + P_{n-1})}{3}$$

We then rearrange the terms to end up with the unknown u_{n+1} on the left side and the known u_n and u_{n-1} on the right:

$$[A_1]\{u_{n+1}\} = [A_2] + [A_3]\{u_n\} + [A_4]\{u_{n-1}\}$$

$$\text{where } [A_1] = \left[\frac{M}{\Delta t^2} + \frac{B}{2\Delta t} + \frac{K}{3}\right]$$

$$[A_2] = \frac{1}{3}\{P_{n+1} + P_n + P_{n-1}\}$$

$$[A_3] = \left[\frac{2M}{\Delta t^2} - \frac{K}{3}\right]$$

$$[A_4] = \left[-\frac{M}{\Delta t^2} + \frac{B}{2\Delta t} - \frac{K}{3}\right]$$

To solve this equation, we need to calculate the four A terms, then decompose (invert) the A_1 term to find u_{n-1}. It should be noted that for a problem with a constant time step A_1 needs to be decomposed only once. However, if the time step changes, it will be necessary to do the calculation again. Thus, it is advisable to maintain a constant time step unless changing it will offset the extra cost.

Modal Transient Response Theory

To run a modal transient response analysis, it is required to transform the physical coordinates to modal coordinates. The natural frequencies and eigenvectors are a good way to do this because of their property of orthogonality. As such, we can replace the physical coordinates u with the modal coordinates:

$$\{x(t)\} = [\phi]\{\xi(t)\}$$

The basic equation of motion (temporarily ignoring the damping term) becomes:

$$[M][\phi]\{\ddot{\xi}(t)\} - [K][\phi]\{\xi(t)\} = \{P(t)\}$$

With a little manipulation, we can rearrange this into something more useful:

$$[\phi]^T[M][\phi]\{\ddot{\xi}(t)\} - [\phi]^T[K][\phi]\{\xi(t)\} = [\phi]^T\{P(t)\}$$

But the mass and stiffness terms are now the generalized modal matrices, diagonal matrices that are easily handled:

$[\phi]^T[M][\phi]$ = modal or generalized mass matrix

$[\phi]^T[K][\phi]$ = modal or generalized stiffness matrix

$[\phi]^T\{P\}$ = modal load vector

The diagonal matrices have the effect of uncoupling the modal degrees of freedom. The load term is a vector and is already uncoupled. As a result, the system is easily solved as a series of uncoupled equations:

$$m_i\ddot{\xi}(t) + k_i\xi(t) = p_i(t)$$

Where m and k are the generalized mass and stiffness values for each modal degree of freedom, and p is the modal load vector.

Once values are found for the modal displacements ξ, the physical displacements can be found from the sum of the modal displacements:

$$\{x(t)\} = [\phi]\{\xi(t)\}$$

This approach will yield the exact same answer as the direct approach, provided that all modal degrees of freedom (DOF) are included in the transformation. However, the strength of the approach comes about because an answer that is very close to exact can usually be obtained with significantly fewer modal degrees of freedom than there are physical degrees of freedom. With fewer DOF, the solution can proceed much faster. This can be especially efficient for large models and for models that require many time steps.

Damping Theory

Various types of damping create the damping matrix [B] in dynamic solutions. Therefore, the damping matrix consists of several matrices:

$$[B] = [B_1] + [B_2] + \alpha[K] + \beta[M]$$

$$[B_1] = [B_{DAMP}] - \frac{G}{W_3}[K] - \frac{1}{W_4} \sum G_{ELEM} K_{ELEM}$$

where:

$[B_1]$ = damping from damping elements (CVISC, CDAMPi) and B2GG DMIG

$[B_2]$ = damping from B2PP DMIG

$[K]$ = global stiffness matrix

$[M]$ = global mass matrix

$[K_{ELEM}]$ = element stiffness matrix

G – overall structural damping coefficient (PARAM, G)

G_{ELEM} = element structural damping coefficient (GE on the MATi entry)

W_3 = frequency of interest in radians per unit time (PARAM, W3) for the conversion of overall structural damping into equivalent viscous damping (see Note)

W_4 = frequency of interest in radians per unit time (PARAM, W4) for the conversion of element structural damping into equivalent viscous damping (see Note)

α = Rayleigh damping stiffness matrix scale factor

β = Rayleigh damping mass matrix scale factor

Note: W3 and W4 in the preceding equations are in the units radians per unit time. However, in the Autodesk Nastran In-CAD user interface, these variables are specified in Hz (cycles per second) and are converted internally to the required units.

Damping in Direct Frequency Response

In a direct frequency response problem, you are using a complex solution. As a result, the complex damping term can be used as is. It is not required to convert the structural damping to equivalent viscous damping. All forms of damping can be used without penalty.

Damping in Modal Frequency Response

In the modal solution, the damping matrix does not generally diagonalize. Further, any structural damping will create a complex stiffness matrix that does not diagonalize either. As a result, if either of those types of damping are included, the solution must be solved in the direct method, but with modal coordinates. It is faster than solving in physical space, but not so fast as solving the uncoupled equations. In order to reap the benefits of the uncoupled solution, it is necessary to ignore the other kinds of damping and use only modal damping, which damps individual modal degrees of freedom individually.

Damping in Direct Transient Response

Transient response does not permit the use of complex coefficients. Therefore, structural damping is included by means of equivalent viscous damping.

The viscous damping force is a damping force that is a function of a damping coefficient b and the velocity. It is an induced force that is represented in the equation of motion using the [B] matrix and velocity vector.

$$[M]\{\ddot{u}(t)\} - [B]\{\dot{u}(t)\} - [K]\{u(t)\} = \{P(t)\}$$

where:

$[M]$ = global mass matrix

$[B]$ = global damping matrix

$[K]$ = global stiffness matrix

$\{P\}$ = global load vector

$\{\ddot{u}\}$ = global acceleration vector

$\{\dot{u}\}$ = global velocity vector

$\{u\}$ = global displacement vector

The structural damping force is a displacement-dependent damping. The structural damping force is a function of a damping coefficient G and a complex component of the structural stiffness matrix.

$$[M]\{\ddot{u}(t)\} - (1 - iG)[K]\{u(t)\} = \{P(t)\}$$

Assuming constant amplitude oscillatory response for a single degree of freedom system, the two damping forces are identical if:

$$Gk = b\omega$$

or

$$b = \frac{Gk}{\omega}$$

Therefore, if structural damping G is to be modeled using equivalent viscous damping b, then the equality holds at only one frequency (see image below).

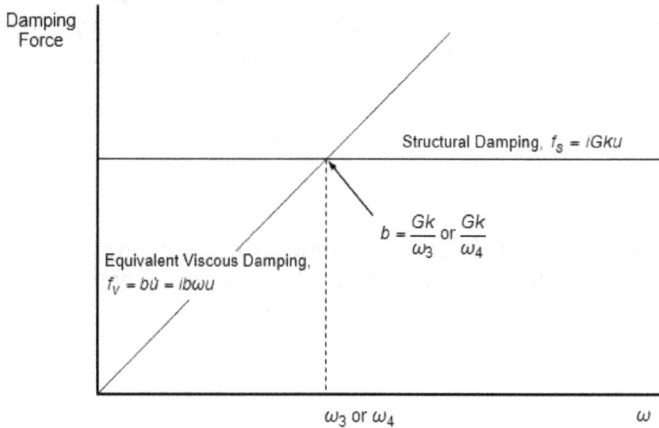

Two parameters are used to convert structural damping to equivalent viscous damping. An overall structural damping coefficient can be applied to the entire system stiffness matrix using PARAM, W3, r, where r is the circular frequency at which damping is made equivalent. This parameter is used along with PARAM, G. The default for W3 is zero, which results in the damping from this source being ignored in transient analysis.

PARAM, W4 is an alternative parameter used to convert element structural damping to equivalent viscous damping. PARAM, W4, r is used, where r is the circular frequency at which damping is to be made equivalent. PARAM, W4 is used along with the GE field on the MATi entry. The default for W4 is zero, which results in the damping from this source being ignored in transient analysis.

Units for PARAM, W3 and PARAM, W4 are in radians per unit time. However, in the Autodesk Nastran In-CAD user interface, you enter the values in Hz (cycles per second) and they are internally converted to the required units. The choice of W3 or W4 is typically the dominant frequency at which damping is active. Often, the first natural frequency is selected, but isolated individual element damping can occur at different frequencies and can be handled by the appropriate data entries.

Damping in Modal Transient Response

Modal transient response analysis uses the mode shapes of the structure to reduce the size, uncouple the equations of motion, and make numerical integration more efficient.

To outline the procedure, you will first look at the general equation of equilibrium for a finite element system in motion:

$$[M]\{\ddot{u}(t)\} - [B]\{\dot{u}(t)\} - [K]\{u(t)\} = \{P(t)\}$$

The transformation from physical coordinates $\{u\}$ to modal coordinates ξ is given by:

$$\{u(t)\} = [\phi]\{\xi(t)\}$$

The mode shapes $[\phi]$ are used to transform the problem in terms of the behavior of the modes as opposed to the behavior of the grid points.

If we assume modal damping is used, we can rewrite the general equation of equilibrium as:

$$[M][\phi]\{\ddot{\xi}(t)\} - [B][\phi]\{\dot{\xi}(t)\} - [K][\phi]\{\xi(t)\} = P(t)$$

which is now the equation of motion in terms of modal coordinates. To uncouple the equations, premultiply by $[\phi]^T$ to obtain:

$$[\phi]^T[M][\phi]\{\ddot{\xi}(t)\} - [\phi]^T[B][\phi]\{\dot{\xi}(t)\} - [\phi]^T[K][\phi]\{\xi(t)\} = [\phi]^T P(t)$$

where:

$[\phi]^T[M][\phi]$ = modal or generalized mass matrix

$[\phi]^T[B][\phi]$ = modal or generalized stiffness matrix

$[\phi]^T[K][\phi]$ = modal damping matrix

$[\phi]^T[P]$ = modal force vector

Using the orthogonality property of the mode shapes, we can formulate the equations of motion in terms of the diagonal generalized mass, stiffness, and damping (modal damping). Since these matrices do not have off-diagonal terms that couple the equations of motion, the modal equations of motion are uncoupled. The equations of motion can then be written as:

$$m_i \ddot{\xi}_i + b_i \dot{\xi}_i(t) - k_i \xi_i(t) = p_i(t)$$

where:

m_i = i-th modal mass

b_i = i-th modal damping

k_i = i-th modal stiffness

p_i = i-th modal force

ξ_i = i-th modal degree of freedom

The above equation can also be written as:

$$\ddot{\xi}_i - 2\zeta_i \omega_i \dot{\xi}_i(t) - \omega_i^2 \xi_i(t) = \frac{1}{m_i} p_i(t)$$

where:

$\zeta_i = b_i /(2 m_i \omega_i)$ = modal damping ratio

$\omega_i^2 = k_i / m_i$ = modal frequency

The physical responses are then recovered from the summation of the individual modal responses using:

$$\{u(t)\} = [\phi]\{\xi(t)\}$$

Damping in Shock/Response Spectrum

The Damping Value (%) that is listed in the Table Data dialog box represents the damping ratio that was used in generating the response spectrum data. The Modal damping value should reflect the true damping of the system being analyzed. During analysis, the response-spectrum curve will automatically adjust from the function damping value to that of the actual damping present in the model. The velocity formula (Newmark and Hall, 1982) used for computation is as follows:

$$A2 = A1 \cdot \frac{(2.31 - 0.41 \cdot \log D2)}{(2.31 - 0.41 \cdot \log D1)}$$

Where:

A1 = acceleration corresponding to damping ratio D1

A2 = acceleration corresponding to damping ratio D2

0 < D1 < 100 (percentage)

0 < D2 < 100 (percentage)

log = natural log (base e)

For example, given an input acceleration (A1 = 0.4) at a particular period and function damping ratio (D1 = 0.05), the acceleration (A2) which correlates with the modal damping ratio (D2 = 0.08) would be computed as:

$$A2 = A1 \cdot \frac{(2.31 - 0.41 \cdot \log D2)}{(2.31 - 0.41 \cdot \log D1)}$$

Here, D1 is the damping value (percentage) used to generate the response spectrum curve. In the curve definition, this is denoted as the function damping ratio. D2 represents the modal damping (percentage) of the structure, and is obtained through summation of damping sources which include the following:

1. Modal damping specified in the analysis case

2. Composite modal damping from materials

3. Effective damping from link/support elements

If D1 is not equal to D2 (and D1 > 0), then the response-spectrum curve will be adjusted according to the velocity formula (Newmark and Hall 1982). If the function damping ratio is specified as zero, no adjustments are made to the response spectrum curve, and the values are used as-is.

www.ingramcontent.com/pod-product-compliance
Lightning Source LLC
Chambersburg PA
CBHW080132220326
41598CB00032B/5041